The Yale Scene: University Series, 2

SCHOOL OF THE PROPHETS

YALE COLLEGE, 1701–1740

by Richard Warch

New Haven and London, Yale University Press

1973

Library of Congress catalog card number: 73-77169
International standard book number: 0-300-01605-0

Designed by John O. C. McCrillis and set in Baskerville type.
Printed in the United States of America by The Colonial Press Inc., Clinton, Massachusetts.

Published in Great Britain, Europe, and Africa by Yale University Press, Ltd., London.
Distributed in Latin America by Kaiman & Polon, Inc., New York City; in Australasia and Southeast Asia by John Wiley & Sons Australasia Pty. Ltd., Sydney; in India by UBS Publishers' Distributors Pvt., Ltd., Delhi; in Japan by John Weatherhill, Inc., Tokyo.

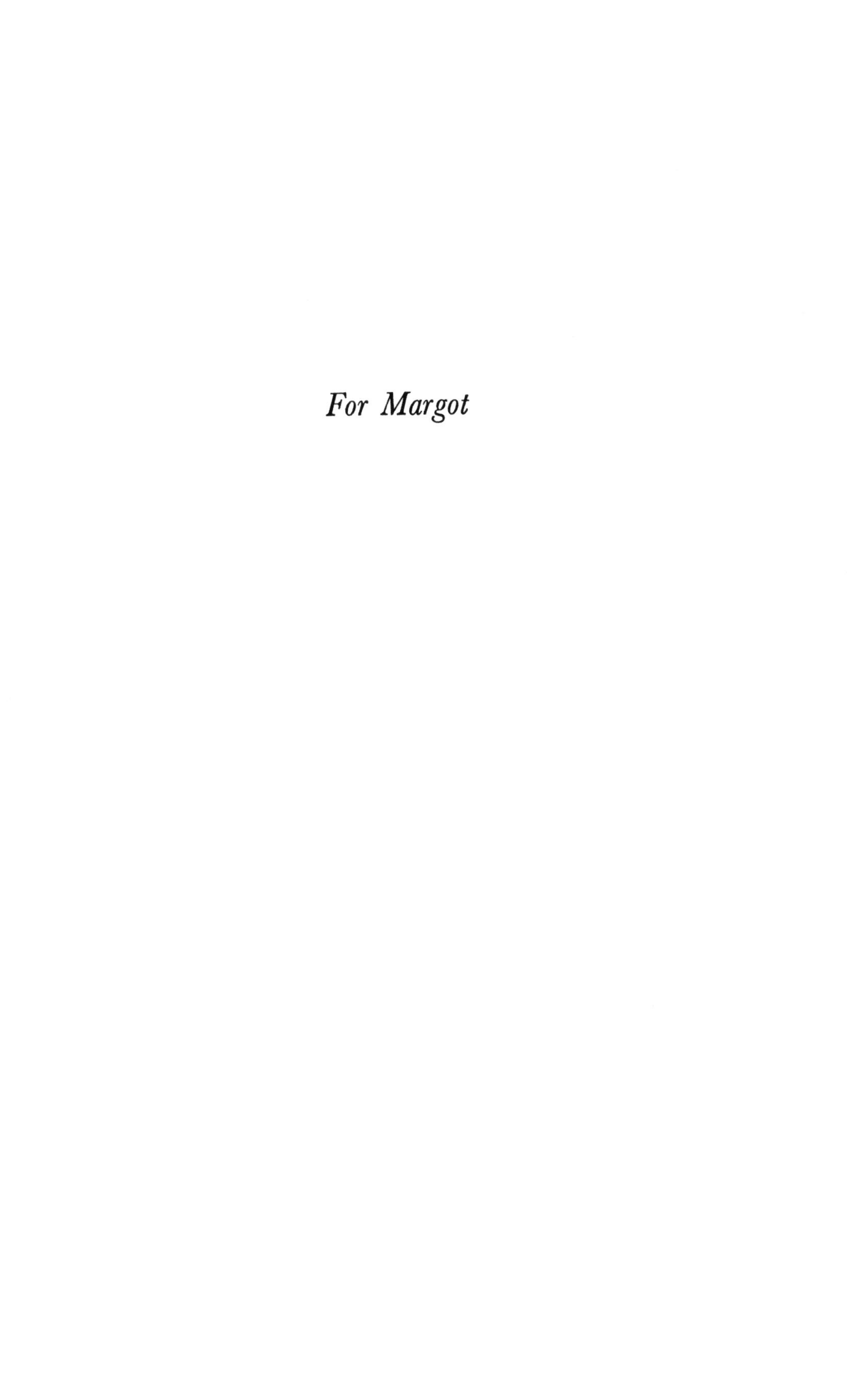

For Margot

Contents

Illustrations

Preface

Yale College has not lacked historians to tell its story. The first history of the college antedates the present account by some 250 years. Between the years 1717 and 1719, Tutor Samuel Johnson, later to be the first president of King's College (now Columbia University), composed "Some Historical Remarks Concerning the Collegiate School of Connecticut in New Haven," which related the history of the school from its founding in 1701 to its settlement in New Haven in 1718. The next account of early Yale was published in 1766 by the college's fifth rector and first president, Thomas Clap, whose *The Annals or History of Yale-College* carried the story down to his own day. Since that time numerous Yale presidents, professors, and graduates have written about the college. The most recent study of colonial Yale per se is Edwin Oviatt's *The Beginnings of Yale, 1701–1726* (New Haven: Yale University Press, 1916).

This book, then, is not on a new topic; it attempts, however, to tell a new story. Previous works on early Yale have, in the main, told the institutional history of the school faithfully. They have not, it seems to me, given the intellectual, social, and religious dimensions of the college their due. The first forty years of the eighteenth century were ones of intellectual and religious transition and tension in the colonies, prior to the so-called American Enlightenment on the one hand and the divisive impact of the evangelical revivals on the other. As an institution that educated men to serve their society and was designed to perpetuate a theological orthodoxy through its graduates, Yale College both reflected and shaped the religious and intellectual trends of the times. These activities—both deliberate and inadvertent—make Yale an illuminating case study of pre-Great Awakening New England. The Collegiate School of Connecticut, the institution's first name, performed a unique role in the colony; my aim has been to delineate that role, the better to understand both the heritage of Yale and the complexity of eighteenth-century society.

What follows is intended to be both a record of Yale's first forty years and a story of the college as intellectual history. Samuel Eliot Morison's three-volume study of seventeenth-century Harvard has demonstrated the validity and value of this approach and I have tried to extend it to the history of Yale. A decade ago Bernard Bailyn stated that "the needs and opportunities for study that eighteenth-century Yale presents are still great." * I have attempted to take advantage of those opportunities and to meet those needs.

In doing so I am fortunate to have been preceded in the task by Franklin Bowditch Dexter (1842–1920), Larned Professor of History at Yale and secretary of the university from 1869 to 1899. Dexter knew more about early Yale than anyone before or since, and recorded his knowledge in numerous articles and in *Biographical Sketches of the Graduates of Yale College with Annals of the College History,* 6 vols. (New York: Henry Holt, 1885–1912), a work which testifies to his dedication and thoroughness. He also collected a large majority of the documents on Yale's early history in *The Documentary History of Yale University under the Original Charter of the Collegiate School of Connecticut, 1701–1745* (New Haven: Yale University Press, 1916), a work which considerably eased my research. While I have checked the originals of the documents in the book, I have quoted the material from Dexter.

My debt to Dexter is overshadowed by my debts to others. This work originated as an American Studies dissertation at Yale in 1968 and owes much to the criticism and encouragement of my adviser, Sydney E. Ahlstrom; at all stages, he has urged me to confront the broader dimensions of the topic. David D. Hall has been consistently and provocatively helpful both as a critic and a friend. George W. Pierson, who has kindly translated his interest in the subject into an interest in this study, has read the manuscript at several points and given me much needed counsel. I have shared many of my thoughts about this project with Joseph Ellis, whose own work on Samuel Johnson touches on early Yale at several places; his ideas have helped me to clarify my own. Many others have assisted me with advice and support at all levels; I wish particularly to thank Edmund S. Morgan, Norman Holmes Pearson, Thomas Schafer, Wallace Anderson, Norman Fiering, Timothy Breen, and Barbara MacEachern.

R.W.

New Haven, Connecticut
September, 1972

* Bernard Bailyn, *Education in the Forming of American Society,* p. 88.

List of Abbreviations

C.A.	The Connecticut Archives in the Connecticut State Library, Hartford, Connecticut; followed by the appropriate collection.
Coll. M.H.S.	The Collections of the Massachusetts Historical Society. The number before the citation refers to the series, the following numeral to the volume; thus, 6 Coll. M.H.S., 2, is the second volume of the sixth series of the Collections.
Conn. Records	J. Hammond Trumbull and Charles J. Hoadly, eds., *Public Records of the Colony of Connecticut,* 15 vols. (Hartford, 1850–1890).
Documentary History	Franklin B. Dexter, ed., *Documentary History of Yale University under the Original Charter of the Collegiate School of Connecticut, 1701–1745* (New Haven: Yale University Press, 1916).
Episcopal Church Documents	Francis L. Hawks and William S. Perry, eds., *Documentary History of the Protestant Episcopal Church in the United States of America Containing Numerous Hitherto Unpublished Documents Concerning the Church in Connecticut,* 2 vols. (New York, 1863–64).
Harvard Graduates	Clifford K. Shipton and John L. Sibley, *Biographical Sketches of Those Who Attended Harvard College,* 14

	vols. (Cambridge, Mass.: Harvard University Press, 1873–1968).
Johnson	Herbert Schneider and Carol Schneider, eds., *Samuel Johnson, President of King's College: His Career and Writings*, 4 vols. (New York: Columbia University Press, 1929).
Proc. M.H.S.	*Proceedings of the Massachusetts Historical Society.*
Pub. C.S.M.	Publications of the Colonial Society of Massachusetts.
Seventeenth-century Harvard	Samuel Eliot Morison, *Harvard College in the Seventeenth Century*, 2 vols. (Cambridge, Mass.: Harvard University Press, 1936).
S.P.G. Correspondence	Transcripts of the Correspondence between the Society for the Propagation of the Gospel in Foreign Parts and Its Missionaries, twenty-six reels of microfilm ("A" Series) covering the years 1701–36.
Yale Annals	Thomas Clap, *The Annals or History of Yale-College, in New-Haven, In the Colony of Connecticut, From the first Founding thereof, in the Year 1700, to the Year 1766* (New Haven, 1766).
Yale Graduates	Franklin B. Dexter, *Biographical Sketches of the Graduates of Yale College with Annals of the College History*, 6 vols. (New York: Henry Holt and Co., 1885–1912).

1 "Liberty to Erect a Collegiate School"

The Collegiate School of Connecticut, renamed Yale College in later years and eventually to become one of the world's great universities, began modestly. Ever since 1636, Harvard had served as New England's only college, although as early as the 1640s certain persons in the New Haven Colony had sought to establish another. These efforts continued for over fifteen years without success. It is impossible to document precisely when the proposal for a second college was revived, but it probably started around 1700 as a topic of casual conversation among several Connecticut clergymen. Soon the talk became more purposeful and the ministers broached the plan to others and sought to make the idea a reality. By the summer of 1701 a nucleus of concerned men began to solicit advice about the school, and by the fall of that year they were ready to announce their plan. All the while, few people outside of the colony seem to have paid any attention to them. The ignorance and indifference of the outside world are understandable. Connecticut was a colony of no more than thirty thousand inhabitants, which had largely avoided controversies with its neighbors or with England. The fact that about a dozen clergymen intended to establish a college there was probably of little significance to anyone.

It was of great significance to the ministers, however. For despite the relative isolation of their colonial society, they consciously stood in a proud tradition of the relationship of religion and learning. What they hoped to do was, quite simply, to perpetuate that tradition in their own colony. The college would be small and remote, to be sure, but its meaning and goals were great and immediate. The ministers designed the collegiate school as a link between two worlds, the one confined and provincial (the colony of Connecticut), the other broad and cosmopolitan (the continent of Europe). On the one side was the new world of Puritanism and politics; on the other side was the old world of Reformation traditions and learning.

This is not to say that Yale College began as the first act in a moral drama of the cultural world, for the Connecticut ministers never articulated their visions in such grandiose contrasts. It is clear, however, that while they thought of themselves as the heirs and perpetuators of the Reformed Protestant tradition, the college they established to further that tradition would have to exist in a milieu in which Reformed ideals were already being modified and would later, in some cases, be denied. The ministers took for granted the fact that the new school would be a vehicle for transmitting the culture of the learned world to New England; yet the atmosphere in which the college would have to function was rather simple and provincial. Finally, they intended their college to serve a homogeneous society and to act as an agent of continuity between the past and the present. However, Connecticut was becoming more culturally diverse, and the young institution was to find itself enmeshed in the political and theological tensions of the colony, and thus unable to perform merely a conserving and transmitting role. As the college proponents were to discover, there would always be an unwelcome gap between their expectations and the realities of the collegiate school's role and purpose.

In 1701, not all of these difficulties were apparent and the ministers viewed the proposed college with optimism. In October of that year they had reached the stage of planning which made it desirable that they seek a charter for the school from the Connecticut General Assembly. The assembly, which had divided into two houses in 1698, met twice a year, at Hartford in May and, starting in 1701, at the cocapital of New Haven in October. Deputies and assistants gathered in New Haven on October 9 and began the week-long business of ordering the colony's affairs and settling its all too many disputes. Not all disputes were external to the assembly, however, for the upper and lower houses were jealous of their own prerogatives and suspicious of each other's. The assembly records reveal none of these conflicts; the only thing they do reveal is that, after forming a committee to settle a boundary dispute with Rhode Island and before adjusting the rates of the New Haven ferry, the legislators granted ten ministers a charter for a collegiate school. There is no evidence of any debate on this matter and it is unlikely that any individuals objected to the plan. It was, in fact, a sensible and prestigious undertaking. Sixty-five years after the founding of Harvard, the way had been cleared for the establishment of a second New England college.

Early College Plans

In some ways, this accomplishment was the fruition of efforts that had begun in the old New Haven Colony as early as the 1640s. New Haven, founded by Theophilus Eaton, John Davenport, and their followers in 1638, included in its jurisdiction most of the present southwestern portion of Connecticut and a few towns on Long Island. To the east was the Connecticut Colony, which extended along the Connecticut River from the Massachusetts border to Long Island Sound. In 1662, Connecticut annexed the New Haven Colony. Throughout the seventeenth century, separate and united, the two colonies sent their young men to Harvard for their education. In New Haven, however, there was an expressed desire for a local college. In part, this hope was a function of colonial pride and practicality and had little to do with any overt dissatisfaction with Harvard. The New Haven colonists not only shared with their Massachusetts brethren a belief in the value and necessity of higher education but took steps to act on that conviction. Within six years of its settlement, the young colony was helping to support the Cambridge college with contributions of corn, and had initiated plans for a free school in New Haven for "the better trayning upp of youth in this towne, that through Gods blessinge they may be fitted for publique service hereafter, either in church or commonweale." [1] In 1647 the colony's assembly met to dispose of vacant lots and formed a committee "to consider and reserve what lott they shall see meette & most commodious for a colledg, which they dissire maye bee sett up so soone as their abillitie will reach therunto." [2]

It is not clear who initiated this proposal for a college, but the agitation for it centered in the town of New Haven and it is probable that the moving force behind the idea was the Reverend John Davenport, minister of the church and a member of the first Harvard board of overseers. Davenport continued as the leader of this movement for the duration of his tenure as the New Haven pastor. But despite his efforts the college issue remained dormant for several years. In 1652 the people of one of the colony towns, Guilford, declared that a college would be too expensive for the New Haven

1. Charles J. Hoadly, ed., *Records of the Colony and Plantation of New Haven, 1638–1649*, p. 210.

2. Ibid., p. 376.

Colony to undertake alone, but expressed a willingness to contribute to such a college if the Connecticut Colony would join the enterprise.[3] Connecticut, however, perhaps because its relative proximity to Harvard made it less concerned with founding a second school, evidently declined to assist New Haven.

In 1655 Governor Theophilus Eaton brought up the college proposal at a New Haven town meeting. He spoke of the merits of having a local college and suggested that recent events at Harvard made this a propitious time to act. President Henry Dunster had just defected to Baptist views, a radical departure from set New England practice which made Harvard suspect in the eyes of many. This was the first—but not the last—time that supporters of a second college were to try to take advantage of Harvard's troubles. John Davenport rose and spoke warmly in favor of a New Haven college; the town responded by forming a committee to assess public opinion on the matter.[4]

Public opinion was favorable. Within nine days Eaton reported to the colonial assembly that the town had pledged £300 for the college. Milford offered to contribute £100, while other communities requested time to consider the issue.[5] By July 4, 1655, these towns had raised £140, giving the proposed college a total of £540. William Leveridge of Oyster Bay on Long Island was nominated as college president, and two young men from prominent families, John Haynes, Jr., son of the Connecticut governor, and Fitz-John Winthrop, grandson of the former Massachusetts governor, made plans to study under him. Governor Eaton presented books valued at £20 for a library and Dr. Thomas Browne of Bermuda, a skilled linguist, offered to be an instructor. Despite these encouraging events, the college was not erected. No firm evidence survives to explain this failure, although the tantalizing hint that Leveridge's wife objected to this career for her husband suggests one reason.[6] The fact that Harvard had quickly recovered from the blow of Dunster's religious decision suggests another. In any event, the flurry of activity in 1655 produced no results and five years elapsed

3. Charles J. Hoadly, ed., *Records of the Colony or Jurisdiction of New Haven, 1653–1665*, p. 370.

4. Franklin B. Dexter and Zara J. Power, eds., *New Haven Town Records*, 1 : 241–42.

5. *Records of the Colony or Jurisdiction of New Haven*, pp. 141–42.

6. Isabel M. Calder, *The New Haven Colony*, p. 138.

before the college issue was again discussed at town or colonial meetings.

In the interval, public officials had considered the need for grammar schools. New Haven and Milford were the only towns that had established such schools of their own, and by 1660 the colonial assembly had decided to create a grammar school for the entire colony. This school was established in 1660 but it, too, ran into trouble. The schoolmaster was dissatisfied with his living arrangements in New Haven, and parents, who a few years earlier had supported the college proposal, were generally apathetic, apparently preferring useful to traditional education. In 1662 the Assembly sadly concluded that, since "the end is not attained for which it was settled," the school would be closed.[7]

The college idea fared even worse. John Davenport continued to support the plan, but with little success. In 1660 he tried again. Davenport had obtained a gift of money from Edward Hopkins, a wealthy Connecticut landowner, "for the furtherance of learning in these parts," the terms of which the minister expounded to the assembly. The legislators received the revived college plan with skepticism. When Governor Francis Newman proposed that a plot of land be set aside for the college, the citizens agreed to do so when the college was established, but not before.[8] They did not intend to donate land for a college that existed only as an idea. But John Davenport persisted. The Hopkins gift, he explained, was to be divided between New Haven and Hartford, and he urged New Haven to use its share "for promoveing the colledg-worke in a graduall way, for the education of youth in good literature." He ended his plea by offering a series of recommendations to the assembly for the erection of a school and college.

The assembly responded favorably. Citing the previous difficulties in establishing town schools in the colony and "the great difficulty & charge to make pay &c, for the maintaining children at the schools or colledg in the Bay" the legislators agreed to set aside funds to erect a colony school. No definite steps were taken on the college issue. Davenport made another plea to the town of New Haven in 1664, again mentioning the Hopkins gift and urging the people to improve the state of learning among them. The towns-

7. *Records of the Colony or Jurisdiction of New Haven*, pp. 374–77, 471.
8. Ibid., p. 356; *New Haven Town Records*, 1 : 457.

men "declared their acceptance with thankefulnes of what Mr. Davenport propounded" but took no action.[9]

Davenport had been prodding his fellow citizens about a second New England college for nearly twenty years. Although he had the will for this endeavor, New Haven colonists failed to find a way. They believed in education, they established grammar schools, and they responded favorably to the *idea* of a college, but they never succeeded in setting up a college of their own. Two factors seem to have affected efforts in this direction. The first was the colonists' apparent reluctance to spend money for a college. The second was the status of Harvard. Since the plan for a second college proceeded furthest in 1655, when Harvard was in trouble over President Dunster's defection, it is reasonable to suppose that Harvard's stability was a crucial factor in determining the interest of New Haveners in creating a second school. As long as Harvard remained sound, serious proposals for another college attracted little support.

By the 1660s, moreover, other problems occupied the colonists' interest and energy. After the Restoration, the New England colonies sought to reestablish congenial relations with the crown. In 1662 the Connecticut Colony applied for and received a charter from Charles II. While New Haven's leaders knew that the neighboring colony was seeking a charter, they believed their own political autonomy was safe. Unfortunately for the colony on the Sound, the new charter placed its own territory under Connecticut's jurisdiction. Although some New Haveners resisted Connecticut's attempts to unify the two colonies, their resistance was futile. One by one, towns that were dissatisfied with the New Haven government accepted Connecticut's invitation to join its dominion. By December, 1664, the New Haven Colony had been irreparably weakened by such defections, and on January 7, 1665, it submitted to Connecticut.[10]

The union of the two colonies was a severe blow to John Davenport. Long suspicious of the less orthodox ecclesiastical and more liberal political structures of Connecticut, he had argued to the end against unification. In addition, Davenport had been an archopponent of the decisions of the Synod of 1662, which permitted

9. *Records of the Colony or Jurisdiction of New Haven,* pp. 370–76; *New Haven Town Records,* 2 : 83–86. For more on the Hopkins bequest, see chapter 2.

10. Calder, *New Haven Colony,* pp. 216–59.

churches to baptize the children of parents who had not experienced God's saving grace in their lives. To men like Davenport, this Half-Way Covenant, as it was called, denied the very nature of a church of the saints. The fact that the churches of Connecticut had received this decision more favorably than those of New Haven only served to confirm the old minister's distrust of the River Colony. So, when the opportunity came, in 1667, for him to go to Boston as the minister of the First Church, he quickly accepted. The Boston pulpit was a better podium from which to denounce the Half-Way Covenant, and with his beloved colony's amalgamation with Connecticut, his bonds of loyalty to New Haven had been severed. Like his friend the Reverend Abraham Pierson, whose distaste for these recent events caused him to move his Branford congregation to Newark, New Jersey, Davenport left New Haven. With his departure the chief voice for the founding of a college also disappeared. Connecticut had never attempted to establish a college within its borders. The River Colony had no advocate comparable to John Davenport and the united colonies produced no spokesman to replace him, so the college idea languished for over thirty years.

Harvard Troubles

Although the New Haven and Connecticut colonies were either unsuccessful or uninterested in establishing and contributing to colleges of their own, they did send students and money to Harvard. Harvard had been founded in 1636 by men whose purpose was "to advance *Learning* and perpetuate it to Posterity; dreading to leave an illiterate Ministry to the Churches, when our present Ministers shall lie in the Dust." This aim was shared by other New England settlers, and it was fitting that those settlers assist in supporting the college. Although most of Harvard's operating revenue came from the people and government of Massachusetts, appeals for funds extended beyond the boundaries of the Bay Colony. In 1644 the Reverend Thomas Shepard asked the United Colonies Commissioners to consider "some way of comfortable mayntenance for that Schoole of the Prophets that now is" and suggested that each family in New England give one-quarter bushel of wheat to the college.[11] Both New Haven and Connecticut re-

11. From *New Englands First Fruits* (London, 1643), quoted in Samuel Eliot Morison, *The Founding of Harvard College*, p. 432; ibid., p. 315.

sponded to the appeal. The Connecticut Colony sent its contributions without much difficulty, but the New Haven government had to prod its people into compliance. In 1647 Governor Eaton urged that the college corn contributions be paid, and added that "it wilbe a reproach that it shalbe said Newhaven is falne off from this service." [12]

New Haven, indeed, did fall off from this service; there is no record of the colony contributing to Harvard after 1652. But the Connecticut Colony, not preoccupied with plans for a college within its own boundaries, continued to donate to the Bay College. In 1652 Connecticut provided £20 for a fellowship at Harvard and in 1665 sent £100 in provisions to the school, the money for which had been taken from Hartford's share of the Edward Hopkins bequest.[13]

What Connecticut gave to Harvard in money it took back, in Harvard's view, in land. In 1652–53 the Massachusetts General Court allotted two thousand acres to the college, which Treasurer Thomas Danforth was allowed to choose at his discretion. He unwisely chose to stake Harvard's claim to land in the Pequot country, located in the present southeastern part of Connecticut. Connecticut refused to recognize the validity of the claim, and disputes arose between the two colonies. In 1683 Danforth bitterly complained of "hard usage from Connecticut" and declared that people from Hartford and Rhode Island had "by violence" dispossessed the college and built on its land.[14]

Despite the complaint of "hard usage," Connecticut relied on Harvard to educate its youth. Between 1642 and 1703, sixty-nine Connecticut boys graduated from the Bay College; thirty-five of them were from the area of the New Haven Colony (seventeen from the town of New Haven) and thirty-four from the old Connecticut Colony (ten from Hartford).[15] No evidence exists to suggest that the Connecticut colonists complained about the education their sons received at Harvard. The cost may have been burdensome but the learning was acceptable. By 1700, however, events had occurred which caused some people to suspect the soundness of a Harvard education.

12. *Records of the Colony and Plantation of New Haven,* pp. 311–12.

13. *Seventeenth-century Harvard,* 2 : 362.

14. Ibid., 1 : 31–34.

15. *Harvard Graduates,* vols. 1–5, passim.

On the surface, the Bay College's problems were political. According to an act of the Massachusetts assembly in 1642 and the charter which the assembly granted the college in 1650, Harvard was administered by two governing bodies: the board of overseers, composed of nearby ministers and magistrates, and a seven-man corporation of the president and fellows. While the corporation was designed as the primary ruling group, with the overseers providing consent to its acts, the overseers were in fact the more powerful entity during most of the seventeenth century. The details of Harvard's governance are less important here than the fact that the college owed its legal corporate status to the Massachusetts Bay government. In 1684, after several years of investigation and debate, the Court of Chancery in London voided the Massachusetts Bay charter of 1629. Two years later, Edward Randolph, who had been instrumental in bringing about this decision, arrived in Boston with a commission that officially made Massachusetts a royal colony to be governed by the king's representative, Joseph Dudley. It was Dudley's opinion—shared by others—that the Harvard charter perished with the colony's; as he purportedly stated, "the Calf died in the Cow's belly." [16]

The tenuous legal status of the college was a severe blow to its supporters, but their most immediate worry was how the new government might deal with it. Fortunately for Harvard, neither Dudley nor his replacement, Dominion of New England Governor Edmund Andros, sought to suppress or royalize the college. On the contrary, except for their later refusal to sanction proposed college charters which either excluded provisions for visitation by the royal governor or included stipulations for religious tests, the royal governors allowed the college to function freely. After the Glorious Revolution of 1688–89, at which time Bostonians took the opportunity to jail and then oust Governor Andros, the colonial status of Massachusetts changed once more. In 1691 Massachusetts became a semiroyal colony, ruled by a royal governor but able to elect its own legislators and officials. College authorities immediately sought a new charter for Harvard. This was by no means an easy matter, since any act passed by the elected colonial assembly was subject to the approval of the royal governor and the further allowance of the King in Council. For a variety of reasons, all five efforts to get a new charter in the 1690s failed. This meant that

16. *Seventeenth-century Harvard,* 2 : 474.

Harvard was continually operating under temporary legal arrangements. But the indefinite status of the Harvard charter proved to be only one of the college's difficulties. What caused some New Englanders the most visible anxiety by 1700 was not just the legal position of the college but the theological and ecclesiastical views of its tutors.

One of those who worried most vocally and most often was Increase Mather, a leading exponent of the New England Way and one of the most illustrious ministers in the colony. Mather had accepted the presidency of Harvard in 1685 on a pro tempore basis, with the understanding that he would not have to resign his Boston pastorate. Mather's "temporary" term in office lasted for sixteen years and he resided in Cambridge for none of them. From 1688 to 1692 he was in England on a successful mission to obtain a provincial charter for the Bay Colony. Upon his return he continued his interest in the college from a distance, making the two-hour trip by horseback and ferry from Boston to Cambridge to pay visits to the school.

In Mather's absence, the effective control of the college was left in the hands of the two tutors, classmates John Leverett and William Brattle, whose terms in office lasted from 1686 to 1697. They served the college well. The years under these two men were genial ones for the scholars in Cambridge. The tutors were catholic in spirit and did not hesitate to permit or suggest departures from the established course of study. A student of these years, Henry Newman (H. 1687), stated later that instead of studying theology for his master's degree he was allowed to learn French and "read chiefly Mathematical Books and Travels." Another of the tutors' charges, Benjamin Colman (H. 1692), looked back on these years with longing, praising the "Catholick Air" of Harvard and recalling the days when the students "received the Writings and Gentlemen of the Church of *England* with the most open Reverence and Affection." [17] Newman retained similar memories; he recalled at another time how Leverett and Brattle

> recomment to their Pupils the reading of Episcopal authors as the best books to form our minds in religious matters and preserve us from those narrow Principles that kept us at a

17. *Harvard Graduates,* 4 : 127.

> Distance from the Church of England and this at a time when there was a President that thunder'd out anathemas upon all that went to the Church of England as apostates from the Primitive Faith.[18]

Newman's recollection of Mather's imprecations is a fair assessment of the president's displeasure with and fear of one feature of a royalized colonial government—the recognition of the Anglican Church. Anglicanism was still the enemy of the New England Way. For the most part, however, Mather was unaware of the fact that the tutors he had recommended to the college were espousing favorable opinions of the Church of England. His more immediate preoccupation, one shared by most members of the lower house of the assembly, was to obtain a charter for the college which would recognize the institution's autonomy and keep it free from the oversight of the crown officials in the colony. The several charters that he proposed in the 1690s all achieved this end by dropping the board of overseers, inflating the size of the clergy-dominated corporation, and omitting provisions for visitatorial power by the royal governor. Mather's desire to protect the college from the external influence of Anglican officials, coupled with his status as a commuting president, effectively blinded him to the internal modifications the tutors were introducing at Harvard. It was not until 1697, when Leverett and Brattle were nearing the end of their tutorships, that Mather first showed any awareness of what was going on.

The first expression of the president's concern came in his introduction to his son Cotton's "Ecclesiastes: The Life of Jonathan Mitchell." Mather spoke of Mitchell, a former tutor at Harvard and pastor in Cambridge, as the model the tutors and students at the school should follow and warned them against deviating from the order of the gospel their forefathers had brought to the new world. He inveighed against the danger of the college becoming apostate and a *"Degenerate Plant,"* and urged the tutors to prevent this. In conclusion, Mather wrote:

> So let me say, If *you* the Students in *Harvard-Colledge,* or any of you, shall deviate and degenerate from the Holy *Principles* and *Practices* of your *Fathers,* the World shall know, and

18. *Seventeenth-century Harvard,* 2 : 505–07.

> Posterity shall know, That the Reason of it is not for want of being otherwise instructed by your Present, as well as by former *Presidents.*[19]

Although Leverett and Brattle had both taken up other careers and were soon to leave their posts as tutors when Mather leveled this criticism against the college, it was largely their influence he was castigating. That influence was not to be far removed. In 1696 Brattle had become minister of the Cambridge church, a place of strategic importance in the battle for young men's minds and souls. What made Brattle's proximity to the college disturbing to the Mathers was the fact that the tutor's ecclesiastical views were more moderate than theirs. He had had the audacity to preach his own ordination sermon and had induced the Cambridge church to do away with the public examination of candidates for membership. These deviations from the established practices of New England bothered the Mathers, and Increase attacked them in the preface to "Ecclesiastes." Cotton Mather revealed his concern over Brattle's position in this important pastorate when he argued that the minister in Cambridge ought to excel in wisdom and orthodoxy "that so the Scholars, which are Devoted to be Preachers of the Gospel, might be seasoned with the Spirit of such an Elijah."[20] Instead, Harvard scholars were being seasoned with the liberal spirit of Brattle, which the Mathers believed to be unsavory.

Not only had Brattle remained in Cambridge, but his brother Thomas was still the college treasurer, and his good friend Ebenezer Pemberton had assumed his mantle as a Harvard tutor. John Leverett, who had turned to the study of law and had been elected a member of the lower house in 1696, also resided in Cambridge. Although Mather was unhappy with the choice of Pemberton, he displayed no further displeasure with Leverett and Brattle for about two years.

In 1698 the so-called liberal forces initiated plans that would make their deviations from the New England Way even more pronounced. Several Boston merchants, with the support of the Brattles, Leverett, and Pemberton, drew up plans to establish a church of their own. They chose as their minister Benjamin Colman, a

19. Cotton Mather, *Magnalia Christi Americana* (London, 1702), bk. 4, pp. 164–65.
20. Ibid., p. 174.

former student of the two tutors whom Leverett thought of as possessing an "enlarged Catholic Spirit." Contemplating trouble in securing Colman's ordination in Boston, the group recommended that he obtain it in England. Colman took their advice and received Presbyterian ordination in England in the summer of 1699. In the fall of that year the founders of the new church were ready to seek recognition by the other Boston churches. They issued a manifesto which declared adherence to the Westminster Confession, the doctrinal standard of the Reformed tradition, and which asked for fellowship with other local churches. The manifesto, however, also revealed that the group was latitudinarian in ecclesiastical polity. The founders announced their intention to read the Scriptures without commentary, to baptize all children, to do away with the public examination of candidates for membership, and to allow the entire congregation (all baptized adults, not only communicants) to elect the minister.[21] To the Mathers the manifesto was nothing less than a subversion of set New England practices. They and their sympathizers initially refused to join in a customary fast of fellowship with the new church, but the mediation of the Reverend Samuel Willard and Judge Samuel Sewall effected a partial reconciliation. On January 31, 1700, all Boston Congregational ministers joined in a fast, giving recognition to the new church.

For the Mathers, recognition of the innovative group did not mean capitulation to it. In fact, the existence of the group alerted Mather to the possibility that Harvard had fostered such views in these men and was now in danger of being influenced by them. The president, who had seen the British authorities defeat three Harvard charters in seven years because they failed to reserve the power of visitation to the royal governor (representing the crown in the colony), attempted in 1699 to pass a fourth one. It included the provision that none be chosen president, vice-president, or fellow of Harvard College except those

> as shall declare and continue their adherence unto the principles of Reformation, which were espoused and intended by those who first settled this country, and founded the College,

21. *Seventeenth-century Harvard,* 2 : 506; Perry Miller, *The New England Mind: From Colony to Province,* p. 242.

> and have hitherto been the profession and practice of the generality of the churches of Christ in New England.[22]

Increase also dropped the names of Thomas Brattle and John Leverett from the corporation. While he undoubtedly intended the religious stipulation to be a warning to the Brattle party, several of whom were on the corporation, the narrow requirement actually doomed the charter. Governor Bellomont saw the provision as an attempt to exclude Anglicans from the government of the college and refused to endorse the charter and send it to London.

Though they failed in 1699, the Mathers nevertheless pressed the issue. In March, 1700, Increase published his *Order of the Gospel,* which attacked the recent innovations. While his frontal assault was against the Brattle Street Church and the inclusive parish system introduced in Northampton by the Reverend Solomon Stoddard (H. 1662), he also censured the wayward thinking at Harvard, which he now perceived to be dangerous: "Let the Churches Pray for the *Colledge* particularly, that God may ever Bless that Society with faithful *Tutors* that will be true to Christs Interest and theirs, and not Hanker after new and loose wayes." [23] But, as Mather well knew, the prayers of the churches were not enough. When the question of drafting a new charter arose later in 1700 the Harvard president was in a quandary. He realized that in order to keep the college free from the influence of the Brattle faction, the charter would have to contain a test for orthodoxy; he also knew that a charter with such a clause would be defeated by the British authorities. Faced with this dilemma, Mather concluded that it would be better for Harvard to exist without a charter than to risk a liberal corporation:

> Is it not much more eligible to have the Colledge turned into a school for Academical Learning without priviledge of Conferring degrees, as in Geneva it has bin where many Eminent divines have had their education, than to consent to such fatal

22. *Seventeenth-century Harvard,* 2 : 524. The complete story of the several attempts to obtain a new charter for Harvard—a business which was far more involved than my account indicates—can be found in ibid., pp. 489–536.

23. Quoted in Williston Walker, *The Creeds and Platforms of Congregationalism,* p. 478.

alterations in the government of the Colledge, as some would have?[24]

The question, as far as the constitution of Harvard was concerned, proved rhetorical. The Massachusetts assembly approved a charter in 1700 which contained no religious test. Furthermore, it was lost and forgotten in the bureaucratic files in London. Nevertheless, the question does indicate that by 1700 Mather was desperately worried about Harvard's role as the preserver of orthodoxy. A Harvard education, he felt, should be conservative, not "broad and catholic." Still, Mather was content to express his concern by verbal laments and charter provisions; he did not choose to exercise that concern by assuming full-time control of the college.

By 1700, the Mathers' hold on Harvard had become very feeble. Increase was still president, but he was now subjected to repeated pressures by the General Court to take up residence in Cambridge. This he refused to do, as he had been refusing for seven years. In 1693, 1695, 1698, and again in 1700 the court had insisted he live at the college. Each time Mather declined to comply, although in 1700 he stayed in Cambridge for several weeks. His unwillingness to obey the court was motivated by his determination to retain his pastorate at Boston's Second Church, a position which gave him a powerful base in the colony's ecclesiastical affairs. Besides, life in Boston was more refined than it was in Cambridge.

In 1701, when the court again ordered him to move to the college town, Increase gave it one more try. He lasted six months. In June, 1701, he wrote Lieutenant-Governor William Stoughton asking that the assembly think of someone else to be president. Mather probably hoped that the court would, as in the past, relent on the residence issue and insist that he remain in charge of Harvard affairs. But the legislators were not inclined to give in again. They turned the control of the college over to Vice-President Samuel Willard, whose moderate temperament and solid orthodoxy made him acceptable to all parties. Furthermore, there was no stipulation requiring the vice-president to reside in Cambridge. Despite Willard's delay in giving his reply, the court ordered him to assume supervision of the college. The fact that Willard, too, would commute to the school from his pastorate at Third (Old

24. *Seventeenth-century Harvard*, 2 : 527.

South) Church in Boston no doubt made the decision all the more irksome to Increase, who ostensibly had been dismissed because he commuted. But whether Mather was dealt with unjustly or not was of small significance. His control over the affairs of Harvard College was at an end.[25]

A Second New England College

It was while the Mathers were feuding with both the liberal and the governmental forces in Massachusetts that, once again, certain Connecticut clergymen were deliberating a scheme for a college in their colony. The connection between these parallel events has been the subject of some controversy. In the 1830s Harvard President Josiah Quincy argued that the Connecticut ministers took advantage of the "crisis of affairs in Massachusetts" and planned their college so it would "be made satisfactory to the predominant religious party in Massachusetts," especially by including in the college constitution "points by that party deemed essential." Yale professor James Luce Kingsley rebutted the particulars of Quincy's statement in the early 1840s. But in his zeal to refute Quincy, Kingsley went too far in minimizing the role of certain Massachusetts men in the early deliberations about the Connecticut college.[26] The accounts of both Quincy and Kingsley suffered by their attempts to make the founding of Yale simpler than the evidence warrants. The proponents of a Connecticut college neither bowed to their Massachusetts correspondents nor ignored their advice.

The surviving evidence does not reveal to us precisely when the renewed interest in a second New England college began. We do know, however, that the leading spirit in the drive for a Connecticut college was the Reverend James Pierpont of New Haven. Graduated from Harvard in 1681, Pierpont came to New Haven as a ministerial candidate in 1684. The committee that called him to the church reported that he was "a godly man, a good scholar, a man of good parts, and likely to make a good instrument." [27] Pierpont's career confirmed those expectations. The New Haven church had been through a period of controversy prior to his as-

25. Ibid., 2 : 530–35. Willard did not become the Harvard president, but remained vice-president until the election of John Leverett to the presidency in 1707.

26. Josiah Quincy, *The History of Harvard University,* 1 : 197–98; [James Luce Kingsley], "Review of Quincy's History of Harvard University," *The American Biblical Repository,* ser. 2, 6 (1841): 177–95.

27. *Harvard Graduates,* 3 : 223.

sumption of the pastorate, but his peaceable disposition and effective ministry soon healed the divisions. Not only did Pierpont's work benefit the church and town, but he extended his interests and activities to include a concern for the general welfare of all Connecticut churches. In this regard he stood firmly in the tradition of his most illustrious predecessor in the New Haven pulpit, John Davenport.

It is impossible to know if Pierpont's wider concerns, and particularly his interest in founding a college, were deliberate attempts to follow in Davenport's footsteps. He undoubtedly knew of his predecessor's efforts from the recollections of some of the older parishioners. Surely Pierpont heard of the college dream from his wife Abigail, Davenport's granddaughter. Perhaps he was told of it by his fellow pastor, Abraham Pierson of Killingworth, whose father had been appointed along with Davenport to select books for the New Haven Colony grammar school in 1659.[28] However the college plan was revived, it is certain that Pierpont and his fellow ministers were aware of Davenport's earlier efforts.

Several factors which had motivated the former New Haven minister were still evident in 1701. One of them was financial. The expense of sending boys to Harvard had not diminished since the New Haven Court had discussed the matter in 1660. In 1678 the Reverend John Bishop of Stamford had voiced a prevalent concern when he complained that none of his sons had been educated; two of them had demonstrated academic promise, "but our Latin schole failing, & my estate too feeble to send them forth, their progresse also failed." Bishop hoped that one of his boys could get a scholarship to attend Harvard.[29] Scholarships, of course, could solve the plight of only a relatively few would-be students. Pierpont and his colleagues were well aware of this fact for, as one commentator wrote later, a principal reason for establishing a Connecticut college was "the Great Difficulty & extream Charges of Educating Children at Harvard Colledge in Cambridge, it being so very remote from us." [30]

Yet a second feature of the Davenport tradition was applicable

28. *Records of the Colony or Jurisdiction of New Haven,* p. 301.

29. 4 Coll. M.H.S., 8 : 305; cf. ibid., p. 660. There was one Harvard fellowship designed specifically for boys from the old New Haven Colony—the Pennoyer scholarship. For a discussion of this topic see *Seventeenth-century Harvard,* 2 : 383–87.

30. *Documentary History,* p. 149.

in 1701. The initial efforts to found a second college had been most promising in 1655 when the Dunster defection had disrupted Harvard. In 1701, many people again perceived Harvard to be in trouble. Increase and Cotton Mather, both of whom took the matter personally, were not the only ones disturbed by the drift of events surrounding the college. Even Solomon Stoddard, who disagreed with the Mathers on ecclesiastical policies, shared their concern over Harvard's affairs. In a 1703 sermon, Stoddard accused the college of being a place of "Riot and Pride . . . profuseness and prodigality" and stated that it was "not worth the while for persons to be sent to the *Colledge* to learn to Complement men, and Court women; they should be sent thither to prepare them for Publick Service, and had need be under the over-sight of wise and holy men." [31] This was a rather general indictment, and although many people might have agreed with Stoddard's fears of worldliness and laxity, there were evidently some Connecticut clergymen who had more specific complaints about Harvard. Moses Noyes, an early trustee of the college, wrote at a later date that the "first Movers for a College in Connecticut alledged this as a Reason, because the College at Cambridge was under the Tutorage of Latitudinarians." [32] These latitudinarians, obviously, were the Brattles, Leverett, and Pemberton. On September 6, 1701, Increase Mather left his post as Harvard president. Nine days later he was writing suggestions to several Connecticut ministers about a second college.

While Harvard's liberal drift bothered both the Mathers and the Connecticut clergy, it is important to note that the initial impulse for founding another college originated in Connecticut. There is no evidence to suggest that what was to become Yale College was conceived by the Mather-dominated party in Massachusetts to counteract the undesirable tendencies in the Bay College. What is clear is that once such a college was planned, the Mather party was in the right frame of mind to encourage and aid the enterprise. Judge Samuel Sewall and Isaac Addington, secretary of the colony, expressed this sentiment in a letter of October 6, 1701, to the college advocates: "We should be very glad to hear

31. Solomon Stoddard, *The Way for a People to Live Long in the Land that God Hath given them,* p. 13.

32. *Documentary History,* p. 242. Moses Noyes, who became a trustee in 1703, wrote this observation in 1723 in reference to Rector Timothy Cutler's defection to Anglicanism. For more on this episode, see below, chapter 4.

of flourishing Schools and a Colledge at Connecticut, and it would be some releife to us against the sorrow we have conceived for the decay of them in this Province." [33]

Ten Connecticut clergymen proposed the second New England college and became its first trustees. Nine of the ministers were graduates of Harvard which they had attended before Increase Mather became president. In the summer and early autumn of 1701, five of these ministers—along with three colleagues—actively engaged in soliciting advice about the structure and legal status of the proposed college. Led by James Pierpont (H. 1681) of New Haven, the active group included James Noyes (H. 1659) of Stonington, Israel Chauncy (H. 1661) of Stratford, Abraham Pierson (H. 1668) of Killingworth (now Clinton), and Thomas Buckingham (no college) of Saybrook. The Reverends Samuel Mather (H. 1671) of Windsor, Samuel Andrew (H. 1675) of Milford, Timothy Woodbridge (H. 1675) of Hartford, Noadiah Russell (H. 1681) of Middletown, and Joseph Webb (H. 1684) of Fairfield, later to be named trustees, did not, so far as we know, engage in the extensive correspondence that was carried on prior to the charter grant of October, 1701.

No evidence survives that reveals how this group of ministers came to be formed. A plausible conjecture is that Pierpont initiated the college idea and proposed it to several of his colleagues. Apparently, Pierpont, Noyes, Pierson, Chauncy, and Buckingham constituted the nucleus of the group, although three ministers who were not to be original trustees also joined in the preliminary discussions: Samuel Russell (H. 1681) of Branford, Gurdon Saltonstall (H. 1681) of New London, and Moses Noyes (H. 1659) of Lyme. In the summer and early fall of 1701, and perhaps earlier, these clergymen met together to discuss the college plan. Meeting at the homes of various members of the group, the men talked about their design and mapped out their strategy. On these occasions they may have lamented Harvard's difficulties and resolved to establish a college that would provide their colony with ministers untainted by latitudinarian theology.

33. Ibid., p. 16. The term "Mather party" is an imprecise one, as included in the group is Judge Samuel Sewall who the Mathers believed had played a damaging role in denying Increase the Harvard presidency in 1701. Yet the term serves to indicate the general outlook and affiliation of those who advised the Connecticut ministers.

But on another level the Connecticut ministers were engaged in a grander enterprise. They were determined, as Thomas Clap later put it, to establish a school in their colony "so the Interest of Religion might be preserved, and the Truth propagated to succeeding Generations." [34] While this motivation dated back to the earliest years of church history, its more immediate and relevant application was found in the Reformed tradition. John Calvin, who stressed the need for an educated ministry—and laity—believed that education was as much a concern of the church as of the state. Ideally, in Calvin's scheme, all three institutions—church, academy, and magistracy—existed harmoniously under the reign of Christ in his roles as priest, prophet (teacher), and king. In fact, the Genevan reformer understood teaching to be a specialized form of ministry and thus reinforced the particular connection between school and church. Calvin's conception of education was reflected in the Academy of Geneva, which he established in 1559, and the same ideal obtained as Calvin's ideas spread. The Huguenots in France established a number of academies through their synods, and in 1560 the Church of Scotland's *First Book of Discipline* proposed a plan of church-supported education from village school to university so that the youth might "have knowledge and erudition to profit and comfort that which ought to be most dear to us, to wit, the Kirk and spouse of Our Lord Jesus." [35] The nonconformists in England followed the same practice, although in a far less systematic fashion, after they were excluded from Oxford and Cambridge in 1662. The Connecticut college proponents were aware of standing in this tradition and, according to one of Yale's first chroniclers, President Thomas Clap, the initial plans for the school were drawn up "in Imitation of the Protestant Colleges and Universities in France, founded by their general Synods." [36]

Unfortunately, the pastors were not in a position to devote all of their thoughts and energies to the religious dimensions of the college. Connecticut's situation in the English colonial system presented the ministers with a more immediate and mundane concern—the legal status of the proposed school. For the moment, the

34. *Yale Annals,* p. 2.

35. R. W. Henderson, *The Teaching Office in the Reformed Tradition,* p. 133; see also George Williams, *Wilderness and Paradise in Christian Thought,* pp. 184–95.

36. *Yale Annals,* p. 2.

clergymen had to put aside the question of purpose and concentrate on this more practical consideration.

Their preoccupation with this issue is understandable. As a corporate colony, Connecticut did not have to send its laws to England for approval and, except for being required to abide by the Navigation Acts, it had no restraints placed on it by the mother country. These were privileges to be jealously guarded and the several pastors did not want to take any steps that might jeopardize their colony's charter. Charters could be revoked, as the case of Massachusetts clearly warned. The clergymen feared that any move on the part of the Connecticut General Assembly to charter a college might endanger the colony's charter. Such a school, moreover, when established, might be declared illegal by Parliament. Since it was not in the power of corporate colonies to incorporate other societies, technically Connecticut could not establish a college.

In 1701 this legal difficulty was a real, not a theoretical, one. The Lords Commissioners of Trade and Plantations, better known as the Board of Trade, had been established in 1696 by King William in an effort to retain royal control over the colonies in the face of Parliament's challenge to that control. The board's influence over colonial affairs was extraordinary; it recommended colonial legislation to Parliament, examined and judged the validity of colonial laws, had a strong voice in the appointment of royal governors, and passed decisions on complaints of oppression and maladministration. Soon after its organization, the board made a survey of the American colonies and concluded that before any uniform control of the colonies could be effected, all corporate and proprietary colonies would have to be converted into royal ones.[37]

On March 29, 1701, the board reported to Parliament that the corporate (or charter) and proprietary colony governments "have not conformed themselves to the several acts of Parliament for regulating trade and navigation, to which they ought to pay the same obedience, and submit to the same restriction, as other plantations, which are subject to his Majesty's immediate government." These colonial governments, the board continued, "have assumed to themselves a power to make laws, contrary and repugnant to the laws of England, . . . some of them haveing refused to send hither

37. David Hawke, *The Colonial Experience* (Indianapolis: Bobbs-Merrill, 1966), pp. 339–40.

such laws as they have there enacted." The board further charged that some colonies had denied appeals by loyal subjects to the King in Council, a criticism which the board leveled against Connecticut in particular a month later. Having stated its case against the proprietary and corporate colonies, the board concluded by recommending that if these colonies were to be "duly subservient and useful to England," their charters must "be reassumed to the crown, and these colonies put into the same state and dependency as those of his Majesty's other plantations." [38]

Although the Board of Trade's subsequent reunification bill failed in 1701, largely due to the effective parliamentary opposition organized by William Penn, the Connecticut clergymen knew that the year was not a propitious one for the colony to enact offensive legislation. For Connecticut to incorporate a college in the face of the Board of Trade's bill would be to court disaster; it would be adding more damaging evidence to the board's case. The problems, then, were real: how to establish the desired college without overstepping legal boundaries; how to achieve the result without risking reprisals?

The Connecticut ministers sought legal counsel and sent inquiries to three men: Gershom Bulkley, a Wethersfield lawyer; Eleazar Kimberly, secretary of the colony; and John Eliot, grandson of the apostle to the Indians and a leading member of the General Assembly. From Eliot's reply it is possible to reconstruct the six questions the ministers had asked.[39] They wanted to know whether the Connecticut government could erect a college that could not be overset by law, the way in which donations to the school should be secured, what the master of the college should be called, whether the college could grant legally valid degrees, whether the government of the college should be placed in the hands of nine trustees and whether there should be an age limit for those trustees, and whether private benefactors could direct their donations to particular officials of the college to be used at their discretion.

38. Leo Francis Stock, ed., *Proceedings and Debates of the British Parliaments respecting North America,* 5 vols. (Washington, D.C.: Carnegie Institution of Washington, 1924–41), 2 : 385–86, 399.

39. I have constructed these six questions by reading back from Eliot's answers. While Bulkley and Kimberly did not deal with all six queries, I assume that they had been asked for an opinion on several issues, as both men referred to questions in the plural.

Obviously, the first of these six queries was paramount: if the proposed college could be overset by law, the other five matters would be academic. Gershom Bulkley addressed himself to the primary question and replied that he had uncovered little legal evidence on which to base an opinion. He cited several Elizabethan statutes that permitted donations for schools of learning and argued that the Act of Indulgence of 1689 overturned the laws prohibiting dissenters from teaching youth. But Bulkley was not sure that the legal precedents would guarantee success and suggested that the safest procedure would be to petition the king "to grant a Liberty, ratified by Act of Parliament, for the founding of a Colledge." [40] While this method may have been legally sound, it was not what the advocates for a college wanted. They had not intended to establish a royally chartered college within a corporately chartered colony.

Eleazar Kimberly had a more optimistic and hence more welcome opinion. He concurred with the view "that the Statutes of England and acts of Parliament are not in force in the forreign Plantations, Excepting only such Statutes &c wherein the Plantations were named." Kimberly therefore thought that the college planners were on safe ground in that no English law applied to their situation. He went on to opine that no properties granted for "the promoting of Good Literature in this Land" would be offensive to the statutes governing religious and charitable corporations, and said that he believed "the Kings of England will always be ready to Promote Good Learning in all their dominions, and to continue any Estates that are given for that use without any alteration as I observe his present Majestie hath done in the Charter of the Massachusetts Province." [41]

Kimberly's encouraging response was echoed by John Eliot, who wrote that to erect a college was "neither Repugnant to the Laws of England nor an entrenchment on the Kings Prerogative," for he knew that "no act of Parliament sais such a Scool may not be erected in the Plantations." While this was ostensibly the line of reasoning taken by Kimberly, Eliot was more positive in his wording. He thought that the existence of Harvard and other societies

40. *Documentary History,* pp. 10–11.

41. Ibid., pp. 11–12. The Statutes of Mortmain prohibited the alienation of lands to ecclesiastical and other corporations in order to protect the feudal rights of the lords.

in Boston and New York proved that at that time the prerogative was not threatened by these kinds of establishments. Eliot, then, considered it safe to proceed with founding a college, but he preached caution. He suggested that the title of the college master be one "which shows Least of Grandeur," as that would be "Least obnoxious," and advised against the college granting degrees because it did not stand "on a Royall foundation." Eliot felt that some kind of certificate would suffice for Connecticut's purposes but counseled prudence even in this, lest "Our enemies will take advantage to injure us." [42]

Though Eliot did not specify to whom a grand name for the college master would be obnoxious or who Connecticut's enemies were, it is clear that he was referring in both cases to those English officials on the Board of Trade who were offended by the colony's autonomy and wished to see Connecticut royalized. These were the men Eliot did not want to provoke, and although he felt the college proposers to be on safe legal ground, he warned them against drawing attention to their school.

Having solicited advice from three of their fellow colonists, the ministers evidently wrote next to two Massachusetts citizens, Judge Samuel Sewall and Isaac Addington, secretary of the colonial government. While the reasons for consulting these men are nowhere mentioned, it is likely that the ministers were motivated by the fact that Sewall and Addington were not only respected officeholders but were orthodox laymen as well. Surely they could offer expert and sound advice about the nature of the proposed college. It is probable that the Connecticut ministers told these men of their concerns, both legal and theological, and requested a model of a college charter. Sewall and Addington complied and sent a draft of a charter to the Reverend Thomas Buckingham on October 6. In the letter accompanying the draft they explained that the charter was cautiously worded so as not to burden the ministers with specific requirements and commitments that might prove detrimental. The draft, therefore, did not mention the particulars of visitation by government representatives for fear "that in little time it might probably prove subversive of your Designe." This remark obviously meant that, if Connecticut was made a royal colony, the government would no longer be in sympathy with the

42. Ibid., pp. 13–15.

aims of the college and visitors could impede the college's operation. The specter of the reunification bill also caused the Boston authors to give the proposed "Accademie as low a name as we could that it might the better stand in wind and weather, not daring to Incorporate it, least it should be liable to be served with a Writ of Quo Warranto." [43]

The college planners heeded the suggestions of prudence and caution. They rejected Gershom Bulkley's opinion that they apply for a royal charter and followed instead the recommendations of Eliot, Sewall, and Addington. The ministers determined to petition the Connecticut government for a charter but to undertake the establishment of a college in the least ostentatious fashion.

It is at this point that the story of Yale's beginnings becomes most confused. In 1766 President Thomas Clap published his *Annals or History of Yale College,* in which he stated that ten ministers officially "founded" the collegiate school as early as 1700 by the act of donating books for the college library.[44] Clap's pur-

43. Ibid., pp. 15, 16. For a discussion of the issues about incorporation that concerned the ministers, see Joseph S. Davis, *Essays in the Earlier History of American Corporations,* 2 vols. (Cambridge, Mass.: Harvard University Press, 1917), 1 : 21–25. Yale was not officially incorporated until 1745. In May, 1758, the governor and upper house vetoed a bill passed in the lower house to incorporate Eleazar Wheelock's Indian School "upon the ground that their action would not be valid if ratified in England, *beyond this Colony,* and that a corporation within a corporation might be troublesome as Yale College has sometimes been." See ibid., 1 : 25.

44. The evolution of Clap's version of the founding of the college developed over a period of nineteen years. He began the work in 1747 and claimed that it was based on records, original papers, and conversations with men "who were contemporary with the Facts related." When he published this history in 1766, Clap said that he was presenting "a just and simple Narration of Facts, without interspersing many Embellishments, Observations or Reflections."

In essence, Clap argued that the first design for a college in Connecticut was begun in 1698 when several ministers met and drew up a plan for a college to be erected by a synod of the consociated churches of the colony. The college was to be called "the *School of the Church*" and was to be supported by the churches. In 1699 the ministers met in several smaller councils and decided on ten of their number to act as trustees. A year later these ten men gathered in New Haven, formed themselves into a body, and agreed to found a college at their next meeting. This was done later in 1700 at Branford, when each minister brought some books, placed them on a table in the Reverend Samuel Russell's house, and said, in effect, "I give these Books for the founding a College in this Colony." This act constituted, for Clap, the actual founding of the school. It was only, he explained, when the trustees began to doubt the legality of their actions that they decided to apply to the Connecticut General Assembly for a charter. The trustees wrote to some friends in Massachusetts and obtained a draft of a charter. The ministers

poses in making this claim were political rather than historical, but the result of his effort was to create a version of Yale's founding which has never been wholly dismissed. No contemporary evidence survives which in any way corroborates Clap's account of ten

---

then petitioned the General Assembly for assistance, and on October 9, 1701, the assembly granted a charter which, according to Clap, was ostensibly the one drawn up by the Massachusetts men, "with some small Additions and Alterations."

There is no surviving documentary evidence to support Clap's claim of an organized founding in 1700. Indeed, the evidence suggests just the opposite. As late as September, 1701, for example, the ministers were still soliciting advice on the number of trustees the college should have; there is no indication that the number ten had been settled upon. Thus, while it is probable that Connecticut clergymen met prior to 1701 to discuss the founding of a college, nothing official had occurred. In 1876 Franklin B. Dexter, the college secretary, challenged Clap's version of the founding of Yale. Dexter pointed out that in the original draft of his history, Clap had made no claim for a pre-1701 founding and had stated that the college trustees gave books for the library in 1702. In 1754, in his *The Religious Constitution of Colleges* (New London, 1754), Clap said that the trustees gave the books and founded the college in November, 1701. In 1766, however, Clap pushed these events back to 1700. The reason for this change, as Dexter suggested, was that President Clap, in 1763, made a successful defense of the college's right "to be exempt from visitatorial power" claimed by the General Assembly as the agency that had founded the college. Clap denied the assembly's claim by insisting that the college founders had obtained books, money, and land before the charter grant and hence they, not the assembly, were the true founders.

The argument worked, and what had been a legal ploy in 1763 became history in 1766. Clap's dating was accepted for over a hundred years. Yale celebrated its 150th anniversary in 1850 but, after Dexter's reevaluation, held the bicentennial in 1901. Despite the alteration in dates, Clap's version persists to this day. Even Dexter placed the important book ceremony before the General Assembly meeting, thus making the ministers the founders of the college, and subsequent historians have followed his lead. The brief "History of Yale University" in the *University Catalogue Number for the Academic Year 1969–1970* states that "ten Connecticut clergymen met in the house of Reverend Samuel Russel at Branford in 1701, and there, according to tradition, made a gift of books 'for the founding of a College in this colony.'" The "History" dates this meeting a month before the General Assembly session and states that the charter made the founders the trustees.

To deny the validity of what appears to be a harmless tradition might seem a petty act of iconoclasm; but as W. H. Cowley, who has researched this issue thoroughly, argues, the Clap history has served to buttress the wholly fallacious notion that somehow Yale has always been, in the modern sense of the term, a "private" college. Perhaps now is as good a time as any to lay this tradition to rest. All the evidence we have supports the fact that the General Assembly founded the collegiate school. For the various versions of this story see: *Yale Annals,* pp. 1–5; Franklin B. Dexter, "The Founding of Yale College," *A Selection from the Miscellaneous Historical Papers of Fifty Years,* pp. 59–83; Charles Henry Smith, "The Founding of Yale College," Papers of the New Haven Colony Historical Society, 7 (1908): 34–64; Edwin Oviatt, *The Beginnings of Yale (1701–1726)*, chap. 4, especially pp. 156–61; and *University Catalogue Number for the Year 1969–1970* (New Haven, 1969), pp. 125–26.

ministers meeting in Branford in 1700 to found the school. Indeed, the documents we do have offer no suggestions that the ministers who proposed the college plan had undertaken any official acts prior to the meeting of the Connecticut General Assembly on October 9, 1701. Subsequent historians, notably Franklin Bowditch Dexter, have recognized the tenuous nature of Clap's claim, but none of them has had the courage of his convictions to dismiss the story as spurious. Dexter, for instance, thought it likely that the event occurred a few weeks before the ministers obtained a charter—a bit later than Clap's dating but still early enough to precede the General Assembly meeting of October. Thus, although with some chronological modifications, Clap's purposes have been perpetuated in the tradition that Yale was founded, not by the Connecticut government but by a group of ministers.

Based on the evidence, the opposite conclusion is the accurate one. This fact should not blind us, however, to the truth that, in every sense but the legal one, clergymen did establish the collegiate school. Ministers conceived the school, planned it, and formulated its nature and destiny. Only after these matters had been settled did they turn to the government for official sanction. Before doing this, they apparently made some political decisions of their own. Of the eight men who worked on the college plan, James Pierpont and Samuel Russell were from New Haven County, Israel Chauncy was from Fairfield County, and James Noyes, Abraham Pierson, Thomas Buckingham, Moses Noyes, and Gurdon Saltonstall were from New London County. The clergymen evidently perceived the difficulties inherent in this imbalance and sought to correct it.

Their solution was to seek a ministerial constituency representing all sections of the colony; Moses Noyes and Saltonstall were dropped from the New London delegation, leaving three men from that county. The pastors also dropped Samuel Russell and replaced him with Samuel Andrew of Milford, thereby retaining two representatives from New Haven County, and added Joseph Webb of Fairfield, giving that county two men as well. Most importantly, the clergymen invited three Hartford County colleagues to join them, Samuel Mather of Windsor, Timothy Woodbridge of Hartford, and Noadiah Russell of Middletown. This last move was a wise one, for Hartford was a center of political power in Connecticut and deserved representation. When the ministers went before the General Assembly in October, then, they represented an evenly distributed geographical area, which served to give the appearance that the college plan was a colony-wide project.

Reassured by the answers to their legal queries and encouraged by the enthusiastic support of friends in the Bay Colony, the pastors were ready to seek the General Assembly's assistance. But these men had more assets than comforting advice and the draft of a charter. The final group of ten ministers also represented an ecclesiastical and social elite and hence wielded considerable influence within the assembly. In the first place, they were ten of the oldest and most respected clergymen in the colony, the only ones of comparable stature being Moses Noyes, Samuel Russell, Gurdon Saltonstall, and Samuel Street of Wallingford. The first three of these had been involved in the pre-October activities and two of them, Noyes and Russell, were soon to become trustees; Saltonstall, in six years' time, became governor, a position that made him a powerful friend of the school.[45]

The group had other strengths as well, for the ministers represented the largest and wealthiest towns in the colony. There were thirty towns on the 1701 tax list and the first fourteen, in order of wealth, were Hartford, New Haven, Windsor, Wethersfield, Fairfield, Milford, Stratford, New London, Guilford, Farmington, Stonington, Stamford, Middletown, and Saybrook. Of these towns, Farmington was without an ordained pastor, Wethersfield, Guilford, and Stamford were served by younger men, and New London by Gurdon Saltonstall, who was an active though unofficial agent in the founding of the college. Each of the remaining nine towns provided one original trustee. The tenth

45. Dexter, "Founding of Yale College," pp. 68–69, 82. In appearance, if not in fact, these men were a closely knit group. Not only did they all share a common vocation, but nine of them claimed the same alma mater. Woodbridge and Andrew had been classmates at Harvard, as had Pierpont and Russell; Noyes and Chauncy overlapped at college for two years, while Mather was a senior when Andrew and Woodbridge were freshmen, and Webb was in his first year when Pierpont and Russell were completing their work for the A.B. The ties of these men extended beyond profession and education, moreover, to include the bonds of family. Webb and Chauncy married sisters, as did Mather and Andrew; Pierpont was Pierson's nephew by one marriage and Buckingham's stepson by another; Noyes and Woodbridge were cousins; and the children of Pierson and Woodbridge intermarried. Noadiah Russell, in fact, was the only minister in the group who had no family connection to another.

man, Abraham Pierson, came from the little town of Killingworth, whose fifty-two rate-payers placed it twenty-fourth on the list.[46]

The ministers not only were men of stature from places of wealth, but they also commanded powerful allies in the government. The governor, Fitz-John Winthrop, who had intended to study at the college proposed by Davenport in 1655, was the parishioner of his friend and advisor, Gurdon Saltonstall; Deputy-Governor Robert Treat counted two would-be trustees as sons-in-law: Samuel Mather of Windsor and his own pastor, Samuel Andrew of Milford. Five of the ten members of the governor's council were parishioners of these ministers, as were Peter Burr (H. 1690) of Fairfield, the speaker of the house, and John Eliot (H. 1685) of Windsor, the only other college graduate in the assembly and a man whose advice the ministers had solicited and followed. The ten clergymen could also count on an acquaintance with, and perhaps the votes from, their town representatives, giving them twenty of the fifty-two men in the lower house.

These factors provided the ministers with ample opportunities to lobby for the college plan, and undoubtedly all of them took pains to solicit the support of their friends in the assembly. Apparently they did their work well, for there is no evidence to suggest that their plea for a charter met with any objections. It is most likely, in fact, that the idea was greeted with unanimous enthusiasm. The Sewall-Addington draft of a charter had arrived in Thomas Buckingham's hands at about the beginning of the assembly session; the ministers, chiefly James Pierpont, revised the draft, changing some words and adding a few phrases. The principal revision was the omission of any specified curriculum in the charter —Sewall and Addington had included a paragraph stipulating that the Westminster Confession and William Ames's *Medulla Theologiae* be required texts.[47] The ministers, while agreeing with this requirement, thought it inappropriate as a charter condition. The alterations in the draft completed, the men turned the document over to the assembly as a model of the desired charter; and the assembly, in effect, ratified that desire.

46. *Conn. Records,* 4 : 360.

47. *Documentary History,* pp. 15, 19. For Pierpont's alterations, see ibid., pp. 17–18.

The charter the General Assembly granted the ten ministers was a benign document. The legislators passed "An act for Liberty to erect a Collegiate School," which gave the clergymen, in effect, carte blanche to form a college in any way they chose. The government did not found or incorporate the college but granted the ten ministers

> full Liberty Right and Priveledge . . . To ERECT form direct, order establish improve and att all times in all suitable wayes for the future to Encourage the said School in such convenient place or Places, & in such form & manner & under such order & Rules as to them shall seem meet & most conducive [to their design].[48]

Control of the college, then, was placed entirely in the hands of the ten trustees (the maximum number of trustees was set at eleven, the minimum at seven, and all were to be Connecticut clergymen above the age of forty) and any successors they elected. The Connecticut government had no legal jurisdiction over the college, as no provision was made for overseers. The absence of this provision marked a decisive break with the practice in Massachusetts, where Harvard was governed by both corporation *and* overseers. The Connecticut college thus established closer—though unofficial—ties with the church than with the state and at the same time anticipated a governing pattern that most nineteenth-century American colleges were to adopt.[49] Although the chief reason for this decision was to safeguard the college against possible intervention by an unsympathetic government, the result was in line with the Reformed ideal of having schools responsible to the church.

Other aspects of the charter reveal the ministers' desire to avoid drawing attention to their school. Following the counsel of Sewall, Addington, and Eliot, the college was called "a Collegiate School," the president was given the title "Rector or Master," and the col-

48. Ibid., p. 21.

49. Richard Hofstadter and Walter P. Metzger, *The Development of Academic Freedom in the United States,* p. 137. Hofstadter was wrong, however, when he argued that the Massachusetts men had urged a dual system on the Connecticut ministers. Sewall and Addington had specifically omitted the provision for visitors from the draft, although they thought such a policy was good.

lege was to grant "degrees or Licenses" instead of legal diplomas.[50] While the language was modest, the intention was bold. The college was proposed by the ten ministers out "of their sincere Regard to & Zeal for upholding & Propagating of the Christian Protestant Religion by a succession of Learned & Orthodox men" and was to be a place "wherein Youth may be instructed in the Arts & Sciences who through the blessing of Almighty God may be fitted for Publick employment both in Church & Civil State." [51] With purposes and goals such as these, what did it matter what the college, its president, or its degrees were called?

The document that the college proponents—now trustees—obtained at New Haven cleared the path for the implementation of their design. They had been granted an annual sum of £120 for the use of the school and were given permission to obtain and use an additional £500 per annum from whatever sources were open to them. In addition, James Fitch, a wealthy landed proprietor and one of the governor's assistants, offered to give the college a deed to a farm which the college could rent for profit.[52] By the time the ministers left the General Assembly meeting in New Haven, they

50. Although the title of *rector* might have been more modest than *president,* the term was also one used by European academies, thus further indicating the trustees' familiarity with and adoption of continental patterns. The term *rector* was used at Yale until the revised charter of 1745, when Thomas Clap changed it to *president.* Literally, then, Clap was Yale's first president.

51. *Documentary History,* pp. 20–21. The language used here, and elsewhere, to describe the purposes of the collegiate school is typical of the Reformed tradition's outlook on education. The *Forms of Prayers and Ministration of the Sacraments, used in the English Congregation at Geneva* (1554), for example, argued for the necessity and purposes of education in terms parallel to those of the collegiate school trustees. Stressing that knowledge of God's word in Scripture was mandatory for ministers of the church, the Genevan Order continued: "But because men cannot so well profit in that knowledge except they be first instructed in the tongues and humane sciences, (for now God worketh not commonly by miracles) it is necessary that seed be sewn for the time to come, to the intent that the Church be not left barren and waste to our posterity; and that schools also be erected and colleges maintained with just and sufficient stipends wherein youth may be trained in the knowledge and fear of God that in their ripe age they may prove worthy members of Our Lord Jesus Christ, whether it be to rule in civil policies, or to serve in spiritual ministry, or else to live in Godly reverence and subjection" (see Henderson, *Teaching Office,* p. 129). Harvard was founded for these same reasons, a fact that Samuel Eliot Morison chose to play down in his excellent works on that college, *The Founding of Harvard College* and *Harvard in the Seventeenth Century.*

52. *Documentary History,* pp. 19–20.

had received the encouragement, the legal right, and the finances to create a college.

The First Trustee Meeting

James Pierpont quickly informed Judge Sewall and Secretary Addington of the successful petition for a charter. Sewall, in his reply, expressed pleasure at the speed with which the ministers had achieved their goal.[53] The trustees did not relax after the charter was obtained; they called their first meeting for November 11 at Thomas Buckingham's house in Saybrook.

Seven of the ten trustees attended the meeting. Timothy Woodbridge was detained in Boston with a leg injury and Samuel Mather, plagued by ill-health all his life, began his unbroken absenteeism by missing the Saybrook gathering.[54] James Noyes was forced to miss the meeting due to an infirmity, but his letter to Pierpont excusing himself indicates that one announced purpose of the first trustee gathering was to collect books for a college library. Noyes empowered his brother, Moses Noyes, "to give out of my books at his house my full proportion, & in nothing I would be behind hand in so publick a good." This book-giving ceremony, which Thomas Clap claimed took place at Branford in 1700, probably had been discussed earlier than the November meeting, but the evidence suggests that the act of starting the college library followed the granting of the charter. We do not know for certain how many works were collected in this fashion, but later estimates place the number in excess of forty, most of them tomes on biblical and theological subjects.[55]

On November 11, 1701, the trustees officially established their college. The occasion was a solemn one. The ministers recalled the purpose of their forefathers who had settled in America "to propagate in this Wilderness, the blessed Reformed, Protestant

53. Ibid., p. 26.

54. Ibid., pp. 23–24. In his letter saying that he could not attend the meeting, Mather stated: "My mind is fully fixt in that New-haven town Plat is the best place for such a Schole." While this opinion had no great impact in 1701, the trustees produced it in 1717 as support for the majority decision to move the college to New Haven. See ibid., p. 122, and below, chap. 3.

55. Ibid., pp. 24–25; Ezra Stiles, "College Records, records of early gifts to the college, 1778–95," pp. 1, 19, Yale Archives, Yale University Library, New Haven, Conn. Several of the volumes given by the first trustees are in the Yale Library of 1742, located in the Beinecke Rare Book Library.

Religion, in the purity of its Order, and Worship." The trustees, in a private jeremiad, recognized their "past neglects of this Grand errand, & Sensible of our equal Obligations better to prosecute the Same end" declared themselves "desirous in our Generation to be Serviceable therunto—Whereunto the Liberal, & Relligious Education of Suitable youth is under the blessing of God, a chief, & most probable expedient." The ministers therefore ordered and appointed "that there shal, & hereby is Erected & formed a Collegiate School, Wherein shal be taught the Liberal Arts, & Languages." [56]

The trustees then established rules for themselves as a body, agreed upon several procedural matters, and made two key appointments. The rectorship of the college was first offered to the oldest trustee present, Israel Chauncy, who declined, probably on account of his age, and then to Abraham Pierson of Killingworth, "who after Consideration was Pleased to take the said proposals into His farther Consideration." The trustees next brought one of the earlier college proponents back into the fold by appointing Samuel Russell (H. 1681) of Branford as a trustee "for Compleating the number of Eleven." The ministers also agreed that, "unless farther Consideration than the reasons now Before us occur and offer themselves," the college would be settled in Saybrook in order to best accommodate Connecticut and "the neighboring Colony." [57]

The chief order of business, however, was to establish and define the duties of the rector, the curriculum of the college, and other matters relating to the function of the school. The founders had solicited advice on these matters from several Massachusetts friends who, in turn, had responded with suggestions and proposals. The Connecticut clergymen had received four responses. The author of the first document is not specified but was probably Cotton

56. *Documentary History*, pp. 27–28.

57. Ibid., p. 31. When Pierson accepted the rectorship he thereby ceased being a trustee. The practice of separating the rector from the trustees continued until 1723 when the General Assembly passed an explanatory act stipulating that a rector was to serve as a trustee during his tenure in office. Elisha Williams was the first to hold this privilege, granted to him somewhat belatedly by the trustees, who did not welcome him to their meetings until several years after he became rector (see ibid., p. 250). The reference to the neighboring colony undoubtedly meant Massachusetts, as travel to Saybrook by way of the Connecticut River made the college accessible to boys from there, especially the western sections.

Mather;[58] Increase Mather wrote the second letter, and Samuel Sewall and Isaac Addington were jointly responsible for the third and fourth.

Cotton Mather's "Proposalls for Erecting an UNIVERSITY," which the ministers probably received in early 1701, stressed the role of the college as a preserver of religious orthodoxy. Mather wanted the college to be founded by a synod of the consociated churches and to be known as *"The School of the Churches."* Increase Mather made a similar proposal in his letter to the college trustees, suggesting that the most satisfactory way of supporting the college president and professors would be to have them maintained by the churches, as was done in France. Cotton's "Proposalls" also stated that the president of the college should be an eminent pastor and he, the tutors, and the trustees be required to "Subscribe certain Articles, relating to the *Purity of Religion,* that shall be by the *Synod* agreed upon." [59]

Here the Mathers were drawing on the tradition of establishing colleges in Reformed communities in Europe. The Calvinists in Geneva, the Huguenots in France, the Reformed churches in Holland, the Presbyterians in Scotland, and the Nonconformists in England either founded new colleges or shaped existing universities to preserve the purity and continue the propagation of the faith as they understood it. Harvard had been created for the identical purpose, and Davenport's dream of a New Haven college had been instigated by the same impulse.

The Connecticut ministers were engaged in a similar enterprise and were in agreement with the tenor of the Mather proposals. But while they concurred with the Mathers' general motivation, the college trustees were not prepared to implement their specific suggestions. Although Thomas Clap later argued that Yale was established by a synod of the consociated churches of the colony, this was not, in any formal sense, the case, as the colony had no

58. Franklin B. Dexter chose to assign this document to Increase Mather on the basis of similarities with his letter of September 15, 1701 (see *Documentary History,* p. 1). William L. Kingsley, offering no reason for his decision, flatly assigned the document to Cotton Mather. See William L. Kingsley, *Yale College: A Sketch of Its History,* 1 : 16. Samuel Eliot Morison, by comparing the proposals with portions of *Magnalia Christi Americana,* concluded that Cotton Mather was the author (see *Seventeenth-century Harvard,* 2 : 500). I find Morison's case most convincing. The comparable sections are found in *Documentary History,* p. 5, and *Magnalia,* bk. 4, p. 126.

59. *Documentary History,* pp. 1–2, 7, 4.

synod. The polity of Congregationalism, unlike that of Presbyterianism, sanctioned no organizational church structure, and hence it was impossible for the Huguenot model to be followed in Connecticut. The college was set up by Congregational ministers, however, so in one sense Yale was a school established *by* the churches but was not officially a school *of* the churches. The colony's congregations neither chose the president and faculty of the school nor contributed toward their or the college's support. Technically, then, the Collegiate School of Connecticut was an independent institution, tied to neither church nor state, though it had a relationship with both.

Another reason why Increase Mather's French model was not strictly applicable to the Connecticut situation was the particular nature of Connecticut's colonial status. The government in France was not sympathetic to the Protestant cause, and thus the churches were forced to found and maintain their own centers of learning. This practice was undoubtedly attractive to Mather because of the political situation in Massachusetts. Although the people of that colony retained the right to elect their own legislators and officials, the governor of the colony was appointed by the crown and Massachusetts had to send all of its laws to England for approval. This semiroyal status meant, in Mather's view, that Harvard's independence had been compromised; his inability to obtain a satisfactory college charter was the most graphic example of this fact.

The former president therefore proposed that the second New England college avoid the possibility of a similar fate by following the Huguenot procedure. The fact was, however, that as a charter colony Connecticut enjoyed practically complete autonomy. The college trustees certainly took pains to protect the college from potential interference from an unsympathetic (i.e. royalized) colonial administration, but on the whole they were confident of the support of what they called the colony's "present Religious Goverment." [60] The Connecticut ministers expected, with some justification, that church, college, and colonial government could operate, as in Geneva, as a working triumvirate, although bound by no literal alliance.

While the trustees failed to follow the first two suggestions made by the Mathers, they adopted a more ambivalent posture on the question of a religious test for college officers. Such tests, too, were

60. Ibid., p. 27.

common Reformed practice. In 1620 the National Synod in France had stipulated that the canons laid down by the Synod of Dort (1618–19) must be "approved, sworn to, and subscribed by the Pastors and the Elders, and by the Doctors and Professors and the Regents, and by all who wish to be admitted into the holy Ministry, or into the Professor's Chair in any of our Academies." At the same time in Holland, the Synod of Dort itself affirmed that all professors, whether of "sacred subjects," the arts, law, or medicine, had to subscribe to the confession and catechism of the church.[61] In making a similar recommendation to the Connecticut ministers, Cotton Mather was trying to impose on the new college, conditions which had been denied Harvard. The Harvard charter of 1699 had been rejected because it contained a religious test, and Increase Mather had considered such a stipulation the sine qua non of the 1700 charter. But the Connecticut ministers were suspicious of required subscription to religious tests and declined to implement them for college officers.

In adopting this stance, the trustees were following an English rather than a European model. Whereas in the aftermath of the Synod of Dort, Reformed communities on the continent imposed subscription requirements, many participants in the Westminster Assembly in England argued against them. The Connecticut clergymen evidently shared this view.[62] The only step the trustees took in this direction was to require that the students not "be Instructed and Grounded in any other Systems or Synopses of Divinity than such as the said Trustees do order and appoint." [63] This meant at the time, and continued to mean until the Revolution, that Yale students would be trained in Reformed theology as set down at the Westminster Assembly and as interpreted chiefly by the theological treatises of William Ames and Johann Wollebius.

61. Henderson, *Teaching Office,* pp. 87, 112.

62. The subscription issue not only raged in England but had its American counterpart in colonial Presbyterianism, where the New England faction (many of them Yale men) took an antisubscription line in the 1720s and 1730s and eventually won a compromise on the matter. For a discussion of this controversy with references to the English situation, see Leonard Trinterud, *The Forming of an American Tradition,* especially chapter 2.

63. *Documentary History,* p. 32. When Rector Timothy Cutler's defection to Anglicanism in 1722 shattered the supposed theological harmony of the college and colony, the trustees established the requirement that all college officers subscribe to the Confession of Faith set down in the Saybrook Platform of 1708 (ostensibly the Westminster Confession). See below, chapter 4.

Increase and Cotton Mather offered two other recommendations to the college proponents. Both men suggested that the new school follow the example of certain Dutch and Swedish universities, which provided an instruction hall but had no living quarters and allowed students to board with families in the college town. The Connecticut ministers did not debate this matter, obviously having agreed among themselves to emulate the student living arrangements of Harvard, which in turn had been copied from the patterns of Oxford and Cambridge. Although the collegiate school operated without any dormitory facilities for several years, it did so out of physical necessity rather than an educational philosophy.

The ministers did, however, adopt the Mathers' second proposal —although perhaps not for the same reasons the Massachusetts men had given. Father and son had both warned against holding elaborate commencements. Increase bewailed the Harvard commencements, which had "of late years proved very expensive & are occasion of much sin." Mather's definition of sin evidently included such relatively harmless pleasures as having plum cake at graduation parties, a custom the president had abolished in 1693. The elder Mather sugested that the Connecticut college avoid such diversions by imitating the example of English Dissenting academies, which "give degrees privately & silently." Cotton agreed. Graduation, he had stated, should be a time "for a Solemn, & Rigid *Examen*, of those that are CANDIDATES OF APPROBATION." Although the Mathers were hypercritical of Harvard and probably saw evil where there was only exuberance, their views on simple commencements made sense to the cost-conscious Connecticut trustees. They ordered that "for the Especial Encouragement of Students in Their industry and good Literature as well as for the Ease of their parents . . . we . . . Disallow of Publick Commencements and forbid the same at all times." [64]

The proposals forwarded to the trustees by Increase and Cotton Mather reflected the writers' dissatisfaction with the institutional and ideological state of Harvard. Not only were they piqued at Increase's loss of the presidency, but they had serious fears about the school's institutional autonomy and theological purity. While the Mathers probably overdramatized the extent of the problem, their unhappiness with their own college explains why they urged

64. Ibid., pp. 5, 6, 7, 3, 33. For the plum cake decision, see *Seventeenth-century Harvard*, 2 : 470.

the Connecticut ministers to imitate the Reformed schools in France, Holland, Sweden, and England. For the most part, these institutions were independent of state control. But the trustees found that it was neither necessary nor desirable to follow European models in establishing their college. While the ministers certainly thought of themselves and their college as participating in the same endeavor as these centers of higher education, their situation dictated other priorities. Since the Collegiate School of Connecticut was to exist in the supportive atmosphere of friendly church-state cooperation, the trustees felt free to turn their attention to more relevant concerns. Chief among these was a course of study that would allow the school to educate learned and orthodox men who would serve their society.

The letters of Cotton Mather, Samuel Sewall, and Isaac Addington all contained proposals for a college curriculum. Mather suggested that the president's duties should be: "Ordinarily once a Day to Entertain the Scholars in a publick Hall, with Prayers, and such other Exercises, (Whether *Expositions* of the Scripture, or Lectures in Divinity, or Church-History, or somewhat Else)," to examine the conduct of the tutors and the progress of the students on frequent occasions, to execute college discipline according to the laws, and to preach in the college town as often as possible. Sewall's idea of an exemplary college was one in which the president and tutors would "Instruct Youth in Academical Learning, and give them Degrees, as the late Reverend & Godly Learned Mr. Charles Chauncey was wont to doe at Cambridge." Sewall wanted the Connecticut ministers to "oblige the President to pray and expound the Scriptures in the Hall Morning and Evening *de die in diem,* and ground the Students in the Principles of Religion by reading to them or making them Recite the Assemblys Confession of Faith which is turned into good Latine, as also the Catechises; and Dr. Ames's Medulla." Sewall explained in a postscript that he specified the Westminster Confession because "Arminianisme is crept even into the Dissenters Annotations." This concern for maintaining religious orthodoxy also appeared in the Sewall-Addington charter draft, in which the authors attempted to legislate the teaching of correct articles of religion by insisting that the Westminster Confession and Ames's *Medulla Theologiae* be the mainstays of the college curriculum.[65]

65. *Documentary History,* pp. 4, 8–9, 18.

The college trustees had not wanted to include curriculum requirements in the charter but they were in accord with the desire for such requirements. At their November meeting, therefore, they formulated a course of study in accordance with the advice of their Massachusetts correspondents. The ministers declared that the students were to be grounded solidly in "Theoretical devinity" and stated that the rector was to

> take Effectual Care that the said students be weekly in such seasons as he shall see Cause to appoint Caused memoriter To recite the Assemblies Catechism in Latin and Ames's Theological Theses of which as Also Ames's Cases, He shall make or Cause to Be made from time to time such Explanations as may be (through the Blessing of God) most Conducive to their Establishment in the Principles of the Christian protestant Religion.

The trustees also stipulated

> That the said Rector shall also Cause the Scriptures Daily (Except the Sabbath) morning and Evening to be read by the Students at the times of prayer in the School according to the Laudable orders and usages in Harvard College making Expositions upon the same, and upon the Sabbath Shall Either Expound practical Theology or Cause the Students non Graduated, to Repeat Sermons, and in all other ways according to his Best Discretion shall at all times studiously Indeavour in the Education of said students to promote the power and Purity of Religion and Best Edification and peace of these New England Churches.[66]

The enumerated duties of the rector thus emphasized the religious orientation of the newly chartered college. The trustees clearly intended to pass on to the rising generation the theological heritage of New England's first settlers. This preoccupation, however, did not make the collegiate school a seminary. The ministers' broad purpose was to educate young men in the arts and sciences in order to equip them to serve the civil state as well as the church. In this respect, their ideas were implicit rather than explicit. The clergymen took for granted the fact that the college would teach

66. Ibid., p. 32. For more on the place of William Ames in the curriculum, see below, chapter 9.

the classical curriculum as defined in English and European universities. The trustees obviously saw no need to legislate this practice; they simply accepted it. In doing so, they again were following the example of their alma mater, for the ministers intended their school to serve as a revitalized Harvard, teaching those subjects and instilling those religious beliefs which would insure that Connecticut would have good laws and solid preaching. The college was to provide for the youth of the colony what Harvard had given the trustees in their undergraduate years. Thus, they copied the "Laudable orders and usages in Harvard College" with regard to daily prayer and Scripture reading and decided, for the time being, to "make use of the orders and institutions of Harvard College for the instructing and Ruling of the Collegiate School." [67]

There were, then, two major features of the trustees' objectives for the new college. In the theological sphere, they were conscious of the laxity and latitudinarianism of Harvard and so were explicit in setting down requirements for religious studies at the collegiate school. As for the intellectual, they were aware of the content and purposes of the classical curriculum as taught at Harvard and in European universities, and therefore they adopted it without question or comment. The Bay College was both a warning and a model for the Connecticut ministers. Samuel Sewall's nostaligic wish for a college that would function like the Harvard of President Chauncy's day was, in fact, a fairly accurate description of what the trustees hoped for the collegiate school.

By the middle of November, 1701, the trustees had firmly established the framework for the Collegiate School of Connecticut. They had obtained a charter, chosen a rector, formulated procedures, and defined a curriculum. All that remained was to enroll some students, settle Pierson in Saybrook, and begin to educate Connecticut youth "in the Arts and Sciences" to fit them "for Publick employment in Church & Civil State."

67. Ibid., p. 32.

2 "A Thing, Which They Call a College"

At the turn of the century Governor Joseph Dudley of Massachusetts sent an account of the state of religion in North America to the London headquarters of the Society for the Propagation of the Gospel in Foreign Parts. His brief entry for Connecticut stated that the colony had "thirty thousand souls, about thirty-three towns, all dissenters, supplied with ministers and schools of their own persuasion." [1] Dudley's letter implied that Connecticut was a homogenous society with a uniform religious posture—so the colony must have appeared from the vantage point of Boston, and certainly of London.

The vast majority of Connecticut's thirty thousand people earned their living as small farmers. Theirs was a difficult existence. A 1680 report on the colony described it as "a mountainous country, full of rocks, swamps, hills and vales. Most that is fitt for planting is taken up. What remaynes must be subdued, and gained out of the fire as it were, by hard blowes and for smal recompence." [2] Despite the terrain the economy was basically agricultural; the colony undertook very little overseas commerce. In 1708 its merchant navy consisted of two brigantines of about sixty tons each and seventeen sloops, ranging in size from around ten to twenty tons. In that year only the two brigantines loaded turpentine, pitch, and tar in Connecticut for direct export to England.

The colony's minimal foreign trade meant that Connecticut was relatively isolated and insulated from outside influences. Connecticut's trade was principally with Boston, New York, and the West Indies, areas which the colony provided with foodstuffs. It sent wheat, peas, rice, barley, corn, pork, and beef as well as turpentine and tar to Boston in return for clothing. To the West Indies the colony shipped horses, pork, beef, staves, and hoops in exchange for sugar, molasses, rum, and cotton wool. Connecticut had only one clothier, as most garments were homemade; the colonists were not wealthy enough to import European goods.[3]

1. Ernst Hawkins, *Historical Notices of the Missions of the Church of England in the North American Colonies* (London, 1845), p. 24.

2. *Conn. Records*, 3 : 296.

3. C.A., Foreign Correspondence, 1 : 126. In 1701 Agent Henry Ashurst, in de-

Connecticut's economic self-sufficiency struck Madame Sarah Knight of Boston, who traveled through Connecticut in 1704 and recorded her impressions of the colony. It was, she opined, "a plentiful Country for provisions of all sorts and its [*sic*] Generally Healthy. No one that can and will be dilligent in this place need fear poverty nor the want of food and Rayment." But while Madame Knight lauded the colony's economic potential, she deplored the lack of refinement among its citizens. She found the inhabitants endowed with "as Large a portion of mother witt, and sometimes a Larger, than those who have bin brought up in Citties" but wanting in education and polite conversation. They stood in awe of merchants, treated their few Negro slaves far too well, and rendered themselves ridiculous by their bumpkinish behavior. "They are generaly very plain in their dress, throuout all the Colony, as I saw, and follow one another in their modes; that You may know where they belong, especially the women, meet them where you will." This simplicity and conformity, however, did not blind Madame Knight to the blessings the colonists enjoyed. "St. Election," she noted, was Connecticut's "Cheif Red Letter day," and she envied the people who enjoyed the privilege of choosing their governor.[4]

This political privilege was one of Connecticut's chief characteristics and set it apart from all other American colonies except Rhode Island. The colony had successfully resisted Governor Edmund Andros's efforts to obtain its charter during the period of the Dominion of New England and fended off similar attempts by the Board of Trade in 1701 and 1706. In the early eighteenth century Connecticut's policy toward Great Britain was one of moderation and caution. When the Anglicans complained about their ill-treatment in the colony in 1708, Connecticut adopted the Toleration Act. In the late 1720s, when the Anglicans, Quakers, and Baptists threatened to cause trouble over the colony's ecclesiastical laws, the General Assembly passed acts exempting members of these churches from taxation for established ministers.[5]

At every turn the Connecticut practice was either to give in to

---

fending Connecticut against Parliament's Reorganization Bill, argued that the colony "lies at a distance from the sea, and the Inhabitants never accused of any maladministration Piraticall or unlawfull Trade, and that their case is different from his Majesties' other Plantations." See ibid., 2 : 68.

4. Sarah Knight, *The Journal of Madame Knight,* pp. 66–67, 43–44.

5. *Conn. Records,* 5 : 50–51; 7 : 106–07, 237, 257.

pressure just enough to satisfy the English authorities or, as was the case with founding the collegiate school, to act in such a way that English suspicions would not be aroused. These tactics worked and Connecticut retained its status as a corporate colony. This political autonomy enhanced the colony's cultural and social uniqueness; unlike the neighboring provinces of Massachusetts and New York, Connecticut never had to adjust its political structure to a royal governor and hence was spared much involvement in imperial affairs and intrigues.

Connecticut's economic and political independence was an important factor in shaping the cultural and social homogeneity which Madame Knight noted and which, to some observers, made the colony appear almost monolithic and impervious to change. A third element in the colony's unique situation was its religious constitution. Governor Dudley, an Anglican, was certainly correct in labeling the Connecticut citizens as "all dissenters." That was a broad description and, from an Anglican viewpoint, an accurate one. But the Connecticut dissenters were unified principally by what they all opposed—Anglicanism, popish forms, latitudinarianism, and laxity. They were not agreed on matters of ecclesiastical polity, and while they offered a united front against all outsiders, they quarreled among themselves over issues of "congregational" versus "presbyterial" church government.

A discerning report to the Lords of Trade in 1676 had referred to Connecticut's ecclesiastical spectrum as composed of some strict Congregationalists, some "large" or revisionist Congregationalists, and some moderate Presbyterians.[6] While none of these groups had formed into parties or were arguing precisely defined positions, the incipient dispute involved those who preferred congregational independence and limited church membership on the one hand, and those who favored presbyterian synods and a modified parish system of inclusive church membership on the other. The Half-Way Covenant of 1662, which authorized baptism for the children of unconverted parents, was one issue between the two groups. But the Half-Way Covenant was only a symptom of what the strict Congregationalists thought of as an ecclesiastical malady. The real disease was Presbyterianism.

6. Leonard Bacon, "Historical Discourse," *Contributions to the Ecclesiastical History of Connecticut*, p. 26. See also Robert G. Pope, "The Half-Way Covenant" (Ph.D. diss., Yale University, 1967), pp. 71–79.

Presbyterianism, in late seventeenth-century Connecticut, seems to have been associated with those ministers who desired a veto control over church decisions and who wanted the fraternity of pastors to participate in the election and ordination of new clergymen. The issue was chiefly one of power in the church plus, more broadly, sacerdotal versus "low" conceptions of the ministry and the church. Many laymen opposed these Presbyterian tendencies because they saw in them a threat to their rights as members of congregations. "Presbyterian" was also used to designate those willing to baptize the children of nonchurch members.[7] As such, the word was, for many ministers and laymen, the foremost pejorative term in Connecticut's ecclesiastical debates. When the Hartford church divided on the Congregational-Presbyterian issue in the 1660s, the Reverend John Davenport of New Haven inveighed against the "parish way" and revealed that the churches of New Haven, Milford, Stratford, Branford, Guilford, Norwalk, Stamford, Farmington, and Windsor were opposed to inclusive membership. (All but the last two were churches in the old New Haven Colony.) But while some men were unalterably opposed to any Presbyterian practices, others wanted to accommodate this segment of the colony's ecclesiastical structure. In 1669 the government asked four ministers to meet and attempt to solve the problems of church polity in the colony. The pastors advocated retention of the Congregational way but expressed a desire to include those who preferred the Presbyterian system.[8]

At the time of the founding of the collegiate school in 1701, Connecticut still had three variants of ecclesiastical polity. While it is difficult to determine which clergymen in the colony held which views, it is probable that among the college trustees there were ministers on at least two sides of the issue; Timothy Woodbridge was in favor of presbyterial forms and had probably published his views to that effect, and James Pierpont was the principal advocate of the large or revisionist position. No doubt the trustees discussed and debated these matters at their meetings, for the polity question was a pressing one and had to be resolved. But whatever the differences over church organization may have been,

7. For much of the above I am indebted to David D. Hall's *The Faithful Shepherd: A History of the New England Ministry in the Seventeenth Century*, which I read in manuscript.

8. Bacon, "Historical Discourse," pp. 23, 27–28.

the trustees did not let them interfere with the establishment of the new school. They put the ecclesiastical question aside for seven years and concentrated their immediate attention on the college.

Even so, the trustees soon found themselves enmeshed in disputes. On November 15, 1701, Thomas Buckingham wrote Governor Fitz-John Winthrop to report on the "very Comfortable unanimous meeting" of the trustees. But Buckingham found it necessary to inform the governor that difficulties had already arisen. The people of Killingworth, he related, "doe not see it their duty to consent unto the parting with Mr Pierson." While Buckingham doubted that the people would persist in an opinion that would hinder and confuse the work of the college, the facts were to be otherwise. Killingworth's refusal to part with Rector Pierson lasted for six years and confounded the issue of a college site.

That issue had already been confounded by the trustees themselves. Buckingham told Winthrop that the ministers had had "no great difficultie" in deciding to settle the school at Saybrook but admitted that the decision had been somewhat provisional. Saybrook had much to recommend it. The town was conveniently located at the mouth of the Connecticut River and was a post-town on all three of the routes between New York and Boston. Besides, it also served as a compromise location between the towns of Hartford and New Haven, the centers for political activity in the colony. Although Hartford does not seem to have been under consideration as the site of the school, New Haven evidently was. In what proved to be a prelude to a more serious rift fifteen years later, the trustees found themselves bickering with each other about the best place to locate the college. By the time of the next trustee meeting on April 8, 1702, the location of the school was still an open question. After much debate the trustees could only arrive at the temporizing conclusion "That the place for the Collegiate School in Connecticut Shall not be farther Eastward Then Say-Brook or westward Than New-Haven, But the farther Determination of the Definitive Place is at present Suspended." [9]

A few weeks later Trustee Buckingham told James Fitch that "A strong designe hath risen up to carry it [the school] farther westward; it is not yet fixed." [10] It is impossible to tell just how

9. *Documentary History*, pp. 36, 39.
10. Ibid., p. 40.

concerted the effort to move the college westward from Saybrook was, but it is likely that James Pierpont, as a chief architect of the college idea, wanted to locate the school in New Haven and thus to realize his predecessor's dream. But Saybrook had the asset of being near Killingworth, where Abraham Pierson was awaiting the arrival of students. With the school in a "hovering posture," Pierpont evidently decided against forcing the issue lest the school collapse before it began to function. In September, 1702, the western faction relinquished the fight and the trustees resolved the debate in favor of Saybrook.

The resolution was only theoretical. Abraham Pierson, who had accepted the rectorship because "He Durst Not Refuse such a Service for God and His Generation," was still unable to obtain his release from Killingworth.[11] Faced with this dilemma, the trustees had only one recourse. Since the rector could not come to the college, the college would have to go to the rector. On September 30, 1702, the trustees agreed to allow the school to continue at the little town of Killingworth (now Clinton), where Rector Pierson was instructing several students.

By this time the collegiate school had issued its first diploma. Nathaniel Chauncy, with the benefit of private tutoring, had come to Rector Pierson in the summer of 1702 and in a few months had demonstrated his proficiency in academic learning. Chauncy acquitted himself so well at the commencement exercises, in fact, that the trustees voted to award him both the B.A. and the M.A.[12] In receiving the latter diploma at the exercises held in the Reverend Thomas Buckingham's home, he was joined by four Harvard graduates who had chosen to take their second degrees from the fledgling college. But Chauncy's brief residence at college was the exception rather than the rule, and Pierson began to welcome scholars who were to spend the required three years studying for their degrees. Jacob Heminway was the first of these full-time students, and he was soon joined by about half a dozen others. To assist the rector in educating these young men the trustees appointed Daniel Hooker (H. 1700) as tutor. Pierson, after all, still had to perform his duties as the Killingworth minister.

From all accounts, Abraham Pierson was admirably suited for

11. Ibid., p. 38.

12. Chauncy's diploma is preserved. See Yale University Library *Gazette,* 9 (1935): 50, for a reproduction of the document.

both his pastoral and educational roles. He was a "well formed and comely looking man," and those who knew him remembered him as "an exceeding pious good man, and an excellent preacher." He had been the minister at Killingworth since 1694 and the small church had prospered under his leadership. One sign of the esteem of his parishioners was their reluctance to lose him to the college. So the college shared him with the church, an arrangement that Pierson seems to have found uncomfortable. Nevertheless, Rector Pierson was a "hard Student, a good Scholar, a great Divine," and he successfully nurtured the collegiate school through its early years. He wrote a system of natural philosophy (physics) that the students used during and after his rectorship; he preached weekly sermons that the townspeople heard and the scholars memorized; and he handled a major part of the instructional responsibilities of the school. Most important of all, he exemplified the theological orthodoxy and the intellectual ideals the college was designed to foster. These traits, although appreciated during his lifetime, were nevertheless taken for granted, only to be recalled in a later time of crisis as remarkable blessings. In 1722 the collegiate school trustees were to pay tribute to the first rector as "a pattern of piety, a man of modest behaviour, of solid learning, and sound principles, free from the least Arminian or Episcopal taint." [13] In the year 1702, however, even Abraham Pierson's piety, learning, and principles could not compensate for the difficulties faced by the new college.

Some of these difficulties were related to the problems of the school's Killingworth location. The college operated in Pierson's home, set on a hillock near the meetinghouse and the burial ground. Here the students performed their recitations and heard the rector's lectures, and from here they went to the Killingworth church and listened to Pierson's sermons. Mrs. Pierson provided the students' board and the townspeople rented them rooms. The absence of a college residence may have bothered some students, but the town itself had other drawbacks. Travel to and from Killingworth was inconvenient—although the erection of a bridge over the Menunketesuc River in 1700 made access to the eastern towns a bit easier—and the students no doubt felt both isolated and trapped in the small community. Attending college at Killingworth was not like going to Cambridge!

13. *Harvard Graduates,* 2 : 257; *Documentary History,* p. 227.

The scholars did not take long to make their discontent known. In 1702 some of them told the rector that they wanted to pursue their studies under "More private opportunities." This was an open challenge to the very purposes of the school, and the trustees rightly refused the request. Awarding college degrees to privately educated young men was not the school's function, and the trustees forbade this practice except in special cases. They required all undergraduates to reside in the college town and not to leave it without permission from the rector or tutor. Violators were to be excluded from the benefits of the school.[14]

Keeping the scholars at the college was not the only difficulty. Finding and keeping suitable tutors was also a chore. Daniel Hooker lasted a few months. In 1703, John Hart (class of 1703) was hired as tutor pro tempore, an appointment the trustees made permanent in February, 1704. They did so in the face of student opposition: Hart's instruction did not please the young Connecticut scholars. While the precise objections to his teaching were not revealed, the trustees found it necessary to issue "A memorial" to the undergraduates reminding them that they, not the students, were in charge of deciding whom to hire as a tutor. The trustees cautioned against "such spirits & methods, as have a tendency to discourage so great & happy an undertakeing" as the collegiate school, and hoped that the "trivial exceptions" taken to Tutor Hart would be forgotten. They also declared their approval of Hart and assured him of all "that support in his trust, & encouragement for his labors we are capable of." [15]

The trustees' stand evidently quelled the student unrest, for Hart continued as tutor for several years with no further trouble. But by the winter of 1705–06 the tutor situation was again dire and Pierson appealed to the trustees for help. Hart had resigned and the rector had been unsuccessful in obtaining a full-time replacement. Samuel Whittelsey (class of 1705) was filling in as a substitute but, Pierson lamented, "the freshmen are not satisfyed to be without a fixed tutor." Of the fifteen or so students at the college at this time, one had left school and was going to give up learning "and more of them may draw off, if they have not a settled tutor, by the want whereof, they may seem to be neglected, as to what they reasonably expect." Outlining this problem to the college

14. *Documentary History*, p. 42.

15. Ibid., p. 49.

trustees in a letter, Pierson revealed that the anti-Harvard bias of the college founders had not abated. Some of the trustees objected to hiring a tutor from Cambridge, a stricture that limited the school's options to a choice between Samuel Whittelsey and Phineas Fiske (class of 1704). Pierson recommended Fiske for the job, as he had "more seniority both in age and standing, than the other, and also hath bin now a considerable time absent from the School, and familiarity with the scholars, and lesse lyable to be objected against by the scholars." The rector pleaded for a quick decision, an indication that student discontent was high.[16] Phineas Fiske was accordingly made a tutor, a post he held for seven years.

While Pierson and the several tutors were attempting to provide the restless undergraduates with good learning, the trustees were trying to get the rector to move to Saybrook. Saybrook was the college's official location and the place where the college had received the deed to a house, about ten acres of land, and donations totaling £50. The donations were contingent on the school's being at Saybrook and thus were useless to Pierson in Killingworth. In 1702 the trustees offered Pierson accommodations in Saybrook, £100 to defray moving expenses, and an annual salary of £120. In 1704 they repeated the offer, urging the rector to move to Saybrook "and there settle for the Better Service of the Collegiate School." [17] None of these inducements bore fruit. The college and its rector remained in Killingworth, and all Saybrook had to show for its selection as the college town was the annual private commencement at Thomas Buckingham's house.

Pierson's failure to leave his Killingworth pastorate was partly a matter of money. In the spring of 1705 he intimated to James Pierpont that additional reimbursements for his services would be welcome, but this suggestion brought him no satisfaction.[18] In September of the same year, Pierson wrote a letter to the inhabitants of Killingworth explaining his position as college rector. He claimed that he had attempted to keep his rectorship "consistant with my ministerial work among you" and that he would not leave the town for Saybrook unless his parishioners consented, "& by

16. Ibid., p. 53.
17. Ibid., pp. 39, 42, 48.
18. Ibid., p. 50. Pierson's request is not extant, but Thomas Buckingham wrote to James Pierpont about this matter; no official action was taken on the rector's request. Pierson evidently intended to move to the college town, as he bought a six-and-a-half-acre plot in Saybrook in November, 1703. See *Yale Graduates,* 1 : 18.

your consent I mean your Genaral and Joynt consent, and not mearly a major part of you consenting." Pierson stipulated that by "consent" he also meant a willingness to offer him some financial reimbursement for his house. This last condition was too much. The people of Killingworth replied to Pierson that "it is our opinion that it is not, or like to be Consistant with your ministeriall worke amongst us to attend said School as heitherto" and added that they did not intend to take any further action on the matter.[19] The people's refusal to buy Pierson's house effectually prevented the rector from leaving town.

The tug-of-war between the trustees and the Killingworth inhabitants over Pierson remained a stalemate for another year. In the autumn of 1706 the trustees again applied pressure on the rector, demanding that he, Tutor Fiske, and the students remove to Saybrook by the next spring. The people of Killingworth, who evidently objected to their pastor's spending time on a dozen and a half students, retaliated by declaring that "they are not willing to allowe that the School should be keept hear as it has been." On November 7, Pierson asked the town to decide under what terms the collegiate school could remain in Killingworth under his care; the town formed a committee to study the matter and draw up terms.[20]

The committee never reported. Rector Pierson died the following March, and the confrontation between the trustees and his parishioners died with him. But, with this problem removed, the trustees were now faced with another—the choice of a new rector. Nobody wanted the job full time, but the trustees did prevail upon one of their number, Samuel Andrew, to serve as rector pro tempore. Andrew was an obvious choice. He had been a teaching fellow at Harvard in 1681 when President Urian Oakes died, and he had in that case been appointed "to execute the office of a Proctor for the commencement week" by the Harvard overseers. He and the other tutor were also chosen to take charge of the college until a new president was elected. Andrew performed this task for one year and in 1682 was congratulated by the Massachusetts General Court for diligently "carrying on the praesidents worke" after Oakes's death.[21] In performing this role, Andrew was

19. *Documentary History,* pp. 51–52.
20. Ibid., pp. 54–55.
21. *Seventeenth-century Harvard,* 2 : 439–40.

the instructor for three of his fellow trustees: James Pierpont (H. 1681), Noadiah Russell (H. 1681), and Joseph Webb (H. 1684). These men were undoubtedly among Andrew's strongest supporters; when, in 1707, the trustees asked him to replace Pierson, the Milford minister agreed. He evidently stipulated, however, that he would not leave his parish, and so in the spring of 1707 the seniors joined him there, where they completed their studies prior to graduation. Tutor Fiske and the rest of the students journeyed to the originally designated college town. Saybrook had a college, or at least part of one, at last.

As a location for the school, Saybrook was slightly preferable to Killingworth. It was a larger town, located at the mouth of the colony's major river, and accessible by water and land. At first the students probably met for classes in Thomas Buckingham's house, but in 1708 the school took possession of a house owned by Nathaniel Lynde and instruction was held there from that time on. Colonial Saybrook was then located on what is now Saybrook Point, a pleasant, compact community surrounded on three sides by water. The collegiate school continued to have its troubles, but at least for the moment its setting was not a principal source of discontent.

The Saybrook Platform

While the college had not flourished under Rector Pierson, it had survived, and under difficult conditions. Aside from the problems of Pierson's residence, the tutors' acceptability, and the students' complaints, the young college was also affected by the political, military, and financial crises of the time. The War of the Spanish Succession (1702–13) was fought in the new world as well as the old, and Connecticut bore a share of the costs both in money and men.[22] Added to the expense of outfitting and paying a militia to defend New England against the French and Indians was the cost of defending the colony's independent status. With Governor Dudley of Massachusetts and Governor Cornbury of New York plotting to have all colonial charters recalled, Connecticut was forced to account for itself before the Board of Trade on several

22. In 1703 the colonial assembly ordered that no student in the collegiate school be entered on the public lists or be rated for his head and that all scholars be exempted from watching, warding, and all public service while in college. See *Documentary History*, p. 45.

occasions. The financial burden was heavy. By 1706 the amount of circulating cash in the colony had dropped to about £2,000 and the General Assembly had to levy a tax to replenish the treasury.[23]

In the face of these concerns the colony was in no position to devote money or attention to the fledgling college. It is no wonder, then, that Madame Sarah Knight, in the journal of her 1704 trip through Connecticut, took no notice of the college. Indeed, it was hardly noticeable. Caleb Heathcote, who made frequent sojourns in the colony on behalf of the Society for the Propagation of the Gospel in Foreign Parts, did, however, notice the school. His suggestion that it had been founded in an attempt to counteract the Anglican thrust into Connecticut flattered the Episcopal cause, but his appraisal of the school as "A thing, which they call a college" was as accurate as it was sarcastic.[24]

Despite the relative obscurity of the college, the trustees were not unhappy with its record. By 1707 it had grown from a school with a single full-time student studying alone with the rector, to a college of seventeen undergraduates. At the time of Pierson's death the graduates numbered only fourteen, but they were fourteen men equipped to serve society in church and state. The trustees, however, were not solely interested in producing educated men. They also wished to revitalize the religious constitution of their colony and to bring order out of its ecclesiastical chaos. Turning out learned and orthodox men might further the first goal, but the issue of church order demanded another solution.

At a meeting at Guilford in March, 1703, the trustees had addressed these larger issues. The participants came to Guilford from as far away as Hartford to do more than transact college business. Meetings of trustees could serve as ministerial gatherings where matters of Connecticut ecclesiastical affairs were discussed. While not representative or authoritative in the ways a synod would be, these meetings nevertheless included the principal clergy of the colony.[25] For this reason the deliberations at the gatherings car-

23. Benjamin Trumbull, *A Complete History of Connecticut, Civil and Ecclesiastical,* 1 : 408–28. For the charges against Connecticut see C.A., Foreign Correspondence, 1 : 116.

24. *Episcopal Church Documents,* 1 : 10.

25. On January 28, 1709, the governor and council of Connecticut sent a report on the colony to their London agent, Sir Henry Ashurst. In a postscript they stated that the colony had forty-six ministers and named the "most Considerable" ones. Of the twelve mentioned, eight were college trustees and two were to become trustees. See C.A., Foreign Correspondence, 2 : 106b.

ried more import than the number of participants would indicate. Meeting at the home of the Reverend Thomas Ruggles, who was to become a trustee several years later, the ministers reflected on the state of religion in Connecticut. If they debated the problem of church order, they evidently failed to reach any accord on a solution. The trustees succeeded, however, in agreeing on at least one course of action. They drew up a declaration proposing that the clergy of Connecticut petition the General Assembly to recommend "to our people & their posterity" the Confession of Faith "agreed to by the Reverend assembly at Westminster, as it is comprised in & Represented by the confession made by the Synod in Boston May 12, 1680 & printed by that Government." [26]

In calling for the government to recommend a statement of faith to Connecticut citizens, the ministers were engaging in an accepted form of church-state cooperation. These men and their counterparts in the General Assembly shared with New England's founders the belief that ecclesiastical and civil authority were, in the words of the Reverend John Davenport of New Haven, "coordinate states, in the same place reaching forth to help mutually each other, for the welfare of both according to God." The support which church and state afforded each other was not precisely defined in legal terms, and each entity retained a clear sense of its own independence and jurisdiction: ministers could not dictate policy to magistrates nor magistrates to ministers.

But while church and state were separate in fact, they were together in spirit, and their partnership was a central factor in the life of the colony. As Gurdon Saltonstall stated in 1697: "God hath designed the Civil Government of his People, to concenter with Ecclesiastical Administrations: and (though by different Mediums) they are both levelled at the same end; the maintaining of Piety and promoting of a Covenant walk with him." Thus the Connecticut General Assembly not only required everyone to attend church and pay taxes for the minister's salary, but it also attempted to support the doctrinal and ecclesiastical purity of the churches.[27]

The ministers who gathered at Guilford in 1703 were aware of this relationship and acted within its context. In this case they

26. Thomas Ruggles, "Att a meeting of Sundry Elders held at Guilford," March 17, 1703, Yale Archives. For more on the various Confessions, see note 29 below.

27. David Hawke, *The Colonial Experience,* p. 138; Richard Bushman, *From Puritan to Yankee,* pp. 14–16.

were simply asking the government to do what it had done before —take steps to shore up the colony's defenses against religious laxity and indifference. The clergymen were not advocating any sort of required subscription to the Westminster Confession, but only proposing that the traditional faith of the colony's churches be reaffirmed. Massachusetts clergy had found such a move desirable in 1680 and now, twenty-three years later, their Connecticut brethren felt the same need. While the declaration failed to gain the assembly's support, it at least revealed the concerns and intentions of its authors. Those intentions would achieve a more systematic expression five years later.

One clergyman who did not attend the trustees' meeting was Gurdon Saltonstall (H. 1684), pastor at New London, adviser and confidant to Governor Winthrop, and a participant in the founding of the collegiate school. When the governor died in 1707, the assembly chose his friend Saltonstall to succeed him. The fact that Saltonstall was not an elected official at the time made this an unprecedented decision, but the Connecticut freemen reaffirmed it in the 1708 election by choosing him for a full term. Saltonstall was a rarity—a clergyman turned politician—and as such was in a unique position to assist his ministerial colleagues. Although he had not attended the Guilford meeting in 1703, Saltonstall knew all of the participants and was privy to their thoughts on ecclesiastical issues. As a minister himself he undoubtedly shared the trustees' concern about Connecticut's difficulties in this area, and he had already expressed his views on the government's responsibility in such matters. As governor he was in a position to act accordingly.

It did not take him long to do so. In May, 1708, the General Assembly, at Saltonstall's urging, called for a synod to meet at the time of the collegiate school commencement at Saybrook in September. In calling for the synod, the assembly declared that it was "sensible of the defects of the discipline of the churches of this government, arising from the want of a more explicite asserting the rules given for that end in the holy scriptures" and asked the synod members to agree to some suitable "methods and rules for the management of ecclesiastical discipline" and submit them to the next General Court.[28] The time and place of the synod

28. *Conn. Records,* 5 : 51.

proved convenient, for eight of the twelve ministers chosen to attend the Saybrook meeting were collegiate school trustees. The trustees not only constituted two-thirds of the ministerial delegates to the synod but they also dominated its proceedings. Thomas Buckingham of Saybrook and James Noyes of Stonington served as joint moderators of the meeting, and James Pierpont of New Haven wrote the chief draft for the crucial section on church polity.

The synod's deliberations resulted in a platform containing three sections. The first was the adoption of the Savoy Confession—practically identical to the Westminster Confession—as it had been restated by the Boston Synod of 1680. Thus, the ministers realized the Guilford proposal of 1703. The second section of the platform was the most significant. It contained fifteen articles of polity and was based on Pierpont's draft, although several clauses were entered at the behest of Timothy Woodbridge and others who desired a more Presbyterian structure. The completed articles provided for the establishment of consociations in each county with oversight of local congregations, county ministerial associations with the responsibility of advising and examining ministerial candidates, and a general ministerial association, its function undefined, which was to meet annually. The section also provided that pastors and churches refusing to attend meetings and to abide by decisions of the consociations would be declared in noncommunion with the established churches. The third section of the platform gave consent to the Heads of Agreement formulated by English Congregationalists and Presbyterians in 1691. This last document, of which Increase Mather had been one of the principal designers, was actually an excellent exposition of current Congregational practice, and its inclusion by the synod made the resulting platform palatable to many ministers who might otherwise have objected to it.[29]

29. Sydney E. Ahlstrom, "The Saybrook Platform: a 250th Anniversary Retrospect," *Bulletin of the Congregational Library* 11, no. 1 (1959–60): 5–10; no. 2 : 3–15; Walker, *Creeds and Platforms*, pp. 495–504. The Savoy Confession, adopted by English Congregationalists in 1658, was a slightly amended version of the Westminster Confession (1646) written by the Presbyterians. While Savoy omitted a few sections of Westminster and added a chapter—"Of the Gospel, and of the extent of the Grace thereof"—the two confessions were substantially the same. The Massachusetts ministers adopted the Savoy Confession in 1680 with few changes. When

While the Saybrook Platform was not unanimously accepted or similarly interpreted by all Connecticut churches and consociations, its chief intent was accomplished. Instead of forty-six separate and independent churches, the colony now had an overall ecclesiastical structure. By April 13, 1709, the four counties of Hartford, New London, Fairfield, and New Haven had ratified the platform and formed consociations. With the support of the General Assembly, which had adopted the platform with the reservation that it was not binding on any church that did not wish to accept its provisions, the Saybrook Platform went into operation in Connecticut.[30]

But the platform was, by and large, a compromise. The revisionist Congregationalists, who occupied the middle ground and held the best bargaining position, accommodated the Presbyterians with the section on polity and mollified the strict Congregationalists by adopting the Heads of Agreement. The platform's most telling effect, however, was that it presbyterianized the colony's churches and provided them with consociations and associations to deal with disciplinary problems. It was a propitious time for the churches to have this power, for, a few months before the Saybrook Synod, the Connecticut General Court had adopted the English Toleration Act. In Great Britain, this act granted the dissenting (non-Anglican) churches certain rights and privileges. In Connecticut, where the so-called dissenting churches were the established ones, the act granted these same rights and privileges to the Anglicans. Since the colonial government could no longer legislate against the Church of England, the Connecticut ministers had further reasons for wanting an established ecclesiastical framework that could act as a bulwark against outside intrusions.[31]

Aside from the platform's design as an affirmation of the ecclesiastical status quo in Connecticut against all other denominations, the agreement was not a restrictive one. It did not impose a uni-

---

the Saybrook delegates accepted Savoy they used the Massachusetts version. The Saybrook Confession, then, was the same as the 1680 Confession except that the Connecticut ministers added biblical proof-texts to each section. See Walker, pp. 340–67, 517–20, 440–52.

30. Walker, *Creeds and Platforms*, pp. 508–13; *Conn. Records*, 5 : 87. Two thousand copies of the platform were published in New London in 1710, the first book to be printed in Connecticut. See *Conn. Records*, 5:97–98.

31. *Conn. Records*, 5 : 50–51; M. Louise Greene, *The Development of Religious Liberty in Connecticut*, pp. 187, 190.

form polity on Connecticut churches but created an establishment within which churches of varying degrees of ecclesiastical formality could coexist. The terms "Presbyterian" and "Congregational" were used interchangeably in the colony from this time on, but with some important regional differences. The counties of New London and Hartford adopted the platform without alteration. New Haven County interpreted the agreement loosely, and its churches retained a more Congregational and independent polity. Fairfield, on the other hand, faced with the direct challenge of Anglican missionaries working out of Rye, New York, chose to stress the Presbyterian aspects of the platform and added excommunication to the consociation's power. By doing this, Fairfield made the most radical departure from the Congregational way.[32]

A few churches refused to abide by the platform at all. The Norwich church was so firmly opposed to the agreement that it finally severed its relationship with its minister, who had been a scribe at the synod. The Reverend Timothy Edwards's East Windsor congregation never approved the platform. In 1729 the church at Guilford divided over the calling of a new minister, and the disaffected minority withdrew from the church, established a second congregation, and disavowed the Saybrook Platform. The New Haven consociation was unable to resolve the Guilford split and the dissenters eventually won recognition as a distinct church. The platform, then, was not a perfect disciplinary tool.[33]

Despite the varying interpretations of the Saybrook Platform and the existence of nonconcurring churches, the document succeeded in giving Connecticut an ecclesiastical structure. The college was intimately affiliated with that structure. The framers of the platform were collegiate school trustees, and the twenty-six ministers who served as trustees from 1708 to 1739 all came from churches which, with differing degrees of rigidity, adopted the agreement. Yale College, then, was identified with the spectrum of Connecticut's ecclesiastical types, not with any one of them. This somewhat latitudinarian commitment to polity was reflected in the fact that many Yale graduates, without any soul-searching, served as ministers in both Presbyterian and Congregational churches in Connecticut and the Middle Colonies.

32. Walker, *Creeds and Platforms,* pp. 510–11; Bacon, "Historical Discourse," pp. 41–42.
33. Walker, *Creeds and Platforms,* p. 508; Bacon, "Historical Discourse," p. 48.

Although the platform did not receive its first real test until the Great Awakening, its adoption in 1708 signaled the beginnings of the bifurcation of New England. In 1705 Increase and Cotton Mather had failed to win acceptance for a similar proposal to institute associations in Massachusetts. The Mathers' failure and Saybrook's success meant that the two colonies would traverse divergent ecclesiastical paths; Connecticut's was to be more ordered, and eventually the colony's churches would have more in common with the Presbyterians of the Middle Colonies than with the Bay Colony Congregationalists. Massachusetts, especially its eastern areas, was to travel a more chaotic route, and its churches were to be helpless in the face of divisive quarrels and liberalizing tendencies.

The distinct characteristics of the two New England colleges prefigured this divergence. The Collegiate School of Connecticut, begun, in part, as an alternative to a heterodox Harvard, was under the trusteeship of the ministers who created the Saybrook Platform and who would, in 1722, demand that all college officers agree to its Confession of Faith. The collegiate school was to exist, therefore, in a relatively stable ecclesiastical milieu, established by the large majority of the colony's clergy and blessed by the government. The college was to draw its trustees, rectors, and, for the most part, students from this milieu and to chart a course consistent with the wishes of the colonial ministry.

Harvard's situation was quite different. The Bay College was under the immediate influence of the colony's royal governor, Joseph Dudley. In 1707 the Harvard Corporation elected John Leverett, former tutor and leading member of the Brattle Street Church, to the college presidency. Increase and Cotton Mather, both of whom had been nominated for the office, opposed Leverett's election, which Cotton saw as a "Violent Essay, to betray the College, and to destroy all the Ch[urche]s of N.E." Mather thought "that, to make a lawyer, and one who never affected the study of Divinity, a praesident for a College of Divines, will be a very preposterous thing, a thing without precedent." Governor Dudley, who approved of Leverett, supported the preposterous and unprecedented election and the Governor's Council voted to accept Leverett. When the House of Deputies vetoed this proposal, Dudley used the power of his office to propose a compromise; he offered to reinstate the Harvard Charter of 1650 in return for a favorable vote on Leverett. Presented with the opportunity to regain a lost privilege, the lower house agreed. Leverett became the Harvard president and the old charter was restored. Dudley cannily took early advantage of the charter provision for a seven-man corporation, to eliminate those who were unacceptable to him in the inflated corporation which had been created by Increase Mather in 1692. When this purge was accomplished, the corporation consisted almost entirely of men who had voted for the new president.[34]

The trend toward a seemingly liberal leadership of the college, which had begun with the ousting of Increase Mather from the Harvard presidency in 1701, was perpetuated by the election of 1707. The changing character of the college caused the Mathers and their supporters to lament. It also dismayed Increase's friend, Sir Henry Ashurst, who was the London agent for the colonies of Massachusetts and Connecticut. In 1709 he wrote a letter to Governor Saltonstall, bitterly complaining of the way in which Dudley had perverted Harvard, "bringing up a strange generation there." He went on to say that he would not donate to the Connecticut college until he saw "a better spirit among you." [35]

Since Ashurst may have been the first to make his donations to the Connecticut college contingent on the acceptability of the school's policies, Saltonstall and the trustees were undoubtedly surprised by his concern about their spirit. They knew that their spirit far excelled that of the Harvard Corporation, for their chief purpose was to bring up a familiar, not a strange, generation. Unfortunately, the institution was not in a position to manifest fully the trustees' spirit. Upon Pierson's death the college had split in two, the seniors residing at Milford with Rector Andrew, the underclassmen at Saybrook with Tutor Fiske. At the 1707 commencement the trustees violated their tacit rule against obtaining tutors from Cambridge and hired James Hale (H. 1703) to assist Fiske. Hale's Harvard education was somewhat offset by the fact that his two uncles, James and Moses Noyes, were college trustees.[36] Tutors Fiske and Hale continued to instruct classes at Saybrook for several years, with Rector Andrew presiding at the commencements. In 1709 Hale left his tutorship "upon some uneasiness" and Aza-

34. *Seventeenth-century Harvard,* 2 : 552, 555.
35. 6 Coll. M.H.S., 5 (1892): 196.
36. *Yale Graduates,* 1 : 80; *Harvard Graduates,* 5 : 216.

riah Mather (class of 1705) was chosen to replace him. By this time Andrew had discontinued his teaching and all the students resided and studied at Saybrook. The college carried on for seven years with this arrangement. It was not the best; the school lacked an adequate building, a functioning rector, and the money to obtain either.

Despite its unhappy circumstances, the collegiate school was a blessing to the colony. At least Stephen Buckingham thought so. In 1711, Buckingham preached the annual election sermon to the colony's legislators. In it he claimed that the college had "not for the Time been unfruitful" in providing Connecticut with "hopeful Persons" to fill its pulpits and "Persons of Worth" to run the government. But the school needed support, and the minister urged the public, "whose advantage is Principally aimed at therein," and men of ability to emulate those whose "Liberal Donations have done Worthily for its Foundation." [37] The people of the colony did not respond to Buckingham's promptings for several years. Rather, the college received some extraordinary donations from a man who had not heard Buckingham's plea and whom few, if any, of the college's supporters knew. His name was Jeremiah Dummer and he was Connecticut's London agent.

Jeremiah Dummer

Dummer (H. 1699) was an outstanding scholar. He was known as the best of his day at college, and in 1702–03 he earned advanced degrees from the universities of Leyden and Utrecht. When he returned to Massachusetts in 1704 he applied, with Increase Mather's help, for a Harvard professorship but was not hired. Disappointed and unable to find a pastorate, Dummer went to England in 1708, his career undecided. In 1710 the scholar turned diplomat: in that year Massachusetts employed him to join with Sir Henry Ashurst as its London agent. Dummer's job, like that of all colonial agents, was to represent the colony's views before crown authorities, chiefly the Board of Trade. In 1712 Connecticut contracted with him to perform the same service.[38]

For the struggling colonial college the choice was a beneficial

37. Stephen Buckingham, *The Unreasonableness and Danger of a Peoples renouncing their subjection to God* (New London, 1711), pp. 21–22.

38. *Harvard Graduates,* 4 : 454–58.

one. Dummer was not only an excellent agent, defending the colony's interests against English intrusions, but was also an active patron of the Collegiate School of Connecticut. As early as 1711, before the colony officially hired him and the Reverend Buckingham pleaded for college donations, Dummer was already working on behalf of the school. The first extant evidence of contact between him and the college is a letter from the London agent to James Pierpont, dated May 22, 1711. But from the content of the letter it is obvious that it was Pierpont, not Dummer, who had initiated the correspondence. Due to the lack of concrete evidence, it is impossible to ascertain precisely how Pierpont came to seek out Dummer. Certainly the New Haven minister knew of the agent and may have been personally acquainted with him; both men at least shared the friendship of Cotton Mather. Although the surviving material is sketchy, it is still possible to reconstruct the probable sequence of events that brought Dummer and the collegiate school together.

The intermediary between Pierpont and Dummer seems to have been John Dixwell, son of one of the judges who had tried and condemned Charles I to death in 1648. The elder Dixwell had subsequently escaped to New England and lived disguised in New Haven as James Davids. The Reverend Pierpont was one of those who had uncovered Davids's true identity. When, in 1708, young John Dixwell decided to make a claim on his family estate in England, the New Haven minister wrote a letter attesting to his lineage. John Alling, the collegiate school treasurer, had also been involved in this process in his capacity as a member of the upper house of the General Assembly. In 1708 Dixwell married Mary Prout of New Haven and settled in Boston as a silversmith and merchant; he also acted as the local agent for the college treasurer, John Alling.[39] In 1710 Dixwell decided to go to England in an attempt to claim a portion of his family estate, and he asked Cotton Mather to provide him with another testimonial letter. Pierpont was interested in Dixwell's mission for personal reasons and commissioned him to undertake two items of business while in England. The first was to inquire about the Pierrepont family, estate, and title; the second was to solicit contributions for the college. It is likely that in both cases Pierpont—perhaps at Cotton

39. Ezra Stiles, *A History of the Three Judges of King Charles I* (Hartford, 1794), pp. 149–50.

Mather's urging—told Dixwell to ask the assistance of Jeremiah Dummer.[40]

Presumably, Dixwell did Pierpont's bidding. It is certain that he went to Dummer for help, but he may have undertaken some solicitations on his own. In any event, when Dummer wrote to Pierpont in May, 1711, the agent had already collected some books for the college and knew about an elderly gentleman by the name of Elihu Yale. Yale, whose family had settled in the old New Haven Colony, had been born in Boston, raised and educated in England, and had made his fortune with the East India Company, where he had served in the post of governor at Fort St. George in the Madras Colony. In 1711 Yale was living a life of comparative ease both in London and on his estate in Wales. It was just at this time that he was trying to find a male heir to inherit his fortune and had hit upon the notion of sending for his cousin's young son, David Yale of North Haven. Since Yale wrote to his North Haven relatives by way of John Dixwell, we may speculate that it was Dixwell who found the old nabob in the first place. Agent Dummer soon seized this opening and conversed with Yale, learning in the process "that he intended to bestow a charity upon some Colledge in Oxford." Dummer thought that Yale might be persuaded to make his donations to the collegiate school instead, "seeing he is a New Englander, & I think a Connecticut man," and urged Pierpont to write Yale a letter on that subject when young David sailed for England.[41]

The Yales of North Haven were pleased with the prospects of an inheritance and sent twelve-year-old David to England in 1712. The boy stayed there for about six years; he even enrolled for a time in Pembroke College, Cambridge. Unfortunately, the purpose of his visit was not realized and he returned home emptyhanded. The only thing David ever reaped from this whole affair was an honorary M.A. from the Connecticut college in 1724. It is not clear whether Pierpont sent the governor a letter with the boy,

40. For evidence that Pierpont commissioned Dixwell, see Jeremiah Dummer's letter to Pierpont, dated May 22, 1711, quoted in part in James Kingsley Blake, "The Lost Dukedom, or the Story of the Pierrepont Claim," Papers of the New Haven Colony Historical Society, 7 (1908): 265–66. Blake's article contains extracts from these important letters, but he erred in dating them and hence mistook the proper sequence of events. Blake thought that the May 22 letter was Dummer's second communication with Pierpont, when in fact it was the first.

41. Ibid.

but the minister did write to Dummer sometime in the winter of 1711–12. In the letter, Pierpont pressed his inquiries about his family title and the possibility of donations for the college. Dummer, in his reply of March 16, 1711–12, reported his difficulty in determining anything definite about the Pierrepont family but encouraged the New Haven minister to persevere. The agent also revealed that he had tried to follow up the contact with Elihu Yale but had been temporarily thwarted. Yale, it seems, was not interested in discussing any financial matters, as he was "very much out of humour on the account of his losing twenty thousand pounds by Sir Stephen Evans, who lately failed, & thereupon retiring to Sir Caesar Childs in the Country hanged himself with a Bed-cord." [42]

Despite his failure with Yale, Dummer did report that he had successfully interested Dr. William Salmon (1644–1713), a prominent English physician who had traveled to New England, in donating his extensive library to the college. Dummer estimated—or boasted—that Salmon's library (which included microscopes, mathematical instruments, West Indian artifacts, and Dutch paintings) was worth six times as much as Harvard's. Salmon, a dissenter, said he would consider giving to the Connecticut collegiate school, but made the one objection "that all Universities follow too much the Study of Heathen learning and corrupt the doctrine of the Gospel." Dummer parried this assertion with the suggestion that, since the college was "a young child," Salmon could influence and shape it "to his own model." The doctor accepted that reasoning, drew up "a long story of directions for the students," and dispatched it to Pierpont. Dummer encouraged Pierpont to reply.[43]

Pierpont probably did respond to Salmon's "directions," for Dummer succeeded in winning the doctor's promise to give to the college. But before he could make out a new will, Salmon died of apoplexy, and under the terms of the old one his "great valuable Library" went to "an absolute Stranger, that he had seen once or twice, & took a fancy to." Dummer tried to recoup the loss by soliciting books from his friends and through his acquaintances. He reported, in January, 1712–13, that he was having some surprising success: "For I have got together a pretty parcell of books already for you to begin with, & I hope in a years time to send you

42. Ibid., p. 264.
43. Ibid., pp. 264–65.

a very valuable collection, with the names of the Benefactors." [44]

Pierpont no doubt told his colleagues of Dummer's activities and the trustees, seeing that the contact with the agent was beginning to pay off, bombarded him with suggestions of other sources to tap on behalf of the school. Their first recommendation was that Dummer seek gifts from one Sir John Davie. Davie, a Harvard classmate of Pierpont and Noadiah Russell, and brother-in-law as well as former neighbor and parishioner of Gurdon Saltonstall, had left Connecticut for England in 1707 to assume his family's baronetcy. He was a reasonably wealthy gentleman, and it was understandable that his New England friends would think of him as a source of assistance. Dummer duly approached Davie, who announced that, if he gave anything to the collegiate school, he would do it on his own. In a year's time, Davie sent the college 170 books.[45]

A second appeal by the college trustees brought less satisfaction. Sometime in 1711, the trustees of the Hopkins Grammar School in New Haven heard, perhaps from John Dixwell, that the will of Governor Edward Hopkins was being contested in court. Hopkins, whose donation of 1660 had so excited and encouraged John Davenport, had put a provision in his will that at his wife's death his estate was to be used in America "to give some encouragement . . . for the breeding up of hopeful youths, both at the grammar school and college, for the public service of the country in future times." Mrs. Hopkins died in 1699, and since the will named no particular beneficiary, various groups laid claim to the legacy. The Corporation for the Propagation of the Gospel in New England petitioned for the estate in 1708, and Harvard initiated action to claim the bequest in 1709. As late as 1711, when Dixwell was in London, the will was still being contested. Dixwell may have passed this information on to his friend John Alling, who was not only the collegiate school treasurer but also a trustee of the Hopkins School. However the news reached New Haven, the Hopkins School Committee became interested in the will and in October, 1711, sent a power of attorney to Jeremiah Dummer for him to work for the recovery of at least part of the legacy. Dummer replied in March, 1712, that he was working on the matter, and in

44. *Documentary History*, pp. 57–58.

45. Anne S. Pratt, "The Books Sent from England by Jeremiah Dummer to Yale College," in *Papers in Honor of Andrew Keogh*, p. 13.

October of that year the Hopkins committee sent a second letter to the agent.[46]

The collegiate school trustees certainly knew of these communications and were enticed by the possibility of tapping the Hopkins bequest themselves. It was at about this time that they, too, sent Dummer power of attorney to claim a portion of the money for the college. Although Dummer had pretty much committed himself to Harvard's cause by this time, he thought that the collegiate school had a strong case and evidently hired a lawyer to investigate its chances. The investigation revealed that legal opinion in London was against "the new Erected Colledge in the province of Conneticott." Matthew Evans, the solicitor handling the Hopkins litigation, told the collegiate school attorney that, since two claims had already been made for the estate, his petition was too late. Besides, Evans continued, it could not "be supposed that Mr. Hopkins could think of any Colledge that was not Existing—when he made his will so that I beleive I have put an End to any further dispute on that account." [47] Dummer, according to the recollection he gave some years later, reported this information to the collegiate school trustees, telling them "that a Suit in Chancery would Swallow up the Whole legacy before it could be ended, if obstinately carry'd on by the parties." He therefore prevailed upon them "to drop the Suit, upon a promise that I would endeavour to make up the loss to them some other way." With Connecticut's claim to the will dropped, Harvard won the estate in March, 1713. A few months later Dummer wrote to John Alling to inform him of the decision.[48]

The agent, however, was as good as his word and continued to solicit donations for the college. Although he complained to Pierpont that he had "almost as many benefactors as books," Dummer managed to do well for the school. He induced Governor Yale to give forty volumes to the college, although, the agent opined, Yale's gift was "very little considering his Estate and particular relation to your Collony." [49] In a few years the old governor would more than make up for his initial parsimony. Dummer worked for other donations too; his boast to Pierpont that his "Acquiantance

46. Ibid., pp. 9–10.
47. Pub. C.S.M., 43 (1966): 323.
48. Pratt, "Books Sent from England by Jeremiah Dummer," pp. 11–13.
49. *Documentary History*, p. 58.

with men of Learning and Estates is very generall" proved accurate, for 181 individuals contributed to the college through him.[50] Richard Blackmore, Richard Steele, and Isaac Newton all gave their own works and Dummer himself contributed 120 volumes. In September, 1714, the trustees received the fruits of Jeremiah Dummer's labors—nine boxes containing more than 800 volumes. The collection was a rich one and contained the best in English thought on every subject from theology and medicine to literature and travel.

The trustees were heartened by Dummer's success, for not only had the agent procured books for the college library but he had also established a link between the provincial school and the intellectual world of England. While the trustees could not be aware of the meaning and potential impact of this link, they nevertheless valued and sought to strengthen it. In 1714 they printed the college's first catalogue and commencement program, no copy of which has survived, and sent it to Dummer in an attempt to obtain further donations of books. Dummer, who continued to send parcels of books and scientific instruments to the college, encouraged the trustees in endeavors of this sort. In 1717 he urged them to insert an item in the *Boston Gazette* about the English donations to the school and send it to him for use in soliciting further gifts.[51]

In 1723 he obtained a donation of books from Dr. Daniel Turner, an English physician of some note, and requested the trustees to send the donor a doctoral diploma. This suggestion no doubt flattered the trustees, who had never awarded an honorary doctorate before, and they readily complied. It had probably never occurred to them that one of their diplomas could be exchanged for gifts. Dummer added to their satisfaction when he wrote back to compliment them on the document which, he said, "both for language & sentiments exceed any thing I ever yet saw from My Own Alma Mater." Though a favorable comparison with Harvard was always welcome, the trustees were displeased to learn, a month later, that the Censors of the College of Physicians in London had refused to honor and ratify the collegiate school diploma. The colonists could take comfort only in the fact that the same policy applied to any diploma offered by other universities to an individ-

50. Pratt, "Books Sent from England by Jeremiah Dummer," p. 12.

51. *Documentary History*, pp. 59, 128, 83–84.

ual who was not a graduate of Oxford or Cambridge. To the eminent physicians of London, it seems, a Scottish degree was as useless as an American one.[52]

Dummer's tenure as Connecticut's official agent and the college's unofficial fund-raiser lasted until 1730. His most significant solicitation on behalf of the school was securing Governor Elihu Yale's timely donation in 1718. In that case Dummer not only helped to rescue the school from financial embarrassment but also to give it a name. But the agent's activities did not always have such harmonious results. In early 1720, Dummer, perhaps flushed by his success with Governor Yale, sought to interest one Thomas Hollis, a well-to-do English nonconformist, in giving to Yale College. Hollis had just begun donating money to Harvard, and when Dummer tried to divert his attention to the New Haven college, both Hollis and various Harvard officials became incensed. Dummer justified his seemingly subversive activities by stating that, since he had done Harvard a favor in 1712–13 by dropping the Connecticut claim to the Hopkins estate, he was within his rights—having promised the trustees that he would "make up the loss"—in trying to enlist Hollis's support for the second New England college.[53]

Despite "Severe reprimands" from his acquaintances at Harvard and disinterest on the part of Hollis, Dummer continued to pester the Englishman for the next few years. Hollis's initial reaction to the matter had been to say that he had never heard of the Connecticut college, but when Dummer persisted he became increasingly annoyed. Dummer, who seems to have been blissfully, even deliberately, ignorant of the furor he was causing, sanguinely told the trustees in February, 1721, that the college would find Hollis "a benefactor e're long." The agent's optimism may have been the result of his confidence in a plan he had hatched. While the evidence is only circumstantial, it seems that Dummer—with the collaboration of Governor Gurdon Saltonstall—had enlisted the support of Cotton Mather, whose disaffection with Harvard and interest in the Connecticut college disposed him to work against the one and for the other. The scheme was to have Mather write elegant and persuasive letters to Hollis.

52. Pub. C.S.M., 6 (1904): 197–98, 201, 203–04.

53. Quincy, *History of Harvard,* 1 : 527; Pratt, "Books Sent from England by Jeremiah Dummer," pp. 11–12.

Starting in February, 1721, Dummer began delivering to Hollis "handsomely worded" but anonymous letters recommending that he give to the Connecticut college. When this procedure was repeated in July and August of that year, Hollis lost his temper and dashed off letters to John White, the Harvard treasurer, asking him to tell the author to desist.[54] The anonymous letters stopped, and Dummer ceased to bother Hollis for over a year, only to return to the fray in the summer of 1723. But, as the agent himself reported, Hollis was something of a "humourist" and Dummer's "Oblique impressions" on him produced no results.[55] Thomas Hollis never donated to the collegiate school, and if this episode can be interpreted as the beginning of a New England college rivalry, the first round was clearly Harvard's.

Dummer's efforts on behalf of the Connecticut college waned in the 1720s and his last donation, consisting of two books, arrived in 1729. But the transplanted colonist, a person of "elegant Taste both in Men and Books," had served Yale well.[56] His solicitations of 1714 had broadened the college library beyond its initial theological bounds and had given the faculty and students their first opportunity to consult and grapple with the most advanced thinking of the time. More importantly, Dummer functioned as a link to the world of culture, a link which offered the trustees the psychological satisfaction of thinking that their college participated in that world.

If the Connecticut collegiate school participated, albeit vicariously, in the old world, it continued to have trouble surviving in the new. The most significant events of the school's early years—the Saybrook Platform and the Dummer donations—had nothing to do with the day-to-day functioning of the college. The library that Dummer provided was, in fact, the school's chief claim to fame; but although it was a source of pleasure to the trustees, it hardly made up for the inadequacies of the Saybrook college. Even the successful resolution of the colony's ecclesiastical questions had little direct impact on the college, and the trustees still had to face the mundane deficiencies of their school.

54. *Documentary History*, pp. 212, 209; Quincy, *History of Harvard*, 1 : 528.

55. *Documentary History*, p. 244. For more on Dummer and Hollis, see Quincy, *History of Harvard*, 1 : 226–29; Pratt, "Books Sent from England by Jeremiah Dummer," p. 25; and Alfred C. Potter, "The Harvard College Library: 1723–1735," Pub. C.S.M., 25 (1924): 7.

56. *Harvard Graduates*, 4 : 465.

After November 22, 1714, the trustees had to confront these problems without the assistance of their most effective colleague, James Pierpont. His death was a severe blow, for he assuredly was, as Cotton Mather eulogized, a "most Valuable" man, a minister of "very Meritorious Character," a "Blessing to his Church, his Neighbourhood, his Colony!" [57] Mather well knew that Pierpont was also a blessing to his college. Indeed, the New Haven minister played the initiating or leading role in practically every major event related to the collegiate school, from its founding in 1701 to the arrival of the Dummer donation in 1714. Almost every piece of correspondence concerning the college was sent to, or by, Pierpont; nearly every decision was cleared through him. Jeremiah Dummer captured the essence of Pierpont's stature when he told an English acquaintance that Pierpont was "the head of a College" and that no one in Connecticut had "a fairer reputation or is better esteemed." [58] His death left the college trustees without a firm and respected leader just at the time when such a man was most needed.

For years the trustees had been unable to remedy the ills of the school's Saybrook settlement; there was not enough money to settle and support a resident rector and no effort was made to get one. Cotton Mather, for whom the well-being of the Connecticut collegiate school was one of many projects, knew that the college was suffering from the lack of a president and privately ruminated about recommending someone for the job.[59] He never did so, and in the absence of a full-time rector, the effectual management of the school rested with the tutors. They not only did the teaching but also arranged and conducted the examinations for degree candidates.[60] Samuel Andrew did little more than send occasional instructions. While this arrangement sufficed to keep the college operating, it was hardly ideal and the trustees knew it. Tutors came and went and the ministers realized that their college would not flourish until it had permanent accommodations and a settled government.

57. Ibid., 3 : 228.

58. Blake, "Lost Dukedom," p. 264.

59. Cotton Mather, *Diary of Cotton Mather, 1709–1724*, 7 Coll. M.H.S. 8 (1918): 64, 70.

60. *Documentary History*, p. 59.

3 "Declining and Unhappy Circumstances"

In 1717, the Reverend Eliphalet Adams, minister at New London, seized the occasion of a recent thunderstorm to preach and publish a sermon. His intention was to improve on the event, that is, to draw meanings and lessons from it for the benefit of his audience. One of the pastor's chief hopes was that the tempest would "tend to allay the Storms that rage in our Breasts and make us Meek, Peaceable, Gentle towards all men." More to the point, Adams prayed that the result of God's meteorological message would be to "still the Noise of Tumult and Contention in the Countrey and Check the spirit of Jealousy, Suspicion and Division that is strangely gone forth to the Disturbance of all Order and which Threatens the Ruin of all that is dear in the midst of us." [1] Adams had in mind a whole range of disturbances and contentions that racked Connecticut society. But included in his catalogue was the collegiate school, which by that time was embroiled in a battle involving political, legal, and personal issues.

The rift occurred just at the time when it seemed that the college's difficulties might be solved. The Peace of Utrecht, ending the War of the Spanish Succession, was signed in 1713. With the war over, Connecticut was relieved of a major drain on its resources and was able to devote capital and energy to other concerns. The collegiate school was an obvious candidate for such attention. In October, 1714, the General Assembly formed a committee to investigate the question of erecting a building for the college. The following May the college trustees told the assembly of the difficulties which beset the school for want of certain advantages, and that the absence of suitable accommodations had impaired the task of educating Connecticut youth. The assembly agreed that the college needed help and authorized a collection to be held throughout the colony for contributions toward a college house. The upper house tried to set an example by alloting £100 to the college, but the lower house vetoed that provision and

1. Eliphalet Adams, *A Discourse Occasioned by the late Distressing Storm* (New London, 1717), p. 32.

the whole bill fell through.[2] In October, 1715, when Connecticut and Massachusetts settled a long-standing boundary dispute in Connecticut's favor, the General Assembly compensated for its previous failure by granting the college £500 out of the money received from the sale of the land.[3]

Two months after the trustees learned of the colony's generosity, the college at Saybrook was rocked by an "unhappy Dissention." Once again the problem centered on the teachers. As long as Phineas Fiske (1706–13) and Joseph Noyes (1710–15) were tutors, the college could always boast of at least one experienced man at Saybrook. When Noyes resigned in 1715 the college was left with two young and inexperienced tutors, Samuel Russell, Jr. (class of 1712) and Benjamin Lord (class of 1714). They displeased the fault-finding undergraduates, who also complained of the lack of a resident rector and of the poor housing arrangements in Saybrook. All of these factors contributed to a strong feeling of unrest, some students maintaining that they could obtain a better education at home.[4]

When the trustees met on April 3, 1716, the student rebellion was in full swing. Realizing that they had to act decisively to quiet the disorder, the trustees voted to use the £500 from the government to build a college house, "with Chambers and Studies as well as a hall and Library," and a house for a rector. They agreed to procure a rector to take charge of the college at a salary of £100 a year in addition to the advantage of boarding the students. In an effort to meet the students' desire for different teachers, the trustees asked Samuel Smith (class of 1713) to be a tutor. These pledges did not calm the dissatisfied students, and the trustees, although stating that the charges against the tutors were "not Sufficient to obliege the Trustees to make another Choice or any further provision for the Instruction of the School," agreed to allow students to pursue their education elsewhere until commencement, when they would be required to reside at the school.[5]

2. *Documentary History*, pp. 60–62. On the cost of the war to Connecticut, see Trumbull, *History of Connecticut*, 1 : 450.

3. *Documentary History*, p. 63.

4. Samuel Johnson, "Some Historical Remarks Concerning the Collegiate School of Connecticut in New Haven," in *Documentary History*, p. 151. Hereafter cited as *Documentary History* (Johnson's "Remarks").

5. *Documentary History*, pp. 64–65; (Johnson's "Remarks"), p. 151.

As events were to prove, this was an unfortunate decision. In making it, the trustees evidently believed that they could solve the conflict by consenting to a temporary disruption of the school, allowing time for tempers to cool, and then reassembling the college in September. The conflict, however, was not so easily resolved. The scope of the problem facing the Connecticut college became manifest when several students, instead of scattering to their respective homes, gathered at Wethersfield to study under Elisha Williams (H. 1711). While many students went home and some stayed in Saybrook, the existence of the Wethersfield contingent pointed to some kind of organized dissent. The organizers revealed themselves on May 10. Without consulting their colleagues, Trustees Timothy Woodbridge and Thomas Buckingham petitioned the General Assembly to settle the collegiate school at Hartford. Nothing could have more drastically illustrated the impact of the loss of James Pierpont. Had he been alive, it is inconceivable that any trustees would have dared to split off from their fellows in so blatant a fashion. But without Pierpont's leadership, gentle spirit, and restraining influence, the two Hartford ministers felt free to make their bold proposal. That proposal initiated a quarrel over the location of the college that was not resolved for three years.

The College Breaks Up

The Hartford representation was prompted, its authors stated, by the "present declining and unhappy circumstances in which that school lies, and the apparent hazard of its being utterly extinguisht unless some speedy remedy be apply'd." While this assessment of the college's troubles was accurate enough, the Hartford proposal was motivated, not only by a concern for the school's welfare, but also by a sectional desire to locate the college in the capital of the old Connecticut colony. Rivalry between the eastern and western parts of Connecticut existed already, due largely to the phenomenal growth, numerical and financial, of the eastern area, and the college issue soon became a symbol of these jealousies. Such conflicts, of course, were never brought out in the subsequent debates, and the upriver ministers couched their arguments in terms of benefiting the college.

Woodbridge and Buckingham claimed that placing the school at or near Hartford would be the best remedy for its current malaise, as that town was in the center of the colony, surrounded by other large towns, and could therefore attract the most students. The petition also stated that some Massachusetts people had agreed to support the college and send young men there if the school were at Hartford. Pledging a good supply of "able and sufficient tutors" for the school, the Hartford trustees revealed that upward of £700 had been subscribed for the venture and that a total of £1,000 was expected.[6] The two ministers believed they had a strong case. Since the assembly had chartered and supported the college, it could certainly designate its location and, in the present situation, the group studying at Wethersfield, located near Hartford, represented the most stable element of the school. Therefore that town could rightfully expect to be named as the best site for the college —or so the Hartford trustees hoped.

The General Assembly responded to the Hartford bid by calling the trustees to appear before it at the May session. Several trustees did meet in Hartford, but they asked the assembly to postpone action until October, with the understanding that the court was to settle the college if the trustees could not unanimously agree on a place for the school before then.[7] Meanwhile, other trustees decided to make their own efforts to relocate the collegiate school. In June, Trustees Andrew, Russell, and Ruggles, along with five other ministers, circulated a petition for subscriptions to settle the college in New Haven. A month later the town of New Haven granted the trustees eight acres of land if the college settled and remained there.[8] By October, New Haven had raised between £1,500 and £2,000. Saybrook, which enjoyed the temporary support of only two trustees, James and Moses Noyes, joined in the bidding and put up £1,200 to £1,400. Hartford evidently had difficulty exceeding its £700 offer. Of course, each town expected to add the colony's £500 grant to its subscription.

While the three towns were soliciting donations to attract the college, the school was continuing in its fragmented state. Tutors Russell and Lord had stayed on at Saybrook with a few students, but in the summer Lord, "seeing how things were disposed," quit. When smallpox broke out in Saybrook at this time, the remaining scholars went to East Guilford, where they were taught by a former

6. Ibid., pp. 65–67. This Thomas Buckingham was from Hartford, not Saybrook. He was elected a trustee in 1709.

7. Ibid. (Johnson's "Remarks"), p. 152.

8. Ibid., pp. 68–70, 71–72.

tutor, the Reverend John Hart (class of 1703).[9] By September 1716, Saybrook was in its old role as a place with a commencement but without a college. It was the last year the town was to enjoy even that privilege.

The trustee meeting in September failed to resolve the locating of the college. Trustees John Davenport and Samuel Russell tried to win agreement for a Saybrook settlement but the two Hartford trustees dissented. A vote to remove the school to Hartford was defeated four to two and a vote to settle it in New Haven was passed five to two, Woodbridge and Buckingham being the minority in both instances. They also dissented in the final vote of the meeting, which called for adjournment until October 17 at New Haven.[10]

The September votes were a prelude to the October transactions. Eight trustees attended the October meeting; James Noyes was unable to attend and Samuel Mather, suffering from a mental disorder, was, as usual, not present. After choosing a moderator and a scribe, the trustees settled down to business. The first item on the agenda was "Whether Considering the Difficulties of Continuing the Collegiate School of Connecticut Colony at Saybrook," the trustees should agree to move it to New Haven "as a very Convenient place for it, and for which the Most Liberal Donations are given, appearing to us, as well as on many other Considerations." The motion carried five to two, with Moses Noyes of Lyme abstaining because he did "not see the necessity of removing the School from Saybrook, but if it must be removed from Saybrook, his mind is, that it be settled at Newhaven."

The vote broke down along geographic lines. In the majority were Samuel Andrew of Milford, John Davenport of Stamford, Joseph Webb of Fairfield, Samuel Russell of Branford, and Thomas Ruggles of Guilford—all ministers of seaside towns near New Haven. The two Hartford trustees made up the minority. James Noyes of Stonington, who signed the trustees' minutes on December 19, 1716, signified that he agreed with the majority on all thirty-two items of business. Noyes's position irritated, among others, John Winthrop, who claimed that the Stonington minister

9. Ibid. (Johnson's "Remarks"), pp. 152–53. See Richard L. Bushman, *From Puritan to Yankee,* p. 141. Bushman wrote: "New Haven and Hartford saw in Yale College a rich supplement for their normal sources of income and perhaps a boost for land prices."

10. *Documentary History,* pp. 72, 127.

had initially been "violent for keeping of it [the school] at Saybrook" in order to retain a £100 legacy granted the college by former Governor Winthrop. Noyes changed his views, said Winthrop, when his son Joseph was ordained pastor of the New Haven church.[11] In this case, family considerations proved more persuasive than financial ones.

The division between the upriver and the seaside trustees remained constant throughout the ensuing debates. At the October meeting the seaside majority had its way. After voting to establish the college in New Haven, the same trustees voted to disallow the vote taken at Hartford in May calling for the General Assembly to settle the school if the trustees could not agree unanimously on a place for it. Those who had not been at Hartford refused to abide by the vote taken there and insisted that "in the faithful discharg of the trust reposed in them, and in Exerting of the power conveyed to them" by the charter they had legally affixed the college at New Haven. Woodbridge and Buckingham voted to retain the Hartford agreement, while Moses Noyes again took a mediating position, saying he did not oppose going to the court.

The trustees next turned their attention to supplying the college with tutors. Samuel Russell had resigned the previous month and the school had no instructors. Samuel Smith (class of 1713) and Samuel Johnson (class of 1714) were chosen, with all but the Hartford trustees assenting. Johnson accepted his election immediately. Smith, who lived in Glastonbury and hence was sympathetic to the Hartford trustees, did not respond but instead joined Samuel Hall (class of 1716) at Wethersfield as a tutor under Elisha Williams.

For the remainder of the October meeting, which lasted three days, Woodbridge and Buckingham listened while their fellow trustees implemented a plan which they opposed. Their lowest moment came when their colleagues voted that the two Hartford trustees were to deliver the colony's £500 donation to Treasurer John Alling for use in New Haven. Finally, with the meeting about two-thirds over, Buckingham and Woodbridge left. The remaining trustees continued their deliberations, formed committees to oversee the building of a college house, and made provisions for moving the school's books and apparatus to New Haven.[12]

11. Ibid., pp. 73, 118.
12. Ibid., pp. 73–78.

When Buckingham and Woodbridge left the meeting they went to the General Assembly to protest the trustees' actions. They reminded the assembly of the May agreement, which called for the court to settle the college in the absence of a unanimous trustee vote, but the assembly did not take any action. Rebuffed but unwilling to admit defeat, the two ministers returned to Hartford to plan their next move. It came on December 18. Prompted by Woodbridge and Buckingham, the town of Hartford voted to offer a remonstrance to the General Assembly protesting the settlement of the collegiate school at New Haven. The upriver town based its objections on three counts: first, it claimed that, since New London and Hartford counties were the largest, paid the most money for the college's subsistence, and provided the greatest number of scholars, the settlement of the college at "remote" New Haven would be inconvenient, "there being but little communication between these counties and New Haven"; second, the May agreement had been violated when the trustees refused to allow the General Assembly to settle the school; third, the decision to move to New Haven had been made "by only an equal part of the Trustees," a reference to the fact that of ten trustees only five were for that town, while three did not concur and two were absent. For these reasons Hartford petitioned the legislators to locate the college "in a place that shall be judged by them most suitable, and where it may be best subsisted, and most accomodable to the greatest part of the government." [13] A few weeks later, Buckingham and Woodbridge circulated this remonstrance throughout Hartford and New London counties.

While Hartford appealed for the General Assembly to intervene, the seaside trustees were allocating money for the college building, buying timber, and receiving land from the town of New Haven. But the Hartford challenge could not be ignored, and in February, 1717, Trustees Andrew and Russell, along with Andrew's son-in-law, Jonathan Law (H. 1695), published a point-by-point response to the upriver remonstrance. It was, they claimed, full of "Inconsistencies Mistakes & Misrepresentations." The seaside trustees stated that the college had been settled by the sea because the coastal towns had the most inhabitants and it was easier for people in the river towns to come down to New Haven than for the coastal scholars to go up to Hartford. They also objected

13. Ibid., pp. 79–80.

that it was misleading to compare the joint donations of Hartford and New London counties with that of New Haven, which had the largest single subscription. As for providing students, the trustees argued that placing the college at New Haven would better accommodate the colonies of New York and New Jersey, which had no means of educating their young men.

Andrew, Russell, and Law also discredited the May agreement, saying that the trustees had the power to settle the college and that to allow the General Assembly to overrule them would mean that every trustee decision could be defeated. Touching an issue dear to Connecticut citizens, the response warned that none should "desire the Assembly to do that to thier Grantees which they would not Others should do to them viz Destroy their Charters & Charter privileges." Finally, the seaside trustees insisted that the college was settled by a clear majority of the trustees. Of the eight ministers present in October, five had been for New Haven, two opposed, and one against moving but for New Haven if the school had to be moved. Samuel Mather, who had been incapable of acting as a trustee for many years, had told James Pierpont as early as 1701 that he favored a New Haven settlement. James Noyes, who was an active trustee, had declared in December 1716 that he was also for New Haven. Thus, of the nine active trustees, six were for New Haven and of the eight voting at the meeting, five favored that town, a clear majority in both cases.[14]

Neither the upriver remonstrance nor the seaside rebuttal prevailed. By the spring of 1717 the Connecticut collegiate school was divided in three. The largest contingent of students (fourteen) was gathered in Wethersfield, taught by Tutors Williams, Smith, and Hall and supported by Trustees Woodbridge and Buckingham. Thirteen scholars were at New Haven, the seniors under Joseph Noyes, a former tutor, and all other classes taught by Samuel Johnson. Four students remained at Saybrook, where the Reverend Azariah Mather, another ex-tutor, supervised their studies. When the trustees met on April 5, there was little they could do to unite the college other than complete the task begun in October. With Buckingham and Woodbridge absent, the trustees declared that they "retained an Unchanged Judgment" on all votes taken at their last meeting. For good measure they reiterated fourteen items of business, repeating the majority vote of October on

14. Ibid., pp. 84–88. For Mather's view, see ibid., p. 24.

each item. The trustees then discussed the task of removing the school's belongings to New Haven and, in a move that consolidated their seaside emphasis, chose John Prout, Jr. of New Haven as treasurer in place of the deceased John Alling.[15]

While the trustee majority systematically implemented the settlement of the college at New Haven, the dissenting minority decided to carry its fight to the General Assembly. In May, 1717, Woodbridge and Buckingham presented a memorial to the court in which they claimed to have been wronged by the actions of their fellow trustees. The memorial recalled the May agreement of 1716 and reiterated that the votes taken in New Haven the previous October were invalid because only five of ten trustees voted affirmatively. Woodbridge and Buckingham also revealed that Thomas Ruggles, who had voted for New Haven, was not legally a trustee since he had been elected before he reached the age of forty, a clear violation of the college charter. The memorial concluded with an appeal for the General Assembly to settle the school, a plea echoed by Moses Noyes in a postscript.[16]

The memorial met with approbation from the lower house. That body resolved to call the trustees to appear at court to explain their doings, but the upper house vetoed the resolution. The lower house then expressed the desire that the college be settled "in sum place at, or neare Connecticut River" and, in the meantime, ordered the colony's annuity to be divided among the tutors at Wethersfield, New Haven, and Saybrook in proportion to the number of scholars taught by each. This proviso was accepted by the entire court. The upper house debated the college issue but declined to interfere; Governor Saltonstall was inclined to think that the upper house would not oppose the trustees' decision. In a letter to James Noyes, Saltonstall said that he heard the lower house favored Saybrook; as for his own stance, the governor found himself "easyly acquiescing in the Prudence of the

15. Ibid., pp. 88–95. Stephen Buckingham of Norwalk, who had been elected a trustee in October, accepted his election in April but did not vote on any of these issues. Perhaps he felt that he was not sufficiently informed to judge the dispute, but his family ties with many Saybrook people may have affected his decision to remain silent.

16. Ibid., pp. 95–98. The objection to Ruggles was technically justified but indicated that the Hartford trustees were groping for issues. As the seaside majority was to point out, Buckingham and Woodbridge had attended several trustee meetings with Ruggles and had never questioned the legality of his election.

Trustees, and Shall be always so perswaded of It, as not to insert my Self into their Affairs till I see further Reason for It." [17]

The lower house's desire to settle the college near the Connecticut River was a decisive factor in the role played by the General Assembly in the college debate. The more populous eastern sections of the colony had more representatives in the lower house than the western parts and thus favored a river settlement. Legal technicalities like charter privileges did not deter the representatives from trying to overrule the trustees and place the school in a location preferred by the lower house. The college issue was also a sectional debate. The ramifications of this debate were far-reaching, as Andrew, Russell, and Law had implied in their February memorial. If the lower house had its way, the Connecticut collegiate school would become subject to the wishes and whims of the colony's government. That was, in part, Harvard's situation. The Connecticut colonists did not know it, but their resolution of the collegiate affair was to set a precedent in assembly-college relations.[18]

The trustee meeting in September, 1717, was relatively uneventful. The Hartford trustees and Moses Noyes were absent, but those who attended had the absentees in mind when they declared that Thomas Ruggles "hath been realy & actually associated to the Collegiate Trustees for divers yeares past," during which time no one had objected to his election. To dispel any further doubt, the

17. Ibid., pp. 99, 100–01. Despite Saltonstall's profession of neutrality, there is some evidence to suggest that he and at least two members of the upper house acted out of self-interest in the college affair. According to Ezra Stiles, both Joseph Talcott and William Pitkin "to secure their Interest joyned with the Western part of the Colony in fixing the College at New Haven." Stiles also recorded that "the Vote for fixing it at Hartford had actually passed the lower & upper houses," but Governor Saltonstall was able to prevent the vote from being recorded. Richard Bushman interprets Saltonstall's motives to have been financial; he wrote that "the weight of the imperious Governor Saltonstall, who owned property in New Haven," influenced the assembly against voting for Hartford. See Franklin B. Dexter, ed., *Extracts from the Itineraries and other Miscellanies of Ezra Stiles,* p. 204; Bushman, *From Puritan to Yankee,* p. 141.

18. Yale experienced the same kind of threat from the Connecticut government in 1763 when the General Assembly claimed visitatorial power over the college. President Clap thwarted this attempt by a questionable interpretation of the college's founding, accompanied by some impressive legal reasoning. The 1763 issue anticipated the Dartmouth College case (1819) as, in a minor way, did the 1717–18 debates over the collegiate school's location and the arguments forwarded by Andrew, Russell, and Law.

ministers declared "we all account him a worthy Trustee & Associate." After answering the Hartford memorial, the trustees, in what was becoming a common affirmation, agreed to all the votes taken at their last meeting.[19]

If the trustee meeting was unexciting, the October session of the General Assembly was the exact opposite. Everyone who had an interest in the settlement of the college offered an opinion, presented a petition, made and answered charges and countercharges. When the debates were over, the issue of the college's location was practically resolved. Or so it seemed.

The October debates were initiated by Justice Daniel Buckingham, a resident of Saybrook who warmly supported the college's settlement there. Buckingham interpreted the initial decision to place the school at Saybrook as a covenant between the trustees and the townspeople that could not be broken unless either party violated its conditions. Since the Saybrook people had been true to the contract, moving the college was an "injustice." In another statement Buckingham argued that the trustees had no charter-sanctioned power to relocate the college. Once it was permanently settled, nothing remained for the trustees to do "But to maintaine &c And so far as the End and designe is obtained the trustees Comision is fulfilled, their worke done & their Power ended." To admit otherwise would allow the trustees to move the school "as many Times, and to as many places as they shall think fit." This notion was obviously foolish, and Buckingham made it more so by suggesting that if the trustees supported the present college move by soliciting private contributions, the trustees might also "at their pleasure set same to sale unto such persons or places as will give most money for it, All which is so far Repugnant to Sence, Reason, Common Right and Justice that if it were in their Charter it were void." [20]

Buckingham's depiction of the removal from Saybrook as illegal and absurd failed to generate any response in the assembly. In fact, with the exception of a later representation from Moses Noyes, which was offered more as a compromise than as a conviction, Buckingham was the only champion of Saybrook. The original college town had few supporters, and it soon became obvious that the river party had no intention of agreeing on Saybrook, located

19. *Documentary History*, pp. 104–05.
20. Ibid., pp. 106–07, 107–08.

at the river's mouth. The fight was between Hartford and New Haven.

The dissenting trustees had convinced the lower house that the decision to move the college to New Haven was irregular. Acting on this conviction, the lower house called the trustees to appear "to Shew the Reasons of Their Late Proceedings and Particularly Why they or any of them Have Ordered a Collegiate School to be Built at New Haven, without the Allowance or Knowledge of this Assembly." While the upper house disagreed with the belligerent wording of this resolve, it accepted the idea behind it. The assembly requested that the trustees come to court in order to facilitate the settling of the school "for the preservation of Order and Peace." [21]

The seaside trustees responded by offering a memorial relating the history of the college at Saybrook and the problems that led to its removal. The memorial stated that New Haven had been chosen as the site of the school because of "the conveniency of its situation, agreeableness of the air & soile, the probability of providing what will be necessary for the subsistence of the Schollars as cheap or cheaper then at other places . . . wherunto may be added the largest sums by farr subscribed by particular Gentlemen for building an house for the School in the said Town." In presenting their reasons for a New Haven settlement, the trustees had a strong case. With a population of about a thousand and with approximately 150 buildings, the New Haven of 1717 was the wealthiest town in Connecticut, with its taxable estates exceeding second-place Hartford's by about £2,000. The townspeople had taken advantage of their prosperity to outbid all rivals for the school, and they had sweetened the pot by granting land adjacent to the town green for the proposed college house. The majority trustees no doubt thought that these facts would be sufficient to stifle all objections to their decision to locate the school there.

Buckingham and Woodbridge, however, found their colleagues' explanations to be irrelevant. The real issue, they insisted, was not the reason for choosing New Haven but the validity of doing so. The Hartford trustees repeated their charge that the choice was invalid because only four out of nine trustees voted for it. The two clergymen arrived at this figure by arguing that Ruggles was not a legitimate trustee, that Noyes's later vote did not count, and that

21. Ibid., pp. 109–10, 111–12.

Mather should still be considered an active trustee since he had not resigned and the trustees had not removed him from office.[22]

On October 23 and 24 the upper house debated the issues raised by the Hartford trustees. The council decided that Ruggles's election as trustee was valid, that Noyes's later vote was invalid, and that Mather, deprived of his reason, ought not be considered capable of either assenting to or dissenting from any trustee decision. This interpretation seemed to affirm that a majority of the trustees had voted for New Haven. The council's resolutions were passed on to the lower house with the instructions that, unless the house had further questions, the matter should be closed and the trustees dismissed.[23]

The lower house did have further questions. Without consulting the upper house, the deputies began to admit pleadings on the issues of the Hartford memorial. The majority trustees answered the charges of their upriver associates by defending the validity of Ruggles's election and Noyes's vote and declaring that Mather had not been an active trustee for many years. The seaside trustees stated that they were innocent of any wrongdoing in moving the college from Saybrook and placed the blame for that trouble on Woodbridge and Buckingham. The lower house was unconvinced. The deputies determined that the charter gave the trustees power only to manage the college, not to move it, and agreed with the Hartford interpretation of the status of the three controversial trustees.[24] As a further case against the seaside trustees, the lower house voted that the trustees must unanimously agree to move the school, thus reviving the May agreement of 1716. The governor's assistants (the upper house) objected to this decision; they told the deputies that it was not "of any Service, to multiply Questions of this Nature," as the only issue was whether or not a *majority* of the trustees agreed to the decision. Finding that to be the case, the upper house voted to support the New Haven settlement.[25]

22. Ibid., pp. 112–14, 114–16. Moses Noyes maintained his mediating posture as a would-be peacemaker by adding a postscript to the remarks of Buckingham and Woodbridge: "I Moses Noyes desire to suspend my opinion concerning some things in these Answers particularly concerning the reverend Mr Rugles, yet if opportunity be given I desire to offer some Plea in behalf of Saybrook." On October 26, Noyes offered such a plea but it was not needed.

23. Ibid., pp. 116–18.

24. Ibid., pp. 121–25, 126–27, 129–30. The trustees replied to the lower house by reiterating their position on all matters to which the deputies dissented.

25. Ibid., pp. 131–32, 132–33.

By this time everyone was growing weary of the debate. The college issue not only involved factions of trustees but also pitted section against section and deputies versus assistants. The arguments about Ruggles, Noyes, and Mather seemed incapable of resolution, so the upper house ceased to look for one. The assistants concluded that, since the trustees believed they had acted properly in moving the school, they should be encouraged to complete the work they had started. But the deputies were not as willing to ignore "the Questions of Right" that the upper house had not found "to be of such Importance." [26] The lower house, having entered the fray, wanted to have the final say in determining the outcome. On October 29, the deputies introduced a new factor into the contest by voting thirty-five to thirty-two in favor of placing the college in Middletown. While Middletown was an appropriate name for a compromise locale, the upper house refused to accept the recommendation.

At this point the deputies bridled. Displaying their fixed animosity toward both New Haven and the upper house, they declared that, if the upper house "did Vote another place for the School then New Haven, they would set down Satisfyed." The assistants did not rise to the bait; no settlement was going to receive universal consent, and the upper house felt that the best solution was to agree to the trustees' decision. The deliberations were, to all intents and purposes, deadlocked. Both sides had stated and restated their positions and neither appeared willing to yield. But the seaside trustees had done more than simply present their case. As evidence of their obstinacy they had gone ahead with the construction of the New Haven college without waiting for the assembly to reach a decision. In fact, by the time the legislators convened in New Haven for the October meeting, workmen had already raised the frame for the college building. Surely the fact that the assembly deliberations took place amidst the sound of carpenters pounding nails must have influenced the final outcome. The physical existence of the college building probably did more to break the deputies' resistance than all the seaside petitions and pleas put together. On the last day of the General Assembly session, the lower house gave in. By a six-vote margin the assembly agreed to tell the trustees "to proceed in that affair, and finish the House, they have built in New Haven, for the Entertainment of

26. Ibid., pp. 134–36.

the Schollars belonging to the Collegiate School." [27] In the end, the entrenched combination of a determined trustee majority backed by the upper house prevailed.

The victory in the assembly, however, did not conclude the dispute. The upriver faction did not take defeat graciously, and although Woodbridge and Buckingham agreed to meet with their fellow trustees in New Haven on the day before the final assembly vote, it was apparent that they were in a sullen mood. When the trustees went over some old business, the two ministers restated their former positions. But the majority party was conciliatory and voted to "use all fair & equal measures in Order to obtain Mr Elisha Williams" as senior tutor, and once more chose Samuel Smith as tutor. They also decided to notify the Wethersfield students to appear for instruction at New Haven, with Samuel Andrew continuing as nonresident rector pro tempore.[28] The conciliation failed. Upon Woodbridge's advice the Wethersfield contingent refused to attend classes at New Haven, and when the trustees sought to remove the college library from Saybrook, they were rebuffed by Daniel Buckingham, who was keeping the books in his house. In the words of Tutor Samuel Johnson, "things looked dark & malencholy & even Spightfull & malicious." In the face of this malice the New Haven trustees did what they had done so well before: they carried on. The Reverend Joseph Moss of Derby joined the Reverend Joseph Noyes of New Haven in instructing the upper classes, while Johnson taught the lower. The college continued with this arrangement for the next year.[29]

It was a bad arrangement. The seaside trustees had received the reluctant support of the General Assembly but found that the Hartford minority, which had appealed to the assembly in the first place, now refused to abide by the decision. The college had gained little from the prolonged court debate if the majority of the scholars stayed away from New Haven. The trustees did not know it, but a partial solution to their problem had been worked out in the mind of Cotton Mather.

Elihu Yale

Cotton Mather was a busy man. When he was not writing books to enlighten and correct his fellow New Englanders he was think-

27. Ibid., pp. 137–40, 145–46.
28. Ibid., pp. 140–45.
29. Ibid. (Johnson's "Remarks"), p. 157.

ing of other ways to serve them. In January, 1718, he conceived a way to help the Connecticut collegiate school. It was not Mather's first gesture on behalf of the struggling college but it certainly was his grandest. He would write to Elihu Yale, the wealthy Londoner who had made a small fortune as governor of the Madras Colony in the East Indies, and suggest that he donate a substantial sum to the Connecticut college. Mather worded the proposal eloquently: "Certainly," he wrote,

> if what is forming at New Haven might wear the name of YALE COLLEGE, it would be better than *a name of sons and daughters*. And your munificence might easily obtain for you such a commemoration and perpetuation of your valuable name, as would indeed be much better than an Egyptian pyramid.[30]

Elihu Yale was not thinking of perpetuating his name with an Egyptian pyramid. But he liked the notion of having a colonial college bear his name and was receptive when Connecticut's London agent, Jeremiah Dummer, visited him in March. We do not know what Dummer said on this occasion, although Yale evidently expressed some concern "whether it was well in him, being a Church man, to promote an Academy of Dissenters." Dummer later wrote of this incident to Governor Saltonstall and explained how he had discussed the matter with Yale, after which

> he appear'd convinc't that the business of good men is to spread religion & learning among mankind without being too fondly attach't to particular Tenets, about which the World never was, nor ever will be agreed. Besides if the Discipline of the Church of England be most agreeable to Scripture & primitive practice, there's no better way to make men sensible of it than by giving them good learning.[31]

With this comforting thought, Governor Yale consented to help the struggling Connecticut college. Though the trustees would hardly have agreed with his proselytizing motives, they were in no position to quarrel. What Yale hoped his gift would accomplish was his business.

At the same time that Agent Dummer was working in England

30. Ibid., pp. 163–64.
31. Ibid., p. 193.

to assist the college, Trustee Woodbridge was hatching a plan in Connecticut to subvert it. Woodbridge had not accepted the victory won by the seaside trustees the preceding October and had succeeded in keeping the Wethersfield students away from New Haven. But this maneuver could not be employed indefinitely. New Haven had the money and the assembly's encouragement to build a college. Wethersfield had about a dozen scholars and £45 from the government to be divided among three tutors. Woodbridge's solution to this problem was bold. In April, 1718, he wrote letters to Harvard President John Leverett and to Harvard Overseer Benjamin Colman asking that the Wethersfield students be allowed to take their first degree at the Bay College.

Woodbridge argued that since the Connecticut collegiate school had split up, the Wethersfield scholars had existed as "an Intire & Separate Company by themselves & their Education is therefore private." He was willing for these students to be subject to Harvard regulations and concluded his request by citing the precedent of admitting privately educated men to degrees at both Harvard and Scottish universities.[32] During the late spring of 1718 Woodbridge awaited the Harvard reply. In the meantime, the lower house offered him yet another tactic to use against the New Haven school.

The Reverend Samuel Estabrook preached the 1718 election sermon, appealing to the assembly to act "for the Healing of our Differences and the Recovery of our Peace and Quietness." [33] The deputies ignored him. They once again injected themselves into the college issue; noting the unsettled state of the school, the deputies voted thirty-five to twenty-one to settle the college near the Connecticut River and, until that was done, to hold commencements interchangeably at Wethersfield and New Haven.[34]

Although the upper house rejected this resolution, Woodbridge and Buckingham accepted it immediately. On June 2 they told their fellow trustees that they "freely comply with the advice [of the lower house] & desire the same of yourselves." If the seaside ministers refused, the Hartford trustees would conclude that "a peaceable composing of our difficulties in a way soe agreable to

32. Woodbridge to [Benjamin Colman], Apr. 10, 1718, Yale Archives.

33. Samuel Estabrook, *A Sermon Shewing that the Peace and Quietness Of a People Is a main part of the Work of Civil Rulers, And That it is the Duty of all to Pray For Them* (New London, 1718), p. 10.

34. *Documentary History*, p. 165.

the greater part of the Country is not enough at heart with you & that you have a purpose of forcing others to a complyance with you which we cannot think is a spirrit should govern christians much less the Ministers of a peaceable Gospel." [35]

Both of Woodbridge's schemes failed. On June 4 Overseer Colman wrote that Harvard would not accept the Wethersfield students:

> the more I think & the more I have enquired into the Circumstances of your College, the more I grow in my Opinion that it is necessary for the Well-being of it that the Classes with Mr. Williams do not desert it. . . . It will I fear weaken & dishearten your Accademy when your Commencement comes on, if several Graduates, it may be of the best Literature should decline receiving their Honours from her. We must in a thousand instances deny our Selves for the common good. I cannot therefore bring my Self to be willing that any number of your Scholars should at this critical time offer themselves to us.[36]

Colman's answer was followed by a similar refusal from the majority trustees. They told Woodbridge and Buckingham that they were welcome to submit proposals "which are likely to be consistent with what we have regularly done," but that it was useless to persist with this kind of opposition.[37] The New Haven trustees admitted no compromise and the Wethersfield renegades, denied sanctuary by Harvard, were forced either to capitulate or to continue alone.

Woodbridge and Buckingham chose to persevere. They did so at the time when Mather's overtures and Dummer's negotiations paid off. In the summer of 1718 Governor Yale's donation arrived in Boston. On hearing this news, the seaside trustees hurriedly decided to scrap the printed commencement program, which referred to the college as the "Collegiate School," and to publish a new set with the name "Yale Colledge" inserted.[38] This minor change was symbolically significant, for it announced to all concerned that the majority trustees not only had the will to settle the school in New Haven, but that they now had the means to do so.

35. Ibid., pp. 166–67.
36. Ibid., pp. 167–68.
37. Ibid., pp. 169–70.
38. Yale University Library *Gazette*, 6 (1932): 16–17.

The Yale gift was timely, coming at a moment when the future of the collegiate school was in doubt. Cotton Mather expressed the hope that the "Yalean assistance to New Haven will prove a decisive circumstance, which will dispose all to an acquiescence there." [39] The hope was not realized. The Hartford trustees were undoubtedly disheartened by New Haven's good fortune, but they were not deterred from pursuing their independent course. On September 10, while the New Haven college was holding an impressive celebration and commencement, the Reverend Timothy Woodbridge awarded degrees to five Wethersfield students.

In New Haven, the mood was jubilant. Master builder Henry Caner, who had been brought from Boston to construct the college building, had been working on the project for nearly a year. He had made good progress; his workmen had put up the frame in October, 1717, and now the structure was nearly complete. Located across from the western corner of the town's center square (on the corner of the present College and Chapel streets), the college was about 170 feet long, 22 feet wide, three stories high, and had six chimneys, three staircases, and a total of sixteen rooms, one of which was the hall on the first floor and above it the library.[40] By commencement time, the hall and the library were finished.

The majority trustees wanted to capitalize on the good fortune of the Yale donation by staging an impressive commencement program. The event attracted a dignified audience. Governor and Madame Gurdon Saltonstall, Lieutenant-Governor Nathan Gold, the entire superior court, and many Connecticut ministers came to New Haven for the exercises. Colonel William Taylor, former lieutenant-governor of Massachusetts, was there as Governor Yale's representative. The day began with a ceremony of recognition for the donation of books, the picture and arms of King George, and £200 sterling sent by Elihu Yale. The college trustees decreed *"that our College House shall be called by the Name of it's Munificent Patron, and shall be named* YALE-COLLEGE." [41] Colonel

39. *Documentary History,* p. 171.

40. Norman M. Isham, "The Original College House at Yale," *The Yale Alumni Weekly,* 26 (1916–17): 114–20. After completing the college house, Henry Caner continued to find gainful employment in New Haven. In 1719 he built a two-story statehouse for the town and in 1722 he erected a rector's house for the college.

41. *Yale Annals,* p. 26. Technically, only the building was named Yale College. The college's name was not changed until 1745, although the whole institution was soon referred to as Yale College. The school was also called—at least by

Taylor responded on behalf of Yale and expressed satisfaction with the proceedings. The company then retired to the New Haven meetinghouse, where the scholars delivered orations and debated their theses; eight men received the B.A. Governor Saltonstall delivered a speech congratulating the trustees on the settlement of the school, after which everyone retired to the college for a "splendid Dinner." The gentlemen dined in the hall and the ladies were entertained in the library, where they were joined by "the Honorable Ingenuous & Generous Coll. Taylor." The day ended with everyone reciting the first four verses of the sixty-fifth Psalm.[42]

But the happy mood of the college commencement did not dispel the difficulties confronting the school. At their September meeting, the trustees attempted to remedy these difficulties; they chose Henry Flynt (H. 1693), a long-standing tutor at the Bay College, as rector, again ordered Daniel Buckingham to send along the library from Saybrook, and told the Wethersfield students that they could return to the college in good standing if they did so before winter. Those who had graduated at Wethersfield were to receive a diploma from the New Haven college if they produced a testimony signed by two trustees—a condition which had already been met, since Woodbridge and Buckingham had signed the commencement certificates of the six upriver graduates.[43] The trustees' proposals were rebuffed in all three instances. When the academic year began in early October, Yale College was still missing one resident rector, several students, and about 1,300 books.

The school received timely help from an unexpected quarter—the General Assembly. At the October session the upper house proposed that, since the settlement of the college at New Haven had worked "a Considerable Hardship upon the Counties of Hartford and New London" and especially upon the town of Hartford, "which was anciently the Seat of the principall administration of power in the Colony," the upriver town should be compensated with a grant of £800 to build a courthouse.[44] After study by an

Harvard men—the "Wooden College," presumably in reference to the structure built by Henry Caner. See William D. Sprague, *Annals of the American Pulpit*, 9 vols. (New York, 1859–69), 1 : 367.

42. *Documentary History* (Johnson's "Remarks"), pp. 157–58; ibid., pp. 176–77; *Yale Annals*, pp. 23–27.

43. *Documentary History*, pp. 173–74, 178–79.

44. C.A., Colleges and Schools, 1 : 200. The upper house had proposed to sell ten square miles of land for £1,000 and to give Hartford £800 for a courthouse and New Haven £200 to complete the college house.

assembly committee, the upper house suggestion was incorporated into "An Act for Encouragement of Yale College." Passed on October 9, the act called for the Wethersfield students to go to New Haven and Saybrook to relinquish the college library, and granted Hartford £500 for a courthouse and Saybrook £50 for a town school.[45]

Prospects for collegiate harmony brightened. With the General Assembly applying pressure in New Haven's favor at last, the upriver dissenters were almost forced to go to the seaside town. When Governor Saltonstall heard that some people intended to persist at Wethersfield anyway, he ordered the assembly's act to be published by the town constable as "sufficient Means to prevent any Such Disorder as is said to be designed there." [46] The feared disorder never erupted. In late November the Wethersfield students moved their chests of clothes and books to New Haven and hired a man to bring their horses back after the journey to the college.[47]

The Dispute Continues

The college's long hoped-for reunification, however, was shortlived. The upriver students arrived looking for trouble, behaved themselves in an obnoxious manner, and made every effort to discredit the college. A few weeks after their arrival the students drew up a "Collection of faults" they found with "the public Expositions & Disputations & managements of the Tutors," especially Tutor Samuel Johnson, who was teaching the juniors and seniors. It is impossible to determine the precise nature of these objections, whether personal or curricular, spurious or real, except that when Trustee Woodbridge learned about them, he approved them "as sufficient" to warrant a challenge to the New Haven college. Woodbridge's motivations are difficult to decipher, but if he did not plan for the students to disrupt the college he certainly was glad to receive their complaints. In late December three parents came to New Haven, perhaps at Woodbridge's suggestion, and decided to remove their sons from the school. Trustees Andrew and Russell tried to forestall an exodus by making a concession. They rearranged the teaching schedule so that two ministers, Joseph Moss and Joseph Noyes, took the two upper classes, and Tutors Samuel

45. *Documentary History*, pp. 179–80.

46. Ibid., pp. 182–83.

47. Esther Edwards to Timothy Edwards, Nov. 20, 1718, Connecticut Historical Society, Hartford, Conn.

Johnson and Daniel Brown (class of 1714) the sophomores and freshmen. While this decision was an attempt to meet the professed objections of the dissidents, in fact it only served to confuse them. Their response indicated how dependent they were on Woodbridge: the students asked the Hartford trustees for advice. Their advice was to leave. On January 10, 1719, a messenger came down from Hartford with horses, and the dissatisfied undergraduates returned to the tutelage of Elisha Williams.[48]

While Woodbridge and his student followers were successfully preventing the college's reunion, Justice Daniel Buckingham was waging a less successful battle for possession of the college library. Until the trustees had built a college house at New Haven, the school's most valuable property had been its books, which had come to the college from many sources; the original trustees had given some, a few donors such as Cotton Mather and Samuel Sewall had sent others, but the large majority of the works had been solicited by Jeremiah Dummer in England. By 1718 the college had about 1,300 books, which the trustees had stored in Daniel Buckingham's house in Saybrook until the school was relocated. Apparently, Buckingham intended to keep them.

The seaside trustees had been trying to get the library for several years. The possibility of losing it entirely first became evident in 1717. On October 31 of that year the trustees had found it necessary to write Agent Dummer asking him to confirm the fact that he had intended the books to advance the cause of learning in Connecticut and "particularly to brighten the Countenances of the Trustees" and "not to furnish many illiterate families in Saybrook with a stock of Books each, as We have heard the uneasy spirits of that Town incline & seem resolved, from an Opinion that your Donation . . . is the Propriety of the School in that Place." [49] That opinion was promulgated by Justice Buckingham and in December, 1718, he attempted to enforce it.

On November 11, Buckingham had turned away a delegation sent to retrieve the library, "declaring he did not know that he had any books belonging to Yale College, but when he did, and should receive authentick orders, he would deliver them." This was sheer sophistry and everyone knew it. When the Governor's

48. *Documentary History* (Johnson's "Remarks"), pp. 159–61. Daniel Brown became a tutor on September 10, 1718.

49. Ibid., p. 147.

Council heard about Buckingham's nonsense it convicted him of a "great misdemeanour and contempt of authority" and ordered him arrested. The justice appeared unrepentant. The council carefully explained to him the legal niceties of how the Connecticut collegiate school at Saybrook had become Yale College at New Haven, but Buckingham was not convinced. Since the library-keeper would not listen to reason, the council voted to use force. The New London County sheriff was ordered to enter Buckingham's house, seize the books, and deliver them to the college trustees.

But Justice Buckingham did not stand alone. When the sheriff went to confiscate the books he was met by a surly mob; one Abraham Chalker, perhaps the head of one of those "illiterate families," told the sheriff "that if he came into the said house it should be upon his peril." The sheriff wisely withdrew, but returned with helpers, who broke into the house and removed the books. The council then ordered the sheriff "to impress men, and carts, and oxen, as shall be sufficient for conveying the said books" to the college. The people of Saybrook, however, had not given up. While the sheriff and his men guarded the books, the "uneasy spirits" of the town broke the carts and turned loose the oxen. The sheriff regrouped his forces and moved the books anyway, but soon discovered that the bridges between Saybrook and Guilford had been destroyed. This vandalism impeded the caravan's progress and it took three days for the library to reach Yale College. When the books were unpacked and counted, the trustees found that the people of Saybrook had won a partial victory. About 260 volumes and "sundry Papers of Importance" were missing, never to be recovered. The remaining thousand works were placed in the college library and the battle of the books was over.[50]

Meanwhile the fight with the Wethersfield faction continued. The dissatisfied students ostensibly had refused to continue at

50. Ibid., pp. 183–87; (Johnson's "Remarks"), p. 160; *Yale Annals,* pp. 28–29. Abraham Chalker was arrested for his behavior in the book affair. The government dealt with Daniel Buckingham the following spring when the upper house demanded that he offer an apology to the assembly before he be allowed to take his seat as a deputy. Buckingham protested that he and others truly thought that the books, "or at lest sum of them [were] given to the coleget Scool at Saybrook," but acknowledged that he had been wrong in not obeying the council's order: "If it were to be acted again I would not do as I have done." See Wyllys Papers, 4 : 4, 5, Connecticut Historical Society.

Yale College for an all too common reason—they did not like the tutors. In this case they specifically did not like Samuel Johnson. The principal complaint against Johnson seems to have been the poor quality of his teaching, although this allegation was certainly overstated, if not trumped up altogether. Johnson himself suspected that he was simply a convenient scapegoat for the general discontent of the Hartford trustees, but whatever the reason, his tenure as tutor was the key issue in the spring of 1719. On March 11 the governor and council met in New Haven to investigate the college dispute, so that "proper measures might be taken to redress what should be found amiss, and prevent the like for the future." Woodbridge and Buckingham refused to attend the meeting and the Wethersfield students, revealing their allegiance to the upriver trustees, replied "that they understood that Mr. Woodbridge and Mr. Buckingham would not be there, and could not tell whether they should be there or not."

Despite the absence of the dissatisfied parties, their allegations of Johnson's "insufficiency" dominated the council meeting. When the trustees were called on to account for the college division, they replied by defending Tutor Johnson against those who "have endavoured to scandalize a gentleman in such a manner, whom much more competent judges highly esteem as a man of good learning, and in that respect very well accomplished for the charge he is in." After listening to the ministers discredit the "pretended cause" of the Wethersfield desertion, the council noted that much of the college's trouble was due to the want of a resident rector. The trustees agreed and pleasantly surprised the assistants by announcing that they had chosen Timothy Cutler (H. 1701), pastor of the Canterbury parish in Stratford, as rector, at least until June. This was encouraging news and the meeting closed on an optimistic note.

On March 29, Timothy Cutler came to New Haven to instruct one class at Yale College; Tutors Johnson and Brown stayed on to teach the other classes.[51] Although the trustees made no formal decision to get rid of Johnson, the Wethersfield students certainly continued to think he should go. One of those students was Jonathan Edwards, who was to become early Yale's most famous graduate and America's greatest theologian. At this time he was a junior in college and he disliked Tutor Johnson; for Edwards,

51. *Documentary History*, pp. 181–91; (Johnson's "Remarks"), pp. 161–62.

Johnson was the sole obstacle to the reunification of the school. It was with some pleasure, therefore, that he wrote his sister Mary that the trustees had "Removed that which was the cause of our coming away viz, Mr Johnson from the Place of a Tutor." The decision to elect Cutler as rector quashed all of the objections to the New Haven college so that, he reported, "All the Scolars belonging to our School Expect to Return there as soon as Our Vacancy after the Election Is over." [52] These expectations were fulfilled; by the time Edwards and his fellow students returned to New Haven, Samuel Johnson had resigned.

In May, the General Assembly, perhaps out of a feeling of relief that the acrimony seemed to be over, granted the college an additional £40 a year for seven years.[53] On June 3 the trustees met and

52. Edwards to Mary Edwards, Mar. 26, 1719, Jonathan Edwards Collection, Andover-Newton Seminary Library, Newton Centre, Mass. The fact that the intellectually inquisitive Edwards was strongly opposed to the learned Johnson suggests the intriguing possibility that Johnson's teaching abilities might not have been the sole source of conflict. By this time Johnson was in the early stages of that spiritual pilgrimage which was to lead him to the refined and dispassionate Christianity of the Church of England; Edwards, on the other hand, and probably his upriver colleagues, partook of a more evangelical tradition and were more experiential in the practice of piety. As an undergraduate Johnson had disparaged the spiritual conceit of those who attended student prayer groups, and it may be that the Wethersfield boys constituted such a group and sensed the tutor's distaste. Having just left the instruction of Elisha Williams, who shared and encouraged an active faith, the students may have found Johnson's reasonable religion objectionable.

This interpretation is, admittedly, a conjecture; no evidence survives to support it. Based on a knowledge of Edwards and Johnson, however, the religious dimension of the 1719 split is plausible. As it is hard to believe that Edwards would have found Johnson's instruction in the new learning anything but stimulating, his obvious dislike for the tutor probably had other foundations. Since Johnson's recent fascination with Anglicanism (see chapter 4 below) contrasted sharply with Edwards's evangelical heritage from his grandfather, Solomon Stoddard, religious differences might have potentially served as those foundations. I am indebted to Wallace Anderson and Thomas Shafer, who spoke of this possibility to me and with whom I have discussed it.

On the surface, however, the objections to Johnson centered around his abilities as a tutor. The seaside trustees felt that Johnson had been unjustly maligned by the upriver faction; at the September meeting they voted him an additional three pounds and their thanks for his "extraordinary service." See *Documentary History*, p. 198.

53. At this assembly Woodbridge and Buckingham launched their last, desperate effort to subvert the New Haven college. Both men were elected representatives from Hartford and, with others, hoped to secure the election of Nathan Gold as governor in place of Saltonstall. The plan was that "if Mr. Gould were at the Head of the upper house & Mr. Woodbridge of the lower, they might effect some-

reaffirmed their choice of Cutler as rector. At the end of the month the Wethersfield students joined the rest of the undergraduates at New Haven. "I Take verry Great Content under my Present Tuition," Jonathan Edwards wrote his father,

> as all the Rest of the Scholars seem to do under their's; Mr Cutler is extraordinary Courteous to Us, Has a verry Good Spirit of Government, Keeps the School in excellent order, seems to Encrease in Learning, and is Lov'd and feared by all that are under him, and when he is spoken of in the school or town He Generally has the title of President. The Scholars all Live in verry Good Peace with the People of the Town, and there is not a word said about our former Carryings on.[54]

Since its founding in 1701, the Connecticut collegiate school had met, at various times, in six towns: Saybrook, Killingworth, Milford, East Guilford, Wethersfield, and New Haven. It was not until the summer of 1719 that the college had, for the first time, a resident rector, a building, and an entire student body in one location. The school's protracted schism was finally healed. Yale College would not move again.

---

thing distructive to the Colledg at N. Haven." The design was foiled when Saltonstall won reelection and Woodbridge was denied his seat in the lower house because of his intemperate remarks against the governor and council. He had accused them of breaking the sixth and eighth commandments in ordering Saybrook to give the college books to Yale. See *Documentary History* (Johnson's "Remarks"), pp. 162–63. For Woodbridge's difficulties and trial in the assembly, see Wyllys Papers, 4 : 6 ff., Connecticut Historical Society.

54. Edwards to Timothy Edwards, July 24, 1719, Jonathan Edwards Collection.

4. "A Most Grevous Rout and Hurle-Burle"

The trustees were pleased with their selection of Timothy Cutler as rector. He was well qualified for the job. In 1709 the Congregational ministers of Connecticut, in an effort to counteract the influence in Stratford of the Church of England's Society for the Propagation of the Gospel in Foreign Parts, had "determined that one of the best preachers that both colonies could afford should be sought out and sent there; and one Mr. Cutler, who lived then at Boston or Cambridge, was accordingly pitched upon." [1] Cutler came to Stratford, a town that had had difficulties finding a minister, and preached as a candidate for settlement; he was well received, and on September 16, 1709, the people of Stratford voted unanimously to have him as their minister. Two years later Cutler married Elizabeth Andrew, daughter of one of the colony's leading clergymen, pro tempore Rector Samuel Andrew.[2]

Cutler's career at Stratford was promising, and in 1717 he was honored by the General Assembly, which invited him to preach the annual election sermon. In it the future rector spoke of the necessity of education: "This Civilizeth Men, and Cultivateth *Good Manners,* and the want of it bringeth in Bestiality and Rudeness, Barbarity and Fierceness, and all those Ill and Crooked Dispositions that make Society less Pleasant and Delightful." [3] With his views and credentials, Cutler was a natural choice to assume the task of overseeing the undergraduates in the newly reunited college. Two other factors in his favor were that he was willing to leave Stratford and become resident rector and that he was acceptable to both the seaside and the upriver trustees. At the September trustee meeting, after Cutler had been in office for several months, the ministers declared their approval of his performance and voted to make his appointment permanent.[4]

1. *Episcopal Church Documents,* 1 : 50.

2. *Harvard Graduates,* 5 : 46.

3. Timothy Cutler, *The Firm Union of a People Represented; and a Concern for it, Urged; upon All Orders and Degrees of Men* (New London, 1717), p. 39.

4. *Documentary History,* p. 196. The vote was not unanimous, however, as a later remark of Trustee John Davenport reveals. See ibid., p. 227.

The Connecticut General Assembly was also pleased by Cutler's election and quickly demonstrated its gratitude by decreeing that the rector "shall have all his estate, as well as polls, freed from any taxes in this government while he is in the aforesaid office." That was not all. In an effort to insure Cutler's permanent residence in New Haven, the court during the next few years voted to donate the proceeds from the rum duty to the college and authorized a colony-wide collection in order to provide money for a rector's house.[5] And in October, 1719, the assembly delegates complimented the newly installed rector by asking him to deliver a sermon at the opening of their session.[6]

When Timothy Cutler took over the position of Yale rector from his father-in-law he inherited a difficult situation. Not only did he have to reunite the college, but he had to correct the downward trend in student discipline caused by three years of neglect. He pursued these ends with dedication. On June 30, 1719, Cutler wrote to the father of one of his students, the Reverend Timothy Edwards of Windsor, to thank him for his good wishes. The rector stated that he wanted to forget old sectional grievances and intended to work hard to serve the young scholars: "They may suffer much from my Weaknesse but they shall not from my Neglect. I am no party-man but shall carry it with an equall hand and affection to the whole Colledge, and I doubt not but the Difficulty and Importance of the Businesse will obtain for me your & all good men's prayers which I do much value and desire." [7] The rector's good intentions proved effective, as Jonathan Edwards testified. Within several months Cutler had established his authority over the school and had brought order to the college routine.

The years of Cutler's tenure were good ones for Yale. One reason for this happy situation was that the college had finally found a home. Compared to the years of makeshift arrangements with Killingworth and Saybrook—to say nothing of the college's three-year division—the school's New Haven settlement was ideal. Not only did it have a resident rector, a building, and a united student body, but it also had the promise of a permanent location. The college itself was built close to the center of New Haven's life and

5. Ibid., pp. 199, 207, 214–16, 220–21.
6. Timothy Cutler, *The Depth of the Divine Thoughts* (New London, 1720).
7. Cutler to Timothy Edwards, June 30, 1719, Jonathan Edwards Collection.

work. Located on the corner of one of the town's original nine squares, the college faced the town green, which contained the meetinghouse (church), grammar school, and market-place. All around the school were the residences and businesses of the town's citizens.

Though New Haven was the wealthiest town in the colony and served as a county seat, it was predominantly an agricultural rather than a mercantile community. The interiors of the eight outer squares of the town contained the orchards, meadows, and cornfields of the many farmers and husbandmen, while the several streets were lined with the homes of artisans and tradesmen. Both farmers and artisans would benefit from having the college in their midst. Soon after Cutler was installed in office, the trustees hired a steward to provide the college "diet"—the provisions for which no doubt came from the fields and pastures of local farmers—and in later years hired various artisans to repair the college and to build the rector's house. While the college laws forbade students from wandering about the town, the trustees did want the undergraduates to participate in one communal activity, and made arrangements with the New Haven church to provide seats for the scholars at weekly worship and lecture services.

But most of the credit for Yale's stability belongs to Timothy Cutler. The rector was, as Ezra Stiles reported years later, "of a commanding Presence & Dignity in Government" and "made a grand Figure as the Head of a College." He was a man of academic as well as administrative abilities. Cutler was widely regarded as an excellent linguist who "spoke Latin with Fluency & Dignity & with great Propriety of Pronunciation." He was also well versed in the traditional disciplines of a collegiate school, so the intellectual life of the college flourished under him. But perhaps Cutler's most enduring trait, one evidenced by the haughty pose of his portrait, was his "high, lofty, & despotic mien." [8] The rector had a belligerent and imperious personality, which may have been an asset in dealing with students but was to plague him during his subsequent career. Only once did the Yale undergraduates dare to defy him openly. That was in 1721, when a sizable group of them violently objected to the quality of the food offered by the steward and voted to boycott commons. The rebellion was brief. Rector Cutler let it be known that he was "exceedingly vex'd, and Dis-

8. Franklin B. Dexter, ed., *The Literary Diary of Ezra Stiles,* 2 : 339–40.

pleased at the Act, which so affrighted the Scholars that they Unanimously agreed to Come into Commons again." [9]

Although one result of Cutler's toughness was to force the students to cause trouble off campus rather than on, the trustees found no cause to doubt the effectiveness and value of the rector's service. However, by the summer of 1722 there were indications that undergraduate decorum was not Yale's only difficulty. The Reverend Joseph Morgan of East Chester, New York, who had received an honorary M.A. from the college, issued the first warning. In a letter to Cotton Mather, he revealed that "some in Conecticut complain that Arminian Books are cryed up in Yale Colledge for Eloquence & Learning, & Calvinists despised for the contrary; & none have the courage to see it redressed." Morgan knew nothing firsthand, but had been so frightened by the rumor that he was considering removing his son from the college.[10]

If this charge was true, there was good reason for Morgan to be concerned, for what was reputedly happening at Yale threatened the very essence of New England's religious heritage. That heritage had two essential components: the Reformed tradition in theology and Congregational church government in polity. Theologically, New England Christians were Calvinists and hence stood in opposition to all deviations from that system. The principal deviation was Arminianism. Deriving its name from the Dutch theologian Jacobus Arminius (1560–1609), the term *Arminianism* technically referred to the heresy of stating that man's redemption does not depend absolutely on God's predestining decrees. The Arminians tended to modify the notion of total depravity and to accent man's freedom to do God's will; their principal attack on Calvinism was to deny the doctrine of irresistible grace and to insist that man could accept or reject his own election.

Although Arminianism had been condemned by the Synod of Dort (1618–19), it had always been one of the inherent deviations in Reformed theology and one that New England clergymen found difficult to expunge. In the Anglican Church of England, however, Arminianism was not viewed with such disfavor. Ever since the 1620s, Arminianism had been steadily gaining ground in the Church of England, and its spokesmen made no attempt to disavow the label. High and low churchmen alike accepted the Ar-

9. Edwards to Timothy Edwards, Mar. 1, 1721, Jonathan Edwards Collection.
10. *Documentary History*, p. 225.

minian scheme, and by 1700 the Anglican communion had hardly a minister of any prominence who declared himself a Calvinist.[11] It was with some justification, then, that New Englanders rightly —and righteously—associated Anglicanism, which they opposed ecclesiastically, with Arminianism, which they attacked theologically.

The troubles brewing at Yale, therefore, threatened both questions of belief and of church government. Morgan, evidently, did not know a great deal about the dimensions of the alleged threat. Strangely, his warning did not cause Mather to sound the alarm and no one took any steps to confront the problem. In August, more rumors circulated about the doings at the college, and these stories gave some hint of what was to come. The Reverend George Pigot, a missionary of the Society for the Propagation of the Gospel (S.P.G.) at Stratford, was the source of these rumors; he had private "expectations of a glorious revolution of the ecclesiastics of this country"—hopes which he obviously could not keep to himself. In the early weeks of September, 1722, talk of the Arminian tendencies of the Yale faculty had reached such proportions that people flocked to the college commencement "expecting strange things." They were not disappointed. At the conclusion of his prayer at the graduation exercises, the rector uttered the words *"and let all the people say, amen."* [12] This phrase came straight from the Anglican prayerbook and its meaning was clear. Timothy Cutler had turned his back on New England's heritage!

The Apostasy

The trustees were scandalized. Yale College was designed to perpetuate the faith of New England's first settlers. Those men had come to America, in part, to flee the corrupt Church of England. Now, nearly a century later, one of New England's own sons seemed ready to return to that church by denouncing the polity of the Saybrook Platform and renouncing the theology of the Westminster Confession.

What made this possibility even more bewildering was that in 1722 there was not one full-time Anglican minister in Connecticut.

11. Roland N. Stromberg, *Religious Liberalism in Eighteenth-century England,* pp. 110–11. The one minister was John Edwards, who had been forced to resign from St. John's College in Cambridge in 1670 because of his views.

12. *Episcopal Church Documents,* 1 : 56; *Johnson,* 1 : 14; *Documentary History,* p. 227.

Not that the Church of England had not tried to settle a minister there. Ever since the first S.P.G. missionaries had ventured into Connecticut in 1702, the Anglicans had been waging a futile battle against the colony's Congregational majority. While the S.P.G. had enjoyed mild success in other American colonies, Connecticut remained impervious to it and the missionaries bitterly complained of the treatment they received there. "The Independents threaten me," one man objected, "and all who are instrumental in bringing me thither, with prison and hard usage. They are very much incensed to see that the Church (Rome's sister, as they ignorantly call her) is likely to gain ground among 'em, and use all the strategems they can invent to defeat my enterprises." [13] It was normal procedure for Connecticut citizens, ministers, and magistrates to harass missionaries, issue pamphlets against the Anglican Church, and threaten to punish anyone who attended an Episcopal service. Caleb Heathcote of Rye, New York, put the matter most succinctly: "I am sorry that anybody should be so unjust in giving the Society [S.P.G.] an account of the people of this colony, as that they are a well-meaning and not heady people, nothing being more true than the contrary." [14]

By 1708 the S.P.G. men had come to the conclusion that there would never be an Anglican minister in Connecticut as long as the "dangerous people" of the colony retained control of their own government. The missionaries had found that it was nearly impossible to proselytize in a colony in which the government actively supported the ecclesiastical status quo. Matters had gotten so bad that service in Connecticut was regarded by the Anglicans as more painful and laborious than anywhere else, and hence deserving of a higher salary. In 1713 Heathcote reported to the London headquarters on the S.P.G.'s singular lack of success in establishing the church in Connecticut; Heathcote was galled that the "dissenters should entirely possess a whole Colony and one of the

13. *Episcopal Church Documents,* 1 : 17. The attitude of the Connecticut ministers toward the Anglican intrusions was expressed in the Reverend Samuel Cooke's funeral discourse on Trustee John Davenport of Stamford. It was, Cooke said, "looked upon by the serious and judicious as a special favor of Divine Providence that a person of such distinction was seated so near the western limits of New England as a bulwark against any irruptions of corrupt doctrines or manners." The reference was obviously to the S.P.G. missionaries who had been most successful in western Connecticut. See Bacon, "Historical Discourse," p. 12.

14. *Episcopal Church Documents,* 1 : 36.

Largest and best Peopled on the main of America & the church to have no manner of footing amongst them." [15]

Despite these discouragements, the S.P.G. could perceive some hopeful signs. There was a small clique of Church of England sympathizers at Stratford, where, in 1707, the Congregational minister, John Read (H. 1697), had lost his job for suspected Anglican leanings. The S.P.G. missionaries had some success in ministering to the Stratford people and continued to do so even after Timothy Cutler was brought in to blunt their influence. A second and, to the missionaries, more promising fact was the widespread practice in Connecticut of denying church membership to all but those who had had a conversion experience. Caleb Heathcote opined that in a town of a hundred sober people, not ten would be admitted to the sacrament and many were denied baptism. He conjectured that there were a thousand unbaptized people in New Haven alone. Here was an opening for the Church of England. Since the Connecticut clergy "stop and hedge up the way to Gods Altar," the S.P.G. should move in to baptize and give communion to all those denied these blessings by the Congregationalists.[16]

Heathcote's plan for establishing the Anglican Church in Connecticut was to work on the laity. He also thought it "of absolute necessity that a College be erected" in New York to train native clergymen, as neither of the New England colleges seemed likely to fulfill that role. As later events were to prove, he was wrong on both counts. By 1717 there were only thirty-six Anglican communicants in Connecticut and, although about one hundred children and adults had beep baptized, the Church of England was not flourishing. In 1718 Connecticut was the only colony in America without a settled Anglican church or ministry.[17]

While conversion of the laity had failed to promote the Church of England in Connecticut, the S.P.G. was to discover that its cause had influenced several of the colony's clergy. Ironically, one of the first ministers to accept the Episcopal way was Timothy Cutler. The fact that his father had been Major John Cutler of Charles-

15. S.P.G. Correspondence, 4 : 36, 32; 8 : 57. In volumes 1, 4, 5, 8, and 16, cited here and below, the second number refers to the number of the document, not the page. Other S.P.G. volumes noted are paginated.

16. Ibid., 5 : 84.

17. Ibid., 4 : 145; 12 : 345–48; *Episcopal Church Documents,* 1 : 53.

town, an adherent of Sir Edmund Andros, governor of the ill-fated Dominion of New England, might have predisposed the young minister to be receptive to the cultured mien and theology of the English missionaries. Whatever the reason, Cutler became interested in the Church of England and its claim as the most scriptural church. Around 1714 he met and conversed with the Reverend John Checkley, who evidently convinced Cutler of the validity of Anglicanism by persuading him of "the invalidity or nullity of the Baptism & other ordinances administered by the Dissenters." In 1715 Cutler borrowed a book from Tutor Henry Flynt of Harvard, entitled "Dr Morrice his discourse of primitive Episcopacy." [18] The more the Stratford minister read and thought about Anglicanism, the unhappier he became with his Congregational ministry. When, in 1719, the Yale trustees asked him to become the college rector, he welcomed the opportunity to leave his congregation.

At Yale, Cutler met other men who shared his views. One of these kindred spirits was Samuel Johnson, who had become disaffected from the prevailing religious modes of the colony while a student at Saybrook. Johnson was impressed by Archbishop William King's attack on the Presbyterians in his *A Discourse Concerning the Inventions of Man in the Worship of God* (London, 1694) and, through conversations with Samuel Smithson, a recent Anglican immigrant, he began to lose his prejudices against the Church of England. With his classmate Daniel Brown and others, Johnson read the works of Anglican divines in the collection of books sent to the Connecticut college by Jeremiah Dummer; convinced by the arguments of the theologians John Scott and Daniel Whitby, Johnson quickly accepted the reasonableness of episcopacy. Such was the state of his mind when he resigned his Yale tutorship to begin his ministry in West Haven in 1719. There he read his parishioners the cold, ethical sermons of Dr. Isaac Bar-

18. *Harvard Graduates,* 5 : 53, 48. I have not been able definitely to identify Dr. Morrice but the reference is probably to Henry Maurice (1648–91), who was evidently a nonjuror. I have not found his work on primitive episcopacy but he did write in defense of the imprisoned nonjuring bishops and published a tract entitled *Twenty-one conclusions further demonstrating The schism of the Church of England* (Oxford, 1688). Since Cutler was accused by Thomas Hollis of being influenced by Dodwell *and* "Morris," one can assume that their views were similar. As Dodwell was a nonjuror, it is likely that Maurice was too. See note 52 below.

rows, offered Church of England prayers, and continued to study Anglican authors.[19]

He did not study alone. Dummer's gift to the Yale library contained a mine of Anglican writings, and not long after Cutler's settlement in New Haven a small group of ministers began meeting at the rector's house to read and discuss these works. The group included Johnson, Cutler, Tutor Daniel Brown, and the Reverends Jared Eliot of Killingworth, John Hart of East Guilford, Samuel Whittelsey of Wallingford, and James Wetmore of North Haven. These seven, six of whom were graduates of the college, invited other ministers to meet with them, and the Reverends John Bulkley of Colchester and Samuel Whiting of Windham attended several gatherings.[20]

The chief topics of conversation at these meetings were the contrast between the ecclesiastical structure in Connecticut and the practices of the primitive apostolic church and the validity of episcopacy. In formulating their opinions on these issues, the group relied on the books in the Yale library. The ministers read the theological works of such men as Isaac Barrows, William Chillingworth, Richard Hooker, John Scott, Edward Stillingfleet, John Tillotson, and Daniel Whitby. These churchmen were all moderate Anglicans, latitudinarian in polity and rationalistic in theology. All save Hooker were professed Arminians. Tillotson, Scott, and Barrows, for instance, thought that heaven and hell were not simply future states but the necessary fruits of man's virtue and vice on earth. Scott insisted that God demanded that man be moral for man's eternal sake, not for God's glory.[21]

In arguing for and defending Episcopal government, these men did not insist that episcopacy was divinely ordained. They stated, instead, that there was no *one* form of church government ordained by God but that, historically, the Episcopal system was closest in form to the ancient church. Thus, Chillingworth argued, "seeing Episcopal Government is confessedly so Ancient and so Catholique, it cannot with reason be denied to be Apostolique." Stillingfleet said that the primitive church was a broad church, and

19. *Johnson,* 1 : 11–12.

20. Bulkley and Whiting attended the meetings but never became members of the group. They both made moderate statements in recognition of the validity of episcopacy at the time of the defection. See *Episcopal Church Documents,* 1 : 59.

21. John Hunt, *Religious Thought in England,* 2 : 91–94, 102, 157.

went on to argue that Episcopal government was a rational and reasonable polity for a state church.[22] While these authors defended the historical validity and desirability of Episcopal church government, they did not seek to impose this polity on others. Their main concern was for peace and order.

The Connecticut ministers also wanted peace and order, but they wanted firmer arguments in favor of the Episcopal way. Since they knew they would have to defend themselves against the attacks of their fellow ministers, the seven men sought to read both sides of the episcopacy issue. They studied Peter King's *An Enquiry into the Constitution, Discipline, Unity and Worship of the Primitive Church* (London, 1691), which set forth the view that the primitive church was organized on congregational principles, and then read William Sclater's *Original Draught of the Primitive Church* (London, 1717), which refuted King and argued for the divine sanction of episcopacy. The Connecticut ministers also read Bishop John Potter's *Discourse of Church Government* (London, 1707), which defended episcopacy by an appeal to the practices of antiquity. Potter, a moderate High Churchman, reiterated the views of two seventeenth-century writers, Joseph Hall and Thomas Bilson, whose arguments for episcopacy were formulated in controversies with the Puritans, not the Roman Catholics. With this heritage, Potter's work was admirably suited to the needs of the Johnson-Cutler group.[23] The Sclater and Potter volumes convinced the seven Connecticut ministers who, after reading the Scriptures and Church Fathers for themselves, concluded "that the episcopal government of the church was universally established by the Apostles wherever they propagated Christianity." [24]

Having decided that the polity of the Church of England came closest to the purity and perfection of the apostolic church, the group went on to discuss the issue of ordination. Again the ministers read both sides of the question. They studied the debate between the moderate nonconformist Edmund Calamy and the moderate churchman Benjamin Hoadly. Calamy, in his *A Defence of Moderate Non-Conformity* (London, 1703–05), argued that

22. William Chillingworth, *The Apostolic Institution of Episcopacy Demonstrated* (London, 1674), p. 322; Hunt, *Religious Thought,* 2 : 135–37.

23. Leslie Stephen and Sidney Lee, eds., *The Dictionary of National Biography* (hereafter cited as *D.N.B.*), 11 : 144, 146; 17 : 937–38; 16 : 216–17; Hunt, *Religious Thought,* 3 : 72–73; 1 : 88–90, 174–78.

24. *Johnson,* 1 : 13.

ordination by bishops, assent to the *Book of Prayer,* canonical obedience, and reordination were not reasonable demands for the Church of England to impose on nonconformists. Hoadly replied with *A Serious Admonition to Mr. Calamy, occasion'd by the first part of his Defence of Moderate Non-conformity* (London, 1705), in which he countered Calamy's views and said that a love for peace and order ought to overcome all scruples about reordination.[25]

25. Hunt, *Religious Thought,* 3 : 31. The many authors the seven Connecticut ministers studied were a varied group. With the exception of Edmund Calamy (1671–1732), the biographical historian of nonconformity, and Peter King (1669–1734), Baron of Ockham and lord chancellor and a lawyer by profession, all of the authors were Anglicans. But they formed no single ecclesiastical or theological party: John Potter and William King were high churchmen, Benjamin Hoadly was a low churchman, and William Sclater was a nonjuror. The inquiring ministers read these many Anglicans for different purposes; Chillingworth, Tillotson, Whitby, and Stillingfleet provided the ministers with a rationalistic theology and a latitudinarian broad church ecclesiastical outlook. The works of Potter, Hoadly, and Sclater answered certain specific questions the ministers had about episcopacy and ordination. In terms of theological and ecclesiastical attitudes, the ministers were most influenced by the minimizing theological and low church ecclesiastical thought of the former group. For the impending debate with their fellow clergymen, the seven men seem to have depended on the precise arguments or the latter group. A division of the Anglican authors into two groups produces the following breakdown:

1. Anglicans read for their theology and ecclesiastical attitude:

Isaac Barrow (1630–77), a graduate of Cambridge, was an eminent mathematician and classical scholar and one of the chief Anglican preachers. He was chaplain to Charles II and, at the end of his life, master of Trinity College, Cambridge. He was most noted as a preacher although he did write against popery (*D.N.B.,* 1 : 1219–25).

William Chillingworth (1602–44), a graduate of Oxford, was briefly (1630–34) a convert to the Church of Rome. He reconverted to protestantism but did not become an Anglican immediately, preferring to rest his beliefs on Scripture interpreted by reason. He opposed the idea of a perfect dogma and for a long time was unable to subscribe to the Thirty-nine Articles; he advocated toleration throughout his life. His greatest work was *The Religion of Protestants a Safe Way to Salvation* (1638), in which he disputed with the Catholics but mainly insisted on the right of free inquiry and the necessity of personal conviction in religion (*D.N.B.,* 4 : 252–57).

Richard Hooker (1554?–1600), a graduate of Oxford, defended the established Church of England against the Puritans. His *Laws of Ecclesiastical Polity* (1594–97) attempted to provide a philosophical basis for the Elizabethan settlement. The work was a rational examination of church government which argued that natural law must be taken with Scripture as a guide to right conduct. In Book 3 he stated that there was no one form of church government but that episcopacy had the firmest historical basis (*D.N.B.,* 9 : 1183–89).

John Scott (1639–95), a graduate of Oxford, published several sermons and a

The Connecticut ministers sided with Hoadly's plea for reasonableness and order but they also examined the New Testament record. The Bible, they discovered, clearly showed that while presbyters preached and administered the sacraments, bishops alone

---

devotional guide as well as defenses of Anglican worship forms. These last were directed against the dissenters. He also wrote against popery (*D.N.B.*, 17 : 979).

Edward Stillingfleet (1635–99), a graduate of Cambridge, was bishop of Worcester. His *Origines Sacrae* (1662) was his most famous work and was an apology for the divine authority of Scripture. He also wrote against the Roman Catholics and, late in life, engaged in a controversy with John Locke on the doctrine of the Trinity (*D.N.B.*, 18 : 1262–65).

John Tillotson (1630–94), a graduate of Cambridge, was archbishop of Canterbury. Born a nonconformist, Tillotson took Anglican orders in 1660–61 but remained friendly to the nonconformists throughout his life. His published works consisted of sermons and some polemical treatises against the Roman Catholics. His arguments were famously (or infamously) reasonable (*D.N.B.*, 19 : 872–78).

Daniel Whitby (1638–1726), a graduate of Oxford, was a noted polemical divine who wrote against the Catholics. He too favored concessions to the nonconformists. In addition to his anti-Roman works he wrote a New Testament commentary, a work on ethics, several tracts on the Trinity, and some attacks on the Calvinists (*D.N.B.*, 21 : 28–30).

With the exception of Hooker, these men tended to be Arminian in theology.

2. Anglicans read for their arguments on episcopacy and ordination:

Benjamin Hoadly (1676–1761), a graduate of Cambridge, was bishop of Bangor, Hereford, Salisbury, and Winchester. The Calamy controversy was his first major polemical exercise. Hoadly was the leader of the extreme latitudinarian low church party, political and ecclesiastical; beginning in 1716 Hoadly attacked the nonjurors and high church party and was engaged in what became known as the Bangorian Controversy for the rest of his life. He was in favor with the Hanovers (*D.N.B.*, 9 : 910–15).

William King (1650–1729), a graduate of Trinity College, Dublin, was archbishop of Dublin. When he was bishop of Meath, the prevalency of Presbyterianism in his diocese caused him to write *The Inventions of Man,* a pamphlet designed to remove the objections of those who refused to attend the established church. He was a high churchman (*D.N.B.*, 11 : 163–67).

John Potter (1674?–1747), a graduate of Oxford, was archbishop of Canterbury. In addition to being a learned classical scholar who published several works on ancient Greece, he was a high churchman and entered the Bangorian Controversy against Hoadly. His work on church government repeated the arguments of Bilson and Hall (*D.N.B.*, 16 : 216–17). Thomas Bilson (1546/47–1616), a graduate of Oxford, was bishop of Winchester. His *The Perpetual Government of Christ's Churches* (1593) emphasized that the power of the keys was placed with the apostles and that the church derived it from them (*D.N.B.*, 2 : 505–06; Hall, *Religious Thought,* 1 : 88–90). Joseph Hall (1574–1656), a graduate of Cambridge, was bishop of Norwich. He attended the Synod of Dort, at which Arminius was condemned, and was a Calvinist Anglican. He advocated peace with the dissenters but, at the suggestion of Archbishop Laud, wrote a defense of the divine right of episcopacy (1637), in which he argued that while episcopacy was not ordained by God, He warranted it and required it when it might be had. The argument was directed

performed ordinations. This evidence, Samuel Johnson thought, was far more persuasive than the New Testament claim for infant baptism or for celebrating the Sabbath on the first day of the week, two practices that New Englanders accepted as biblical. The result of these inquiries was that the seven men came "to be considerably dubious of the lawfulness of their ordination." [26] What made them even more dubious, however, was the Connecticut practice of having laymen participate in ordinations. While this practice had been discontinued some years before, the fact that laymen had once taken part in such services broke the chain of apostolic succession in which even the Connecticut ministers believed.

The seven men fully realized the import of these views; they knew that to announce them publicly would shock their friends and be "very grievous to their country." [27] But the men were determined to pursue their new commitment to the end of adopting Episcopal discipline and seeking Anglican orders. Toward this purpose they asked George Pigot, the S.P.G. missionary in Stratford, to meet with them. At the meeting, held sometime in August, 1722, the ministers expressed their charity and veneration for the Church of England and asked Pigot to secure the support of the mother church for their proposed undertaking.[28] Pigot assured them that the church would back their move, and the seven ministers resolved to make their opinions known in a dramatic fashion.

The scene they chose was the Yale commencement. After Cutler had provocatively closed his prayer with the Anglican form, the trustees, now fearing that the rumors about the ministers might be true, summoned the seven to "clear themselves from these suspicions" so that "the dark apprehensions of the people" might be quelled. Although the trustees had no ecclesiastical authority to sit in judgment on these men, the would-be Anglicans consented to the meeting. Here was an opportunity to make their views known openly. On September 13, the day after commencement,

---

against the Scottish Presbyterians (*D.N.B.,* 8 : 959–64; Hunt, *Religious Thought,* 1 : 175).

William Sclater (d. 1717?), a graduate of Oxford, was ejected after the Revolution of 1688 when he refused to take the oath of allegiance. *The Original Draught* is the only work that can definitely be attributed to him (*D.N.B.,* 17 : 937–38).

26. *Johnson,* 1 : 13.

27. Ibid., pp. 13–15. Johnson, for one, agonized over his doubts about ordination and his impending decision to declare for episcopacy. See ibid., pp. 61–62.

28. *Episcopal Church Documents,* 1 : 56–57; *Johnson,* 1 : 13–14.

the ministers delivered a statement to the trustees, declaring "that some of us [Hart and Whittelsey] doubt the validity, and the rest are more persuaded of the invalidity of the Presbyterian ordination, in opposition to the Episcopal" and saying they would welcome any light the trustees might shed on this matter.

The trustees were shocked. Their only response was to urge Hart and Whittelsey to resolve their doubts but to continue their ministerial duties, and to order Cutler, Johnson, Brown, Eliot, and Wetmore to cease all duties until the next trustee meeting, scheduled for October 16. After the confrontation, Rector Cutler added insult to injury by telling the trustees "that he had for many years been of this persuasion . . . and that therefore he was the more uneasy in performing the acts of his ministry at Stratford, and the more readily accepted the call to a college improvement at N. Haven." [29]

The reaction to the defections came swiftly and reflected the astonishment of the colonists. Richard and Benjamin Franklin's *The New-England Courant* poked fun at the event in a report of one "Jethro Standfast of Nuhaven." His words graphically and humorously represented New England's response: "Thare has bein a most grevous rout and hurle-burle amung us, ever sense the nine Ministurs are turn'd *Hi-Church-men.*" [30] The hurly-burly was not confined to New Haven. Judge Samuel Sewall was astonished when the "Thunder-Claps" from Yale reached Boston: "The Colony, the Town, the Society from whence it came, Accented every Sound. It quickly brought to my mind Rev. 16.15." At a Fast Day, Increase

29. *Johnson,* 1 : 14; *Episcopal Church Documents,* 1 : 65; *Documentary History,* p. 228. Cutler was accused of biding his time at Yale while waiting for the best opportunity to leave. The rector added his own testimony to this view in a letter to Thomas Hollis written in January, 1723. Hollis, a benefactor of Harvard, had tried to speak with the former rector in an effort to win him away from Anglicanism. Cutler declined to meet with the Englishman and told him: "I was never in judgment heartily with the Dissenters, but bore it patiently until a favorable opportunity offered. This has opened at Boston, and I now declare publicly what I before believed privately" (see Quincy, *History of Harvard,* 1 : 365). That Cutler was slated for the Boston church and knew so before his declaration for Anglicanism is confirmed in a letter of Samuel Sewall to Gurdon Saltonstall of September 15, 1722, in which the judge said: "Before the Smoke of Yale-College was discerned, I was shew'd a piece of Ground bought to build an Episcopal Church on in Boston; and the same person whispered to me, that Mr. Cutler your Rector was to preach in it." See 6 Coll. M.H.S. 2 (1888): 143.

30. *The New-England Courant,* Oct. 1–8, 1722. Standfast obviously included Bulkley and Whiting in the group.

Mather "pray'd, much bewail'd the Connecticut Apostacie." [31] But the laments heard in Boston were insignificant compared to the groans of dismay that emitted from Connecticut. In this time of trouble the college trustees and colonial ministers turned for help to the leading exponents of "the good old cause"—Increase and Cotton Mather. In fact, one of the first things that at least one trustee did was to write surreptitiously to Cotton Mather asking him to become the Yale rector.[32]

Although the letter of invitation to Cotton Mather has not survived, several others have. Trustees John Davenport and Stephen Buckingham wrote a lengthy letter to both Mathers on September 25, explaining the Cutler affair and relating it to the avowed purposes of Yale College:

> we are willing to make our mournful report, how it hath been a matter of suprize to us . . . to find how great a change a few years have made appear among us, and how our fountain, hoped to have been and continued the repository of truth, and the reserve of pure and sound principles, doctrine and education, in case of a change in our mother Harvard, shews itself in so little a time so corrupt. How is the gold become dim! and the silver becomes dross. and the wine mixt with water!

The two trustees regretted Cutler's "unhappy election" and wondered "with what good faith" he could have accepted the rectorship of a college "erected for the education of such as dissented from the church of England" when he himself held Anglican views. Davenport and Buckingham accused Cutler of the "foul frustration" of the confidence extended to him by the trustees and feared for the number of students who might have been infected by his opinions. Evidently, several parents had the same fear; two students, Samuel Seabury and Dudley Woodbridge, left Yale after the Cutler defection and enrolled at Harvard. Their decision was

31. 6 Coll. M.H.S. 2 (1888): 144; Samuel Sewall, *Diary of Samuel Sewall,* 5 Coll. M.H.S. 7 (1882): 309. A month later Sewall attended a meeting at Harvard at which "Mr. [Benjamin] Colman pray'd, bewail'd what was befallen Yale College" (see 5 Coll. M.H.S. 7 : 311). Colman also wrote the famous English Dissenter, Isaac Watts, about the Cutler affair. Watts replied: "I am sorry you should have any persons amongst you that affect our Episcopal forms. So far as I can hear it makes very little noise in London, & I hope will do you in New England but very little injury." See 2 *Proc. M.H.S.* 9 (1895): 339.

32. Kenneth Murdock, "Cotton Mather and the Rectorship of Yale College," Pub. C.S.M. 26 (1927): 388–401.

symptomatic of the college's plight. The only encouragement Davenport and Buckingham could relate to the Mathers about the whole sorry business was that the trustees "shewed themselves constant to your principles, and affected to the trust committed to them." [33] There was still hope for Yale.

Other ministers were not so sanguine. Disturbed by their inability to refute the episcopal position, several of them appealed to Cotton Mather for help. It "is now a time with us," wrote the Reverend Joseph Moss, "that we must put on our armour and fight, or else let the good old cause, for which our fathers came into this land, sink and be deserted." Moss admitted his ignorance of the issues raised by the Anglicans and wanted Mather to send him some books "as with most strength of reason and argument, plead our cause; especially in this point, of the validity of Presbyterian ordination." Trustee Joseph Webb also asked Mather for some good arguments in favor of presbyterial ordination. But Webb feared that arguments would not suffice; the churchmen were certain to emphasize that "in the more ancient days" laymen participated in ordinations, thereby nullifying any Presbyterian claims made by the Connecticut ministers. Webb could not understand what had possessed his forefathers to allow such a practice and thought that ordinations by laymen would do "more damage than all the arguments that can be brought for the necessity of Episcopal ordination. Our condition I look upon, as very deplorable and sad." [34]

The Mathers took steps to remedy Connecticut's sad condition. Cotton Mather sent a circular letter to the clergymen of the colony, "exhorting them to trace the pious steps of their forefathers." The letter contained little in the way of learned arguments with which to refute the Anglicans, although Mather did say that Christ himself had confuted "that vile, senseless, wretched whimsey of an uninterrupted succession." The main thrust of the letter was a call to reaffirm New England's Reformation heritage against those "unhappy men" who had "cast a vile indignity" upon Congrega-

33. *Documentary History*, pp. 226–28. For the cases of Seabury and Woodbridge, see *Harvard Graduates*, 7 : 432, 448. Seabury's departure, in retrospect, was ironic, as he became a leading Connecticut Anglican.

34. 2 Coll. M.H.S. 2 (1814): 130, 132–33. One humorous aspect of this issue, at least to the Anglicans, was the so-called leather mitten ordination of the Reverend Israel Chauncy, at which one of the laymen, a Deacon Brinsmead, wore a leather glove during the laying on of hands.

tional ministers and had thrown the New England churches into "disturbance and confusion." [35]

A few weeks after the defection, Governor Saltonstall called a meeting of trustees and clergymen to confront the apostates in the hope of mitigating the ecclesiastical confusion and winning the defectors back to the Congregational way. The ensuing debate, held in the Yale library, was no contest. The would-be Anglicans "had weighed things with much care and so were ready with their answers," while the Connecticut ministers, despite Cotton Mather's hurried reassurances, "had never well considered" the ordination issue. Samuel Johnson defended episcopal ordination by an appeal to Scripture and demonstrated—to his satisfaction at least—that Timothy, as bishop, was superior to both the clergy and the people at Ephesus, as was Titus at Crete. The apostates also presented the point that the New Testament only warranted ordination by bishops. The assembled clergy had no arguments to refute these statements and were soon reduced to railing against their opponents. When this happened, Saltonstall quickly ended the conference, saying he had "only designed a friendly argument." [36]

But there was nothing friendly about this whole episode. George Pigot reported to the S.P.G. secretary that the Congregationalists soon mounted an ambitious counteroffensive against the Anglicans. Some clergymen, he reported, promulgated the view that there were "*two* Churches of England, the high and the low; with the low they pretend to hold full communion, but the high are rank *Papists;* they terming us no less." Towns were "glutted" with books, thousands of which had been printed at Boston, all casting aspersions on the Church of England and defending New England's ecclesiastical practices.[37]

Yale's condition was as deplorable as the colony's. Of the seven men who had signed the September 13 declaration to the Yale trustees, six had graduated from the college (Brown, Eliot, Hart, Johnson, Whittelsey, and Wetmore) and five had taught there at one time or another (Brown, Cutler, Hart, Johnson, and Whittelsey). The most telling blow, however, was that the rector had defected. To men like Major James Fitch, who had been one of the college's first benefactors, Cutler's apostasy was a staggering setback. While other friends of Yale wrote appeals for help and

35. Ibid., pp. 133–36.
36. *Johnson,* 1 : 14–15.
37. S.P.G. Correspondence, 17 : 346–48.

privately lamented the college's fallen state, Major Fitch composed poetry. His doggerel verse poked fun at the pretensions of the defectors ("*Wetmore* and *Whitelsie,* are turned to Episcopacie, /And the Fellow *Brown,* wants he a fine Church Gown?") and, in a more serious vein, captured the sentiments of those who deplored Yale's role in the affair.

And is it not to our Sorrow a Great Aggravation,
That such in our College had their Education?
That out of that Mother of Learning did spring,
That should her Sons and Churches mortally sting.
Alas for us, who gave to the College so willingly,
Could we in that Day such a great Evil espy?
And to the Rector my Donation,
Was it to go and get a new Ordination?
No, no, nothing so.
But we hope God will accept our good Will therein;
So it is not ours, but theirs great Sin.[38]

The trustees were eager to demonstrate their "good will" and to remove all suspicions about their complicity in the Cutler affair. At their October meeting they, "in Faithfulness to the Trust reposed in them," dismissed the rector from his post. It was the only thing they could do. Cutler's apostasy had made the college itself suspect. An article in *The Boston News-Letter* bemoaned the fact that the college in Connecticut, "the Fountain and Nursery of Truth and Learning, set up there according to Scripture Rule, Free of Humane Traditions and Impositions (for which their and our Fathers left the Pleasant Land of our Fore-Fathers to enjoy the same, came by Voluntary exile into this rude Wilderness) is now become Corrupt." Some people viewed the events at Yale as part of a "plot." One pamphleteer portrayed Cutler as the chief culprit, one who had seized the offer of the Yale rectorship as "an opportunity privately to destroy the principal intention of the academy, and blow up the churches which he appeared a friend unto." The writer went on to relate that the Yale library had not helped matters since it was stocked with "Episcopalian things" and "little or nothing of the antidote." [39]

38. *The New-England Courant,* Mar. 4–11, 1723.

39. *Documentary History,* p. 232; *The Boston News-Letter,* Oct. 8–15, 1722; "A Faithful Relation of a late Occurence in the Churches of New England," 2 Coll. M.H.S. 2 (1814): 137–38.

The college trustees took decisive steps to prevent anything like the Cutler apostasy from occurring in the future. To their credit, they did not purge the library of Anglican books.[40] They did, however, stipulate that all college officers must give assent to the Confession of Faith in the Saybrook Platform. The collegiate school founders had declined to provide a test for religious orthodoxy. After the rude shock of the defection, the trustees felt differently. At the same meeting at which they dismissed Cutler and Brown, the trustees voted that all future rectors, tutors, trustees, and officers were to give satisfaction "of the Soundness of their Faith in opposition to Armenian & prelatical Corruptions or any other of Dangerous Consequences to the Purity & Peace of our Churches." The agreement provided for mutual checks for doctrinal soundness—the rector and tutors could examine suspicious officers and the officers could question the rector and tutors. The new provision went into effect immediately. James Pierpont (Y. 1718) and William Smith (Y. 1719) were chosen tutors, and "before the Trustees declared their Assent to our said Confession & the soundness of their Faith." [41]

The decision to institute a religious requirement for college officers indicates the radical nature of the Cutler apostasy. Yale College had been founded and had existed for twenty years in a relatively stable religious environment. That milieu was a broad one and allowed for a range of theological and ecclesiastical opinion within the scope of Reformed orthodoxy. To be sure, there had been uneasiness and debate about the precise nature of that orthodoxy, and the Saybrook Platform, which was a result of that debate, served to define the accepted limits of orthodox practice

40. At least one New England minister donated to the college library with the Cutler affair in mind. The Reverend William Cooper of Boston gave the college John Reynolds's *Zeal a Virtue; or, a Discourse concerning Sacred Zeal.* In the front of the book Cooper wrote: "The Dissenters' Cause, as it relates to Ordination consider'd and vindicated, from p. 120 to p. 130." See Yale Library of 1742, Beinecke Rare Book Library, Yale University.

41. *Documentary History*, pp. 233–34. The requirement that the faculty assent to the Saybrook Platform remained in effect until 1823. Further evidence of the attempt to ensure Yale a proper religious milieu is found in a letter of Tutor James Pierpont to Trustee Timothy Woodbridge, written in 1723. Pierpont urged that Jonathan Edwards be encouraged to settle in North Haven, where James Wetmore had ministered before the defection, as it would be "both for the interest of the Trustees & safety of the Colledge to have the neighbouring Clergy both able & well principled both which in my account Mr Edwards bids very fair for." See Pub. C.S.M. 6 (1904): 199–200.

and belief. It was generally agreed that Anglicanism lay outside of those limits. The uneasiness, however, persisted and the defection, in one sense, was a culmination of the continuing ecclesiastical arguments in Connecticut over power and authority in the church. The quest for church order led men like Cutler, Johnson, Brown, and Wetmore to renounce the colony's established polity and join the Church of England.[42] The Anglicans certainly had order. What made the defection so disturbing to the majority of Connecticut ministers was that they, like the Anglicans, considered polity an integral part of their faith.

But there was more at stake than church order. While the defectors had made their break with the established church of Connecticut on ecclesiastical rather than religious grounds, their choice of Anglican polity implied a choice of Arminian theology. It was the coupling of these two hated systems that made the defection so onerous to the colonial clergy. When Joseph Morgan told Cotton Mather about the popularity of Arminian books at Yale, he was referring to books by Anglican authors. After the event, commentators blamed these books for all the trouble, and Benjamin Colman dashed off a letter to Jeremiah Dummer, taking him to task for sending so many Anglican (Arminian) books to the college. This accusation so unnerved Dummer that he rushed to Thomas Hollis with a list showing that Dissenting authors outnumbered Anglicans in the collection of books he had sent to Yale. Dummer hoped to publish this list in Boston to clear his name of the charge that he was indirectly responsible for the defection.[43]

The apostasy shook Yale out of its lethargy. The trustees and their fellow ministers had always taken the college's religious heritage for granted. When the founders had voiced their understanding of the collegiate school's role as the preserver and perpetuator of Reformed orthodoxy, everyone knew and believed in the value of that role. For twenty-one years, that role had gone unchallenged. But the Cutler defection dramatized the extent to

42. For some indications of the former rector's unease with the prevailing ecclesiastical set-up in Connecticut, see Cutler, *The Firm Union of a People Represented,* pp. 51–52, and Cutler, *The Depth of the Divine Thoughts,* p. 35.

43. Thomas Hollis to Benjamin Colman, Mar. 2, 1723, Harvard College Library, Cambridge, Mass. Dummer later defended himself in a letter to Trustee Woodbridge written on June 3, 1723: "there never was an Eminent Dissenter & Author whose works are not in that Collection." See *Documentary History,* p. 241.

which the understanding of the college's business had become a rhetorical form without literal substance. Simply stated, Connecticut clergymen had become complacent about their theology, their ecclesiology, and their traditions. The ministers had continued to speak the familiar language, the colony had withstood Anglican intrusions, and no one in the churches had professed heretical views. There seemed nothing to fear. Cutler's declaration shattered that complacency.

It also shattered the clergy's confidence in themselves. In response, ministers desperately sought information about the very heritage they supposedly professed and transmitted. The trustees and others became curiously self-conscious about their beliefs and practices. This sudden introspection had a confining effect; the clergymen, particularly the trustees, turned back to their own local experience, rejected any ties with England, and acted unashamedly as provincials. The events of 1722 drove them back to their past, forced them to speak of primitive practices and the good old cause. Connecticut, which the S.P.G. had always viewed as a closed society, became even more so. Ironically, this posture was to prove a liability rather than an asset in combating Anglicanism, for as the ecclesiastical establishment sought to reaffirm its solidarity, some of the laity and a few of the clergy looked for a way out—a way which the Church of England was all too willing to provide.

These consequences of the Cutler affair took years to unfold. The most immediate result was the damage done to the college. The new requirement that all Yale officers were hereafter to assent to the Saybrook Confession and declare their opposition to all Arminian and prelatical corruptions was the most obvious way to repair some of the damage. But rumors of the college's decline and fall persisted. Yale's role as the preserver of orthodoxy had been compromised and some New Englanders suggested that the college had become corrupt. Even Englishmen questioned the college's ecclesiastical stance. As late as 1725 Jeremiah Dummer told Trustee Timothy Woodbridge there was a "foolish Story" in London that Yale College was designed to be "a Nursery for the Church of England." Woodbridge passed this information on to Governor Joseph Talcott, who quickly responded to the charge; he admitted that the Cutler affair "might be a sufficient cause for the rise and life of such a notion" but declared that the rector's dismissal must convince everyone "that our College was not set up, nor is not intended to uphold the Church principles, but the Church here by law established." [44]

Rumors of this sort in England were not of the utmost importance to the Yale trustees. Their immediate concern was to cleanse the college of the taint of corruption and restore it as a fortress of orthodoxy to the satisfaction of the colonists. The religious test was a step in this direction. A more significant problem was to find a strong and suitable rector.

Anglicans and Yale

While the trustees were reaffirming Yale's religious position and beginning the search for a new rector, four of the defectors were making plans to realize the intent of their declaration. Of the original seven ministers, Hart, Whittelsey, and Eliot had been swayed by the arguments of their fellow Congregationalists and had decided to continue their respective ministries. Cutler, Johnson, Brown, and Wetmore intended to go to England to obtain orders, the first three immediately, Wetmore to follow several months later. Before leaving, Cutler, Johnson, and Brown applied for Anglican parishes they hoped to serve on their return; Cutler wanted to go to Boston, Johnson to Stratford, and Brown to either Bristol or Providence, Rhode Island.[45] The scorn and contempt that New Englanders heaped on the Church of England and its new converts only dramatized the significance of the Anglican victory. By one declaration the Yale defectors had established the Episcopal cause in Connecticut where the S.P.G. had been frustrated for twenty years. The converts might be slandered as "cudweeds" and "degenerate offspring," the church might be labeled the "enemy" and "mother of harlots," but the American Anglicans rejoiced in these epithets and gloated over their triumph.[46]

George Pigot heralded the defection as the beginning of "a reformation in this deluded country" and Francis Nicholson, a colonial governor and benefactor of Yale, correctly predicted that the Yale affair "if Rightly Managed & Encouraged may be of great Service to our Holy Mother the Church of England." [47] Timothy Cutler, whose college rectorship was interpreted by one S.P.G.

44. *Documentary History*, pp. 257–58, 259.

45. 2 Coll. M.H.S. 2 (1814): 140; S.P.G. Correspondence, 16 : 303.

46. "A Faithful Relation," 2 Coll. M.H.S. 2 (1814): 138–39.

47. *Episcopal Church Documents*, 1 : 59; Francis Nicholson to David Humphreys, Jan. 11, 1723, Yale Archives.

missionary as "the most creditable and profitable employment of any in this country," was generally regarded as the most important convert. He was so highly esteemed, in fact, that some American Anglicans fantasized about the potential benefits of his conversion. The Vestry of the Episcopal Church in Newport, Rhode Island, for example, thought that the church hierarchy ought to utilize Cutler's presidential talents. Referring to Cutler's position at Yale, the vestry suggested that, if it could "be obtained by the favour and authority of the Crown that he should be re-established in it, and return in holy orders, it is more than probable that his influence over the youth, and distilling good principles in them, would be of great service to religion and the Church in this country." [48] Intoxicated by their well-publicized success, American Anglicans were eager to capitalize on the Cutler defection and Yale's supposed vulnerability. While the Newport proposal was unrealistic —it would have required royal interference in colonial affairs of drastic proportions—it nevertheless symbolized the dramatic importance of the Yale apostasy.

Although that importance was more evident in New England than in the old, Cutler, Johnson, and Brown were enthusiastically received by Anglican churchmen when they arrived in December, 1722. The following March the three converts were ordained deacons and priests in the Church of England.[49] A week later, Brown was fatally stricken by the smallpox. Saddened by his death, John-

48. *Episcopal Church Documents,* 1 : 79, 91. The trustees, however, had an opportunity to strike back at the Anglicans. Most Anglican missionary efforts in Connecticut had originated in New York. In 1727 the people of Rye, New York, sent a petition to the Yale trustees asking them to plead with the Connecticut General Assembly to send a Congregational minister to Rye. In that town the Congregationalists were in the minority and as a result were, they said, "under havey Bonds and taxes to the Church of England being forced to pay Annualy a Considerable Salery and also to help them Build their Church or Rather Rebuild the Same." The trustees assured the people of their support and informed the Connecticut Assembly that it would be good if a church "according to the manner of the Churches in New-England be erected in the Town of Rye, to be Improved by a Minister of like persuasion with ourselves." The assembly agreed and appointed John Davenport of Stamford and the Fairfield Association to oversee the establishment of a dissenting church in Rye. See C.A., Ecclesiastical Affairs, 3 : 16, 17, 18.

49. One individual who did not give the three men a warm welcome was Jeremiah Dummer. Having heard that the large concentration of Anglican books in his donations to Yale was held partly responsible for the defections, Dummer was civil but "cautious" in his deportment toward the new churchmen. See *Documentary History,* p. 241.

son and Cutler completed their preparations for the return to America, including visits to Oxford and Cambridge, where both men received honorary degrees. The S.P.G. had decided to send Cutler to Boston and Johnson to Stratford. But Cutler, at least, had not forgotten Yale. He volunteered to visit New Haven to promote the Anglican cause, saying he still retained "some share in the affections of many of the people and scholars there." The S.P.G. accepted this dubious claim and gave the former rector "conditional orders" to visit the college town. Although Cutler thought he could work "to good Advantage" in New Haven, there is no evidence that he ever went there.[50] Unhappily for the college, the conveniently located Samuel Johnson took his place.

In mid-September, 1723, Johnson and Cutler arrived in Boston. Judge Samuel Sewall, who held the conviction that "Episcopacy is that upon which the Fifth Vial is poured out," was curious enough to attend Cutler's first preaching engagement. He was not impressed. Cutler preached on the text "For this Cause left I Thee at Creet" but, the judge noted sourly, he "Mention'd Forty One." [51] Sewall's sarcastic appraisal of Cutler's first performance was an accurate prelude to the latter's Boston career. Hardly anyone liked him. His opinionated and argumentative nature quickly antagonized both the established Congregationalists and his fellow Anglicans. One of Cutler's chief enemies was the Reverend Henry Harris, an S.P.G. minister at King's Chapel in Boston, who had enjoyed some success with the Congregationalists by pursuing a policy of moderation and using "all the gentle methods of persuasion" to bring them to the Church of England. Cutler's approach was much less charitable, and his appetite for controversy angered Harris. Harris thought that the church would never flourish under Cutler and informed the Bishop of London that there was "not so much as one person of tolerable note & distinction whom he has brought off from the congregational persuasion." Harris avoided any contact with Cutler lest all Anglicans be associated with the former rector's "indiscretion." Cutler, in turn, attacked Harris as a slanderer, and the Boston Congregationalists rejoiced in the spectacle of churchman fighting churchman.[52]

50. *Episcopal Church Documents,* 1 : 80; William S. Perry, ed., *Historical Collections Relating to the American Colonial Church,* 3 : 143–44.

51. 6 Coll. M.H.S. 2 (1888): 144; 5 Coll. M.H.S. 7 (1888): 326.

52. Perry, *Historical Collections,* 3 : 158–61, 162–65. From the outset, Cutler proved to be the most ecclesiastically conservative of the signers of the 1722 declaration.

Cotton Mather, who shared Judge Sewall's antipathy toward the former rector, reveled in Cutler's difficulties. In 1724 Mather wrote to Gurdon Saltonstall with good news for the Yale trustees. "That miserable Apostate Cutler," Mather exulted, "Experimentally finds the Frowns of our glorious Lord, upon his Apostasy." His church was peopled by "shabby" parishioners and Cutler's "High Principles" were "out of fashion" with the Church in England.[53] While these remarks were sheer gossip, the trustees undoubtedly were glad to hear of Cutler's troubles.

Although Cutler's Boston settlement safely prevented him from influencing Yale, the college still had to contend with the enthusiasm of Samuel Johnson. Settled in Stratford, Johnson made many forays from this base, preaching in other Connecticut towns and recruiting young men for the S.P.G. The colony government continued to make life hard for the Anglicans, but Johnson was still able to achieve success for the church at many points. By 1725 he reported to the society that many ministerial candidates had come to him for books and conversation, and that he hoped to enlist some of them in the church's service. Johnson told the S.P.G. that young men, mostly Yale graduates, who adhered to the Anglican

---

While the others were convinced by the arguments of men like Hoadly and Potter, the rector followed the reasoning of the nonjuror Henry Dodwell (1641–1711), a graduate of Trinity College, Dublin and, until he refused to take the oath of allegiance in 1691, a professor of history at Oxford. Dodwell's belief in apostolic succession had led him to announce that all who heard the Gospel but were in noncommunion with the Church of England were—like pagans—eternally damned. Dodwell not only insisted that ministers must be reordained but that all non-Anglicans must be rebaptized (see *D.N.B.*, 5 : 1084–86; Hunt, *Religious Thought*, 2 : 85–86).

While Cutler never sought rebaptism, his acceptance of Dodwell marked him as an extremist in the group of defectors. The rector evidently voiced these high church opinions before leaving for England. New Englanders accused him of denying the validity of all sacraments performed by the dissenters, and Johnson, Brown, and Wetmore had to defend Cutler against the charges that he said all churches without diocesan bishops were damned (see *The New-England Courant*, Oct. 29–Nov. 5, 1722). In England, Cutler told Thomas Hollis that he had read Dodwell and "Morris" (see note 18 above) and never read books his father had liked. Hollis thought that Cutler's "narrow uncharitable and Dodwelian Principles" were inconsistent, as he was prepared to baptize others without having been rebaptized himself. These notions antagonized his more moderate Anglican colleagues in Boston. See Thomas Hollis to Benjamin Colman, Jan. 14, 1723, and Thomas Hollis to John Leverett, Aug. 16, 1723, Harvard College Library.

53. 7 Coll. M.H.S. 8 (1917): 806. In another letter, Mather described Cutler's congregation as "a Little sorry, Scandalous Drove, which have Little but Baseness and Impiety and Jacobism to distinguish them." See ibid., p. 804.

communion usually were unable to find employment in Connecticut. Johnson hoped that the society could provide "encouragement and relief for such young men of the College from time to time as are neglected in the country" by offering them jobs as Anglican schoolmasters.[54]

But the Church of England could not supply its missionary needs by waiting for young men to seek it out. The Anglicans knew that the church's success depended on influencing young men during their college years. The S.P.G. had long recognized the need for college-educated native clergymen and had tried several tactics to obtain them. As early as 1703 one missionary had suggested that the society send some "pious and able scholars" from Oxford or Cambridge to reside near Harvard and proselytize among the students there.[55] In 1708 Caleb Heathcote proposed that the church erect a college in New York, a suggestion that was not to be realized until the founding of King's College (now Columbia) in 1754. In the meantime, the Anglicans concentrated on influencing the students at Harvard and Yale.

Timothy Cutler had the unpleasant task of dealing with the Bay College. He tried unsuccessfully to have a say in Harvard affairs, complaining that without any Episcopalian control "all the Education of this Country is begun & compleated in prejudice to our Excellent Church." Harvard, he told the S.P.G. secretary, was "a Battery planted against the Grand Designs" of the S.P.G. "in Erecting Missions & sending Missionaries into these parts." Cutler entertained a low opinion of Harvard and Yale, however, and the best he could say of them was that New England was free from atheism and deism because "our poor starved Colleges here will not afford us any thing very strong for or against Religion."[56]

Samuel Johnson had a better opinion of his alma mater. Although he recognized the "low advantages for learning" at Yale, Johnson thought that a Yale degree was sufficient proof that a man was educated enough to become an S.P.G. missionary. The Stratford minister enjoyed more success with Yale than Cutler did with Harvard. The college officers tried to hinder his work in New Haven, but despite these efforts Johnson found an audience in the college town. In 1728 he preached before a congregation of

54. *Episcopal Church Documents,* 1 : 105, 117–18, 120–21.

55. S.P.G. Correspondence, 1 : 88.

56. Ibid., 20 : 258–62, 275–76; John Nichols, *Illustrations of the Literary History of the Eighteenth Century,* 4 : 291.

one hundred, "among them several of the scholars, who are very inquisitive about the principles of our Church." [57] By October, 1730, Johnson could report to the S.P.G. secretary that his efforts in New Haven had been rewarded:

> One thing I have particularly to rejoice in, and that is, that I have a very considerable influence in the College in my neighbourhood; and that a love to the Church gains ground greatly in it. Several young men that are graduates, and some young ministers, I have prevailed with to read and consider the matter so far, that they are very uneasy out of the communion of the Church, and some seem much disposed to come into her service; and those that are best affected to the Church are the brightest and most studious of any that are educated in the country.[58]

While this last claim was somewhat overblown, Johnson had good reason to be proud of his work. He rightly saw his most important contribution to the Anglican cause as helping Yale students in the "Reading of Good Books in Directing their Studyes and leading them into a Good Affection to our Excellent Church." By 1732 his successes had reached such proportions that he told the S.P.G. secretary to let him know if he was converting more potential missionaries than the society could provide for.[59]

Johnson's proselytizing irritated Cutler's successor, Rector Elisha Williams. Not only had Johnson printed a rebuttal to one of the rector's Calvinistic sermons, but he had been personally responsible for recruiting at least seven Yale students for the Anglican priesthood. But the Stratford pastor's interest in Yale was not entirely subversive. He still retained an affection for the college, and in 1732 he and Jared Eliot, by intimating that Yale was on the verge of becoming Episcopalian, persuaded George Berkeley to make a substantial donation of books and land to the school. Although Johnson felt that Rector Williams was not sufficiently appreciative of this gift, the rector welcomed the windfall, Anglican donor or no.[60]

57. S.P.G. Correspondence, 24 : 407–09; cf. ibid., 21 : 467–68; *Episcopal Church Documents,* 1 : 127, 128.

58. *Episcopal Church Documents,* 1 : 145.

59. S.P.G. Correspondence, 24 : 121–24.

60. Nichols, *Literary History,* 4 : 287. A discussion of the Berkeley gift appears below, chapter 7.

The one objective Johnson was unable to achieve in New Haven was the building of an Anglican church. He had hoped for one for many years. In 1738 it appeared his dream would be realized. Several years before, one William Gregson of London had given the Reverend Jonathan Arnold (Y. 1723), an S.P.G. missionary, the deed to a tract of land in New Haven as the site for a church. Timothy Cutler was excited by this prospect, as a church so near to the college would "be very instrumental to ferret schism out of that nest of it." Cutler's enthusiasm was not shared by the people of New Haven. When Arnold and his servants tried to take possession of the land and clear it for the builders, he was opposed by a mob of students and local people, "who in a riotous and tumultuous manner" beat his servants and forced them to withdraw. The Anglicans suspected that the "chief men of the town" had instigated the mob and complained to their superiors in England that the civil authorities refused to punish the offenders.[61]

Arnold's treatment in New Haven typified the colony's reaction to the Anglicans. Connecticut's ecclesiastical structure, ordered by the Saybrook Platform, was such that Anglicanism was the chief refuge for those disaffected with the prevalent religious constitution of the colony. In a way, the established ministers had to accept some of the responsibility for this fact, for their ecclesiastical parochialism after the Cutler defection undoubtedly alienated a number of their parishioners. The ministers themselves, however, interpreted the Church of England's role in slightly different terms. To the Congregational majority, Anglicanism was a refuge for those from whom the established churches were disaffected. The most frequent charge the ministers leveled against the Anglicans was that their church had deliberately become "a Sanctuary to the contentious, refractory and ungovernable" people who had been disciplined by the established churches.[62]

Those who joined the Anglican church were, in a sense, religious deviates and were treated accordingly. The colonial government, for all its rhetoric to the contrary, never treated the Episcopalians as equal partners in Connecticut religious affairs.[63] De-

61. Nichols, *Literary History*, 4 : 299; *Johnson*, 1 : 97, 98.

62. [John Graham], *Some Remarks Upon a late Pamphlet entitled, A Letter from a minister of the Church of England to his dissenting parishioners* ([Boston], 1733), p. 35.

63. The Anglicans constantly complained of the ill-treatment they received from the Connecticut government. In 1724 Samuel Johnson complained to the bishop of

spite such mild persecution, the Church of England made substantial gains after 1722, and the Yale defection obviously marked the crucial turning point in its success. At the time of the Cutler apostasy, there had not been one settled Anglican minister in Connecticut and only a few scattered adherents of the church. When Samuel Johnson returned from England in 1723 he became the only Church of England minister in the colony. Twenty years later there were over two thousand communicants and seven priests in the Connecticut Church.[64] All of the ministers had graduated from Yale. Ironically, the collegiate school, established as a bulwark against latitudinarianism and requiring all its officers to denounce episcopacy, turned out to be the principal provider of native Church of England ministers.[65]

Yale College was an unwilling provider. At no time did the college verge on becoming Anglican. In 1732 Timothy Cutler implied that Rector Elisha Williams was in trouble in Connecticut for "dodging about" and flirting with the Church of England, but this was wishful thinking.[66] Samuel Johnson, for one, saw Williams as one of the church's chief opponents; Johnson's testimony about his New Haven troubles is ample proof of Yale's continuing stance as an orthodox college. To be sure, Yale demanded no denomina-

London of the "unreasonable demands of the government in exacting taxes from [Anglicans] to the support of the Independent teachers." In 1728 the Reverend Henry Caner told the bishop that although the government had freed the churchmen from paying these taxes, the act was interpreted so that only those Anglicans who lived not more than a mile from a Church of England were so freed. Caner stated that two-thirds of his parishioners still had to pay the tax. See *Episcopal Church Documents,* 1 : 95, 126.

64. *Johnson,* 1 : 109. Johnson was not only a central figure in the events related in this chapter but was involved in many aspects of early Yale as a student, tutor, and graduate. For an excellent treatment of Johnson's life and thought during these years, see Joseph J. Ellis, *The New England Mind in Transition: Samuel Johnson of Connecticut (1696–1772).*

65. Between 1701 and 1785, forty-five Anglican ministers worked in Connecticut. Of these, twenty-six graduated from Yale; King's and Harvard Colleges only provided five each. Forty-seven deacons and prominent laymen labored in the colony during this same period, thirty-one of whom were Yale graduates. Thus, of ninety-two principal Connecticut Anglicans, fifty-seven were products of a Yale education. See Hector G.L.M. Kinloch, "Anglican Clergy in Connecticut, 1701–1785" (Ph.D. diss., Yale University, 1959).

66. Nichols, *Literary History,* 4 : 294: "Mr. Johnson has the pleasure of bettering the College in his neighbourhood, and seeing several of its Regents and Students advancing towards the Church of England, insomuch as the Rector, who would save his bacon whilst he is getting light, is in danger of having his public salary taken from him whilst he is dodging about."

tional profession of belief from its students, so the undergraduate body included members of the Church of England.[67] But the college rector, tutors, and trustees were all professing adherents of the Saybrook Platform and had publicly stated their opposition to all "Armenian & prelatical Corruptions." As long as Yale College was governed by officers drawn from Connecticut's religious establishment, there was little danger that the school would again deviate from "the good old way."

67. S.P.G. Correspondence, 25 : 150–53.

5 "A Repairer of the Breach"

Following the defection and dismissal of Timothy Cutler, Yale entered a period of drift. The college's reputation had been tarnished and the trustees felt obliged to act quickly to arrest the corrosion before it went too far. Their first task was to keep the college functioning, their first priority to find a new and suitable rector. Both jobs were difficult, and the trustees did not accomplish either of them quickly.

Once again, the tutors handled the day-to-day administration of the school, a role they were to fill for the next four years. This was not a happy arrangement, for in two instances in the recent past, government by tutors had caused unrest at the college. Whether this cause and effect syndrome prevailed in these years is impossible to say, but it is clear that the need for student discipline was a dreary constant in Yale's existence. In the period from November, 1722 to October, 1723, the trustees had to enact five additional college rules, over and above the existing regulations, to deal with student misbehavior. In the absence of a resident rector, the tutors were deputized to enact all punishments save expulsion, which required the assent of at least two trustees.

With the tutors running the school, their comings and goings took on added importance for the trustees. James Pierpont, son of the former New Haven minister, and William Smith were the first to hold these positions. When, in 1723, both of them considered leaving, Governor Saltonstall wrote Trustee Timothy Woodbridge that it would "be a great disadvantage to the Colledge to loose them both at Once" and urged that pressure be applied to Smith, at least, to stay on a few years longer.[1] It may be that the trustees appealed to both men to stay, for Smith remained for another six months and Pierpont for another year and a half. In 1724, Robert Treat and Jonathan Edwards became tutors; in 1725 Daniel Edwards took on the job. These young men kept the college going and, in the case of Jonathan Edwards if not the others, provided undergraduates with a first-rate education.

But the college needed a president and the trustees had no

1. Pub. C.S.M. 6 (1904): 197.

candidates in mind. As was mentioned earlier, someone sought to solve Yale's plight in a dramatic fashion by trying to get Cotton Mather for the job. But, although the evidence is sketchy at best, it appears that the attempt to obtain Mather was an informal query rather than an official invitation, for the trustee records do not contain any mention of the offer.[2] Still, it was a good idea. Mather was the living embodiment of the good old cause, and his election as rector would have symbolized Yale's fidelity to its heritage. But Mather probably discouraged the suggestion, preferring to remain in Boston clinging to the idle hope that someday Harvard might ask him to become its president.

Not knowing whom to choose as Cutler's successor, the trustees temporized. They turned first to one of their own number and asked Timothy Woodbridge to fill in as temporary rector until the next April. On the surface, this seems a remarkable decision, for only a few years earlier Woodbridge had been the leader of the anti-New Haven faction. It is impossible to know precisely how the reconciliation was effected, although it is an index of the good will among the trustee fraternity that both sides had been willing to forget old quarrels and join forces to promote the school's welfare. To have Woodbridge lead the college at this time would, if nothing else, demonstrate the solidarity of the trustees. But Woodbridge gave no immediate reply, and in the meantime the trustees appointed the Reverends Joseph Moss of Derby and Joseph Noyes of New Haven to visit the college until a permanent solution could be worked out. Soon thereafter, Woodbridge declined his election and the trustees met again in November, 1722 to arrange another method of overseeing the school. They decided to have "some meet Persons," usually trustees, act as temporary

2. *The New England Courant*, Sept. 24–Oct. 1, 1722: "We hear the Reverend Dr. Cotton Mather has been desir'd to take the Charge of the College at Newhaven, in the room of the Reverend Mr. Timothy Cutler who has resign'd that Place." The one piece of corroborating evidence is a letter of Joseph Green, a friend and parishioner of Mather, to Stephen Williams, Boston, Oct. 1, 1722. Green told Williams of the defection at Yale and added: "Dr Mather has an invitation to the Rector-ship there, but whether he will go we are uncertain, but as to my own part I am full of hopes he will not, I believe the Contumelies and unworthy treatment he has mett with in Boston would facilitate his parting with it, but the Church & his good Father will never part with him I hope." See Kenneth Murdock, "Cotton Mather and the Rectorship of Yale College," Pub. C.S.M. 26 (1927): 388–401. In his essay on this issue, Murdock concluded that the offer, though tentative and informal, was probably made, despite Mather's personal silence on the matter.

rectors for a month each until the following spring. This procedure was adopted and, when the trustees were unable to settle a resident rector, continued for several years.[3]

In April, 1723, the trustees met to elect a full-time rector and called to the post the Reverend Nathaniel Williams (H. 1693), headmaster of the Public Free Grammar School in Boston. Less than a month later Williams declined. Though he was flattered by the offer and, he said, "would think my self obliged to sacrifice my own ease and private Satisfaction to the Service of God and the great interests of Religion, yet I cannot think my self obliged to urge my Wife and Family to that which may hereafter make them uneasie." [4] The trustees were certainly disheartened to learn that the acceptance of the rectorship was considered a sacrifice, but since Mrs. Williams refused to leave Boston, they had no choice but to find another man for the job.

In the summer of 1723 the search turned up three more candidates: Elisha Williams, former tutor of the Wethersfield faction and minister of the Newington parish in that town; Nicholas Sever (H. 1701), a one-time pastor, then a tutor at Harvard; and Edward Wigglesworth (H. 1710), the Hollis Professor of Divinity at the Cambridge college. Gurdon Saltonstall, whose recommendations for the future rector had been solicited by Timothy Woodbridge, thought Williams was a good choice but believed that his Wethersfield pastorate might preclude his acceptance of the job. The governor had heard both positive and negative reactions to Sever, whose principal attribute seems to have been a delight in controversy, and felt that calling Wigglesworth from his service at Harvard might be ill-advised.[5] But the trustees made no immediate overtures to any of these men, and it was nearly a year before they again tried to find a rector.

In October, 1723, the governor's council asked the trustees to explain the delay in finding a replacement for Cutler. They re-

3. *Documentary History*, pp. 234, 235.

4. Ibid., pp. 239–40.

5. That Williams was under consideration for the rectorship in 1723 can be inferred from a letter of Governor Gurdon Saltonstall to an unnamed correspondent. Saltonstall referred to a "hint concerning the Supply of the Rectorship" by a man who had been recommended as "a Senior Tutor" in 1718–19 with an eye to making him the rector. Saltonstall stated that this individual was now (1723) a minister. These particulars could refer only to Elisha Williams. See Saltonstall to [?], July 9, 1723, Yale Archives.

plied that they had been hampered in their search by the scarcity of qualified men, the difficulty in winning the qualified ones away from their present employments, and some disagreements among themselves about their rules of procedure as a governing body. The issues that had caused most of the technical difficulties in the protracted debates over the location of the college from 1716 to 1718 had still not been resolved, and the trustees asked the assembly to help settle them. The ministers sent a list of questions to the assembly, and within a few days the legislators answered in the form of "An Act in Explanation of and Addition to the Act for Erecting a Collegiate School in this Colony." The purpose of this explanatory act was to clarify certain points in the original charter so that the trustees could better carry out the affairs of the college, "for Want of which It has Laboured under great difficulties Very much to the prevention of that Order and good Education which is to be desired there." The act contained five provisions, the first four of which virtually affirmed the positions taken by the seaside trustees six years earlier: first, the trustees could choose another person to replace an incapacitated or inactive trustee; second, the trustees could make decisions by a majority vote of those attending a meeting; third, a meeting could be called by any three trustees, with seven making a quorum; fourth, the minimum age for a trustee was reduced from forty to thirty; and fifth, anyone chosen rector of the college "shall by Vertue thereof become a Trustee of the same" for his term of office.[6]

There is no way of knowing whether these amendments facilitated the deliberations, but when the trustees next met in April, 1724, they officially elected a rector for the second time. This time they chose a fellow trustee, Eliphalet Adams, the minister at New London and a staunch supporter of the college. Adams was willing to take the job but his parishioners were reluctant to let him go. On April 15 the town of New London held a public fast to seek God's guidance in the impending decision over Adams's election. Joshua Hempstead, a local farmer, recorded in his diary that on April 16 "wee had a Sort of Town meeting to Consider if wee were Willing to part with Mr Adams. I was most of the day on it & it is Negatived." [7]

6. *Documentary History,* pp. 247–48, 248–50.

7. Ibid., p. 251; *Diary of Joshua Hempstead of New London, Connecticut,* The New London Historical Society Collections, 1 (1901): 142.

Having failed to obtain Adams, the trustees met again in May and held two more elections. They chose the Reverend Edward Wigglesworth of Harvard, whose name had been mentioned a year earlier and, in case he refused, the Reverend William Russell (Y. 1709), of Middletown, the first Yale graduate to be offered the job.[8] By this time the General Assembly had again become alarmed over the college's failure to find a rector and asked the trustees to relate what they had done toward filling that position, a matter "of great Necesity to the flourishing of that Society." The trustees responded that they had elected Wigglesworth and Russell and, as a third choice, assented to, by "the Major part of the Trustees here present," Elisha Williams.[9]

By August 13, Wigglesworth, citing reasons of health, had declined the invitation to leave Harvard for Yale, and Trustees Woodbridge and Russell made overtures to the people of Middletown about William Russell's election. Russell accepted the trustees' offer but his parishioners balked at releasing him. Negotiations with Middletown continued into October but ultimately met with failure.[10] There is no record that the trustees ever contacted Elisha Williams about the job. Perhaps the lack of unanimity in his election existed because there were still those who had doubts about offering the rectorship to the man who had taught the dissenting students several years before.

While there is no evidence in the Yale records that the trustees invited anyone else to take the job, there was at least one other man who aspired to it. In 1724 Gilbert Tennent resided at the college, probably as a postgraduate student, and received an M.A. in 1725. Gilbert's father William, a recent immigrant from Scotland and, with his four sons, a future leader of the Great Awakening in Pennsylvania, was the minister of a Presbyterian church in Bedford, New York. In this capacity he evidently became acquainted with some Connecticut ministers, probably as a result of the frequent interest and accompanying contacts those ministers

8. *Documentary History*, p. 252. According to his son, William Smith (Y. 1719) was offered the rectorship in 1723–24 while a tutor at the college. If this statement is true, the offer must have been very tentative, as there is no record of it. See *Yale Graduates*, 1 : 207.

9. *Documentary History*, pp. 253–54.

10. Timothy Woodbridge to Yale Trustees, Aug. 13, 1724, Yale Archives. See also *Yale Graduates*, 1 : 312; *Harvard Graduates*, 5 : 550. For a newspaper reference to Russell's election, see *Documentary History*, p. 255.

had with the religious affairs of the Middle Colonies. In any event, William knew enough about Yale to send his son there and, according to a close friend, had "some hopes of being made principal of the College." [11] Tennent's credentials for the job were certainly respectable, although his Anglican ordination in 1704 might have offset his otherwise Reformed profile as the holder of an Edinburgh degree and a member of the Synod of Philadelphia. It is impossible to know if Tennent's hopes for the rectorship were conveyed to the trustees, but it is clear that they never approached him about the position. The Scottish minister made up for his dashed aspirations in 1735, however, when he opened his "Log College" in Nesheminy, Pennsylvania, to train young men for the ministry.[12]

Because of their inability to obtain Wigglesworth and Russell, their indecision about Williams, and the fact that Tennent's hopes bore no fruit for either himself or the college, the trustees were forced once more to turn to one of their own number for assistance. Samuel Andrew, who had served as rector pro tempore during the college's troubled early years, again offered his services to the school and officiated at the 1724 commencement. In April, 1725, the trustees made no efforts to secure anyone else for the rectorship and asked Andrew to continue as acting rector through the next graduation.[13]

It was now three years since Cutler's dismissal. In that time the trustees had chosen four men for the rectorship and had been turned down by all of them. The General Assembly, disturbed by these failures, had been applying pressure on the college to set its administrative house in order, and no doubt the trustees felt both embarrassed and frustrated by their inability to do so. Unfortunately, the records do not reveal the trustee discussions about a new rector, but it seems that for several years they had been considering Elisha Williams for the job. His name had first

11. Thomas C. Pears, Jr. and Guy S. Klett, eds., *Documentary History of William Tennent and the Log College* (Department of History, Presbyterian Historical Society [Philadelphia], 1940), p. 39a.

12. William Tennent's "Log College" was built in 1735 and closed in about 1744. During its brief existence Tennent trained "possibly twenty-one men, many of whom were of unique usefulness in the American Presbyterian Church." For more on Tennent's school, see Trinterud, *Forming of an American Tradition,* pp. 63–64, 74, 82, 123, 169–95.

13. *Documentary History,* p. 258.

come up in the summer of 1723 and again in the spring of 1724. He had not been a unanimous choice at either time and it is probable that the opposition to his election came from one or more trustees who had favored the New Haven settlement in 1716–18. But Williams had one decided asset in his favor—he was available. This fact kept his candidacy alive, and in September, 1725, out of either desperation or conviction, the trustees unanimously elected him rector. This decision was particularly pleasing to the upriver trustees, who had certainly been Williams's chief supporters, but all of the trustees closed ranks and announced that they judged the young minister "well qualified for the work we have called him to, and in him have a fair prospect that he will be a repairer of the breach that has been made in that Society." Trustees Woodbridge, Buckingham, and Whitman were appointed to treat with Williams and his parishioners about removing the minister to Yale.[14]

In October, 1725 the trustees informed the General Assembly that they had "a likely prospect" of getting Williams for the job but said that his removal from Newington would place the parish in considerable financial hardship. The college did not have the money to compensate the town fully and asked the assembly for help. The representatives responded favorably. They were eager to reestablish the college on a sound basis and they congratulated the trustees on their choice of a man "so agreeable to the country, and so very acceptable to the Assembly." To assure the success of this latest election, the legislators decreed that the people of Newington would be freed from taxes for four years on the condition that the money be used "towards settling another minister in said parish." By the spring of 1726 the trustees, after some negotiations, obtained the consent of Mr. Williams and his church to his election as rector. But the people of Newington were still not satisfied with the financial compensations awarded the previous October, and the trustees again had to appeal to the assembly for assistance. Again the assembly reacted favorably. It granted Yale £100.16.0 to facilitate the settlement of Mr. Williams.[15]

Completion of the financial arrangements with Newington took time, and Rector-elect Williams did not assume his post until the day after the 1726 commencement. On September 13, four years

14. Ibid., pp. 260, 261.
15. Ibid., pp. 261–62, 263–64.

to the day after Timothy Cutler had made his shocking declaration to the trustees, Elisha Williams gave his consent to the Saybrook Confession and announced his opposition to all Arminian and prelatical corruptions. That evening he delivered an oration in the college hall, after which he was greeted by each trustee and formally installed as Yale's fourth rector.[16] Even though Williams was the trustees' fifth choice as a replacement for Cutler, his election and installation were warmly received by all who had an interest in the college.

Elisha Williams came to the Yale rectorship as a man with varied experiences. The son of the Reverend William Williams of Hatfield, Massachusetts, young Elisha had gone through Harvard in three years and was Scholar of the House in his senior year. As this record indicates, Williams was a capable scholar; a friend remembered him as a man with "uncommon Strength of Memory and Judgment, a vigorous and lively Imagination, and early made a happy Proficiency in Classical Learning, Logic and Geography." Ezra Stiles concurred in that opinion, describing Williams as "a good classical Scholar, well versed in Logic, Metaphysics & Ethics, & in Rhetoric & Oratory."[17] After graduating from college in 1711, Williams taught school for a time but then returned home to study theology with his father. In 1714 he married Eunice Chester of Wethersfield, took up residence in that town, and began to read law. In 1716 he gave up the law to become the senior tutor of the Wethersfield faction; he had the intellect for the task and his instruction satisfied the students under his care. In 1717 Williams was chosen a deputy to the General Assembly, where he cast his votes to settle the collegiate school at or near Hartford and, as clerk, recorded the assembly's debates on this issue. The eventual settlement of the college in New Haven coincided with a period of illness for Williams, which may explain why he refused the offer to become the senior tutor at the reunited school. Instead, he accepted the invitation of the recently organized Newington Church in Wethersfield to become its first pastor. It was from this position that he accepted the call from Yale. Since Williams had been intimately affiliated with the upriver trustees dur-

16. Ibid., p. 266; *Yale Annals,* p. 35. Williams was technically the third rector, as Samuel Andrew only served on a pro tempore basis, even though he did so for twelve years (1707–19), plus his stint from 1724 to 1726.

17. *Harvard Graduates,* 5 : 588; *Literary Diary of Ezra Stiles,* 2 : 336.

ing the troubled years 1716–18, his acceptance by all the trustees in 1726 signified the healing of this old breach.

Williams, like his predecessor, took over the college at a time when student behavior was a problem. Rector Cutler had never completely controlled the undergraduates, and the interregnum policy of monthly visitations by various trustees had not remedied the situation. While the tutors disciplined some offenders, "the ill Habits formerly contracted by the Students were not easily and suddenly eradicated," so Williams had to impose order on a school where none had existed for four years. Student misbehavior, of course, occurred at other colleges in the colonies and abroad and would persist at Yale even in times of administrative stability. Nevertheless, restoring some propriety to undergraduate life was one of the rector's first tasks and, according to his successor, Thomas Clap, he succeeded in this endeavor. After his settlement in New Haven, Williams "began, by Degrees, more effectually to suppress Vice and Disorder among the Students; and to introduce and settle a Number of good Customs." [18]

Williams obviously had a way with students, for within three years he had guided the college to a position of stability. John Sergeant, in the valedictory oration for 1729, lavishly praised the rector for his wise and prudent government of the college: "By your kind influences this seminary once so drooping begins to flourish." Sergeant called for God's blessings on Williams's efforts "for the happy promotion of the dearest interest of your beloved country, in forming the converted youth of this academy for the service of Church and State." [19] While the purple prose of a commencement address might have overstated the case, Williams had, in fact, provided Yale with the stability which allowed it to grow and prosper. Students were coming to the college in increasing numbers and from more distant places. During Williams's tenure, Yale averaged a yearly enrollment of seventy students, with an apex in 1735 when it had a student body of eighty-two and graduated twenty-four bachelors of arts.

This increase in size practically demanded that Yale have a functioning administration, and here again Williams was successful. The rector managed to get the various college offices operating

18. *Yale Annals,* pp. 35–36.

19. John Sergeant, *A Valedictorian Oration, delivered at Yale College in the Year 1729,* p. 17.

regularly, particularly those of butler, scholar of the house, and monitor. The office of college butler, given to a graduate, had existed for several years, Jonathan Edwards being the first known holder of the job. His duties were to serve the beer at morning and afternoon "sizings" and generally to assist the college steward. In 1723 the butler was also delegated to keep a quarterly account of the condition of student chambers. In 1726 this latter role was assumed by the scholar of the house, his duty being "to observe & note down all Detriment the College receives in its Windows Doors Studies Tables Locks" and to report the damage quarterly. Sometime in 1727 the trustees created the office of monitor. The Yale records do not specify the monitor's duties, but he probably performed the same job as his Harvard counterpart, namely, to "observe them that are fayling, eyther by absence from prayers or Sermons, or come tardy to the same" and report the delinquents to the rector.[20]

Although the monitor was the only position created under Rector Williams, the several offices had not really functioned until he assumed control of Yale. By 1730, then, Williams supervised an active administrative hierarchy that ran the college: eleven trustees dictated Yale policy; the rector and two tutors did the teaching, one tutor acting as librarian; a steward provided the food in commons; a treasurer handled all financial accounts; and the butler, scholar of the house, and monitor all performed their assigned duties. Yale College had acquired a working institutional framework.

While this organizational achievement was significant, a far more serious challenge was the matter of college finances. With the exception of the three years of Cutler's tenure, the institutional history of early Yale revolved around the search for a resident rector, a college building and site, and money to pay for both. By the time Elisha Williams settled in New Haven the college had technically solved these problems. In doing so, however, the school had exhausted its funds and, at the same time, incurred new expenses. While Yale was without a resident rector, the trustees did not have to pay a rector's salary; without a college building, they did not have to spend money for repairs and upkeep. Now they

20. *Documentary History*, pp. 246, 265, 281; *Seventeenth-century Harvard*, 1 : 108. For an example of a Harvard monitor's bill, see Franklin B. Dexter, "Harvard-College Monitor's Bill," in *Miscellaneous Historical Essays*, pp. 1–5.

had to do both, and the result was that the college was in financial hardship. The plight of the school was reflected in the fact that it did not have the funds to pay for Williams's removal from Newington and had to appeal to the government for assistance. One of Williams's first tasks, therefore, was to set Yale's financial house in order—no small job, as from the collegiate school's earliest years, financial support had been chaotic and scanty.

6 "Ballance in Favour of the College"

Yale may have been founded as a school of the church, but financially it was a college of the colony government. Ministers created and shaped the collegiate school; legislators paid for it. In October, 1701, when it granted the ten ministers a college charter, the Connecticut General Assembly pledged the school a yearly donation of £120 and the permission to "accept acquire purchase or otherwise lawfully enter upon Any Lands Tenements & Hereditaments to the use of the said School not exceeding the value of five hundred Pounds per Annum." The theory behind this limitation on donations is unknown, but in any case the £500 ceiling on annual donations did not pose a problem for the original trustees or their successors. On the contrary, the chief problem was to obtain enough rather than too much income. An early index of the college's financial picture was contained in the first gift to the school, 637 acres of land, which according to the donor, Major James Fitch, might bring the college an annual profit of only £20. Still, when the trustees left New Haven in October, 1701, they already had some contributions to the school. And at their first official meeting on November 11, the clergymen brought some of their own, a number of them donating books to help start the college library. These forty volumes were the beginning of what, by 1739, was to be a library of 2,500 books.[1]

These three items—the colony annuity, land, and books—were the principal types of donations to the college during its first forty years. Of the three, books were the least important economically; though an intellectual necessity, they were a financial luxury. Their value could be and was computed, but the college treasurer could not use them to pay for the school's needs. However, the fact that many books were donated meant, of course, that Yale did not have to purchase them, so these gifts did save the college money. At times, in fact, the books actually brought in money; in 1731 the trustees ordered the rector to sell library duplicates and buy new books, and in 1739 Rector Williams

1. *Documentary History*, pp. 22–23, 19–20, 25; *Yale Annals*, p. 94.

earned the college £14.0.10 from volumes sold.[2] For the most part, however, books had a small role in Yale's financial dealings.

A second category of gifts to the college was land. As with books, the treasurer rarely included property donations in his yearly accounts. But land was an important asset which, if it did not bring any immediate income, was still a source of potential funds. In 1701, Nathaniel Lynde, the newly elected treasurer, gave the collegiate school a house in the town plot of Saybrook, along with eight or ten acres of adjacent land. Lynde intended this gift for the college as long as it was located in Saybrook. Rector Pierson's refusal to leave Killingworth prevented the trustees from using the gift until 1707, at which time the house probably served as the place of instruction. In 1714 the trustees leased the land for a three-year period and allowed each tutor to graze one horse in the plot's pasture. The Lynde gift brought the college a little income, but when the school moved from Saybrook in 1716, Lynde retracted his donation.[3] The trustees soon compensated for the loss.

At the time of the college's division in 1716, the towns of Hartford, New Haven, and Saybrook all bid for the school. On July 30, 1716, the proprietors of the town land in New Haven granted the trustees eight acres of land if the college "Should be Setled here and So long at is Shall Continue here." The proprietors also stipulated that individuals would be allowed to donate up to forty acres to the college,[4] and when Trustees Andrew, Russell, and Ruggles circulated a subscription for the school, at least twelve men pledged from one to five acres each to further the college's settlement. Once the college came to New Haven, the trustees received other land donations: Joseph Peck gave two acres, Joseph Moss bestowed six acres, his father seven, and Captain Samuel Smith eight. In 1721 the trustees decided to convert these scattered holdings to cash and voted to sell all but ten acres of the land. They sold Rector Cutler the forty acres given by several gentlemen in New Haven, but the rector had little time to profit from his new holdings; Cutler kept the land for one year and then sold it back to the trustees after his dismissal.[5]

2. *Documentary History*, pp. 290, 336.

3. Ibid., pp. 36, 60; C.A., Colleges and Schools, 1 : 181; *Documentary History*, p. 106.

4. *New Haven Town Records*, 3 : 387, 391, 396, 401.

5. *Documentary History*, pp. 69–70, 213; *Yale Annals*, p. 96; Joseph Moss, Quit

With the exception of a few acres, then, the treasurer sold the New Haven land donations to acquire working capital. But the college did not sell all of its real estate. In 1732, for example, the trustees petitioned for and received a land grant of 1,500 acres from the General Assembly, lands which they pledged to retain and improve. In the same year, the college received a ninety-six-acre farm in Rhode Island from George Berkeley, who stipulated in the deed that the college keep and rent the land. In the case of the 637 acres given by James Fitch, however, the trustees never had to worry about whether to sell or rent. Their main concern was possession.

Major James Fitch was one of the shrewdest land speculators in the colony and a man of some political influence. For many years the New London county voters had elected him to the upper house where, despite the opposition of such established families as the Winthrops, who considered him something of a renegade, Fitch wielded considerable power. While he acted the role of the people's champion in political matters, the major was a keen operator when the stakes involved land. In 1684 he had obtained a deed from the Indians to extensive tracts of property in southeastern and northeastern Connecticut. As with most Indian lands, the boundaries of this territory were poorly defined and, as it turned out, overlapped properties that the Winthrops had received from other Indians. The subsequent disputes were bitter and were not resolved for decades. To complicate matters, both Fitch and the Winthrops proceeded to sell portions of this land, further tangling the web of ownership and title.

Yale College became involved in this real estate conflict when, in 1701, Fitch gave the school a tract of land in Killingly, located in northeastern Connecticut. Had the college made use of this land immediately, its claim might have gone unchallenged. As it was, the trustees made no attempt to utilize the property until the college was settled in New Haven. By that time, Fitch had lost most of his political power; in 1707 the assembly had deprived

Claim Deed, July 27, 1719, Yale Archives; *Documentary History*, pp. 213, 232. In 1722 the New Haven Church, in return for a donation of forty-three pounds, granted the trustees the use of one-and-a-half acres next to the college. The church pledged to use the money in ways agreeable to the trustees. See New Haven First Congregational Church Records, 1639–1926, C1 : 32, Center Church, New Haven, Conn.; New Haven Church, Lease for One and a Half Acres, Oct. 20, 1722, Yale Archives.

him of his lands in northeastern Connecticut, and after that date the major never again served in the upper house. In 1717, however, Fitch returned to the fray and began selling land in the territory. Although challenged by the government, Fitch persisted, only to be served a warrant to appear before the assembly. Fitch refused to come, but he later apologized for his disrespect and the matter was dropped. It was in this somewhat hostile climate that the trustees decided to take possession of the 1701 gift. In 1719 they met with Fitch in order to arrange the college's title to the acreage. Fitch drew up a quit claim granting Yale the land, with the single proviso "that it be to School or Colledge Use so long as said Colledge shall be under the Instruction of Rector or Tutors or Instructors, that are of the Presbyterian or Congregational persuasion." [6] Fitch was evidently a staunch supporter of the Saybrook Platform and, as it turned out, an archfoe of the Church of England. When Cutler defected to Anglicanism in 1722, the old major was extremely upset, so much so that Yale nearly lost his donation.

The college almost lost the gift anyway. The college farm, as it was called, was surveyed in 1719, but the boundaries were indistinct and the college was unsure of its exact holdings. Given the haphazard nature of the original boundaries and the subsequent conflicts that had surrounded the property, this was an understandable problem, but in 1720 the trustees decided to go ahead and claim the tract, and ordered all other people off it. In 1721 the college earned a paltry £6 from rental of the lands, and that was as much as it earned for some time. In 1721 two men, John Fiske and James Leavins, each brought suit against the college, claiming that they held title to over 140 acres within the Fitch farm. A protracted series of court proceedings ensued for a period of several years, with other men entering similar claims of overlapping grants. At first the college lost the case when its

6. *Documentary History,* pp. 198–99; The Agreement between Major James Fitch and Samuel Russell and Thomas Ruggles, New Haven, Sept. 9, 1719, MS, Yale. The Agreement also stipulated that the trustees would pay Fitch thirty pounds and would order an additional thirty pounds "to be Disposed (by said Major Fitch to the good Satisfaction of Said Trustees & Rector) to some pious uses in Said Colledge." In 1724 Fitch instructed the trustees to send the thirty pounds to Rhode Island to help settle a Presbyterian minister there. See James Fitch to Yale Trustees, Sept. 4, 1724, Yale Archives. For a sketch of Fitch's tumultuous career, see Bushman, *From Puritan to Yankee,* pp. 83–103.

lawyer failed to appear at the New London court, but the school won a new hearing. In 1724 the General Assembly agreed to a trustee proposal to allow the disputants to exchange land, the college to take other acreage of equal size and value.[7] But James Fitch objected. His 637-acre grant, he argued, contained the proviso that the college must have Congregational or Presbyterian governors. If the college exchanged his grant for other lands, Fitch feared that his stipulation would become invalid. "Pray, Gentlemen," he wrote the trustees, "consider what if within a few years yor Great masters over the watter should take the Coladge into their hands & put in a churchman to be a Rector & such Tutors: what say you, must my farme goe to them; surely not, verily my Record is on high I never entended or why els did I lay in that proviso." [8]

The trustees, however, were able to convince Fitch that his wishes for the college would be respected even if the land were exchanged, so the major finally agreed to the transfer. The transaction was disputed for six years until finally, in 1730, the trustees declared that they were satisfied with the alternate plot near the Housatonic River offered by Fiske and Leavins.[9] Twenty-nine years after the donation, Yale College took possession of the land. The plot does not appear to have been rented, for the treasurer never recorded any income from the farm during Rector Williams's tenure.

By 1733, then, Yale College held the title to approximately 2,243 widely scattered acres of New England soil (consisting of the tracts given by Fitch, Berkeley, and the General Assembly). This was a substantial asset for the school, but only the Berkeley farm in Rhode Island seems to have brought in any money before 1740. The potential income from the lands was not to be realized until the rectorship of Thomas Clap.

7. Thomas Kimberly, Description of Major Fitch's Farm at Killingly, October, 1719, Yale Archives; Yale Trustees, Power of Attorney granted to John Read, Apr. 20, 1720, Yale Archives; *Documentary History*, p. 214; C.A., Colleges and Schools, 1 : 207a, 208a, 209, 210, 211, 212, 213, 216, 217, 43; ibid., Towns and Lands, 6 : 113, 162, 163. The General Assembly allowed the petition of Henry Green in 1726 and granted him equivalent lands, but when Jonathan Mansfield entered a plea in 1734, several years after the matter had been settled, the court rejected his request for compensation for two hundred acres. See Towns and Lands, 4 : 162; and 6 : 146.

8. James Fitch to Yale Trustees, Sept. 3, 1724, Yale Archives. Fitch was author of the poem about the Cutler defection cited in chapter 4.

9. *Documentary History*, pp. 265, 270, 281, 285.

Books and land provided the school with a library and property, but neither had much to do with the yearly finances of the collegiate school. When it came to paying salaries and meeting expenses, the treasurer had to rely on the annual donation from the Connecticut General Assembly. Without this money the college would not have survived.

Treasurers Alling and Prout

During the school's unsettled years at Killingworth and Saybrook, college finances were minimal and, at the same time, complex. In 1701 the trustees elected Nathaniel Lynde of Saybrook college treasurer, deputizing him "to ask, demand, sue for, recover & receiv for our use in the Service of said School all donations, bequests, annuities whatsoever that are or shall be bestowed on us as Trustees for the use of said School." [10] After first accepting the election, Lynde then declined it, and the trustees chose in his stead Richard Rosewel of New Haven, who accepted the post but died the next spring. These events might have boded ill for the collegiate school's finances, but the trustees chose to ignore such signs and kept looking for a treasurer. On April 8, 1702, they found one, John Alling, a New Haven merchant; he accepted, and lived and served for fifteen years.[11]

Alling's duties, as spelled out in the charge to Lynde, were simple. He was to obtain and hold all college monies and disburse them at the direction of the trustees. In September, 1702, the trustees expanded his duties to permit him to "put out into safe hands upon Good Security the Several Donations That are or shall Be made to said School as may be profitable to the same." [12]

Since the college met in Killingworth, Alling's sole spending responsibility was to pay the rector and tutors. Because Pierson

10. Ibid., pp. 34, 35. There were undoubtedly private donations to the college but few records of them survive. The will of Samuel Jones of Saybrook, dated February 20, 1704, gave all of Jones's corn to his son "in consideration of his discharging my obligation to the Collegiate School in Say Brook" (see Henry C. Jones to Franklin B. Dexter, July 14, 1888, Yale Archives). The will of Nathaniel Boykin of New Haven, dated September 11, 1705, ordered "that my Brother Denison his heirs assignes do pay unto the use of the Colledge Six pounds in provision pay." The college was the only legatee outside of Boykin's family and received the second largest bequest. See "An Early Benefactor of Yale College," Yale University Library *Gazette,* 12 (1938): 58–62.

11. *Documentary History,* pp. 34, 39.

12. Ibid., p. 42.

did not move to Saybrook and because his teaching duties depended on the number of students and the availability of tutors, his salary was never fixed. The treasurer paid Pierson a sum commensurate with the time he expended. The tutor, at first, was allotted £50 a year plus the tuition of the students in his care (30s. a year per student). In 1704 the tutor's salary was lowered to £50, with tuition fees included.[13] Alling, therefore, did not collect tuition from the several undergraduates, and since the college had no collegiate living, the scholars made their own arrangements for room and board in Killingworth. This same arrangement was evidently continued when the college moved to Saybrook.

With the internal finances of the college so simple, Alling's chief job was to collect and utilize any donations to the college. While there were a few private donations, the bulk of the school's operating income came from the General Assembly. The annual colony grant was £120 in "country pay," in other words, items designated each year by the General Assembly as acceptable payments for taxes. The prices of these commodities—usually farm products—were set 50 percent higher than New England currency. The college's annual grant, therefore, was worth £80 in money.[14] John Alling's responsibility was to convert the country pay to cash.

13. Ibid., pp. 41, 46. The treasurer's records for this period are difficult to decipher. Alling did not keep an ordered yearly account of income and expenditures and probably carried much information in his head. According to his ledger, the payment of tutors' salaries was erratic. Tutor Phineas Fiske, for example, received payments of £12.8.6 in 1705, £33.10.9 in 1706, £35.7.9 in 1707, £17.19.10 in 1708, and £86.3.6 in 1709. His total earnings for eight salaried years, however, was £392.16.10 or an average annual wage of nearly £50. Tutor Joseph Noyes also received an annual salary that averaged to £50 over five years, but his wages varied from £4.4.6 in 1711–12 to £67.10.0 in 1713–14. Thus, while payments were inconsistent, they did average out to the £50 stipulated by the trustees in 1702 and 1704. See Yale College Treasury Book, 1701–1828, Yale Archives.

14. Henry Bronson, "A Historical Account of Connecticut Currency, Continental Money, and the Finances of the Revolution," Papers of the New Haven Historical Society, 1 (1865): 23. The country pay rates were established whenever the assembly set a tax. In 1701, for instance, the court set a tax of 2½d. on the pound "to be paid in wheat, pease, Indian corn, rye and pork; winter wheat at five shillings per bushell, pease and rye at three shillings per bushell, Indian corne at two shillings and sixe pence per bushell, porke at three pounds 10 shillings per barrell; all the grain to be good and merchantable, the pork to be repackt by a sworn packer, and marked with his mark, and if any will pay their proportions or part thereof in money it shall be accepted at two thirds. It is also ordered that no person shall pay above one third part of his rate in rye" (see *Conn. Records,* 4 : 360–61). Bron-

The General Assembly, in granting the annuity, had stipulated that the sum was to be "raised & Paid in such ways & manners & att such a value as the Country Rates of said Colony are & have been usually raised & Paid." The usual manner of raising and paying rates in Connecticut was through the local constables. According to a General Assembly enactment of 1703, the colony employed "listers" who appraised the rateable estates of Connecticut every August. The assembly declared a tax annually, at this time usually two-and-a-half pennies on the pound, which the citizens were to pay to the constables in certain items designated as country pay—wheat, peas, Indian corn, rye, pork, and beef. The tax was computed on the country pay value, but if an individual chose to pay his rates in money he received a one-third reduction. The assembly ordered the constables to keep the specie brought to them (not to convert it to either money or country pay) and to use it "for the service of the countrey and for payment of the countrey debts [the colony's financial disbursements]." [15] The college, therefore, received the colony's annuity from the constables. After collecting taxes, the constables would pay the colony's grant to the collegiate school by transferring a certain amount of country pay items to Treasurer Alling. Prior to 1710, when the colony stopped country pay payments, the college received allotments from the various constables. In 1703, for example, Alling recorded:

Received of the Constable of Wallingford in
grain sent to Boston per Mr atwater: ——24-16-9

. . .

new haven constable 92 bush ½ indian corn
at the ware House 13-17-6 [16]

Having received the products, Alling then had to arrange for their sale. He paid men to measure the grain and to transport it

son gave an example of the country pay-money ratio in a 1705 New Haven inventory which read: "money, £4.16.1, in pay £7.4.1½." To convert pay and money to sterling, one would deduct one-fifth of the New England money price. For example, £200 sterling converted to £250 New England money, which converted to £375 country pay. By 1718 the New England money price seems to have been figured at double the sterling value.

15. *Documentary History,* p. 22; *Conn. Records,* 4 : 439–40.

16. Yale College Treasury Book, 1701–1828, p. 31 (left-hand pagination), Yale Archives. Pages 1–37 contain data for this period. Pagination is erratic throughout.

to the wharf. In readying the products for shipment, some amounts invariably were lost and Alling had to compute the cost of this "shrinking of measure." The loss of two-and-a-half bushels of corn out of an original consignment of ninety-two-and-a-half bushels, for instance, cost the college 7s. 6d. The final stage in the transaction was to send the goods to a market—usually Boston—for sale. Only after this sale was made did Alling know how much money the college had earned. A 1703 shipment of "122 & a half of indian corn & thirty one bushels of wheat & four bushel & three pecks Rye sent to boston by Mr Rich Hall" brought the college a cash return of £15.4.0.[17]

In addition to using the services of Messers. Atwater and Hall, Treasurer Alling also sent goods to Boston by way of Enos Talmadge and Francis Browne. Browne made several trips a year in his sloop the *Speedwell,* sailing from New Haven and usually making a stop at either Saybrook or New London; the one-way voyage normally took seven to nine days. Since Browne's account book for these voyages still survives, it is possible to piece together an approximate idea of how this procedure worked. Browne received an allotment of goods from Alling which he then transported to Boston and sold through the agency of John Dixwell. Dixwell, son of one of the three judges who had sentenced King Charles I to die in 1648, was a native of New Haven who had settled in Boston around 1707 and soon "became a merchant in good and flourishing circumstances." [18] In 1708 Dixwell married Mary Prout of New Haven (whose brother became college treasurer in 1717), and in 1710 he sailed for England in an attempt to lay partial claim to the family estate. While in London, Dixwell seems to have assisted James Pierpont in initiating a search for donations for the collegiate school.

In Boston, Dixwell's job was more prosaic. He acted as the college's agent, selling its produce and either lending out money or purchasing supplies with the proceeds. Browne kept records of how the college money was used, and his accounting shows that either he or Dixwell "laid out" the cash, or else he returned to New Haven with money and/or supplies. On almost every voyage, Browne came back with some items for Treasurer Alling; these included such things as seventeen yards of crepe (perhaps for com-

17. Ibid.
18. Stiles, *Three Judges,* pp. 149–50.

mencement gowns?), various quantities of rum and green wine, and smaller objects like a brass skillet, a pewter basin, and a steel candlestick.[19] Although some of these items might have been designed for the collegiate school, it may be that Alling resold them and used the profits either to pay the college's bills or to lend out on the college's behalf.

This last activity was a fairly frequent one in the college's early years. Since Alling rarely spent the colony annuity, he took what was left over and put it "out into safe hands upon Good Security." This moneylending activity enriched the college treasury. In 1707, for example, Alling recorded loans to three men of six, eight, and five pounds. Between 1709 and 1717 the treasurer received the return of this money plus interest. In 1717, for instance, he noted: "To so much Received of Ephraim Morris for the Interest of Six Pounds 2 years & 5 months—00 17 3." During his tenure as treasurer, Alling recorded interest payments of at least £57.7.1.[20]

Although the collegiate school's early financial status was satisfactory, the trustees' complaints of lack of funds were not mere rhetoric. The college was able to subsist on the colony's yearly grant, but it subsisted without a resident rector or a college building. Even Alling's lending activities could not pay for those necessities. Matters changed somewhat in 1709 when Connecticut decided to emit bills of credit to help pay for the expenses of the War of the Spanish Succession. In 1710 the colony disallowed country pay as a medium of public exchange and began paying the college annuity in bills of credit. In both 1711 and 1712 the college received grants of £80 in bills (comparable to the old country pay rate of £120). In 1713, with the costly War of the Spanish Succession over, the government raised the annuity to £100.[21] It remained at this level until 1755.

19. Francis Browne, Account Book, 1706–16, Yale Archives. The book is not paginated so the college entries can be found by date only: Apr. 6, 1707, Sept. 16, 1707, Apr. 10, 1708, June 18, 1708, Oct. 14, 1708, and Sept. 20, 1709. The need for Browne's services abated in 1710 when the colony discontinued country pay as a medium of public exchange.

20. Yale College Treasury Book, pp. 28 and reverse, 6, 2a, 2b, 3–37 passim, Yale Archives.

21. C.A., Finances, vol. 1: Treasurer's Accounts 1709–36, Audits, pp. 34, 50, 52. The colony annuity was not as steady a source of income as might be imagined. Colony Treasurer John Whiting was not above doctoring the books, and when he died bankrupt in 1717 he owed the colony £2,060. While treasurer, he had failed to pay the college one of its annual grants. This oversight or deliberate omission

The annuity was adequate for the Saybrook college's limited needs but insufficient for extraordinary expenditures. When the trustees informed the assembly in 1714 and 1715 that the college needed additional funds for a building, the court responded by ordering a brief (public subscription) to be conducted in the colony. The proposed subscription was never held, as an upper house amendment of a £100 assembly grant caused the lower house to veto the bill. The court favored some aid to the school, however, and in October, 1715 it ordered that 105,793 acres of land be sold and that the trustees be granted £500 out of the proceeds.[22] The sale was made and in October, 1716 the trustees received the money. Because of the troubles attending the college's removal to New Haven, it was all they got. The lower house, angered by its inability to control college affairs, voted in 1717 to grant no additional funds to the trustees until the school had been located in a satisfactory place. With the £100 annuity divided among the tutors at Wethersfield, Saybrook, and New Haven, the trustees could not count on additional government money to pay for the college house.

Treasurer Alling died in late 1716. He had managed the college finances well and, according to the later figures of Rector Thomas Clap, had left the treasury with a surplus of approximately £250. In April, 1717 the trustees chose as his successor John Prout, Jr. (Y. 1708) of New Haven, who had been acting as unofficial treasurer since February 7.[23] Prout accepted the appointment, beginning a service as treasurer that was to last until his retirement in 1765.

Prout took over from Alling at a time of great financial activity. The trustees were committed to their plan to build a college house in New Haven and had received government and private

was rectified in 1719. See Bushman, *From Puritan to Yankee*, p. 138; C.A., Finances, vol. 1: Treasurer's Accounts, 1709–36, Audits, p. 171.

22. *Documentary History*, pp. 60–62, 63. William Pitkin, who was in charge of the transaction, sold the land for £683 in April, 1716. The lower house was dissatisfied with this price and called upon Pitkin to justify his actions. He appeared before the assembly in October, 1716, at which time the upper house insisted that Pitkin had faithfully discharged his trust; the lower house took no action either for or against him. See *Conn. Records*, 5 : 529.

23. *Yale Annals*, p. 96; *Documentary History*, p. 94; Samuel Russell to John Prout, Jr., Feb. 7, 1717, Yale Archives. Prout was a merchant in New Haven and held some public offices during his career.

donations for the task. The private bequests were the result of an appeal circulated in 1716 by Trustees Andrew, Russell, and Ruggles and five other ministers for funds to help locate the college in New Haven. Subscription lists were circulated in various New Haven County towns, with individuals pledging to give their donations to the college within one year of its settlement in New Haven. The donations ranged from 10s. from Samuel Clark, Sr. and £3 in work from Thomas Sperry to forty acres of land from several New Haven gentlemen and £100 from Jahleel Brinton, Esq., who lived in Rhode Island. While not all of the subscription lists have survived, the total of these gifts was declared at the time to be in excess of £1,500.[24]

Added to the colony's £500 grant, the New Haven donations enabled the seaside trustees to commence building the college house in October, 1717.[25] But construction costs exceeded contributions and by 1718 the trustees did not have the money to complete the building. They were rescued from this embarrassing position by Governor Elihu Yale. Yale's gifts to the Connecticut collegiate school arrived in New England in the summer of 1718 and in New Haven the following October. Although the goods were not all sold immediately, the prospect of the potential income was enough to encourage the trustees to complete the college house and name it after the old governor. When sold, the materials brought the college about £800, a substantial but hardly overwhelming sum. Governor Yale, it seems, won immortality more for the timeliness than for the munificence of his gift.[26]

The final sale of the Yale donation was not made until 1721, at which time a second shipment of goods arrived from England. The trunks of muslin, calico, Spanish poplins, black and white

24. *Documentary History,* pp. 68–70; Yale College Treasury Book, pp. 3a, 3b, Yale Archives. Brinton, of Newport, Rhode Island, gave the money to one of the Hartford representatives to the General Assembly and asked him to deliver it to the trustees in New Haven at the time of the court meeting. As the Hartford delegates had been courting Brinton to give the money to help settle the school in the upriver town, this maneuver was a blow to Hartford's hopes. See *Documentary History* (Johnson's "Remarks"), pp. 159, 152–53.

25. For a discussion of the architectural dimensions of "Yale College," see Norman M. Isham, "The Original College House at Yale," pp. 114–20.

26. Still, Elihu Yale was the greatest contributor to the college for over a century. He was superceded in 1837 by Dr. Alfred E. Perkins, who willed the college ten thousand dollars for the library. See Franklin B. Dexter, "Governor Elihu Yale," *Miscellaneous Historical Papers,* p. 97. For more on Yale's gifts, see chapters 2 and 3.

silk crepe, camlett, and stufe (worsted goods) brought the college £562.12.0.[27] The trustees hoped for more gifts from Elihu Yale and were pleased by Jeremiah Dummer's report that he had elicited a promise from Yale that he would give the Connecticut college £200 sterling a year during his lifetime and would arrange for a settled annual provision after his death. "But," Dummer lamented to Governor Saltonstall, "old Gentlemen are forgetfull." The agent had visited with Yale on several occasions in an effort to speed matters along but had been unsuccessful. In March, 1721, Dummer wrote that he was afraid Yale might die before making out a new will and urged the trustees to continue writing to the old governor.[28]

Dummer's warning came too late. Elihu Yale died on July 8, 1721, in his house in London. The governor's will was imperfect and his sons-in-law were able to protract its probate over several years. Agent Dummer dutifully attended the court proceedings, arguing the college's case. At first he thought the legacy to Yale College had a good chance of standing, but his reports to the trustees grew steadily more pessimistic. Finally, the legacy was defeated. Dummer suspected that the college lost the suit "by the vile decree of the Dean of the Arches, who, I verily beleive was corrupted." But the bribery charge could not be proven, and since an appeal would be too expensive, the agent advised the trustees to drop the matter.[29] Yale College had heard the last of its first great benefactor.

Elihu Yale's gifts had enabled the college to complete the building in New Haven, but the school had other needs, primarily a house for Rector Cutler. Timothy Cutler had assumed the Yale rectorship in 1719 at an annual salary of £140. The trustees had made an agreeable settlement with Cutler's Stratford parishioners, had paid the rector £190 for his old home and home lot, and had agreed to lodge him and his family in New Haven until a rector's house was built.[30] In 1719 the General Assembly aided both

27. *Documentary History,* pp. 216–18. Rector Cutler wrote Trustee Timothy Woodbridge about the sale of the Yale gift and discussed the relative merits of selling the goods in Boston or Connecticut. Cutler did not want news of the gift to spread for fear that it might "totally hinder the Good Effects of the Brief" for a rector's house. See ibid., pp. 219–20.

28. Ibid., pp. 209, 212.

29. Ibid., pp. 237, 241, 242, 244, 257.

30. Ibid., pp. 200–01, 203. Seven years later the Old Society in Stratford petitioned the General Assembly that it had been promised aid after it lost Cutler to Yale

Cutler and Yale by freeing the rector from all taxes and by ordering that a committee be empowered to sell colony lands up to the amount of £300 in order to provide Yale with an additional £40 a year for seven years. A year and a half later the assembly ordered that the committee complete the sale of land and pay the rest of the £300 to the college outright. In May, 1721, the court again acted to help the college and called for a colony-wide brief to be held in July to raise money for the rector's house.[31] The brief netted about £100 and in October, 1721, as a further encouragement to the college, the assembly decreed that the impost on rum for the next two years was to go toward building a rector's house at Yale. The impost enhanced the college treasury by almost £230.[32]

This rash of colony-sponsored measures gave the trustees enough money to erect Cutler's home. They again employed Henry Caner as the builder, and by September, 1722 he had nearly completed a structure forty-four-and-a-half feet long, thirty-eight feet wide, and eighteen feet to the studs. The building and an adjacent barn cost approximately £600.[33] However, Timothy Cutler never resided in the house. After his defection and dismissal it, too, stood without a resident rector for four years.

The years 1717–22 were busy ones for Treasurer Prout. He had to keep track of private and government donations and pay for

but had not been recompensed fully. The request for money to alleviate the society's suffering was turned down by both houses. See C.A., Ecclesiastical Affairs, 3 : 19.

31. *Documentary History,* p. 199; *Conn. Records,* 6 : 125–26, 130, 214–15, 256, 260; *Documentary History,* pp. 214–16. One amusing aspect of the 1721 brief was the report that one Jonathan Hill of New London had told his fellow townsmen that the assembly had *not* ordered a subscription. The Governor's Council charged Hill with a misdemeanor and ordered him arrested. He was acquitted by a jury in September, 1722 (see *Conn. Records,* 6 : 267–68). The brief was held in New London without incident. Joshua Hempstead recorded in his diary for July 23, 1721: "a Contribution to build a house for the Rector of Yale Colledge. a very Small one." See *The Diary of Joshua Hempstead,* p. 111.

32. *Documentary History,* pp. 221, 220–21; *Yale Annals,* p. 96.

33. *Documentary History,* p. 223. The treasurer's records for this period are not extant and it is difficult to tell the exact income and expenditures for the rector's house. Gurdon Saltonstall claimed that the colony brief netted about £100, but Thomas Clap, writing at a later time, thought that it only brought in £35 sterling, or £70 in money. Clap's figures for this entire monetary matter stated that the brief earned £70, donations £110, the rum impost £230, and the sale of land £240, for a total of £650. Clap estimated that the cost of the rector's house was £520 (all figures translated to New England money). See *Yale Annals,* pp. 95, 96.

two major pieces of construction. But the influx of money had not made Yale College wealthy by any means. Much of the treasurer's time was spent tracking down delinquent contributors and, by order of the trustees, prosecuting errant donors in court if necessary. Even Governor Saltonstall helped out in this endeavor, writing to one George Lucas of Antigua in 1722 to remind him that he had, when living in Hartford, pledged the college £20-worth of corn. Saltonstall said the college needed the money and that Lucas could send his contribution to any Connecticut port.[34] But there is no indication that Lucas ever heeded the governor's plea.

College Costs

The completion of the rector's house in 1722 marked the end of a period of extraordinary expenditures by the college. Yale's New Haven settlement and the rectorship of Elisha Williams imposed a normality on both the college routine and college finances. Yale's need for money had not diminished, but the sources and disbursements of college funds became more orderly. Yale now had collegiate living, which meant that the students paid room rent. The steward and butler provided commons and sizings, for which undergraduates paid a price. Treasurer Prout collected tuition himself and gave the tutors and rector fixed salaries. The colony annuity of £100 became an accepted part of Yale's financial picture, and even the success of the trustees' annual appeals for additional funds took on a pleasing regularity.

At their meeting on September 9, 1719, the trustees established undergraduate fees for the reunited college. They set tuition at 30s. per year and stipulated that all nonresident scholars were to pay an annual fee of 20s. All students, except those with special permission, were to reside at the college and pay a yearly rental of 20s. Board cost 5s. per week, although affluent students could pay more and eat better; there was no set fee for sizings in the buttery, each student paying the butler according to his consumption of beer and bread. At commencement, every graduate paid the rector 20s. for his diploma. The graduate also paid a sum for the commencement dinner, although the cost was not set until 1727 when the dinner was priced at 20s. While it is difficult to reconcile

34. *Documentary History,* p. 223; Pub. C.S.M., 6 (1904): 193–94. See *Conn. Records,* 6 : 325, 337. There is no evidence that Prout ever took a donor to court.

these fees with the cost of tuition, it is probable that the diploma and dinner expenses reflected the overall cost of the graduation exercises and also constituted a way for the college to gain a little extra income. The trustees altered some fees during the interregnum period; tuition was raised to 40s. in 1726, and board was lowered to 4s. 4d. in 1721 and raised to 4s. 8d. in 1724, obviously reflecting a fluctuation in food costs.[35]

Shortly after Elisha Williams assumed the rectorship, the trustees revised college costs. In 1727 they raised tuition to 50s., board to the 1719 level of 5s. per week, and set room rent at 5s. per quarter for an upper chamber and 7s. 6d. per quarter for all other rooms. A detriment of 5s. per quarter was required of all students who boarded out of the college. During Williams's tenure, the trustees raised all fees except room rent. They increased board to 6s. a week in 1730, the commencement dinner and diploma to 30s. each in 1736, and tuition to 60s. in 1737.[36] Throughout this entire period an undergraduate also paid 2s. a year for his seat in the New Haven church.

During the course of an academic year, then, a Yale student paid four required fees—tuition, room rent, board, and the seating money. According to the established costs, a student in 1720 would have paid a minimum of £15.12.0 a year, with the addition of £2 if he graduated. In 1728 a student would have paid £16.17.0 plus £2 at commencement, and in 1737, £19.19.0 and £3 at graduation. The few surviving quarter bills indicate, however, that the average undergraduate spent more than the set fees. In the second quarter of 1728–29, for example, the average payment was approximately £5.12.0 per student, and in the third quarter the average was £5.16.0. Commons and buttery expenses were responsible for the inflated bills; David Rowland (Y. 1732) spent £11.1.2 in the buttery and £14.10.0 in all during the second quarter, and Ebenezer Devotion (Y. 1732) spent a total of £11.19.10 in the third quarter. While some students spent nothing in either commons or the buttery, there were enough spendthrifts to raise the average.[37]

35. *Documentary History,* pp. 195, 197, 268, 267, 213, 256.

36. Ibid., pp. 268–69, 286, 320, 325.

37. Quarter bills, Dec.–Mar., 1728–1729, Mar.–June, 1729, Yale Archives. Figures rounded off to the shilling. Yale has five quarter bills for this period: Sept.–Dec., 1727; Dec.–Mar., 1728–1729; Mar.–June, 1729; June–Sept., 1732; Sept.–Dec., 1733.

Taking the two 1728–29 quarter bills as a base, the average student in that academic year would have spent £22.16.0, almost £6 more than the set fees. Using the same base, a student would have spent £91.4.0 at Yale over a four-year course, plus the £2 at commencement. These figures are supported by the testimony of the father of John Browne (Y. 1728), who stated that he spent £100 on John's college education.[38] This was a substantial sum but does not seem to have excluded less wealthy boys from attending the college, for most students were the sons of farmers and artisans. The trustees deliberately kept college costs low and relied on the General Assembly for money to sustain the school. Yale, however, did educate some boys who were relatively impoverished. Joseph Adams (Y. 1740) was not only in arrears to the steward during his sophomore year but also had a depleted and dilapidated wardrobe. "I am affraid I must come home before Commincement for want of close," he wrote his father,

> I having none sent me have wore these raigged & shant have none but ragged close to ware at Commencement and shall be asshamed to be here then, unles I have some from home, I have sent for a hat by Hatheway, for mine wore threw the Crown, all which I hope you will provide for me, & send them by Hatheway.[39]

Presumably, few students were in such dire financial straits as this, and most could pay for both college costs and commencement clothes.

All student charges, except commencement fees, were collected quarterly. The steward was responsible for receiving the student's money and turning it over to the treasurer. The treasurer would then take out the college's due—tuition, room rent, punishment assessments, glass breakage costs, and the fee for a seat in the New Haven church—and return the commons and buttery money to the steward. This procedure continued until at least May, 1732, at which time the quarter bills contained only those items paid to the treasurer; all commons and buttery costs were paid directly to the steward or butler. Treasurer Prout, therefore, never counted commons and sizing costs in his annual reports. The only

38. *Yale Graduates,* 1 : 368.
39. Joseph Adams to Abraham Adams, July 20, 1738, Yale Archives.

constant sources of income from students were tuition and room rent; in 1726–27 the college earned £163.0.0 from these sources and in 1738–39, the most profitable year, £369.18.3.[40]

In addition to the tuition and room rent, the treasurer also collected punishment and glass breakage charges. Yale College made money only on the former. In 1701, and periodically thereafter, the trustees established monetary penalties, to be assessed by the rector and tutors, for certain undergraduate offenses. Any student absenting himself from study periods could be amerced 6d., for missing Sunday worship 8d. and daily prayer 2d.; cutting classes cost the delinquent scholar 4d. Noting absences from services was the monitor's job; a boy's teacher kept track of his missed classes. The maximum monetary penalty for a crime in the college was 5s.; bringing a pack of cards to school earned this fine, while playing cards only cost a student 3s. Although the total punishment income rarely exceeded 35s. per quarter, it was collected from about one-third of the student body. In 1729 one rambunctious undergraduate, William Partridge (Y. 1729), accounted for one-fifth of the total punishment income for the third quarter by drawing fines totaling 7s.[41]

The fines for glass breakage, which were noted down by the scholar of the house, were not really income, as Treasurer Prout had to spend the money to replace the shattered panes. Breaking windows was a favorite undergraduate pastime. In the summer of 1732, sixty-nine out of eighty-two students paid fines for this offense. One particularly mischievous student, Jonathan Hunting (Y. 1735), paid 13s. 3d. for breakage, and the total of all fines was £11.18.2.[42] The rate of glass breakage declined considerably in the winter months, perhaps indicating that creature comfort often took precedence over the urge to destroy.

After the treasurer, the most important financial officer in the college was the steward. He was responsible for collecting all quarter bills as well as for providing commons for the students, sweeping the chambers and halls daily, and making the scholars'

40. *Documentary History,* pp. 201–02; quarter bill, June–Sept., 1732, Yale Archives; *Documentary History,* pp. 272–73, 334–36.

41. Ibid., pp. 47, 238, 309; quarter bill, Mar.–June, 1729, Yale Archives.

42. Quarter bill, June–Sept., 1732, Yale Archives.

beds.[43] He collected and kept the money paid by the students for commons and buttery sizings. Neither the minutes of trustee meetings nor the surviving quarter bills indicate the steward's profit in this transaction. Food costs were easily the most expensive item in a student's budget, and some gluttonous undergraduates spent five, eight, or even eleven pounds a quarter in the buttery alone.[44]

From 1718 through 1740 the Yale trustees hired five different stewards. Captain John Munson was the first to hold the job, serving from 1718 to 1721. Munson's years in office were unhappy ones; although a committee of trustees met with him annually to work out the terms of feeding the students for the following year, Munson was barely able to make ends meet. In April, 1720, the students complained of the fare in commons and, when Munson failed to obey a trustee directive to hire a cook, the trustees hired

43. *Documentary History,* p. 268. In 1741 the trustees described the fare the steward was to provide the students in commons: "For Breakfast One Loaf of Bread for 4, which (the Dough) Shall weigh one Pound. For Dinner for 4 One Loaf of Bread as aforesaid; 2½ pounds of Beef, Veal or Mutton or 1¾ pounds of Salt Pork about twice a Week in the Summer Time; one Quart of Beer; 2 penny Worth of Sauce. For Supper for 4. 2 Quarts of Milk & one Loaf of Bread, when Milk can conveniently be had, and when it cannot then an Apple-Pye which shall be made of 1¾ lb Dough, ¼ lb Hogs fat, 2 oz Sugar & ½ peck of Apples" (see ibid., p. 351). In 1733 the trustees stipulated that every barrel of beer delivered to the butler "shall be made of Half a Bushell of good Barley Malt after it is ground or a Bushell of good Oat Malt after it is ground or a peck of good Barley Malt after it is ground and a Quart of good Molosses or half a Bushell of good Oat Malt after it is ground & a quart of good Molosses & be mash't and well brewed & hopped" (see ibid., p. 304).

44. Quarter bills, Sept.–Dec., 1727, Dec.–Mar., 1728–1729, Mar.–June, 1729, Yale Archives. Commons and buttery income is available for these three quarters only. In 1727 the steward recorded payments of £53.18.1 in commons and £3.16.2 in the buttery. This last figure bears no relation to the expenses of the undergraduates, for a computation of the buttery payments of sixty students shows that a total of £67.7.4 was spent. The £3 figure, therefore, must refer to outstanding bills or to the surplus. In 1728–29 the commons's income was £112.16.5 and the buttery's £208.2.10 (with a written figure of £10.19.2). In 1729 commons's was £151.18.5 and the buttery's £184.7.8 (£9.7.2 outstanding). In all three bills the commons total equaled the computation of all student expenses. Individual students spent varying amounts in commons and the buttery; some scholars spent as much as £5.17.7 in commons and £8.0.2 or even £11.1.2 in the buttery. Other undergraduates spent as little as a few shillings, and some spent nothing at all. Obviously a student could spend as little or as much as he wanted on food. In 1737 the trustees ordered that, due to the rise in meat prices, the steward could collect additional money from every student who ate in commons: 6d. per week for the third quarter, 1d. per week for the second quarter, and 2d. per week for the fourth quarter. See *Documentary History,* pp. 323–24.

one themselves, deducting her wages from Munson's bill.[45] Widow Beacher's culinary skills were not sufficient to quiet the students, however, and in early 1721 the undergraduates declared a food strike. While Rector Cutler was able to restore order and return the scholars to commons, the daily meals evidently got no better —Jonathan Edwards reported to his father that the students had resorted to stealing hens, geese, turkeys, pigs, and meat! A few months later the trustees dismissed Munson and hired in his stead John Punderson. Munson had not only failed to provide an adequate diet for the students but had lost money as well. In April, 1722, he appealed to the trustees for some reimbursement for the losses he had sustained while serving as steward. A year later the trustees awarded him ten pounds "on Account of his Complaint of extraordinary Difficulties in his serving the College in its Beginning Times." [46]

John Punderson fared no better than Munson. Four years after he took over the job, Punderson asked for and received ten pounds "towards the repairing of his Losses in former Years." Punderson left the stewardship in 1728 without the pressure of student discontent with commons, but his successor, Daniel Edwards, was not so lucky. In 1733 the students complained "of the Insufficiency and Faultiness of their Commons and Sizings" and the trustees held a meeting to deal with the matter. The outcome was unfavorable to Steward Edwards, for the trustees dismissed him the following year.[47] Samuel Cooke was chosen as Edwards's replacement and he served the college for five years without incident. Upon his resignation, Aaron Day took the job.

Stewards Edwards and Cooke may have had more financial success than Munson and Punderson: there is no record of either of them asking the trustees for money. But their solvency depended, in large part, on annual advances from Treasurer Prout. Between 1727 and 1738 Prout recorded payments to the stewards of from £34 to £72 a year. Whether this money was an advance to cover costs or a compensation for losses is not clear, but it was most likely the former. In 1741 the trustees appointed a committee to set the price of commons and agreed to "allow the Steward 50 per Cent. Advance for his Care & Trouble." The 1741 provision un-

45. *Documentary History,* pp. 173, 197, 201, 204. Mrs. Beacher was instructed to provide the scholars with fresh meat three times a week throughout the summer.

46. Ibid., pp. 210–11, 224, 245.

47. Ibid., pp. 256, 304–05, 308–09.

doubtedly made explicit a long-standing practice. In 1732 the trustees allotted the steward extra money to compensate for the increased cost of wheat and in 1737 they raised his allotment to offset the rise in meat prices.[48]

The college was also plagued by the inability or failure of some students to pay their quarter bills. Since students themselves paid most of their food bills, the steward probably suffered the most. To rectify this problem the trustees, in 1738, stipulated that

> no Person for the time to come be admitted an undergraduate in this College, untill his Father or Guardian or some proper Person hath given a Sufficient Bond unto the Steward of Said College to pay the Quarter Bills of the said Schollar allowed by the Authority of the College from time to time as long as he shall continue a Member of Said College.

If any student failed to provide security, the steward was instructed to tell the rector and tutors, who could expel the student from college.[49] There is no telling how many boys were affected by this new regulation, but at least one undergraduate felt its impact immediately. Joseph Adams (Y. 1740), who wrote to his father for a new hat and decent clothes, also pleaded for money:

> I have right to you & told you what money I want & the perticulars for which I want it but I shant tell here but tell you when I come home, I cannot do without 26 £ and pray send it by Hatheway or Mr Coock wil go to the trustees at Commincement and complain, it will be about 20 £ to him & six to others.[50]

As Adams stayed at Yale and earned his degree it is probable that his father sent him the needed money. The 1738 provision, however, did not protect the steward from all delinquent students. In 1739 the trustees had to reimburse the steward £6.14.2 for one Timothy Allen, who had not paid his bills.[51] The records do not indicate if Allen was penalized for this financial failure.

48. [John Prout], Treasurer's Accounts, 1727–38, Yale Archives; *Documentary History*, pp. 351, 297, 323–24.

49. *Documentary History*, p. 327.

50. Adams to Abraham Adams, July 20, 1738, Yale Archives.

51. *Documentary History*, p. 333. Part of the steward's problem may have been the fact that students ate in commons irregularly, thereby upsetting his projected expenses. In 1743 the trustees "Voted That all undergraduate living in College shall be in Commons." See ibid., p. 362.

Subsidizing the steward in these ways cost the college money, but Treasurer Prout recouped a part of that expense by collecting that portion of the graduates' commencement dinner fee which the steward did not spend. This amount ranged from £8.15.0 in 1734 to £47.7.3 in 1730. In every year except 1737, however, the allotment to the steward exceeded the income from the dinner money. The treasury also received, beginning in 1734, £8 a year from the butler as payment for the extra beer and bread he was allowed to take from commons.[52]

Public Support

Yale College, then, had four constant sources of income: the quarter bills (mainly tuition and room rent), the colony's £100 annuity, the dinner money, and the butler's payment. College expenditures, on the other hand, were more varied. All college officers except the butler and the steward received annual wages. Rector Williams's salary rose from £140 in 1726–27 to £300 in 1729–30 and remained at that level, with some special additions in 1737–38, for the duration of his tenure.[53] The tutors earned £65 a year, the senior tutor receiving an extra £5 for being the librarian. These salaries fluctuated, however, as occasionally one tutor would undertake additional responsibilities when his colleague was ill or absent. In 1738–39 the tutors' wages were raised to £80. The monitor and the scholar of the house, two student officers who were supposed to keep track of the absences and indiscretions of their peers, each received a yearly stipend of £3; the treasurer earned a salary of £8. Of the other disbursements, the most numerous were to local laborers for repairing the college house, the rector's home, or the school's wells and pumps. These costs ranged from a mere 7s. to a substantial £61.10.0.[54]

52. Treasurer's Accounts, 1727–38, Yale Archives; *Documentary History*, pp. 334–36, 304. The butler did not lose money, as the steward was ordered to pay him eight pounds a year for serving the bread and beer.

53. Treasurer's Accounts, 1727–38, Yale Archives. The rector also collected the diploma fee from all candidates for both the first and second degrees. The fee was raised from 20s. to 30s. in 1736 (see *Documentary History*, p. 320). For the rector's salary, see ibid., pp. 272, 277–78, 281, 286, 290, 296, 305, 311, 313, 318, 324, 327, 335.

54. Treasurer's Accounts, 1727–38, Yale Archives. For the tutors' salaries, see

The net result of this financial picture was a bleak one for Treasurer Prout. From 1726 to 1739 expenditures ranged from an admittedly curtailed budget of £315.16.4 in 1726–27 to a substantial £701.9.6 in 1737–38. Disbursements usually exceeded income by more than £100 every year. The trustees were well aware of this constant disparity and year after year they turned to the Connecticut General Assembly for help.

The assembly's yearly grants had aided the collegiate school since its founding. At several times the colony had bestowed substantial sums of extra money on the college—in 1716 for the college house and in 1721 for the rector's house. During the interregnum period Yale operated on a somewhat reduced budget and was able to meet its expenses. The settlement of Elisha Williams in the rectorship marked the beginning of annual deficits in the college treasury. The colony had helped the college settle Williams by freeing Newington from taxes for four years and by granting the trustees £100.16.0 to reimburse the parish for the loss of its minister.[55] But these gifts were not sufficient to make Yale solvent and the college soon appealed for aid.

In October, 1727, the trustees informed the assembly that expenses exceeded receipts by £52.16.4 and that the college needed an extra £185 for additions to the rector's salary and to pay for another tutor. Noting that "the usuall Salary allowed from the publick Treasury with the standing perquesites from the Schollars,

---

Documentary History, pp. 270, 273, 277–78, 281, 286, 290, 296, 305, 311, 313, 318, 324, 327, 334.

55. Elisha Williams hoped for some personal help from the assembly. In October, 1727, he asked that he, like Cutler, be exempt from taxes while serving as Yale rector. The upper house supported this plea but the lower house rejected it. In 1729 Williams renewed the request, stating that he had assumed he would be freed from rates when he accepted the rectorship. Noting that Cutler had been excused from paying taxes, Williams wondered if his service to the college was less acceptable than his predecessor's—a rhetorical question to which Williams knew the answer only too well. The rector claimed to have been disadvantaged in his personal estate by his move to New Haven. Again the lower house vetoed the request. In 1737, however, the General Assembly ordered that all ministers should have their estates in their places of residence freed from taxes and included Rector Williams on the list. The assembly also excluded him, the tutors, and the students from personal taxes. See *Documentary History*, pp. 274–75, 282–84; *Conn. Records*, 8 : 131–33.

is not sufficient to support the Rector, and the necessary Tutorage of the Students, & not being willing to make the Charges of Tuition, and Chamber Rent, unreasonable burthensome, which would prove a means to sink the Credit of our Colledg," the trustees asked for relief. They called upon those legislators who were alumni or fathers of Yale students to "Sympathize with our straitned Circumstances" and grant the college the impost on rum for an indefinite period of time. The petition was granted; a compromise bill allotted Yale the rum duty for the next year. Though the rum impost seems to have been as much a protective as a revenue-producing tariff, Yale did well by this grant.[56] In 1727–28 the college received £222 from the rum impost and showed a healthy surplus, after expenses, of £114.1.5.

The trustees failed to obtain an additional grant from the court in 1728 due to some confusion between the two houses, and the 1727 surplus was almost entirely spent. In 1729 the college renewed its request for funds and the assembly granted it £80 a year for the next two years. In 1730 the trustees again petitioned for aid, asking that the £100 annuity be raised to £250 "by Reason of the sinking Value of Bills of Credit." Like other New England colonies, Connecticut was suffering from inflation and the college felt the squeeze. An ounce of silver was worth 8s. in 1708 but 18s. in 1732.[57] The trustees hoped that the assembly would compensate for this inflation by increasing the colony's grant. The General Court, however, preferred to retain the basic annuity of £100 and only granted the college an additional £100 in bills for each of the next two years, the sum to be paid in four installments of £50 each.

The significant feature of the 1730 petition, however, was its confident assessment of the college's position. The trustees admitted that Yale had languished in the past, but proudly reported that "more lately to the great Satisfaction of Yourselvs, Us & our Country in general it has arrived at & appears in a flourishing State by a full Supply of Officers Academical, vizt: an accomplisht & agreeable Rector, & Worthy Tutors, & a pleasing Increase of Students hopeful for a publick Improvement to the Credit of said

56. *Documentary History*, pp. 271–74; *Conn. Records*, 7 : 133; 5 : 56, 84, 160; 6 : 36, 224, 282, and especially 350–52.

57. Bronson, "Connecticut Currency," pp. 51–52.

Colony." The trustees, then, were not asking for money to get the college going, but for funds to maintain it in a flourishing state. The legislators were receptive to this argument and Yale received the extra allotment from the court for the remainder of Williams's tenure. Although the additional £100 was granted retroactively in 1733, and for a period of three years in 1735 and 1738, Yale College obtained a steady £200 annually throughout Williams's rectorship.[58]

The rector's success in establishing Yale on a firm academic and administrative footing helped to convince the colony government that it should make other donations to the college during these years. In 1732 the trustees, seeking a more permanent endowment than the assembly annuity, asked the court for grants of land in the new townships east of the Housatonic River. The trustees argued that the college would improve the land and eventually derive an income from it, whereas others would only buy the land for speculative purposes. The assembly favored this request and gave the college three hundred acres in each of the five new townships for the school's permanent use. In 1738 the colony gave the trustees forty pounds to defray the cost of surveying and staking out the five college plots.[59] The farms were eventually rented and provided Yale with an annual income, although the trustees did not complete these arrangements until the rectorship of Thomas Clap.

In 1735 the trustees again petitioned the court for extra funds. The college building was in a state of decay and the trustees did not have the money to make the necessary repairs. The college had been paying for building maintenance since at least 1726, but the present damages were beyond the ordinary. The assembly delegated some men to examine the building and they agreed with the trustees' assessment. The college, they reported, was

> much out of Repair And are of Opinion t'will be Best to Mend the Roof and Some Part of the Back Side and End with the Kitchen the Doors and Back Windows, also that the fore

58. *Documentary History,* pp. 287–88; 278–80, 287–88, 302–03, 306–07, 310–12, 314–17, 328–29; *Conn. Records,* 7 : 178, 229, 302, 472, 523; 8 : 24, 203.

59. *Documentary History,* pp. 292–94; *Conn. Records,* 7 : 412–13. For the surveying of the land see *Documentary History,* pp. 319, 329; *Conn. Records,* 8 : 203; C.A., Colleges and Schools, 1 : 249.

> Side of the House and Back Windows be new Coullered, and the fence new Sett the Posts Being Rotten.[60]

The court hired Isaac Dickerman and John Punderson to make the needed repairs to the college, and in 1736–37 the assembly paid them a total of £134.7.0 for material and labor.[61]

The financial history of early Yale reveals a special working relationship between the college and the colony. On the one hand, the trustees had complete charter-sanctioned autonomy to control college affairs and had retained that autonomy in spite of a lower house challenge in 1717–18. On the other hand, the General Assembly, which had no official voice in Yale policy, contributed between one-third and one-half of the college's annual income, helped to settle its rectors, and donated nearly one-fourth of the cost of the college building and almost the entire cost of the rector's house. As their annual petitions to the court indicate, the trustees were well aware "That the Support of the said College is necessarily dependant upon those Supplies which this Honorable Assembly hath been pleased to Grant from time to time." [62] Yale College was, then, a privately controlled but publicly supported school.

This arrangement worked to the satisfaction of both parties. Except during the battle over the school's location in 1717–18, the General Assembly made no attempt to interfere with the college it had helped to create. For their own part, the trustees freely professed that the college had been "erected at first and ever since patronized by" the assembly. Elisha Williams, in addressing the court, referred to his rectorship as *"this Service to which you have seen fit to call me."* [63] This statement was not only an attempt by the rector to make the legislators feel responsible for his financial well-being, but was an accurate reflection of the assembly's understanding of Williams's job. The rector's work, after all, was a service to the colony, for Yale supplied Connecticut pulpits with

60. C.A., Colleges and Schools, 1 : 243a.

61. *Documentary History*, pp. 315–16, 317, 321–22, 330–31; *Conn. Records*, 8 : 15, 75. In painting the college, the workmen used lampblack and white ocher, a combination that gave the building a bluish color.

62. *Documentary History*, p. 310.

63. Ibid., pp. 315, 283.

Elihu Yale (1717), by Enoch Zeeman. Yale University Art Gallery, gift of Dudley Long North, M.P., in 1789.

Timothy Cutler, by Henry Willard. Yale University Art Gallery.

Elisha Williams, by Ruben Moulthrop. Yale University Art Gallery.

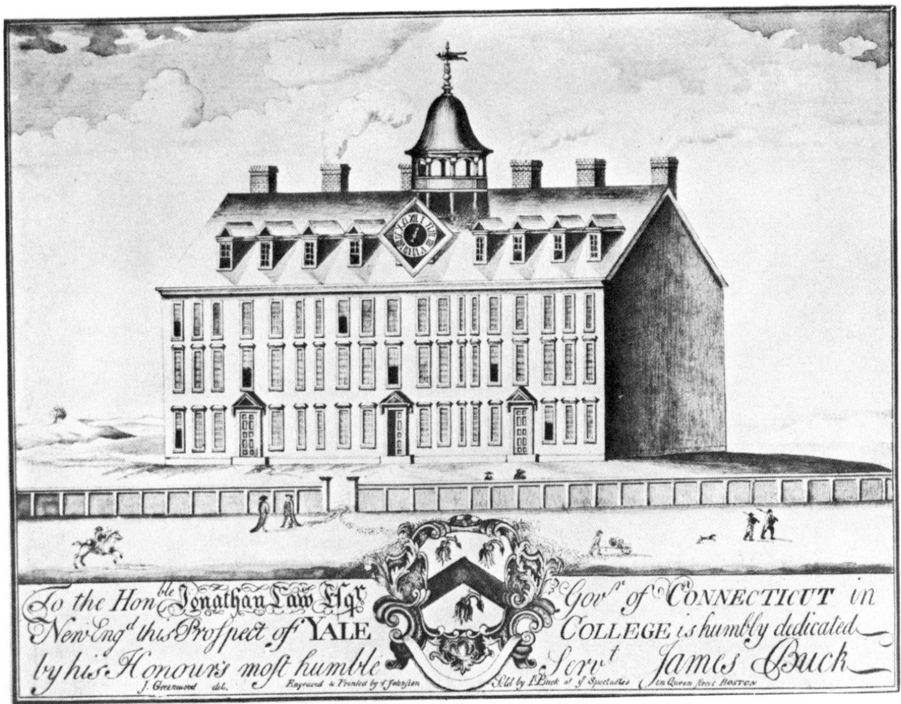

Thomas Johnston's engraving of Yale College, after John Greenwood's design.

HONORATISSIMO
Ac insigni Virtute, Doctrina, et Omnigena Scientia Clarissimo Viro,
D. D. Gurdono Saltonstall, Armigero,
GUBERNATORI Coloniæ Connecticutensis Celeberrimo;
HONORATISSIMOQUE
Nec minus Pietate, Doctrina, et Liberalitate Præclarissimo,
D. D. ELIHU YALE, Londinensi, Armigero,
Mecænati, COLLEGII YALENSIS, in NOVI-PORTO CONNECTICUTENSI, Munificentissimo;
Nec non Perquam Honorando D. NATHAN GOLD, Vice-Gubernatori Coloniæ supradictæ, Armigero;
Una cum Proceribus hujus Politiæ consultissimis et Spectatissimis, Curatoribus Scholæ Academicæ Venerandis & Vigilantissimis, Ecclesiarchis Reverendis, Evangelii Ministris Pietate et Eruditione Conspicuis, Omnibus & Singulis Artium Liberalium Studiosis, et Musarum Alumnis, Universis denique Reipublicæ Literariæ Patronis, et Fautoribus Benignissimis;
THESES hasce jam in Lucem editas, quas, Deo favente, sub Moderamine Reverendi D. SAMUELIS ANDREW, COLLEGII Ejusdem YALENSIS pro Tempore Rectoris, Pro Viribus defendere, conabuntur Juvenes in Artibus Initiati, tam submisse, quam humillime,
D. D. D. Q.

Jacobus Pierpont
Samuel Pierpont
Ebenezer Rossetter
Robertus Treat
Timotheus Collens
Samuel Hopkins
Ebenezer Prime
Daniel Newell.

Theses TECHNOLOGICÆ.

Theses LOGICÆ.

Theses GRAMMATICÆ.

Theses RHETORICÆ.

Theses MATHEMATICÆ.

Theses PHYSICÆ.

His Antecedit Oratio Salutatoria.

Habita in Comitiis NOVI-PORTI CONNECTICUTENSIS, Die Decimo Septembris. MDCCXVIII.

[C]ATALOGUS Eorum qui in COLLEGIO YALENSI, quod est NOVI-PORTI apud CONNECTICUT, ab Anno 1702, ad Annum 1718. Alicujus gradus Laurea donati sunt.

1702.
Stephanus Buckingham Mr.
Salmon Treat Mr.
Josephus Coit Mr.
Josephus Moss Mr.
Nathanael Chauncey Mr.
1703.
Johannes Hart Mr. Tutor.
1704.
Johannes Russel Mr. Cur. Nov.
Phineas Fisk Mr. Tutor.
Jacob Hemingway Mr.
1705.
Azariah Mather Mr. Tutor.
Samuel Whittelsey Mr.
Samuel Cook Mr.
David Parsons Mr.
Samuel Pumery.
1706.
Jared Eliot Mr. Cur. Nov.
Timotheus Woodbridge Mr.
Jonathan Dickinson Mr.
1707.
Samuel Lynde Mr.
Samuel Wells Mr.
Daniel Chapman Mr.
Thomas Tousey
Daniel Taylor Mr.
1708.
Jonathan Russel Mr.
Johannes Prout Mr.
Benjamin Allen Mr.
1709.
Jeremiah Miller Mr.
Gulielmus Russel Mr. Tutor.
Josephus Smith Mr.
Nathanael Burnham Mr.
Benjamin Woolsey
Richardus Sacket Mr.
Josephus Noyes Mr.
Daniel Bordman Mr.
Josiah Deming Mr.
1710.
Benjamin Colton Mr.
Johannes Bliss Mr.
1711.
Johannes Pierson Mr.
Johannes Gardiner Mr.
Samuel Andrew Mr. Cur. Nov.
1712.
Samuel Russel Mr. Tutor.
Samuel Maltbie.
1713.
Samuel Smith Mr.
Daniel Elmer
David Evan.
1714.
* Josephus Haynes
Nathanael Clark
Jedidiah Buckingham Mr.
Benjamin Lord Tutor.
Josephus Willard
Josephus Blague
Jacobus Wetmore Mr.
Samuel Johnson Mr. Tutor.
Daniel Brown Mr.
1715.
Nathanael Mather
Josephus Webb Mr.
Henricus Willes.
1716.
Samuel Hall
Gulielmus Worthington
Benjamin Doolittle.
1717.
Georgius Griswold
Hezekiah Lord
Josephus Lamb
Isaacus Burr
Moses Dickinson.
1718.
Jacobus Pierpont
Samuel Pierpont
Ebenezer Rossetter
Robertus Treat
Timotheus Collens
Samuel Hopkins
Ebenezer Prime
Daniel Newell.

Numerus Integer——72
E vivis cessit [illegible]——1

NOVI-LONDINI: Excudebat Timotheus Green, MDCCXVIII.

1718 Commencement broadside, Yale University Archives, Yale University Library.

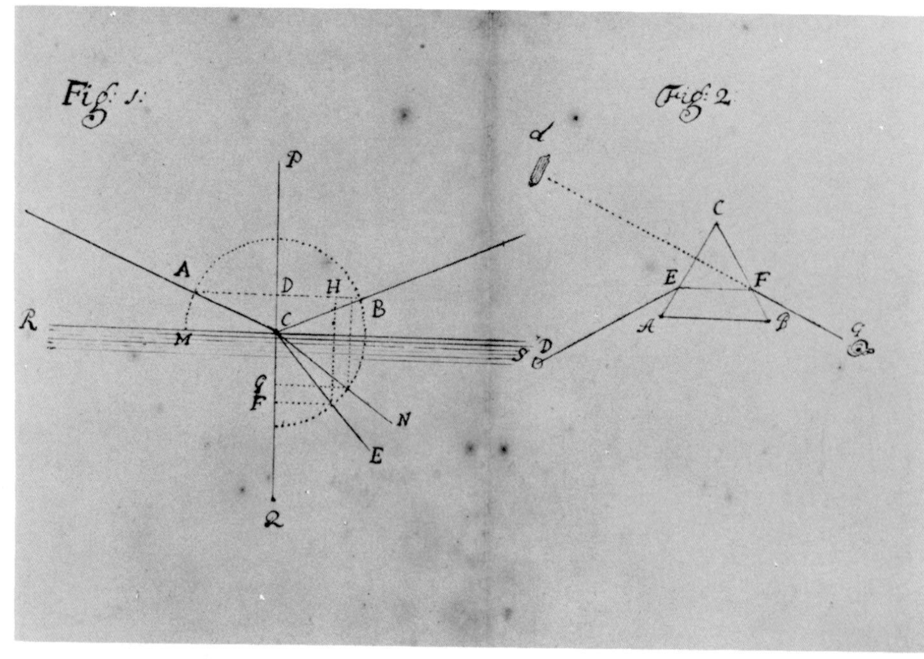

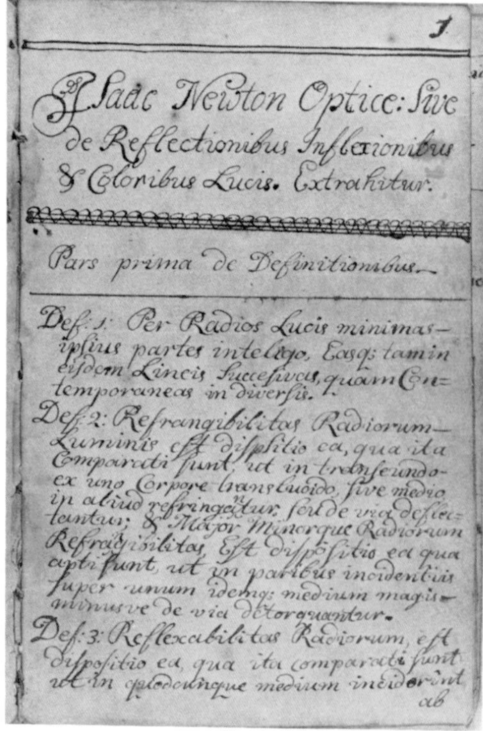
1

Isaac Newton Optice: Sive
de Reflectionibus Inflexionibus
& Coloribus Lucis. Extrahitur.

Pars prima de Definitionibus.

Def: 1. Per Radios Lucis minimas
ipsius partes inteligo, Easq: tamin
eisdem Lineis succesivas, quam Con-
temporaneas in diversis.
Def: 2: Refrangibilitas Radiorum
Luminis est dispositio ea, qua ita
Comparati sunt, ut in transeundo
ex uno Corpore translucido, sive medio
in aliud refringentur, seu de via deflec-
tantur; & Major Minorque Radiorum
Refrangibilitas, Est dispositio ea qua
apti sunt, ut in paribus incidentiis
super unum idemq: medium magis
minusve de via detorqueantur.
Def: 3. Reflexabilitas Radiorum, est
dispositio ea, qua ita comparati sunt
ut in quodcunque medium inciderint
ab

Pages from Matthew Rockwell's student notebook (1727), The Beinecke Rare Book and Manuscript Library, Yale University.

educated ministers and the assembly and towns with learned legislators. College and colony needed one another.

As far as Treasurer Prout was concerned, however, the college's need was greater. During the thirteen years of Williams's rectorship, Prout recorded a slight annual deficit on six occasions, prefacing the entry in the ledger with the words "ballance in favour of the Treasurer." Were it not for the assembly's £100 annuity and the yearly £100 bonus, he would have recorded thirteen huge deficits and Yale College probably would have collapsed. On October 31, 1739, John Prout presented his accounts to the college trustees. After the deduction of the most recent expenditures, his ledger showed a "Ballance in Favour of the College" of £10.15.1.[64] At this trustee meeting Rector Elisha Williams resigned, and it undoubtedly pleased him to know that his successor would inherit, at the very least, a solvent treasury.

64. Ibid., pp. 336–39. For Prout's more detailed report, which he offered the trustees in September, see pp. 334–36.

7 "A Most Valuable Man"

In 1725, the Reverend Joseph Morgan published a discourse entitled *The Only Effectual Remedy Against Mortal Errors.* He had preached this sermon in Freehold, New Jersey, a few years earlier in response to the Cutler defection. His decision to print it in Connecticut was an attempt to present his position to the citizens of that colony. Morgan's principal theme was the pressing need for ministers who had themselves experienced God's grace in their lives. Since the Presbyterian and Congregational churches of the colonies insisted that ministers be educated men, Morgan devoted a portion of his sermon to the life and work of the two New England colleges. He urged the faculties to "teach your *Pupils* to know the *Cross of Christ*" and called for lectures in the college town to be given by "the most *Heart-searching* Ministers we have." Only by such actions could the leaders of the colleges be sure that they had done all in their power "to procure GOD's Grace upon the Students." Morgan concluded this section of his sermon with the plea that trustees choose not only "men of the best Learning but also of the greatest Experience in the Cross of Christ, to be *Rectors* and *Tutors* in the Colleges." [1]

While Morgan's references were to the two New England colleges, it is probable that his chief concern was with Yale. He had received an honorary degree from the school in 1719 and his son was a student there when the Cutler apostasy occurred; in fact, Morgan had been the first to sound the warning about Arminian tendencies at Yale in 1722. Three years later, when he called for an experiential Christian to be the college rector, Morgan voiced a sentiment shared by the Yale trustees. The Cutler defection had not only caused a disruption of the normal functioning of the college, but had severely shaken Yale's religious foundations. As one way of refuting the Arminian-Anglican label that some had attached to the college, the trustees had required all officers to subscribe to the Saybrook Confession. The more immediate need, however, was to find a rector who could not only assent to an

1. Joseph Morgan, *The Only Effectual Remedy Against Mortal Errors Held Forth in a Discourse* (New London, 1725), p. 45.

orthodox statement of faith but who was both a learned man and an experiential Christian. The choice of Elisha Williams in 1726 brought Yale an excellent approximation of this ideal.

It did not take Williams long to convince the trustees that his election had been a sound decision. The new rector worked quickly to restore order to the college routine and steadily to bring stability and health to the school budget. But his principal task, as everyone understood it, was to reestablish Yale's commitment to the traditional faith. Shortly after assuming the office of rector, Williams preached a sermon before the General Assembly which indicated that he was the right man for the job. Indeed, the rector may have solely intended the sermon as proof of his theological soundness, for unlike most discourses preached to legislators, it was devoid of practical advice, dwelling exclusively on free grace, election, and the mediation of Christ. In dealing with these matters, Williams preached a strict form of Reformed orthodoxy. The rector's legal mind obviously found the logical and uncompromising doctrines of Calvinism attractive, and in his sermon he spoke of them with firm conviction:

> IF our Salvation be wholly of Grace, how can any thing of Self come in, as a Cause or Motive thereto; or any thing we are or can do, be a ground why it is bestowed? They will Exclude one the other. If any Thing of ours be the Cause, Motive or ground of Salvation, then it is not wholly of Grace: And if it be wholly of Grace, then all of Self is wholly Excluded, As the Apostle shews, *If it be of Works, then it is not of Grace; but if it be of Grace, then it is not of Works. Otherwise Grace were no more grace. . . .* Grace, can have no Partner.

Williams renounced works of any kind and denied any human agency in the process of redemption. "By various methods natural Men attempt to bring GOD under some Tie or Inducement to bestow Salvation upon them," the rector said, and went on to condemn such tactics. Grace, he reiterated, was wholly free and unearned.[2] In this sermon Williams confronted the main theological tenet of the Reformed tradition and presented it accurately and starkly. The rector's statement provided no comforting equiv-

2. Elisha Williams, *Divine Grace Illustrious, in the Salvation of Sinners* (New London, 1728), pp. 36, 37–38, 40.

ocations to any would-be Arminians; Williams had delineated the Reformed position and virtually dared anyone to disagree.

A few people did. Timothy Cutler either read or heard about the sermon in Boston and referred to it as an exposition of "Calvin's 'Horribile Decretum' "; he reported to an English correspondent that Samuel Johnson planned to publish a rebuttal to it.[3] These reactions, of course, played right into Williams's hands. Cutler and Johnson were the best of all possible enemies, for their opposition enhanced the rector's position—they had instigated Yale's religious difficulties and it was significant that they objected when Williams attempted to remedy them. The General Assembly, however, felt otherwise. The legislators were pleased with the rector's performance and ordered the discourse published, as it would be "of great service to religion, in confirming the people in the great truths by him delivered." [4]

It was one thing for Williams to announce that he understood and supported the theological tradition of Yale, Connecticut, and New England but quite another for him to demonstrate that support. A year later he got his chance. One of the stipulations that defined Connecticut's status as a charter colony was that it could not pass laws repugnant to the laws of England; but Connecticut did not always adhere to this rule. The colony's intestacy law, for example, did not conform to England's. In England, intestate estates were granted entirely to the eldest son, while in Connecticut the estate was divided among all heirs, the eldest receiving a double portion. Connecticut had adopted this procedure in its earliest years and it had existed as tradition until 1699, when it was made law. The reason for this practice was that Connecticut had a plethora of land but a paucity of settlers, and the intestate law was intended to keep as many people landed as possible. In 1728, John Winthrop, the nephew of one Connecticut governor and grandson of another, challenged this law and appealed to the King in Council to award him his father's entire estate. He won the case.[5]

The Connecticut colonists received this news with consternation, for if the ruling was to be enforced retroactively, the colony's

3. Perry, ed., *Historical Collections,* 3 : 670.

4. *Conn. Records,* 7 : 138.

5. Charles M. Andrews, "The Connecticut Intestacy Law," *Yale Review* 3 (1894): 261–94. For the Winthrop case, see p. 276.

landowning system would be thrown into confusion. Although the Winthrop decision did not immediately affect Yale, Rector Williams perceived possible trouble and moved quickly to head it off. "For my own part," he wrote Timothy Woodbridge, "I must Confess my fears are greater with relation to our religious than Civil Interests." The rector dreaded that once the king and council discovered Connecticut's violation of the intestacy law, they would pursue the inquiry further and declare that

> we have had Little power to do many other Things We have Done as in the other Instance; when we presumed we had power Enough
>
> Will they not Say our Ecclesiastical Establishment is a Nullity? Our College Charter a Nullity? (Can we plead & make it Good when we have done that the Governour & Company have a power to Make a Body Politick?) and may we not fear we Shall in a Little Time be in no better Circumstances than our Dissenting Brethren in England? [6]

Rector Williams had had enough legal training to realize that Connecticut and Yale were in a precarious situation. To make matters worse, the increasingly emboldened Connecticut Anglicans had been agitating against the colony's ecclesiastical structure. Williams thought that the Anglicans would love "to Defeat the Intention of Erecting the College" by having its charter overturned, and he wanted the colony to take steps to prevent this. In 1701, Gershom Bulkley had advised the college founders to petition the king for a charter, but his suggestion had been ignored.[7] The original trustees had wanted to keep the college free from imperial control so they could shape its religious stance to their liking. Twenty-seven years later, with Yale's recently threatened commitment to orthodoxy reestablished, Rector Williams reiterated Bulkley's plan as a way of perpetuating that commitment.

> Now what I would propose to Your Consideration is whither it would not be adviseable That The Agent The Government now Sends, be directed in the Prudentist Methods Possible, to *obtain a Charter for the College from the King.* and if it might be, also, Something in favour of our Ecclesiastick Constitution.

6. Pub. C.S.M., 6 (1904): 207–08.
7. *Documentary History,* pp. 10–11.

Williams thought such a plan might succeed in that the king had just come to the throne and might "do us a favour in another Matter as that of a Charter for the College," as it was not uncommon for a king "to Shew an act of Grace when he has manifested Severity." The rector urged the governor to act alone in directing the colony's agent on this matter, for he feared that debate in the General Assembly would so publicize the proposal "as That our Bigotted Churchmen would get it, & endeavour all ways Possible to Defeat it." [8]

Trustee Timothy Woodbridge, now applying his energies for the betterment of the college, discussed the rector's suggestion with Governor Joseph Talcott, who had succeeded the deceased Gurdon Saltonstall in 1724. Talcott evidently understood the reasons for Williams's fear but did not agree to the proposed petition to the king. In November, 1729, Talcott wrote to Connecticut's agents in London, urging them to seek redress for the colony from the King in Council rather than Parliament; like Williams, he felt that a full-scale inquiry into Connecticut affairs would hurt the colony. His instructions referred to the colony's fears of losing the college charter but said nothing of seeking a new one.[9] Fortunately for Connecticut, neither the King's Council nor Parliament chose to pursue their inquiries to the end of revoking Connecticut's ecclesiastical arrangements or Yale's charter. The council issued a report that severely chastised the colony for its independent behavior, but no substantive intervention resulted. Within several years Connecticut had resumed its traditional intestacy practices and, in a later case, the colony's law was upheld by the King in Council.[10]

This episode, while in fact peripheral to the college, tested Rector Williams's mettle. Although his radical proposal proved unnecessary, it nevertheless reflected his intense commitment to Yale's traditional religious posture. This commitment, which was shared by the trustees and other colonial ministers and officials, can be construed as a form of parochialism. The Cutler affair had been the most graphic example of this phenomenon. In that case, supporters of the college were made peculiarly sensitive to the

8. Pub. C.S.M., 6 (1904): 208–09.

9. Collections of the Connecticut Historical Society, 4 (1892): 175–76.

10. Andrews, "Intestacy Law," pp. 289–94. For further correspondence on the intestacy suit, see C.A., Foreign Correspondence, 1 : 145; 2 : 148, 153.

dimensions of their religious heritage—a heritage which they belatedly realized had been taken for granted and not revitalized. For men like Williams, Connecticut's religious heritage was intimately bound up with its political autonomy. Their greatest fear was that England would intrude on their local institutions and threaten their most cherished beliefs. Such concerns placed the college officials in an ambivalent position. Intellectually, they desired contact and affiliation with England and Europe; in that case they posed as cosmopolitans. Religiously, they wanted to preserve and perpetuate those forms and doctrines which had been developed in New England; in that case they acted as provincials. In the years after the Cutler apostasy, their provincialism was dominant. Williams and his colleagues were convinced that their first job was to retain and revivify Yale's and Connecticut's allegiance to the Reformed tradition.

But Yale's religious constitution and the rector's vigorous orthodoxy were no guarantees that the college would be spared theological deviations and divisions. These personal and institutional commitments certainly set the prevailing mood of the college, but no attempt was made to enforce that mood. For this reason, and because no religious credo was demanded of entering students, it was always possible that Yale would harbor some young men with extreme theological views. And while this possibility had always existed, it was not until the rectorship of Elisha Williams that such deviations became a serious problem.

In the early 1730s, in a prelude to the divisions of the Great Awakening, the Yale student body included a coterie of enthusiasts and a group of undergraduates who espoused Arminian views. The enthusiasts, led by David Ferris of Milford, a nongraduating member of the class of 1733, were six in number and banded together as a club. According to one of their college contemporaries:

> They laid great Stress upon *Impressions* and *Impulses;* particularly, upon any *Sense of Scripture* that was suddenly and *strongly suggested* to their Minds.—They were strangely *uncharitable;* expressing *themselves censoriously* of most others: They had indeed *no Opinion* of any but *themselves* on a *religious Account*.[11]

11. Charles Chauncy, *Seasonable Thoughts on the State of Religion in New England,* p. 213. The six students were Ferris, James Davenport, Eleazar Wheelock, Benjamin Pomeroy, Timothy Allen, and Daniel Bliss. Davenport was the most

Their fellow students found the six enthusiasts obnoxious and haughty, but they did not cause the college administration any visible anxiety. Rector Williams had been warned about Ferris by one of the boy's grammar school teachers but had admitted him anyway. Indeed, the six students had little impact on the college except that their animadversions against their less pious colleagues may have, in part, resurrected the issue of Arminianism at Yale.[12]

James Pierpont (Y. 1718), a former tutor who had taken up the vocation of an apothecary in Boston, was one of the first to rediscover Arminianism at the college. The issue had been dormant since the Cutler apostasy, but in about 1730 Pierpont visited the school and, after conversing with the tutors and students, declared that Yale "was corrupted & ruined with Arminianism & Heresy." Rector Williams, hearing of the charge, evidently investigated it, but no record survives that he took any action. Ezra Stiles, who recorded this event in 1790, thought that Pierpont's claim was a false aspersion against the college, but others voiced similar fears.[13] In his 1731 funeral sermon for Trustee Moses Noyes, Azariah Mather noted that the deceased minister had lamented the erroneous doctrines he "feared prevailing among our *Schools* & *Young Candidates for the Ministry,*" especially Arminianism and Pelagianism.[14]

It is difficult to determine precisely what caused Pierpont and Noyes to fear Arminianism at Yale. This heresy was over a century old, had been forthrightly condemned by the Synod of Dort, and by this time had become a difficult position to define. The term had lost much of its precision and seems to have been used as a pejorative definition of any theological position that ignored

---

notorious of the six; as a radical New Light, his religious excesses led to trials in both Connecticut and Massachusetts at which he was declared non compos mentis. Pomeroy and Wheelock shared the Berkeley scholarship in 1733–34, so their participation in this group did not count against them at the college. Ferris left Yale in 1732 and returned to Milford where he rejoined a company of Quakers. In 1742 he was thought to be an itinerant Quaker preacher. For more on this group see chapter 10.

12. This view cannot be proved. I have inferred it from evidence that refers to the group's disparagement of nonmembers and the rumors of Arminianism alive at this time.

13. Franklin B. Dexter, ed., *Extracts from the Itineraries and other Miscellanies of Ezra Stiles*, p. 408.

14. Azariah Mather, *A Discourse Concerning the Death of the Righteous* (New London, 1731), pp. 21–22.

rather than denied the doctrines of free grace and innate depravity. The term was also used, as it had been during the Cutler affair, to castigate anyone who leaned toward Anglicanism, since the Church of England was notoriously favorable to the Arminian scheme. In the early 1730s, certain Yale students must have been toying with such ideas. Although no students were arguing a cogently defined Arminian position, it may be that some of them were propounding a vague theology that tended to stress man's ability rather than his depravity and to suggest that man's role, not God's, was the key to salvation. Other students may simply have professed an interest in Anglicanism. This last was certainly an issue, for Samuel Johnson had been recruiting Yale men to the Church of England for some years. Not only were his two stepsons, Benjamin and William Nicoll, attending the college at this time, but in 1731–32 three Yale graduates—John Beach (Y. 1721), Isaac Browne (Y. 1729), and John Pierson (Y. 1729), the nephew of the first rector—were converted to the doctrines of the Church of England. These examples served as warnings to Trustees Woodbridge and Adams that the college might be tending toward heresy. Both ministers voiced their concern. In December, 1732, Benjamin Colman wrote to Adams that "the Bruit of the Prevalence of Arminianism in the College" had reached Boston and was causing alarm among friends of the school there.[15] The rumors even prompted Williams's predecessor, Timothy Cutler, to declare that the rector was "dodging about" on the issue of Anglicanism. Although this charge was completely unwarranted, it nevertheless pointed to the persistent legacy of the 1722 defection. Despite Williams's professed and unquestioned stance as a spokesman of Reformed orthodoxy, the school had never completely removed the stain of heresy from its image.

The residual suspicion fostered by Yale's previous difficulties was reinforced by the events of the early 1730s. With Samuel Johnson enjoying some success in winning Yale men over to the Church of England, and with David Ferris and his friends openly questioning the quality of their fellow students' faith, it was perhaps natural that the vague and convenient accusation of Arminianism should be hurled at the school. As was most often the case, the term also pointed to the threat of Anglicanism. While this fear

15. *Documentary History*, p. 298. For students, see *Yale Graduates*, 1 : 240, 380, 389, 394, 430, 432, 509–11.

proved to be groundless—indeed, the trustees never recorded a discussion of the issue at their meetings—it ironically helped the college to get a sizable gift. That gift, in turn, reconfirmed the old fear.

George Berkeley

George Berkeley, a graduate of Trinity College in Dublin in 1704 and a fellow of that college for twenty years, had sailed for America in 1728. Landing in Virginia, he had made his way to Newport, Rhode Island, and bought a farm where he resided for three years. Berkeley's reason for coming to the colonies was to establish a college in Bermuda, a project he had conceived as early as 1722. The purpose of the college, which he had outlined in 1724 in "A Proposal for the Better Supplying of Churches in Our Foreign Plantations and for Converting the Savage Americans to Christianity," was to prepare young men for service in the Church of England in America and to convert Indians who would serve as missionaries to their people. Berkeley, whose ecclesiastical title was Dean of Londonderry, had chosen Bermuda as the site for the college on account of its good climate, plentiful provisions, and ideal location. In 1725 he obtained a royal charter for the college and by the end of that year had received donations totaling £3,400. The crown also granted him £20,000 for the venture on the stipulation that the college be located in Bermuda.

Berkeley settled in Newport to further the plans for the college and to await the crown's munificent grant. He waited in vain. Rumors that the dean was wavering as to the location of the college allowed the opponents of the scheme, among them Sir Robert Walpole, to delay the allocation of the grant indefinitely. Responding to an inquiry from the Bishop of London about the funds, Walpole is rumored to have said:

> If you put this question to me as a Minister, I must and can assure you that the money shall undoubtedly be paid, as soon as suits with public convenience; but if you ask me as a friend, whether Dean Berkeley should continue in America, expecting the payment of £20,000, I advise him by all means to return to Europe, and give up his present expectations.[16]

Berkeley learned the substance of these remarks and in September, 1731, he gave up his project and sailed for England.

16. Yale University Library *Gazette,* 28 (1954): 7. See pp. 2–9 for more on Berkeley.

Berkeley's years in Newport were not totally wasted, however. He did further philosophical work, wrote *Alciphron; or The Minute Philosopher,* and met and conversed with a few American colonists. While he never traveled in New England, his circle of acquaintances was large enough to include two Yale graduates, Samuel Johnson (Y. 1714) and Jared Eliot (Y. 1706).[17] Johnson, the senior Episcopal missionary in Connecticut, and Eliot, who had expressed his interest in Anglicanism in the 1722 declaration, visited Berkeley at his Rhode Island farm and undoubtedly told the dean about Yale. Johnson, who had been enjoying some success in bringing Yale graduates into the Church of England, emphasized this fact to Berkeley. Ezra Stiles recorded that Johnson persuaded the dean that Yale "would soon become Episcopal, and that they had received his *immaterial philosophy.*"[18]

Berkeley was more interested in the first possibility than in the second, and in 1730 he asked Johnson if the trustees "would admit the writings of Hooker and Chillingworth into the library of the College in New Haven."[19] The dean took no steps to bestow books on Yale, however, until his departure for England in 1731. Just before leaving Newport, Berkeley wrote to Johnson and said that he would like to help Yale College, "the more as you were once a member of it, and have still an influence there." Berkeley sent Johnson some books, including several Latin and Greek texts, for him to distribute "to such lads as you think will make the best use of them in the College."[20]

On the return voyage to England, Berkeley may have mulled over the failure of his Bermuda scheme and wondered what to do with the donations he had received for his proposed college. By January 12, 1732, he made his decision. On that date he dined with his friend Sir John Percival, who suggested that Berkeley donate

17. Berkeley lived a retired life at Newport and saw little of New England. He never visited Connecticut. See Daniel C. Gilman, "Bishop Berkeley's Gifts to Yale College," Papers of the New Haven Colony Historical Society, 1 (1865): 153. Samuel Johnson hoped that Berkeley might become the Anglican bishop for America. See *Johnson,* 3 : 222.

18. *Literary Diary of Ezra Stiles,* 1 : 205–06. Stiles also stated that one Colonel Updike, who was intimately acquainted with the dean, said that Berkeley's "Motive was the greater prospect that Yale College would become episcopal than Harvard."

19. *Johnson,* 2 : 284. The library had received these works in the Dummer collection.

20. Ibid., 1 : 81. Timothy Cutler hoped that Berkeley would place his college in New England, as that would be "some compensation for the loss the Church has sustained as to Harvard College." See Perry, *Historical Collections,* 3 : 671.

the subscriptions for his Bermuda college to further James Oglethorpe's altruistic plan for the colony of Georgia. But the dean had other intentions. According to Percival, Berkeley said that many of his friends had urged him to keep the money for himself, but that he had refused and had

> recommended to them the letting their subscriptions go to the support of a College in Connecticut, erected about thirty years ago by private subscription, and which breeds the best clergymen and most learned of any college in America. That the clergymen who left the Presbyterian Church and came over to ours last year were educated there. That as this college, or rather academy, came nearest to his own plan, he was desirous to encourage it.[21]

Berkeley had visited both Harvard and William and Mary but had never seen Yale. Yet Johnson's friendship, coupled with the recent conversion of three more Yale graduates to Anglicanism, seems to have convinced the dean that he should compensate for his Bermuda failure by assisting the Connecticut college.

Enough of his friends and subscribers supported Berkeley's plan to allow him, by the summer of 1732, to convey the deed to his Rhode Island farm to Yale. In his instructions for the use of this gift, sent in detail a year later, Berkeley stipulated that the annual rent from the farm be used by the college to support several students, adjudged most competent in Latin and Greek, as scholars of the house between their first and second degrees. The competition was to be held each May, with the rector and senior Anglican missionary of the colony acting as the examiners. In his letter to Johnson about this matter, Berkeley revealed both his motives for the gift and his high regard for the former Yale tutor:

> It is my opinion that as human learning and the improvements of reason are of no small use in religion, so it would very much forward those ends, if some of your students were enabled to subsist longer at their studies, and if by a public trial and premium an emulation were inspired into all. This method of encouragement hath been found useful in other learned Societies, and I think it cannot fail of being so in one where a person so well qualified as yourself, has such an influence, and will bear a share in the elections.

21. Yale University Library *Gazette,* 8 (1934): 2–3.

In closing his letter, Berkeley revealed that he was going to "endeavor to procure a benefaction of books for the College Library" and had hopes for success.[22]

Samuel Johnson conveyed Berkeley's deed and instructions to the college trustees, who, on December 20, 1732, asked Rector Williams to write a letter of thanks to the dean. In making his contribution to Yale, Berkeley demonstrated his generosity; in accepting it, Williams displayed his boldness. The rector must have realized that a donation to Yale from a prominent Anglican would certainly arouse suspicion. It would confirm, in the eyes of some, that the college was still in the grips of precisely that trend which Williams had been hired to reverse. Recent events at the college had already aroused some criticism along these lines, and the Berkeley gift prompted more. Benjamin Colman, who had been fearful of Arminianism at Yale anyway, worried about the implications of the donation and on December 2, 1732, at the behest of some "superior Friends" in Boston, wrote several letters of inquiry about it. Colman and his friends hoped that the benefaction came to Yale "without the Clog of any Condition that is inconsistent with or subversive of the known and true Intent of the Honourable Founders of your College; and that the Reverend Trustees will carefully see that it does so before they accept of that or any other Donation." [23]

Rector Williams, having read Colman's letter, hastened to assure him that no harm would come of the Berkeley gift:

> I entirely concur with your Sentiments with regard to the Revd Dean Berkeley's Donation. Were it clogged in the manner you hint so as it would be subversive of the true Interest of the College, it would be unworthy of Him, and the acceptance of it, Treachery in us who have the Care of it. The Gift is made to us in such a Manner as bespeaks a true Catholick Spirit, as much (if I mistake not) as Mr Hollis's to Harvard College.

Williams told Colman that the intention of the gift was to encourage learning and that the premium would be "very likely to excite the Students to Industry, and a Laudable ambition to Excell." Williams thought that the dean's instructions safely limited

22. *Johnson,* 1 : 82–83.
23. *Documentary History,* pp. 299, 298.

the influence of the colony's Anglican missionary, showing that Berkeley was "taking as little notice of those of his own Communion as can reasonably be Imagined." All told, the rector concluded, the donation ought to serve, as Berkeley intended, "in the *Promoting Charity, Learning and Piety in this part of the World.*" [24]

Williams's detailed reply to Colman is an indication that the rector appreciated the Boston minister's fears. In some ways, those fears were justified, as Berkeley gave the deed to Yale because he had heard and hoped that the college might become Anglican. Fortunately, Berkeley never spelled out his somewhat subversive hopes in his instructions, so Williams was free to accept the gift openly. As it turned out, the donation did accomplish those lofty pedagogical ends which the dean *had* spelled out. Samuel Johnson reported later that classical learning at Yale had prospered through the annual competition for the Berkeley stipend.[25]

In the winter of 1732–33 the trustees took possession of the Rhode Island farm and rented it; in May, 1733, they held the first competition. Benjamin Pomeroy and Eleazar Wheelock won the contest and were awarded the Berkeley scholarship for 1733–34, each receiving a stipend of sixteen pounds from the rental of the farm.[26] By 1739 Johnson could report to Berkeley that "it is very agreeable to see to what perfection classical learning is advanced in comparison to what it was before your Lordship's donation to this College." The Anglican pastor complained, however, that one of the rector's sons, "who had manifestly the advantage of the rest," won the prize in 1739; although Johnson did not say whether young Williams's advantage was in learning or in favor, he undoubtedly meant the latter.[27] Despite such nepotism, the Berkeley prize—in a sense, the first graduate scholarship at Yale—had accomplished its stated purpose; it had spurred some undergraduates on to excellence in Latin and Greek.

The dean's munificence did not end with the donation of his

24. Elisha Williams to [Benjamin Colman], January 11, 1733, Harvard College Library.

25. *Johnson,* 1 : 98.

26. *Literary Diary of Ezra Stiles,* 2 : 534–35. The rent from the farm was seventy pounds, but after expenses only thirty-two pounds remained. It was divided equally between the two recipients. Wheelock and Pomeroy resided at the college for only one year.

27. *Johnson,* 1 : 98.

farm. In May, 1733, aided by "the liberality of certain publick spirited persons," Berkeley shipped eight cases of "well chosen" books to the Yale College Library. The dean hoped that the volumes would "shed a copious light in that remote wilderness" and would be used "for the increase of Religion and Learning" at Yale. The books, along with some classics destined for Harvard, arrived in Boston in August, 1733, and at Yale in early September.[28] The donation was, Thomas Clap later opined, "the finest Collection of Books that ever came together at one Time into *America.* The Number was near 1000 Volumes, (including those which he had sent before) whereof 260 were Folios, and generally very large." Clap estimated that the books were worth about four hundred pounds sterling.[29]

The trustees were grateful for Berkeley's generosity and sent him a letter of thanks. They placed the books in a special part of the library but ignored the dean's impractical suggestion that all who borrowed the books leave a deposit equal to or double the price of the volume.[30] The Berkeley donation increased the value of Yale's already substantial library, and visitors to the college were impressed by the size and scope of the collection. An Austrian traveler commented that the library "for a beginning is large enough" and the Reverend Ebenezer Parkman (H. 1721), who spent several hours perusing the books, marveled at the "most Curious and Costly Collection." [31] In fact, the most curious thing about the collection was that it contained numerous works by Anglican divines. While this was understandable considering that the donor was an English churchman, it was not especially pleasing to the college officers. At a later date, Rector Williams was to use this fact to solicit more suitable books for the Yale library.

George Berkeley was Yale's greatest, though not its only, bene-

28. Pub. C.S.M., 28 : 106–07, 105–06. See *Boston News-Letter,* Aug. 2–9 and Aug. 10–17, 1733, for an account of the arrival of the books. The books for Harvard were lost in the burning of Harvard Hall in 1764; the lost volumes were described as "The Greek and Roman Classics, presented by the late excellent and catholic-spirited Bishop Berkeley, most of them the best editions." See Quincy, *History of Harvard,* 2 : 481.

29. *Yale Annals,* p. 38.

30. Pub. C.S.M., 28 (1935): 106–07.

31. Yale University Library *Gazette,* 9 (1935): 62, contains a selection from the diary of Phillip Georg Friedrich von Reck, who visited New Haven around 1734; Ebenezer Parkman, *Diary, Proceedings of the American Antiquarian Society,* n.s. 71 (1961): 433. Parkman visited Yale in 1738.

factor during Williams's tenure. Nevertheless, his donations never earned the dean the friendship of the college officers. The case was quite the opposite with English Dissenter and hymn-writer Isaac Watts. Compared to Berkeley, Watts was a minor donor to Yale, but his few gifts meant more to Rector Williams than all of the Berkeley volumes put together.

Benjamin Colman was the man who first interested Watts in donating to Yale. Colman had what Connecticut ministers lacked, namely, contacts with Englishmen. He had been ordained in England and his son and a number of his acquaintances frequently went there. Like Cotton Mather, Colman was interested in assisting the Connecticut college, but he did so without the sense of urgency and import that Mather had attached to the task. In 1730 Watts, using his correspondent Colman as an intermediary, sent all of his published works to Yale except for his study on the Trinity, which had been criticized as Arian, lest, he said, he "be charged with leading youth into heresie." [32] Watts's candor must have convinced the trustees that this donor, at least, had the college's best interests at heart. Colman also interested two other Englishmen in Yale, and in 1730 Joseph Thompson and Samuel Holden contributed to the college. Thompson sent forty-six books and Holden gave Richard Baxter's *Works* in five volumes. The trustees sent letters of gratitude for all these gifts and Rector Williams, seizing the opening, appealed for more. He wrote to Benjamin Colman expressing the hope that Samuel Holden would help the college settle a professor of divinity, and asked if Isaac Watts might solicit further donations from Thompson.[33]

32. Anne Stokley Pratt, *Isaac Watts and his Gifts of Books to Yale College,* p. 10. Ezra Stiles placed Watts's controversial work in the college library in 1777 and remarked in his diary: "When Dr. Watts set out in Life he was clearly a Calvinist. . . . When the Arian Controversy got hold of the Dissenters . . . about 1720: Dr. Watts entered the Arian Researches, *became plunged as to the real Divinity of J.C.* . . . But tho' he was an Arian on the Divinity of Christ, yet he never relinquished any of the other evangelical Doctrines" (see ibid., p. 14). Arianism is a Christian heresy deriving its name from Arius, a fourth-century presbyter of Alexandria, who promulgated the notion that the Logos, the medium of God's creation, was not coeternal with the Godhead and that there was a time when the Logos was not. Motivated by a monarchian view of God, Arius argued that the Logos (the Son) was created by God. Arianism was condemned by the Council of Nicea in 325 A.D.

33. Ibid., pp. 16–18. I have not been able to find biographical information on Joseph Thompson. Samuel Holden, a benefactor of Harvard College, was an English Dissenter and governor of the Bank of England. For the efforts of Jonathan

Neither wish was realized. Watts replied that he rarely saw Thompson and could be of little service in asking him for gifts, and Samuel Holden never responded to the rector's suggestion. Isaac Watts, however, emboldened by Williams's statement that his writings were "so usefull to the College," kept up his interest in Yale and continued to send occasional books for its library. In 1734, the same year in which Joseph Thompson and some citizens of New Haven jointly contributed to the start of Yale's collection of scientific instruments, he ordered a pair of seventeen-inch globes, painted to his specifications, for the college. In 1735 and 1736 Watts sent the college several of his recent publications. Watts's sermons, Williams said, "have done great service to our youth, as I hope those now sent will, which I purpose shall be read in the *College-hall* every Sabbath evening." [34] Needless to say, Dean Berkeley's books never received this compliment.

In 1737, Williams told Watts that the college needed Calvinistic books; the Englishman responded by sending the works of three "moderate men." Williams, in his reply, excused himself for being so forward in telling Watts of Yale's wants, but explained that the library had been filled by "Writers of the Arminian stamp—from whom I have always . . . feared some unhappy Influence on the minds of our Youth," and that Watts's gifts "Will I trust be standing Helps in the Cause of Truth." [35]

In his correspondence with Watts, Elisha Williams showed his true colors. Whereas Berkeley's gifts had increased the college's assets considerably, Watts's donations had an additional value; they helped the cause of truth—Reformed truth. This was Yale's cause, and when Williams solicited Watts's aid he was fulfilling his chief task as champion of that cause. Indeed, much of Williams's career as rector was spent advancing it. To be sure, the rector had a variety of roles—administrator, disciplinarian, teacher, pastor—but his most visible function was to be the standard-bearer for the

---

Belcher to secure gifts for Yale, see Collections of the Connecticut Historical Society, 4 (1892): 192.

34. *Documentary History*, pp. 307–08; Yale University Library *Gazette*, 22 (1948): 15; Ezra Stiles, "College Records," p. 99, Yale Archives; Pratt, *Isaac Watts*, pp. 29–30.

35. Pratt, *Isaac Watts*, pp. 50, 52. Watts was interested in both Yale and Harvard but was most fascinated by the revivals of 1734–35, especially the one in Northampton led by Jonathan Edwards. Watts supervised the English publication of Edwards's narrative of the revival.

college's religious position. He had done this in private ways—as when he advocated getting a royal charter in 1728 to protect the college's religious constitution, or when he sought books from Isaac Watts—and he had done it in the public forum—as in his 1727 sermon to the General Assembly.

Defending the Faith

Perhaps the rector's most dramatic gesture of this sort occurred in 1735. In that year there was a furor in Springfield, Massachusetts, over the proposed ordination of one Robert Breck, who was charged with suspected Arminianism as well as devious behavior. The troubles of Robert Breck (H. 1730) began when he was expelled from college for stealing books. In 1733 he started preaching in the third parish of Windham, Connecticut, where he espoused some questionable doctrines, including the notion that "Heathen that liv'd up to the Light of Nature should be Saved." This declaration aroused the curiosity of Thomas Clap, pastor in Windham, who questioned Breck about his theology. In the course of the discussion, Breck denied Clap's charge that he had been suspended from Harvard. Soon after this confrontation, Breck left Windham and began preaching as a ministerial candidate in Springfield. The rumors of his Connecticut troubles caught up with him, and the Hampshire County ministers refused to ordain him until he obtained a certificate of orthodoxy from Clap. When Clap refused, Breck went to Boston and tried to get testimonies of his soundness of faith from that city's more liberal ministers. On the advice of one of them, William Cooper, Breck arranged to have some of the Boston ministers sit in on the ecclesiastical council that was to examine him in Springfield. The Hampshire County ministers solicited the assistance of some of their Connecticut colleagues, so when the council convened in 1735, clergymen from both Boston and Connecticut were present.[36]

Rector Elisha Williams was one of the Connecticut contingent. He was a logical person to attend the meeting for two reasons: first, his family was well known in the Connecticut Valley and several of his relatives were ministers in the Hampshire County association; second, the rector was irrevocably opposed to the Ar-

36. *Harvard Graduates,* 8 : 663–73, is an excellent account of the Breck case. For Thomas Clap's role in the affair, see Louis L. Tucker, *Puritan Protagonist,* pp. 47–59.

minian doctrines that Breck allegedly held. Although Thomas Clap was the chief advocate of the "Yale-Calvinist-conservative faction which opposed Breck," Williams also played a leading role. No sooner had the ordaining council convened than things began to happen. Responding to a charge that it was irregular to have outside ministers on the council without the expressed consent of the church that had called Breck, several Springfield justices of the peace ordered the Boston ministers arrested. For some reason, however, one of the justices talked his colleagues into arresting Breck instead on the charge that his preaching "had been a violation of the Massachusetts Act against atheism and blasphemy." But since Breck had voiced his heresy in Connecticut, the justices ordered he be sent there to answer charges. These proceedings were of dubious legality at best and, as later events seemed to indicate, were probably little more than attempts at harassment. Nevertheless, the pro-Breck faction accused Williams of attempting to "hinder the Ordination" by advocating the arrest and of sitting "with a singular Air of Pleasure in his Countenance" when Breck was seized.[37]

Although Williams denied the charge that he had tried to stop the ordination by force, he made no effort to hide his sympathies. He wrote to his kinsmen in Longmeadow and Lebanon urging that Breck be denied ordination and referring to his case as evidence that "Satan seems to have been let loose and to have made Ministers (who should always be upon their Guard and approve themselves good Soldiers of Christ in fighting against the Interests of his Kingdom of Darkness) his Tools to do Infinite mischief to religion."[38] Although Breck forfeited his bond in Connecticut and never appeared for his court hearing, the publicity and pressure of the 1735 meeting had some effects. A year later, after passions had cooled, Breck offered a public profession of his orthodoxy and was ordained in Springfield.

37. Harvard Graduates, 8 : 664, 669–71; [Robert Breck], *An Examination of the Proceedings of those Ministers of the County of Hampshire . . . that have Disapproved of the late Measures taken in order to the settlement of Mr. Robert Breck* (Boston, 1736), pp. 75–76. For more on the Breck affair, see *A Narrative of the Proceedings* (Boston, 1736) and *A Letter to the Author of the Pamphlet Called an Answer to the Hampshire Narrative* (Boston, 1737).

38. *An Examination,* pp. 72–73; Elisha Williams to Solomon Williams, Dec. 30, 1735, Yale Archives. For a criticism of Williams's role in this episode, see William Cooper to Benjamin Colman, Nov. 25, 1735, Massachusetts Historical Society, Boston, Mass.

While Williams did not represent Yale in any official capacity at the Breck inquiry, his participation there was a public demonstration of his theological beliefs. Indeed, Williams's religious activities during his rectorship serve as a good index of the religious attitudes propagated at the college. In addition to his Reformed orthodoxy, which he displayed both in word and deed, the rector was also a warm supporter of the revivals that had begun in Jonathan Edwards's Northampton parish in 1734 and that had soon spread to eleven other river towns in Massachusetts, as well as to fourteen communities in Connecticut, including New Haven.[39] These revivals stressed the experiential aspect of the life of faith; that is, they awakened the individual to a personal sense of sin and a personal relationship to a gracious God. It was one thing to know *about* God, it was another to know and experience him. The revivals fostered this latter phenomenon.

The experiential aspect of religion was an essential ingredient of the Reformed tradition in New England. Orthodox ministers had always insisted that right belief alone was not enough; a person also had to experience God in his life. Thus, Williams welcomed the revivals—a "Wonderful Blessing," he called them—which brought this desirable and necessary element of faith. In 1735, when the revival took hold in the college town, Rector Williams supported it;[40] a year later, he wrote a long letter to Isaac Watts describing the revival in Hatfield, Massachusetts (where his father was the minister), and relating the success of John Sergeant (Y. 1729) in converting the Indians. "Would to God," Williams

39. Sereno E. Dwight, ed., *The Writings of President Edwards,* 4 : 25–27. The Connecticut towns were Windsor, East Windsor, Coventry, Lebanon, Durham, Stratford, Ripton, Guilford, Mansfield, Tolland, Hebron, Preston, Woodbury, and New Haven.

40. Elisha Williams to Solomon Williams, Dec. 30, 1735, Yale Archives. When the revival swept New Haven, Rector and Mrs. Williams joined the New Haven church. They did so despite the fact that Williams evidently did not get along with the pastor, Joseph Noyes, whom the rector seems to have found wanting in experiential piety. At least that was the opinion of Benjamin Gale (Y. 1733), who later recalled that the rector bore Noyes a personal grudge and was his "professed Inemy, & Imployed his whole powers to render his publick Performances Despicable . . . & he Effectually Accomplished it within the walls of the Colledge." Gale went on to state that the college tutors shared this opinion, and evidently convinced many students that Noyes was a poor minister. Whatever the dimensions of the conflict, it never came into the open; it is probable that Williams held stricter views on theology and piety than did the New Haven minister. See Benjamin Gale to [?], [c. 1755?], Yale Archives.

concluded, "this blessing might be extended not only through our land and nation but the whole world." [41]

By these words and actions, then, the rector proved to be all that the trustees had hoped for in 1726. He was an orthodox Calvinist, a vigorous opponent of Arminianism, and a warm friend of the revivals and experiential religion. The only time Williams's theological convictions might have been called into question was when he accepted Dean Berkeley's donations, but even then he soon demonstrated his true temperament. Shortly after receiving the bequests, Williams joined with the ministers of Hampshire County, Massachusetts, in roundly condemning the S.P.G. for its tactics, a maneuver which reassured his would-be critics and angered Samuel Johnson, who thought that gratitude to Berkeley should have precluded such sentiments.[42] But Johnson soon learned that the rector was not one to treat Anglican advances in Connecticut lightly—and that the Berkeley gifts were not going to deter him from acting on his convictions.

Elisha Williams had good reason to be proud of his record as Yale rector and the trustees were certainly pleased by the length and quality of his service. But in 1739 he informed the trustees of the "Necessity of his Resignation of his Rectoral Relation to the College on the Account of the Impairs of his Bodily Health." According to Benjamin Colman, Williams had suffered "a dreadful headache, which had greatly endangered the loss of his sight," a malady he blamed on the sea air and his sedentary life at the college. Some critics—Samuel Johnson among them—argued that the rector's chief aim was to succeed Joseph Talcott as governor, since the old gentleman was in his declining years.[43] This allegation is impossible to prove or disprove, although Williams did seek and win political offices after his retirement.

In November, 1739, Williams left Yale and returned to Wethersfield, where, in several months, his health improved. The trustees elected as his replacement Thomas Clap (H. 1722), the minister at Windham. Clap's intellectual and religious credentials were solid and it may be that the trustees were attracted to him because

41. Pratt, *Isaac Watts*, pp. 29–31.

42. Perry, *Historical Collections*, 3 : 299–301; *Johnson*, 1 : 27; see also, E. B. O'Callaghan, ed., *Documents Relative to the Colonial History of the State of New York*, 15 vols. (Albany, 1853–87), 7 : 372, for another letter of Johnson on this matter.

43. *Documentary History*, p. 337; Pratt, *Isaac Watts*, p. 57; *Johnson*, 1 : 101–02.

of his vigorous defense of orthodoxy during the Breck affair in 1735. He certainly seemed to be the right man to represent Yale's religious tradition. Clap gladly accepted the call and, after a settlement had been worked out with his parish, he moved to New Haven and was installed as Yale's fifth rector, in April, 1740.

The reaction to Williams's departure was varied. Samuel Johnson, who saw the rector as a "zealous dissenter, a great enemy to the Church and of a very insidious temper," was not sorry to see him go; he hoped the Connecticut Anglicans would fare better under his successor. Benjamin Colman, however, thought otherwise: "He is a most valuable man, and his sickness or retirement would be a great loss to us." [44] Given the different points of view, both evaluations of Williams were valid, although neither prediction of his retirement was entirely accurate. Thomas Clap, possessed of an imperious personality that was as often a handicap as an asset, proved to be as dedicated an adversary to the Church of England as Williams had been and, like his predecessor, a staunch supporter of Reformed orthodoxy.

The transfer of the rectorship to Thomas Clap was made smoothly and the college was without a resident rector for only a few months. When Clap took over, he was the first Yale rector to assume control of a settled and prospering college. Elisha Williams had headed the college for thirteen years. By remaining at the helm of Yale affairs for such a period, Williams had given the school a continuity and stability that it had previously lacked. With this stability came better relations and more advantageous financial arrangements with the General Assembly, benefits which made Clap's job considerably easier. Williams had also put the college into communication with other colonists and Englishmen; Watts and Berkeley, for example, continued their interest in Yale into the 1740s, so that Clap inherited established contacts with a wider intellectual world, which he both cultivated and expanded. A chief result of these contacts was that, under Williams, the college had nearly doubled the size of its library and had begun the acquisition of scientific apparatus, making a more up-to-date and sophisticated academic program possible. In addition, Williams had supervised the growth of the college's student population; during his rectorship Yale began drawing a more geographically diversified group of young men, taking significant numbers of

44. *Johnson,* 1 : 26; Pratt, *Isaac Watts,* p. 57.

undergraduates from the Connecticut River Valley in Massachusetts. The graduates of the College, 215 under Williams, engaged in a variety of occupations and carried Yale's name to their new residences throughout the colonies. By 1740, Yale College was an established academic institution and had assumed a place in the intellectual community of America.

These were remarkable achievements, but Williams's most outstanding service was rescuing the college from the religious doldrums brought on by the Cutler apostasy. Almost singlehandedly he revivified Yale's theological credentials as a perpetuator of Reformed orthodoxy. Although several people suspected that some form of Arminianism lingered at the college in the early 1730s, the rector's rigorous Calvinism, his personal distaste for theological laxity, and his advocacy of experiential religion all served to negate those suspicions. By the time he resigned his rectorship, Yale's official religious position was firmly reestablished. Within a year's time, that position was to be tested and shaken by the emotional fervor of the Great Awakening.

8 "Wherein Youth May Be Instructed in the Arts & Sciences"

The Curriculum: Part 1

The clergymen who established the Collegiate School of Connecticut intended the college to educate a "succession of Learned & Orthodox men" who would serve their society though "Publick employment both in Church & Civil State." The ministers chose the phrase "Learned & Orthodox" deliberately, for the Connecticut colonists believed in the Reformation ideal of the mutual relationship and dependence of religion and learning. Ministers preached this theme often. John Bulkley, in his 1713 election sermon, reminded the General Assembly that the Roman emperor Julian had tried to suppress Christianity by "shutting up all Schools of Learning, and forbidding to Christians the Liberty of instructing their Youth in the Liberal Arts and Sciences." "To neglect the Religious and good Education of our Youth," John Woodward had argued the previous year, "is a very direct way to betray Religion and all that is Good, into the hands of a Succeeding Ignorant and Barbarous Generation." To allow learning to wane, William Burnham stated in 1722, was to court the "danger that our religion will soon sink into Paganism." Samuel Woodbridge, speaking in 1724, referred to the larger implications of the college's task: "The Education of our Youth is of the last Importance to our future flourishing in Vertue, in Piety, in Arts, in Wisdom & Reputation." [1]

Ministers argued that Connecticut's young men had to be provided with "good Learning" and furnished with "sound Principles of Religion and Piety" so that they would be useful members of society. Indeed, as Eliphalet Adams pointed out in 1720, education was the necessary foundation for useful men. To be leaders

1. John Bulkley, *The Necessity of Religion in Societies* ([New London], 1713), p. 48; John Woodward, *Civil Rulers are God's Ministers for the People's Good* (Boston, 1712), p. 44; William Burnham, *God's Providence in Placing Men In their Respective Stations & Conditions Asserted & Shewed* (New London, 1722), p. 29; Samuel Woodbridge, *Obedience To The Divine Law, Urged on all Orders of Men, And the Advantage of it shew'd* (New London, 1724), p. 22.

of their community, men *"must have a good stock of Knowledge, an Intimate acquaintance with things both Divine & Humane."* They should know the Scriptures and the principles of religion, be "capable of penetrating into the secrets of Nature & have made successful Enquiries into the several Arts and Sciences which are meant to let us into the Knowledge of things." Such wisdom, Adams went on, "advanceth persons to a very high degree above their Brethren." Educated men "have very much the advantage of them who are destitute thereof" and hence should be the most valuable men in the colony.[2]

From its inception, then, Yale was intended to train leaders and, naturally, the course of study was one of the chief means by which this task was accomplished. But the curriculum was far more than a vehicle for producing educated men for society. By teaching the arts and sciences, the collegiate school perpetuated in America the learning and culture of Europe. In the early eighteenth century, a colonial scholar received an education that was almost entirely derived from the old world; a Yale student examined the same subjects and often the same texts as his peers on the Continent and in England. This was no accident. European standards of learning were the accepted standards, and colonial Yale followed them with willingness, if not complete understanding. An examination of the curriculum, therefore, offers the best insight into the very being of the early college. The course of study reveals what the colonists deemed the proper diet for an educated man, and its evolution during Yale's first forty years demonstrates the slow and subtle ways in which that diet was enriched by the influx of new ideas.

At their first official meeting after obtaining a charter for the college in 1701, the trustees established admission requirements for entering freshmen. These decreed that the rector and either a trustee or a neighboring minister were to examine the candidates, "And finding them Duly prepared And Expert In Latin and Greek Authors both Poetick and oratorial As also ready in making Good Latin Shall Grant them admission Into Said School." By 1718 the

2. Eliphalet Adams, *A Discourse Shewing That so long as there is any Prospect of a Sinful People's yielding good Fruit hereafter, there is hope that they may be Spared* (New London, 1734), p. 74; Eliphalet Adams, *Eminently Good and Useful Men, The Glory and Defence of the Places Where They Live* (New London, 1720), pp. 10–11.

entrance examination was more fully defined and demanded that a candidate "be found expert in both the Greek and lattin Grammer as also Grammatically Resolving both lattin and Greek Authors and in making Good and true lattin." This requirement remained in effect until 1745, when the trustees added to a knowledge of the classics the need for an understanding of "the Rules of . . . Common Arithmetick." [3]

In 1700 Connecticut had only four schools designed to equip young men for college. In that year the General Assembly ordered all towns of seventy families or more to keep a common school to teach reading, writing, and some arithmetic. The court also ordered the four county towns of Fairfield, Hartford, New Haven, and New London to maintain grammar schools. Normally, no student was admitted to a grammar school unless he already knew how to spell, read, write, and do ciphers. The business of the grammar school was to improve these skills and to teach the students "after they can first read the psalter, reading, writeing, and arithmetick, the Lattin and Greek tongues." [4]

Although the Connecticut assembly contributed forty shillings on every thousand pounds of rateable real estate within a town's limits to support the town school, the amount rarely sufficed to meet the costs of educating local youth. Common schools in the towns, therefore, were open irregularly. The four county grammar schools, which also received the colony's rebate, fared a little better. The Hopkins Grammar School in New Haven, aided by the private donation of its benefactor, remained open consistently, as did the well-endowed New London school. The Hopkins School in Hartford and the Fairfield school, one plagued by poor financial management and the other by lack of funds, were in session sporadically. A few smaller towns took up the slack in precollege education by hiring Yale graduates to teach in the common schools, but these schoolteachers stayed for only a few years and probably prepared very few boys for college. Secondary education in the colony, then, was ill-equipped to provide scholars for the collegiate school.[5]

3. *Documentary History*, pp. 29–30; *Yale Graduates*, 1 : 347; 2 : 2.

4. Bernard C. Steiner, *The History of Education in Connecticut*, Bureau of Education, Circular of Information no. 2 (Washington, D.C.: Government Printing Office, 1893), p. 28.

5. Robert Middlekauf, *Ancients and Axioms: Secondary Education in Eighteenth-century New England*, pp. 24, 40–45.

Most freshmen entering Yale College probably received their preparatory education privately, the most popular manner being to study with the local minister.[6] As college graduates themselves, clergymen were the best equipped to teach boys the rudimentary knowledge of the learned languages needed to enter Yale. Timothy Edwards (H. 1691), pastor of East Windsor, not only readied his son Jonathan for Yale but also supervised the preparatory studies of at least five other Yale graduates. The normal procedure was for a father to agree to pay Edwards a fixed amount to educate his son "in the Tongues." William Wolcott, for example, paid Edwards three shillings a week to educate William, Jr. (Y. 1734). Edwards also stipulated that young Wolcott "must do Some Chores for me" over and above the weekly tuition. John Hart (Y. 1703), minister at East Guilford, also prepared boys for Yale, leaving records of four youths whom he boarded and educated.[7] Edwards and Hart are undoubtedly typical of many pastors who served their communities in this manner. The sons of clergymen, obviously, received their preparation at home.

Some boys were well prepared for the entrance examination. Samuel Johnson (Y. 1714) entered the collegiate school in 1710 having mastered Latin and Greek and commenced Hebrew; Jonathan Edwards (Y. 1720), who began his studies in 1716, already knew the languages; and at the tender age of twelve, James Davenport (Y. 1732) had transcribed the college laws from English to Latin.[8]

Precocious boys were rare, however, and the majority of prospective students were not well prepared for college. For most lads the entrance examination was a rigorous exercise. Isaac Stiles (Y. 1722), for example, after studying with Timothy Edwards, presented himself as a candidate for admission in June, 1719. Jonathan Edwards wrote to his father about the examination and

6. *Yale Graduates,* vol. 1, passim. Of the 386 graduates in the years 1702–39, Dexter gives preparatory education data for only fourteen. Of these, two were privately educated, two went to a grammar school, and ten studied with a minister. The compilations are mine.

7. Timothy Edwards, Account Book, 1715–1750, pp. 82–85, Yale Archives; John Hart, Notebook, Yale Archives.

8. *Johnson,* 1 : 5–6; Thomas H. Johnson, "Jonathan Edwards' Background of Reading," Pub. C.S.M., 28 (1935): 196; James Davenport, *Leges Colegii Yalensis,* 1728, Yale Archives. John Davenport, a trustee, wrote to Rector Williams about his son's efforts; see Davenport to Williams, Oct. 23, 1728, Yale Archives.

told him that Rector Cutler tested Stiles in Latin, Greek, and even Hebrew and, despite the fact that Cutler used Tully's Orations, which Stiles had never construed, the boy did rather well —he made only one error in Virgil during the entire examination. Timothy Cutler's assessment of young Isaac's abilities was a bit more critical. The rector's letter to Edwards describing the boy's performance is the only extant evidence concerning early Yale's admission policy.

> The young man whom you have sent down I have examined. I find him, Sir, to have made advances but small in Learning, but I look upon them Considerable with respect to the Time he hath had, & Disadvantages he hath lyen [?] under; & look upon his natural parts as not mean. And tho' I think we may be too lax in admission yet I know not but that all things consider'd he ought to be encouraged. I look not upon my Self to have power of admission, & did therefore send him to Mr Andrew to know his sentiments, He sent me word he had nothing against favouring such a person. I have therefore ordered this Isaack Stiles to attend Recitations with the Freshmen under Mr. Brown till the Commencement, when we might know the Pleasure of the Trustees, which (I scruple it not,) will be in his favour.[9]

Cutler's reference to easy admission standards indicates that Yale could count on its freshmen to have had only minimal preparation for the college course of study. This concern for laxity had some basis in fact. Both Peleg Heath (Y. 1721) and Benjamin Ruggles (Y. 1721) were admitted to Yale after being rejected on scholastic grounds by Harvard. The Connecticut college retained this reputation for leniency for over a decade. In 1733 Peter Thacher, who was having difficulty getting his son into Harvard, complained to Nathan Prince that unless the boy was accepted at the college where his father and grandfather were educated, "I may be forc'd to go to New Haven with him for sure I am many

9. Jonathan Edwards to Timothy Edwards, July 24, 1719, Jonathan Edwards Collection; Cutler to Timothy Edwards, June 30, 1719, Jonathan Edwards Collection. Stiles was originally brought up to be a weaver and began his studies late. He entered Yale at the age of twenty-two and graduated in three years. See *Yale Graduates,* 1 : 264.

much Inferior to what he was last year (& his proficiency is not smal since) have been frequently Admitted." [10]

Freshmen entered college in September, writing out a copy of the Yale laws as a sign of their admittance. These laws, entitled "Orders and Appointments to be Observed in the Collegiate School in Connecticut," spelled out the college routine. There is no other evidence with which to reconstruct the student's day, so the schedule set down in the laws must be taken as the ideal arrangement. An undergraduate's day began at sunrise or, from March 10 to September 10, at six o'clock. He went first to morning prayers, at which the Holy Scriptures were read with the rector offering an exposition on the text. After prayers came breakfast, which lasted half an hour. Classroom exercises occupied the rest of the morning. There was a break for snacks (called "sizings") from the buttery at mid-morning and recitations were held just before dinner. The student had an hour and a half of free time after the noon dinner before returning to classes for the afternoon. Evening prayers were held from four to five in the afternoon, again with Bible reading and an exposition and occasionally an "analysis" of the Scripture by one of the older students. Evening recitations probably followed, then supper. The scholar was then free until nine o'clock, at which time he had to be in his chamber for study until eleven, when all lights were to be extinguished.[11] It was a long and full day and there were probably many students who chose to put out their candles before the designated hour.

The college laws stated that "Every student shall consider the main end of his study to wit to know God in Jesus Christ and answerably to lead a Godly sober life." Toward this end the students were ordered to read the Scriptures daily, to attend daily prayers and weekly worship, and to engage in secret prayer. This emphasis was repeated in the section of the laws on the curriculum, which stipulated that "Such authors are to be used as agree best with the Scriptures wherein the Special Care of the Rector & Tutor is to be Exercised & their Directions attended." [12]

10. *Harvard Graduates,* 6 : 99; 7 : 646; Peter Thacher to Nathan Prince, July 11, 1733, Massachusetts Historical Society.

11. *Yale Graduates,* 1 : 347–49. The laws stipulated that lights could not be on before 4 A.M.

12. Ibid., pp. 347–48; Jeremiah Curtis, Orders and Appointments to be Observed

The college trustees had established this pattern at their initial meeting in 1701. While they had ignored Samuel Sewall's suggestion that the charter designate the teaching of William Ames's *Medulla Theologiae* and the Westminster Assembly's Statement of Faith and Catechism in Latin, they were quick to reinstate these requirements in their orders about the rector's duties. The trustees directed the rector to ground the students in only those synopses or systems of theoretical divinity of which the trustees approved —namely, Ames and Westminster, two standard expressions of the Reformed tradition as it was understood in New England. In addition, the rector was to expound practical theology on the Sabbath and have the scholars repeat sermons and memorize the catechism in order to establish the undergraduates "in the Principles of the Christian protestant Religion" and "to promote the power and Purity of Religion and Best Edification and peace of these New England Churches." [13]

Despite the initial and continued emphasis on religious orthodoxy, the collegiate school curriculum contained much more than biblical and theological studies. The college was designed to train men for the ministry, but the school was not a seminary. A Yale degree did not automatically qualify a man to be a pastor, although it did qualify him to prepare for the ministry. If a student chose a career in the church he had to pursue the study of divinity beyond the college course, usually by attaching himself to an ordained clergyman who would supervise his biblical and theological investigations.

The original college trustees had stipulated that the collegiate school was to be a place "wherein Youth may be instructed in the Arts & Sciences." The trustees never stated what the content of

---

in the Collegiate School in Connecticut, 1720, Yale Archives. Yale has copies of the college laws transcribed by entering freshmen for the years 1718, 1720, 1721, 1726, and 1728. I have also examined a copy for 1725 at the Massachusetts Historical Society and one for 1737 at the Connecticut Historical Society. Franklin B. Dexter reprinted the 1726 laws in full in *Yale Graduates,* 1 : 347–51. I have used his transcription for most quotations. Unfortunately, Dexter chose to reproduce the one extant copy of the laws which does not contain the proviso about authors agreeing with Scripture. The other six copies of the college laws I have examined all contain this phrase, so its omission in 1726 must have been an oversight of the freshman who transcribed the laws, Jonathan Ashley (Y. 1730). The laws were revised in 1745; Dexter reproduced the revised version in *Yale Graduates,* 2 : 2–18.

13. *Documentary History,* p. 32. See chapter 1 for more information about this meeting.

the arts and sciences was, but it is clear that they intended the course of study to be the same as the classical curriculum of the great European universities. The Connecticut ministers took this heritage for granted and valued it implicitly. Theological subjects required their close attention; the rest of the curriculum received only their assent.

The first prescription of the precise content of the college curriculum appeared in the "Orders and Appointments" of the collegiate school. According to these laws—again the chief source of information—freshmen spent the first four days of the week studying grammar, especially Greek and Hebrew, but also reviewing their Latin. Toward the end of the year, unless the tutor felt they were ready for it sooner, they began some logic in the mornings. The freshmen were also required, at the time of morning and evening recitations, to translate biblical passages from English into Greek. Sophomores primarily studied logic, although they continued to have language exercises. Juniors concentrated on physics (natural philosophy) and seniors devoted their time to mathematics and metaphysics, although both upper classes continued some language and logic studies. The three upper classes also performed daily recitations, reading the Old Testament out of Hebrew into Greek in the mornings and the New Testament out of English or Latin into Greek in the evenings.

From Monday through Thursday the four classes devoted time to these separate disciplines. On Friday and Saturday all undergraduates studied rhetoric, oratory, ethics, and theology. These last two subjects had been of chief concern to the college founders and they had stipulated the texts for theology and ethics at their meeting in November, 1701. At some time during the school's first decade, the trustees added Johann Wollebius's *Compendium Theologiae Christianae* to the list and reserved Friday afternoons for its use. On Saturday mornings the students recited from William Ames's *Medulla Theologiae,* and Saturday evenings from the Westminster Assembly's catechism. On Sundays the undergraduates attended worship services and heard the rector explicate sections of Ames's *Cases of Conscience.*[14]

14. In Killingworth, the students attended services conducted by the rector in his church; in Saybrook they heard Thomas Buckingham (until 1709) and Azariah Mather (Y. 1706). The seniors who resided in Milford for a time heard Rector pro tempore Samuel Andrew. When the college divided in 1716, the few scholars in East Guilford attended the preaching of their tutor John Hart (Y. 1703); those

In addition to these fixed daily requirements, students also had to perform disputations and recitations. Upperclassmen and resident candidates for the M.A. took turns offering an analysis of Scripture at evening prayers, and all undergraduates had to give recitations of sermons in the college hall, dispute syllogistically five times a week, and offer declamations once every six weeks.[15] At these occasions, one or more students performed but all students listened to the speeches or debates; in this way the younger students received glimpses of what their future studies would entail.

The pattern of the course of study made sense. In the first year a student improved the language skills he had needed for admittance, perfecting his Latin so that he could read the texts in his next three years, and began to study logic. In the second year he studied logic in depth, thereby equipping himself with a method for analyzing the ideas and facts that he would examine in his final years. The virtue of this format was that a scholar examined one subject at a time in his liberal arts studies. Throughout his college course he studied theology and ethics, the subjects about which the trustees had expressed the most concern. Public disputations and declamations gave undergraduates an opportunity to use the skills of rhetoric, oratory, and logic learned in the classroom in defense of propositions in any of the liberal arts. At the end of four years' study, the graduating seniors, in consultation with the faculty, prepared a topical list of theses for the commencement program. Several theses were defended publicly by preselected members of the class, although all seniors had to be able to defend any thesis, if called upon to do so. Taken together, the theses served as a summation of what the seniors had studied and learned.[16] This evidence demonstrates that on the whole, and by

in Wethersfield probably heard Stephen Mix (H. 1690). In New Haven the scholars attended Joseph Noyes's (Y. 1709) church. They also heard visiting preachers, usually trustees.

15. *Yale Graduates,* 1 : 348–49.

16. The Yale Library has commencement theses broadsides for the years 1718, 1720, 1723, 1727, 1728, 1730, 1733, 1735, 1737, 1738, 1739, 1740, and for years thereafter. The first commencement broadside was printed in 1714 in Boston under the direction of Cotton Mather and was to be sent to Jeremiah Dummer to aid him in soliciting books for the collegiate school—perhaps by serving as evidence that the school actually existed! The document has not survived. For more on the first theses sheet, see above, chapter 2 (see *Yale Graduates,* 1 : 116). The next broadside appeared in 1718.

standards then prevailing in Great Britain and on the Continent, Yale College offered a broad and well-integrated curriculum.

The curriculum remained relatively constant through the tenure of Elisha Williams. There were a few changes; in 1730 the commencement theses included metaphysics as a separate category, and those of 1733 included ethics for the first time, indicating that Rector Williams had established these subjects as discrete topics for debate. But since both metaphysics and ethics had always been in the curriculum, the change was chiefly one of emphasis. Rector Thomas Clap, who was more skilled in the sciences than any of his predecessors, amplified the course of study during his early years in office. By 1745 he had added geometry and geography to the sophomore requirement and astronomy and mathematics to the third-year course. Again, the change was minor, as it merely made explicit what the curriculum had always contained by implication. Logic, rhetoric, grammar (Latin, Hebrew, Greek), geometry, astronomy, and arithmetic—six of the seven subjects in the ancient trivium and quadrivium—were the basic topics in a Yale education, supplemented by the weekly study of ethics and theology.[17]

In 1701 and again in 1718 the trustees stipulated that the normal course of study was four years for the B.A. and three more years for the M.A. The ancient quadrivium and trivium was a seven-year course and Yale, like Harvard, adhered to the conviction that that was how long it took to produce a fully educated man. Most students agreed; only 46 of the 386 graduates of these years failed to take the second degree and therefore fell short of complete education. In addition to the four-year requirement, candidates for the B.A. also had to take an examination in July of their senior year. If a student proved himself expert "in Reading the Hebrew into Greek and into lattin and Grammatically Resolving the said languages and in answering such questions in their systems of logick and in the principles of naturall phylosophy and metaphysicks" asked by the rector, he could receive the B.A.

After graduation, only a few men stayed on at college to study for the M.A., and those who did normally remained in residence

17. In 1737 an Austrian visitor to Yale described the curriculum as follows: "They teach languages here, especially Greek, Hebrew, mathematics, history, geography, Latin, etc." (see Yale University Library *Gazette*, 9 (1935): 62). The reference to history is odd, as I have found no record of this subject being taught at Yale at this time. The reference may be to occasional lectures in church history.

for only a year or two. Master's candidates who resided at the school performed occasional exercises, such as Scripture analyses, but basically the only requirement for the degree was for the individual to present "a written synopsis either of logick or naturall phylosophy or metaphysicks as also a Common place on some Divinity thesis and the solution of two or three problems" proposed to him by the rector. The vast majority of men fulfilled these obligations just prior to applying for the degree. Satisfactory completion of the work for both degrees usually meant that the student was "not Culpable and Convicted of Gross Ignorance" (a rather negative objective for a college!) and therefore eligible for his diploma; if he was also free from "Grose immoralities and scandals" he then received it.[18]

The trustees also made provision for an accelerated course of study, reducing the time needed for a B.A. to three years and for an M.A. to two. This provision was drawn up at the first trustee meeting in 1701 and seems to have been in effect during the college's early years; there was a tradition that until 1709 or 1710 the school had only three classes—senior sophisters, sophomores, and freshmen. It is impossible to substantiate this tradition but it is clear that some students took an abbreviated course. Nathaniel Chauncy (Y. 1702), who entered college after several years of private study, took both degrees after studying with Pierson for a few months, but his was a special case. John Hart (Y. 1703) came to the collegiate school in 1702 after two years at Harvard and thus graduated after just three years of college work. Jacob Heminway (Y. 1704) did the same, beginning his studies in Killingworth in 1702 as the first full-time student under Rector Pierson after one year at Cambridge. Isaac Stiles (Y. 1722) and William Wolcott (Y. 1734) both resided at the college for only three years. The fact that Stiles and Wolcott took an abbreviated course of study may be testimony to the excellent preparation they had received from Timothy Edwards.[19] Whatever the reason, these men seem to be

18. *Yale Graduates,* 1 : 350; *Documentary History,* p. 33. The only surviving M.A. thesis from this period is the one delivered by Jonathan Edwards in 1723 and entitled "A Sinner is not Justified before God except through the Righteousness of Christ acquired by Faith," Yale Archives.

19. *Documentary History,* pp. 33–34; *Yale Graduates,* 1 : 18; for Chauncy, Hart, and Heminway see *Yale Graduates,* 1 : 9–10, 14, 23, and *Harvard Graduates,* 5 : 253, 263. Hart was originally in the class of 1704 at Harvard, Heminway in the class of 1705. Isaac Stiles was admitted in June, 1719, and graduated in September, 1722;

the exceptions; most Yale students spent four years studying for the B.A.

While the course of study remained fixed between 1701 and 1739, the books used for the various subjects did not. It is difficult to determine precisely which books were used as texts in the various courses at the college. The trustees never recorded a discussion of required texts and the several rectors left no records of the books they used to instruct the students. In 1879 Theodore Dwight Woolsey wrote a short essay entitled "The Course of Instruction in Yale College in the Eighteenth Century," in which he named the texts used during the school's early years. In the latter part of the nineteenth century John Christopher Schwab prepared a list of eighteenth-century Yale texts, and in the 1930s Edward Parmlee Morris used the Schwab list to prepare a manuscript on the Yale curriculum. Unfortunately, not one of these men indicated his source of information on college books. Most of the works they mentioned, however, can be substantiated by primary evidence such as student notebooks, letters, and reminiscences, and in two instances the writings of Ezra Stiles.[20] In some cases, the printed commencement theses reveal ideas that can be traced to specific thinkers and texts. Beyond this, however, the theses serve as a prime source of information about student learning in general; they will be cited extensively in the following discussion of the curriculum.[21]

William Wolcott went to Yale in July, 1731, and graduated in September, 1734 (see *Yale Graduates,* 1 : 264, 519). For the time of entrance for these two students, see Jonathan Edwards to Timothy Edwards, July 24, 1719, Jonathan Edwards Collection, and Timothy Edwards, Account Book, 1715–1750, pp. 82–85, Yale Archives.

20. See Theodore D. Woolsey, "The Course of Instruction in Yale College in the Eighteenth Century," in William L. Kingsley, ed., *Yale College: A Sketch of Its History,* 2 : 495–502; [John C. Schwab], *A Partial List of the Text-books used in Yale College in the Eighteenth Century* [New Haven?, 1901?]; Edward P. Morris, Manuscript Drafts of Unfinished Work on the Yale Curriculum, 1701–1850, Yale Archives. Morris's work was of little value.

21. See note 16 above. Miss Anne Accardo has translated these broadsides for me and all quotations in the text are based on her work. I do not footnote any commencement theses, but give the years in which they appeared; except when noted to the contrary, all quoted theses are taken from the section of the broadside devoted to the topic under discussion: thus, all logic theses are taken from the section entitled *Logicae.* Unlike the broadsides for Masters' *Quaestiones* (first printed in 1740), the commencement sheets do not indicate whether a thesis was

Grammar

All languages were taught under the broad rubric of grammar, a discipline the commencement theses defined as "the art which establishes the use of each language" (1738, 1739). At the Connecticut collegiate school, those languages were Latin, Greek, and Hebrew. Tully (Cicero) and Virgil were the chief texts in Latin, the New Testament served as the text in Greek, and the study of Hebrew was confined to the Psalms. Students may have used the Septuagint (the Old Testament in Greek), especially for the daily recitations. Only those seniors who were competing for the Berkeley prize, awarded to those most proficient in the classics, seem to have read Homer.[22]

Latin was the most important language of the three, as many lectures and most texts were in the Roman tongue. Although the freshman course emphasized Greek and Hebrew, the students also reviewed their Latin. As a first-year student, Asher Rosseter (Y. 1742) kept a notebook in which he transcribed dictated Latin, which was then corrected by his tutor. The subjects of the dictations ranged from axioms about the diligent student, the proper choice of wise friends, and the correct use of time at school, to brief paragraphs about historical figures such as Alexander the Great and Julius Caesar. Occasionally the tutor dictated a pious statement about God's goodness and man's duty to praise and admire Him. Students, therefore, not only improved their ear for spoken Latin and their written work but also garnered some incidental information and some rules for right living.[23]

The college laws forbade the undergraduates to talk English in school, requiring them to converse with each other in Latin at all times, both in class and in their chambers, but this rule was probably more honored in the breach than the observance.[24] Though Yale students were able to use Latin, they did not necessarily like

---

argued affirmatively or negatively. I have cited the theses as affirmative statements, although for purposes of debate they may have been argued in the negative. The important point, however, is that the theses indicate the substance and, in some cases, the origin of the learning disseminated at the college.

22. Benjamin Lord to Ezra Stiles, Norwich, May 28, 1779, reprinted in *Yale Graduates*, 1 : 115–16; Woolsey, "Course of Instruction," p. 500.

23. Asher Rosseter, Notebook, Yale Archives.

24. *Yale Graduates*, 1 : 349.

to do so. The author of this complaint recorded in a library book very probably spoke for his fellow students when he wrote:

> This Book if Translated would abundantly better answer the End to be read by the Students of the College, I believe, for . . . I must Judge other Folks by my Self, and I believe that, they understand their mother Tongue better than the Latin.[25]

Next to Latin, the most important language was Greek. The students certainly had to use it in their biblical studies, as the requirement for daily recitations implied. The scholars were expected to sight-read Latin but this most likely was not the case with Greek and Hebrew. The requirement for freshmen to read English into Greek perhaps involved translation, but the upperclassmen who read Hebrew into Greek, or Latin into Greek probably used a multilingual Bible, memorizing corresponding verses in each language. Such exercise allowed a student to practice his oral mastery of a language and to improve his vocabulary, but it is doubtful that undergraduate knowledge of Greek was as extensive as that of Latin.

Hebrew was the least studied language, probably owing to its difficulty and the amount of time needed to master it. One of the few students to excel in the language was Samuel Johnson (Y. 1714), who demonstrated his facility by taking some of his college notes in Hebrew. The one rector proficient in it was Timothy Cutler, whom Ezra Stiles praised as "an excellent Linguist" and "a great Hebrician." [26] But neither Johnson's example nor Cutler's excellence had much influence on the place of Hebrew in the first-year course. To be sure, the commencement theses contain numerous references to this language, but the seniors were probably hiding their inadequacies by offering generalizations about the nature of Hebrew. "The Hebrew tongue designates the essence of all things before all others" was argued in 1727, and in 1739 the graduates proclaimed that "The Hebraic language excels all others in brevity of construction." There were no theses about Latin in

25. An unsigned, undated remark written in the back of George Berkeley's *De Motu,* Yale Library of 1742, Beinecke Rare Book Library, Yale.

26. Samuel Johnson, Notebook, Samuel Johnson Manuscripts, Columbia University, New York; *Literary Diary of Ezra Stiles,* 2 : 339–40.

this period—although the entire commencement program was in Latin—and Greek was not so honored until 1740. In that year, after stating that Hebrew versification was "wavering and arbitrary," the scholars announced that "The Greek language excels all others in poetry."

The study of grammar did not undergo any changes in the college's first forty years. The fact that Rectors Cutler and Williams were good classical scholars might have motivated some students to pursue language study more diligently, but George Berkeley's prize for excellence in Latin and Greek probably did the most to upgrade the grammar course. Such, at least, was Samuel Johnson's opinion. According to him, language study at the collegiate school before the Berkeley competition was minimal; the most that was aimed at was "to construe five or six of Tulley's Orations and as many books of Virgil poorly and most of the Greek Testament and a very superficial knowledge of part of the Hebrew Psalter." [27] Still, the young scholars knew enough Latin by the end of their freshman year to read the assigned texts in logic, physics, and theology, and enough Greek to make sense of the New Testament. The superficial acquaintance with Hebrew was no doubt quickly forgotten.[28]

Logic

Unlike the language texts, the books used in the second-year logic course varied during the years 1701–39. The broad definition of logic, however, remained constant. In 1718 the graduates offered the thesis, "Logic is the art which directs reason in the investigation of truth," a definition that was retained and repeated through 1740, when the proposition read, "Logic is the art of investigating and communicating the truth." Yale students learned this art from many sources, the chief one being Petrus Ramus's *Dialecticae Libri Duo*. Students at the Killingworth college may have learned Ramus through Amandus Polanus's *Syntagma Logicum Aristo-*

27. *Johnson,* 1 : 6.

28. It is not clear that grammar was intended to improve a man's use of English, but at least one Yale graduate was accused of deficiency in this respect. In 1742 an anonymous pamphleteer charged that Samuel Buell (Y. 1741) was "not able to speak two sentences without transgressing the common Rules of Grammar." The accusation, however, may have simply been a way to discredit Buell's revivalistic sermons. See Edwin Gaustad, *The Great Awakening in New England,* p. 44.

telico & Rameum, as Rector Abraham Pierson owned a copy of this work. Although Ramus was the core of the logic course at the early college, his work was supplemented by the use of Franco Burgersdijck's *Institutionum Logicarum Libri Duo,* Adrian Heereboord's *Logica* and, in the early 1720s, by a manuscript version of William Brattle's compendium of logic. During the tenure of Elisha Williams the logic course also included John Locke's *Essay on Human Understanding.* While there is no evidence that this work was a required text, references to its contents in the commencement theses indicate that the graduates from 1728 to 1739 were familiar with its ideas.[29]

The several logic texts were usually used concurrently. Benjamin Lord (Y. 1714) claimed that while he was at college he read Burgersdijck, Ramus, and Heereboord. In 1721–22 Jeremiah Curtis (Y. 1724) took copious notes on Ramus's *Dialecticae Libri Duo* as an introduction to logic and the next year wrote sixty-five pages of notes on Descartes. Yale College was not wedded to one system of logic and no single text was ever used exclusively. Yale students, like their Harvard counterparts, were "pledged to the words of no particular master." [30]

The logic course, therefore, was an admixture of various systems, the Ramean, Aristotelian, Cartesian, and Lockean. While these differing philosophies existed side by side at Yale without causing any apparent stir, the chief among them was, at first, the Ramean. Peter Ramus (1515–72) initiated his intellectual career in 1536 when he maintained in his master of arts thesis at the University of Paris that "Whatever has been said from Aristotle is forged." [31] The thesis shocked his fellow scholars, and for the remainder of his life Ramus, a professor at the University of Paris, elucidated a system of logic that successfully challenged Aristotle's supremacy.

29. *Yale Graduates,* 1 : 115; *Johnson,* 1 : 6; Jeremiah Curtis, Notebook, Yale Archives. Pierson's copy of the work of Amandus Polanus (1561–1610) is in the Beinecke Rare Book Library. While Locke's *Essay* was not a logic text, it was used in the logic course, as the testimonies of Samuel Johnson and Jonathan Edwards indicate (see notes 40 and 41 below). Theodore Woolsey stated that the logic texts of Richard Crakanthorpe and Bartholomew Keckermann were used prior to 1740, but I have found no contemporary evidence to support this claim. See Woolsey, "Course of Instruction," p. 499.

30. Quoted in Perry Miller, *The New England Mind: The Seventeenth Century,* p. 118.

31. Ibid., p. 116.

Ramus freed the study of logic from the Aristotelian categories, which he believed to be inconsistent and unreliable, putting in their place "arguments," by which he meant "that which is affected to argue something" either as an opposite or in a relationship (thus, cause argues effect, hot argues cold, father argues son, etc.). Logic, he claimed, was simply "the art of discoursing well," and his system endeavored to base this art on common sense and reason. The primary characteristic of his logic was its classification of concepts in a rational order by the use of dichotomies. Ramus presented logic in a schematic framework, beginning with the general definition, which he then dichotomized into "Invention" and "Judgment," each of which again divided, and so on. The various dichotomies are not as significant as is the overall method. The student taught the Ramean method was trained to perceive and distinguish the various components of any art. Most importantly, Ramus grounded his logic on realities. The first part of his logic, Invention, was not the creation of categories in the mind but the discovery of arguments in reality. Since, for Ramus, such arguments could be both things and the relationships, acts, and descriptions of things, they thus encompassed matters both natural and spiritual and hence were as applicable to physics as to theology.[32]

Ramus's logic had been the mainstay of the logic course at Harvard. "That Great Scholar and Blessed Martyr," as Increase Mather called him, was held in great esteem in New England. Leonard Hoar advised his nephew Josiah Flynt (H. 1664) to write his college notebook in the Ramean style:

> Let all those heads be in the method of the incomparable P. Ramus, as to every art which he hath wrot upon. Get his definitions and distributions into your mind and memory. . . . He that is ready in these of P. Ramus, may refer all things to them And he may know where again to fetch any thing that he hath judiciously referred; for there is not one axiom of truth ever uttered, that doth not fall under some speciall rule of art.[33]

By 1723 the logic of Peter Ramus was still a basic text in the Harvard curriculum, although its elevated place had been some-

32. Ibid., pp. 146–51.

33. Leonard Hoar to Josiah Flynt, March 27, 1667, quoted in *Seventeenth-century Harvard,* 2 : 640.

what reduced. In 1719 a Harvard commencement thesis had maintained only that Ramean logic should not be deemed inferior to the Aristotelian, a sign that Hoar's high opinion of a half-century before was no longer universally held.[34]

Ramus also occupied a key position in the Connecticut collegiate school curriculum. Samuel Johnson, in the introduction to the "Encyclopedia of Philosophy" that he prepared for his graduation in 1714, traced the history of philosophy from the Greek schools of Socrates, Plato, and Aristotle to Europe, where, he argued, philosophy was bettered because the philosophers were Christians.

> Among these innumerable men the principal sects were Platonists, Peripatetics, and Eclectics. The leader of the eclectic sect was that great man, Ramus, at whose feet, as it were, there followed Richardson and then Ames, the greatest of them, followed him and we follow Ames.[35]

The collegiate school student of 1714 understood himself to be the intellectual heir of Ramus. Indeed, Johnson's "Encyclopedia" dealt with logic exclusively in Ramean categories and used the Ramean method to analyze the other arts and sciences.

While Ramus served as an introduction to the study of logic, Aristotelian texts were, quantitatively, more important. When Benjamin Lord read Ramus at the Saybrook college he also studied two Peripatetics, Franco Burgersdijck and Adrian Heereboord. The foremost of these two was Burgersdijck, whose works bore his Latinized name, Burgersdicius. Born in 1590, he studied at the University of Leyden and was professor of logic there from 1620 until his death in 1636. Although he incorporated some Ramean tendencies in his work, Burgersdicius was an Aristotelian and his *Institutionum Logicarum* (1626) was an abridgment of Aristotle's work. This book enjoyed a place in the Harvard curriculum as late as 1723 and had been popular in English universities in the seventeenth century. Adrian Heereboord (1614–61) was Burgersdicius's pupil and succeeded him in the Leyden professorship. Beginning his career as an Aristotelian, Heereboord had eventu-

34. Ibid., 1 : 146, 188.

35. *Johnson*, 2 : 61. Alexander Richardson (fl. 1620s) was the author of *Logicians School-Master; or a Comment upon Ramus Logick* (1657), which was used as an introduction for freshmen at Harvard. Richardson is an obscure figure, but was a tutor at Queen's College, Cambridge. See Miller, *The Seventeenth Century*, p. 500.

ally become a syncretist, combining Aristotelian and Ramean ideas. He was converted to the Cartesian point of view in the 1640s and spent the rest of his life trying to reconcile the two schools of thought. The Yale students, however, read his semi-Ramean work.[36]

For Burgersdicius, logic was not the art of discoursing well but rather had to do with *"Definitions, Divisions, Syllogisms* and *Method,"* and its purpose was to search out the meanings of words and things.[37] In protest against Ramus, Burgersdicius's *Logicarum* reintroduced the Aristotelian emphasis on categories but, like Ramus, retained the methodological approach of proceeding from universals to particulars. The second part of his work dealt exclusively with the syllogism, a form that Ramus had suggested be used sparingly. Faced with these two alternative views in the logic course, a student, having paid his tuition, could take his choice. Some, like Samuel Johnson, chose Ramus; others, apparently Jonathan Edwards among them, adopted Burgersdicius and Heereboord.

The two types of logic, however, were not radically different. Whether a student used the simpler, experience-oriented approach of Ramus with its attendant emphasis on dichotomies, or the categorical system of Burgersdicius, he still learned to view the world as an ordered and reasonable entity that he could discern and understand. He also learned to order his own thoughts. Even Jonathan Edwards, whose understanding and appropriation of the new learning was one of the most significant intellectual achievements in eighteenth-century America, admitted that one reason why

> before I knew other Logick, I used to be mightily pleased with the study of the Old Logick, was, because it was very pleasant to see my thoughts, that before lay in my mind jumbled without any distinction, ranged into order and distributed into classes and subdivisions, so that I could tell where they all belonged, and run them up to their general heads.

36. *Seventeenth-century Harvard,* 1 : 191–92. Walter J. Ong, in his *Ramus and Talon Inventory,* categorizes Heereboord as semi-Ramist, holding a combination of Aristotelian and Ramean ideas, and Burgersdicius as a thinker with some Ramean tendencies, but fewer than Heereboord. Ong considers Polanus a semi-Ramist too. Ong has also written the best account of Ramus: *Ramus, Method, and the Decay of Dialogue: From the Art of Discourse to the Art of Reason.*

37. William S. Morris, "The Genius of Jonathan Edwards," in *Reinterpretation in American Church History,* ed. Jerald C. Brauer, pp. 31–32.

It has been argued that Edwards's subsequent intellectual career was conditioned by this early acceptance of Burgersdicius, an acceptance he never wholly renounced, and that his particular genius lay in the way in which he combined the old scholastic logic with the new Lockean empiricism.[38]

The Cartesian logic used at the college in about 1721 was probably based on a manuscript written at Harvard ca. 1687 by Tutor William Brattle (H. 1680). Brattle, who had shared the teaching responsibilities at the Bay College from 1686 to 1697 with his classmate John Leverett, prepared for his pupils a manuscript, *Compendium Logicae,* based on Descartes, Legrand, and Pascal. This work was used as a text at Harvard until 1765 and no doubt came to Yale by way of Rector Timothy Cutler (H. 1701). Cutler probably introduced the text himself, but it remained at the college after his departure. Tutors Robert Treat (Y. 1718) and Jonathan Edwards owned copies of the Brattle manual. Jonathan wrote notes in the back of his copy, suggesting that perhaps he used the book in his classes; Treat may have taught from it also.[39] With its stress on the supremacy and sufficiency of human reason in judging truth and its rejection of the authority of any given system, Cartesian logic was more liberalizing than that of either Ramus or Burgersdicius. Its student users, therefore, were pre-

38. *Works of President Edwards,* 1 : 682–83; Morris, "Genius of Jonathan Edwards," pp. 29–34.

39. Edwards owned a copy of the Brattle volume that had been given to his father by William Partridge (H. 1689). The Partridge manuscript contained several items: "Expositiones Georgii Dounami, In Petri Rami Dialecticum catechismus" and "A compendium of logick, according to the modern philosophy, extracted from Le-grand and others their systems." The latter was the Brattle logic, a manual that evidently went under several titles. Its contents correspond closely to Harvard Tutor Henry Flynt's "Manuscript called the New Logick Extracted from Legrand and Ars Cogitandi," used at the Bay College in 1723 (see *Seventeenth-century Harvard,* 1 : 192–93). During his tutorship, Edwards wanted to borrow Treat's copy of the manual, perhaps in order to compare it with his (see Jonathan Edwards, "Catalogue" of books, p. ii, Yale Archives). The eclectic nature of logic studies during this period is exemplified by Edwards, who owned copies of Downame's Ramist logic, Brattle's Cartesian manual, a manuscript of Charles Morton's System of Logick (which was Aristotelian), and a published version of the Port Royal Logic, Antoine Arnauld's *Logic; or, the Art of Thinking* (London, 1717). Jonathan requested this last volume from his father in 1719 as a book that would be "Profitable" in his studies. See Edwards to Timothy Edwards, July 24, 1719, Jonathan Edwards Collection. Wallace Anderson provided the information on Edwards's ownership of Morton. Edwards's copy of Arnauld is in the Beinecke Rare Book Library, Yale.

pared to some degree to be receptive to the philosophy and physics of Locke and Newton, which were to become dominant in the next few decades.

The commencement theses reflected the inherent variety of the logic course. In 1718 the graduates defended the Ramean notion that "The criterion of the proposition of truth is the evidence of its harmony with the things themselves," but also defined logic in traditional Aristotelian terms: "Logic must be distributed according to the distinct operations of the mind." "The operations of the mind are distinct; they are apprehension, composition and discourse." In 1718 the syllogism was praised—"Syllogistic discourse is the most accurate"—but in 1733 the students defended the more Ramean idea that "A syllogism is not helpful in seeking out the truth." The influence of Ramus appeared as late as 1737 when the students, referring to the two aspects of his *Dialecticae,* declared that "Invention and judgment agree in method."

The Cartesian influence was represented almost immediately after its introduction by Cutler, for in 1723 a thesis stated that "The senses are lacking in power for judging the truth." By 1728, however, this Cartesian idea had been contradicted by a knowledge of John Locke (1632–1704), although the latter's work was not officially included in the required course of study until the 1740s. Yale undergraduates knew of him, though, and Samuel Johnson claimed that as a tutor in 1717–18 he had introduced Locke to his students. In this, Johnson was somewhat successful, as Lockean propositions appeared in the 1718 theses under *Physicae* and in the 1720 *Logicae* theses.[40] But this initial introduction does not seem to have been a permanent one. No Lockean theses appeared in 1723 and the next group occurred in 1728. The lack of commencement sheets for 1724–26, however, prohibits any firm statement on the status of Locke during that period.

Jonathan Edwards read Locke while he was in New Haven, but not as part of his logic course and most likely after he had graduated and was residing at the school as the college butler. His "Notes on the Mind," written at about this time and while he was a tutor, reveal a thorough acquaintance with Locke's *Human Understanding* and probably formed the basis of much of his class-

40. *Johnson,* 1 : 8. A possible substantiation of Johnson's claim to have introduced Locke into the logic course is the fact that in 1720 Johnson had completed a manuscript, "Logic," which includes Lockean ideas. See ibid., 2 : 218–43.

room teaching.[41] Edwards, therefore, was undoubtedly responsible for reintroducing Locke during his tutorship (1724–26), as the first major group of Lockean theses appeared after his tenure. In 1728 the students—who would have studied logic with Edwards during their sophomore year—argued that "Nothing is afforded in the mind which did not preexist in the senses" and "Simple ideas derive primarily from the senses, secondarily from the memory." The graduates also offered a thesis that demonstrated a knowledge of Locke even while contradicting him: "No simple ideas received from two senses are afforded." This proposition may have been argued negatively. Lockean theses are scattered through the commencement sheets for the remainder of Elisha Williams's tenure as rector, the most popular being "The ideas of sensations are at the root of all learning" (1730, 1737, 1739). Some theses were more substantial: "The names of simple ideas signify not only the real but nominal essence" and "A change in relation is able to exist without [a change in] subject," both argued in 1738, reveal a more thorough acquaintance with the *Essay*.[42]

By the 1730s, then, Locke had become a fixed and central figure in the logic course. In 1730 the graduates treated the commencement audience to a public disputation on a Lockean thesis. Under the *Physicae* section of the broadside the students chose to debate the proposition "No ideas are common to touch and sight." In 1733 John Hubbard, in his poem entitled *The Benefactors of Yale-College,* implied that Locke was of chief importance in the school curriculum:

> Now Logick gives a pondrous weight to sound
> And Nonsense quits the long possessed ground:
> Here nervous *Locke* the sure foundation lays
> Of sterling reason, and *his* lasting praise.[43]

Hubbard also intimated that Isaac Watts's *Logic* was studied but, like Locke, Watts did not become an announced requirement un-

41. Jonathan Edwards, "Catalogue" of books, pp. i, 1, Yale Archives; *Works of President Edwards,* 1 : 664–702. I am indebted to Thomas Schaefer for the dating of Edwards's reading of Locke. For more on Edwards and Locke, see Perry Miller, *Jonathan Edwards,* pp. 52–68, and William S. Morris, "Genius of Jonathan Edwards," pp. 29–65.

42. For the comparable sections in Locke, see *An Essay Concerning Human Understanding,* 2 vols. (Oxford, 1894), vol. 1: bk. 2, chaps. 1 and 2, bk. 3, chaps. 2 and 4, bk. 2, chap. 25.

43. John Hubbard, *The Benefactors of Yale-College* (New London, 1733), p. 3.

til the 1740s.[44] The preeminence of Locke is reflected in the change in the *Logicae* theses during this period. Prior to 1728 the theses dealt almost exclusively with the systematic preoccupations of Ramean and Aristotelian logic. In the 1730s, however, the theses became almost entirely epistemological.

The progression from Burgersdicius and Ramus to Locke was an important if uneven one. Lockean theses appeared as early as 1718 and Ramean ideas were in currency as late as 1737. Still, the curriculum of 1710–14, which Samuel Johnson called "the scholastic cobwebs of a few little English and Dutch systems," had been largely replaced in the logic course by 1730. While students like William Adams (Y. 1730), who came to college with an impressive personal library that included Locke's *Human Understanding* and *On Education,* were rare, Yale scholars under Rector Williams were acquainted with these works of the new learning and were thus, in some sense, intellectually modern.[45]

Natural Philosophy

The modernization of logic studies was duplicated, in a more clear-cut fashion, in the physics course. Physics, or natural philosophy, was defined in the 1718 commencement theses as "the art of seeking out the imprints of nature." Studying the imprints or physical manifestations of nature was a wide-ranging task and the natural philosophy course comprised many different fields—astronomy, geography, biology, physics, and even metaphysics.

Prior to the rectorship of Timothy Cutler, the collegiate school scholars learned these subjects from a manuscript prepared by Abraham Pierson, who based his notes on two works, John Magirus's *Physiologiae Peripateticae Libri Sex* and the "Notes of Physicks" in Alexander Richardson's *Logicians School-Master,* which were used at Harvard during the 1660s. Magirus's book, discarded at Harvard several years after Pierson's graduation, was an Aristotelian text presenting little but a compilation of medieval lore.[46] Selecting most of his passages from Aristotle and adding

44. It appears that Jonathan Edwards read Watts's *Logic* during his tutorship. See Edwards, "Catalogue" of books, p. 3, Yale Archives. The students also may have read Watts; Ezra Stiles stated that Eleazar Wheelock (Y. 1733) was acquainted with the work. See *Literary Diary of Ezra Stiles,* 2 : 338.

45. *Johnson,* 1 : 6; 4 Coll. M.H.S., 1 (1852): 44.

46. *Seventeenth-century Harvard,* 1 : 226–27, 233, 155, 157; Miller, *The Seventeenth Century,* p. 218. In 1671 Edward Taylor, a Harvard student, recorded that his class

glosses by various commentators, Magirus progressed from a general description of natural bodies, the world, stars, and planets, the four elements (fire, air, water, and earth), meteors (fiery, mixed, aqueous), to metals, stones, animals, and plants through a discussion of the vegetable, animal, and rational souls and the faculties of each.[47]

Pierson's manuscript, based on his college notes, was largely a reproduction of what he had learned at Harvard and as such was, almost at the moment he wrote it, obsolete. Samuel Johnson's *"Synopsis Philosophiae Naturalis,"* prepared during his last year at the Saybrook college, reflected Pierson's work and shows that Johnson was taught nothing of seventeenth-century physics or astronomy. Indeed, one of the chief characteristics of the synopsis is that it only departed "from the heathen Aristotle" in order to account for the many things he had excluded from physics, "as for example, the highest heaven and the angels, whose nature is nowhere considered." [48] Pierson's manuscript, however, followed the Bible in these matters and included a section on the angels, which the rector defined as "a spirit, not made of one of the elements, but of rare medium, endowed with reason and will, and ministers of God, having always existed from the beginning, of least materiality but of many forms." [49] That this kind of material was included in a physics course is testimony to the idea of scientific method and knowledge prevailing at the young Connecticut college. This coexistence of biblical and scientific knowledge was to continue in collegiate curricula generally into the nineteenth

had refused to read Magirus "which was reputed none of the best." The students' refusal marked the end of the use of the Magirus text at the Bay College. It was replaced by such works as Adrian Heereboord's, which presented the Cartesian critique of scholastic physics (see *Seventeenth-century Harvard,* 1 : 233; Miller, *The Seventeenth Century,* p. 221). Magirus (d. 1596) was a professor of physics at the University of Marburg. Pierson's college notebook, which probably formed the basis of his classroom teaching and his text, is in the Beinecke Rare Book Library, Yale.

47. Johanni Magiri, *Physiologiae Peripateticae Libri Sex* (Cambridge, 1642).

48. *Johnson,* 2 : 27. For evaluations of Johnson's synopsis and "Encyclopedia of Philosophy," see Theodore Hornberger, "Samuel Johnson of Yale and King's College: A Note on the Relation of Science and Religion in Provincial America," *The New England Quarterly* 8 (1935): 379, and Edmund S. Morgan, *The Gentle Puritan: A Life of Ezra Stiles, 1727–1795,* p. 48.

49. Pierson's notebook on physics, translated and quoted in part by Collyer Meriwether, *Our Colonial Curriculum: 1607–1776,* p. 192. For Samuel Johnson's notes on this topic, see *Johnson,* 2 : 42–45.

century. Most important, however, is the fact that the acceptance of Aristotle lasted so long in New England.

Pierson's system remained the chief text in physics until the early 1720s. Jeremiah Curtis's notebook entries on natural philosophy, written around 1722, still reflected the concern for categories and metaphysics that characterized the Magirus and Pierson texts. Curtis defined physics as a science which has as its object "a natural body that it is a substantial composite of matter and form," having "in itself principles of motion and rest." He then went on to discuss "the principles of being which concur to the *esse* of natural bodies," the nature of prime and secondary matter, and the qualities of each. Curtis obviously knew nothing of scientific method; he studied nature in purely scholastic terms.[50]

At least one portion of the physics course had been improved prior to the rectorship of Timothy Cutler, when Tutors Samuel Johnson and Daniel Brown introduced the undergraduates to the Copernican interpretation of the universe. The tutors used William Whiston's *Astronomical Lectures, read in the Public Schools at Cambridge* (London, 1715) and William Derham's *Astro-Theology: Or a Demonstration of the Being and Attributes of God, from a Survey of the Heavens* (London, 1715) as the bases for their presentation of the new astronomy to the students.[51] It is doubtful that the scholars read the Whiston and Derham books themselves.

Timothy Cutler built on the foundation laid by the two tutors and upgraded the astronomy section of the natural philosophy course by introducing Pierre Gassendi's *Institutio Astronomica* as a required text.[52] The work of Gassendi (1592–1655), a pro-

50. Jeremiah Curtis, Notebook, Yale Archives. By 1722, however, the natural philosophy course had advanced to the stage where Curtis could state that "God and angels do not pertain to physics." Mr. Gerald Fogerty, S.J., has translated this portion of the Curtis notebook for me.

51. *Johnson,* 1 : 8–9; Morgan, *Gentle Puritan,* pp. 54–55. Whiston's book also served as an introduction to Newton; see Jonathan Edwards, "Catalogue" of books, p. 1, Yale Archives.

52. Woolsey stated that the undergraduates at this time also read the *Physica* of Jean LeClerc, but I have not been able to substantiate this by primary evidence. In 1716 Samuel Johnson read LeClerc—he called him "Mr. J. Clark, professor of philosophy in Amsterdam." Johnson read the first two volumes of LeClerc's four-volume work on "Logic, Ontology, Pneumatic, and Physic," and recommended the work to his friend and classmate Daniel Brown (see *Johnson,* 2 : 197). The work referred to was Jean LeClerc, *Opera philosophica in quatuor volumina digesta*

fessor of mathematics at the College Royal in Paris, was more specialized than those of Magirus, Whiston, and Derham. Gassendi contributed little directly to the progress of science but he had aided the anti-Aristotelian movement in France and had publicized the works of Kepler and Galileo. The decision to use the Gassendi text was an important intellectual step in Yale's early history. His *Astronomica* was ostensibly an impartial exposition of the Ptolemaic, Tychonian, and Copernican systems, but he clearly preferred the last, making his book a convincing presentation of the new astronomy.

The book, which Cutler used with the seniors, required little mathematical knowledge from the reader, and the volume itself contained the simple geometry needed to understand the astronomy. The work was short, only 177 pages, and dealt mostly with mathematical geography; it explained how the astronomer made his observations, offered a historical synopsis of the hypotheses proferred to explain the observed phenomena, and then discussed the movements of the sun, moon, earth, and planets in terms of the heliocentric hypothesis. The final section of the book presented the arguments for and against this hypothesis but clearly favored the Copernican. Gassendi's work contained many references to its numerous diagrams and figures, which clarified the text. The Yale undergraduates were also aided in the study of the movement of heavenly bodies by the use of the pair of globes that Jeremiah Dummer had sent the college around 1716.[53]

(Amsterdam, 1704), which arrived as part of the Dummer collection in 1714. Brown later read LeClerc himself (see below, chapter 9).

LeClerc, a professor of theology at the Remonstrant College in Amsterdam, was a popularizer of Locke. His work on physics, however, which he wrote for his students in Holland, was basically scholastic. It was an improvement over Magirus but little more. LeClerc presented his readers with expositions and diagrams of both the Ptolemaic and Copernican systems and referred to Galileo, but his work essentially followed the old pattern, dealing with the earth and sea, air and meteors, plants and animals, and bodies in general (see Joan Clerici, *Physica sive de Rebus Corporeis Libri Quinque* [London, 1696]). Tutor Brown may have used LeClerc in his instruction in physics.

53. Pietro Gassendo, *Institutio Astronomica* (London, 1675). This book was required for seniors in 1720; see Jonathan Edwards to Timothy Edwards, July 24, 1719, Jonathan Edwards Collection. Jeremiah Dummer solicited "some mathematical instruments, & glasses for making philosophical Experiments, as Microscopes, Telescopes, & other glasses" from Elihu Yale in 1719, but the items were never sent to the college. Yale did not obtain such instruments until 1734. See *Documentary History*, p. 193.

The Gassendi text enjoyed only a brief currency at Yale, however. It may have been used through the interregnum period, but the evidence suggests that the tutors probably relied on other works too. Robert Treat possessed some astronomical lectures that he lent to his colleague Jonathan Edwards; astronomy was Treat's specialty and he used it in composing almanacs. The tutors also catalogued the library during these years and this task made them even more familiar with the various books it contained. Edwards's "Catalogue" of books undoubtedly reflects this familiarity and shows that he was aware of and may have read in such authors as Whiston and Watts on astronomy, Williams James Gravesande's introduction to the work of Newton, and "Jacob Rohaults Phisica, Amplified and Adorned by Samuel Clark." [54] This last book seems to have become the standard text in the physics course under Rector Elisha Williams.

Rohault (1620–72), a professor at the University of Paris and one of the greatest expositors of Cartesian physics, wrote his *Traite de Physique* in 1671. The book was divided into four parts. The first, more than half of the whole, dealt with physics per se, the second with astronomy, the third with the earth and the air, and the fourth with the human body (anatomy and physiology). Students at Yale undoubtedly studied the entire book, for the commencement theses contained propositions on all of these topics. The most important section of the book, however, was the first.

Cartesian physics started with the assumptions that there are no occult forces in nature, that the universe is completely filled with matter, and went on to create a mechanistic and corpuscularian view of the physical universe. According to Descartes, matter was composed of three species of minute particles (roughly equivalent to the Aristotelian elements of fire, air, and earth), by which one could explain the natural world.[55] Rohault delineated this view in his book, but for Yale students the work was even more complicated. In 1697 Samuel Clarke, the noted English theological controversialist, translated Rohault into Latin and added footnotes based on the work of Isaac Newton (1642–1727) to correct and refute the Cartesian text. One John Clark put this revision into English under the title *System of Natural Philosophy*; Yale students used this edition. Rohault's book, although full of quali-

54. Jonathan Edwards, "Catalogue" of books, pp. 1–2, Yale Archives.
55. Alfred Rupert Hall, *The Scientific Revolution: 1500–1800*, pp. 205–10.

tative experiments, was fundamentally nonmathematical, a fault which Clarke's footnotes corrected (especially those on optics). Clarke also balanced Descartes's corpuscularian ideas with the more precise ones of Newton. Whether or not Yale undergraduates fully grasped the conflicting viewpoints of the text and notes in Rohault's *Natural Philosophy* is questionable. It is significant, however, that by 1727 Newtonian science was being disseminated at Yale, albeit indirectly.[56]

Teachers and students at the collegiate school had an opportunity to consult Newton as early as 1714 when several of his works —which he gave himself—arrived in the Dummer collection. Few, however, were ready to use them as texts and, when Samuel Johnson decided to do so as a tutor in 1717–18, he found that he did not know the mathematics required to understand them. Johnson claimed that he and Daniel Brown "joined their utmost endeavors to improve the education of their pupils" and toward this end "introduced the study of Mr. Locke and Sir Isaac Newton as fast as they could and in order to this the study of mathematics." Johnson himself was averse to mathematics, but he persevered and studied Euclid, algebra, and conic sections so that he could "read Sir Isaac with understanding." [57]

These innovations took place at the time of the college's fragmentation and did not constitute permanent changes in the curriculum. Johnson and Brown succeeded to a remarkable degree in introducing algebra to the students, but seem to have barely scratched the surface with Newton. In 1718 the graduates paraphrased Newton's second law of mathematical principles in a commencement thesis which stated that "Movement is proportional to a force moving by having been pushed." Newton was again repre-

56. See Jacques Rohault, *System of Natural Philosophy* (London, 1735); see also *Literary Diary of Ezra Stiles*, 2 : 338, for Stiles's statement that Eleazar Wheelock (Y. 1733) studied Rohault's physics. An interesting corroboration of the fact that Rohault's book was used, is that Willoughby Lynde (Y. 1732) left an estate of £5,600 and one book—Rohault. See *Yale Graduates*, 1 : 460.

57. *Johnson*, 1 : 8–9. See Lao G. Simons, *Introduction of Algebra into American Schools in the Eighteenth Century*, Bureau of Education Bulletin no. 18 : 34–35; Frederick E. Brasch, "The Newtonian Epoch in the American Colonies (1680–1783)," *Proceedings of the American Antiquarian Society*, n.s. 49 (1939): 314–32. Brasch stated that "From 1714 the college [Yale] accepted the new order of Newtonian philosophy." He overstates the case to the point of error. Newtonian philosophy was not "accepted" in 1714 and, in fact, made its way into the curriculum only gradually.

sented in the 1720 theses, this time with a concise rendition of his third law: "Action and reaction are always equal." Since these are the only two Newtonian theses prior to 1727 (again with the hiatus from 1724 to 1726), it can be assumed that Johnson only offered an introduction to *Mathematical Principles* and that the superficial acquaintance with this work did not last beyond the immediate influence of his tutorship. In other words, a more thorough knowledge of Newton did not come until the introduction of the Rohault text.

The use of Clarke's Rohault did not mean that undergraduate knowledge of Newton was entirely second-hand. In the early 1720s Jonathan Edwards made it his business to become more fully acquainted with the great thinker. Edwards may have read some introductions to Newton by Clarke, Whiston, and Gravesande but he also confronted the *Principia* and *Optics* themselves; his "Notes on Natural Science," which he wrote while he was butler and more fully as a tutor, reveal a familiarity with the English scientist's ideas. Like his "Notes on the Mind," Edwards's scientific speculations were probably transmitted to the scholars under his tutorship.[58]

At least one student pursued his interest in Newton beyond the scope of the physics course. In 1727 Matthew Rockwell (Y. 1728) composed a two-part notebook entitled "Isaac Newton *Optice: Sive de Reflectionibus Inflexionibus & Coloribus Lucis Extrahitus*" and *"Philosophia Naturalis Principia Mathematica."* The book, ten pages in length with seven figures at the end, consisted of Newton's eight definitions, eight axioms, and eight propositions on optics and his eight definitions and three laws of mathematical principles. Rockwell may have simply transcribed the main headings from these books to his own, for there is no evidence that Newton was a required text at the college.[59] Still, the fact that Rockwell prepared such a notebook indicates that he had learned something about Newton while he was at Yale.

By the 1730s, then, Newton was an established figure in the Yale

58. Jonathan Edwards, "Catalogue" of books, pp. 1–2, Yale Archives; *Works of President Edwards,* 1 : 41–54, 702–61. See also Miller, *Jonathan Edwards,* pp. 70–99. Edwards also desired to read the Philosophical Transactions of the Royal Society; see "Catalogue," p. 2.

59. Matthew Rockwell, Notebook, Yale Archives. I have compared the Rockwell notebook with the 1730 edition of *Optics* and the 1729 edition of *Mathematical Principles.*

curriculum and John Hubbard, in his commemorative poem, devoted three stanzas to the "Great *Newton*." Hubbard's verse paid tribute to the English scientist for the revolution he had wrought in human knowledge:

> Labor'ous *Angels* turn the globes no more,
> But an almighty moving *Cause* explore,
> That rolls the worlds their proper centres round
> By laws which *that* ordain'd and *Newton* found,
> *Surpriz'd* at mortal skill, but *pleas'd they* view
> Their own vast schemes in those that *Newton* drew.
>
> Wide as the universal laws are known
> That govern nature, *Newton's* name is shown,
> Which still shall live, when time and motion die,
> If saint and angel in sweat [*sic*] symphony
> Concordant sing *creation* and it's *laws*
> Tho' then no more to their almighty *Cause*.[60]

Later commencement theses reflected the graduates' acquaintance with Newton. The theses of 1727 and 1728 each contained a Newtonian statement taken, as in 1718 and 1720, from *Mathematical Principles*. In 1730 the students displayed an acquaintance with *Optics*, arguing that "Refraction and reflection are proportional to the density of the medium" (Newton's fourth axiom) and "The lines of reflection and incidence are in the same plane" (Newton's first axiom). These theses appeared under the *Physicae* section in the commencement sheet, but in 1735 the scholars included Newton's first and second optical axioms under *Mathematicae*. In 1737 the students accorded Newton the honor of singling out a thesis based on his second and third definitions of *Optics* for public disputation. Those who attended the commencement exercises that year heard the Yale graduates argue that "Reflection and refraction of rays of light occur by the same cause." By 1740 the scholars had progressed to the propositions in Newton's work on optics and offered the thesis that "Colors are as simple as degrees of refrangibility are different." Statements taken from Newton, however, constituted a small percentage of the physics theses, and it is probable that students spent relatively little time on him directly. The commencement theses indicate that the scholars also

60. Hubbard, *Benefactors of Yale-College*, pp. 7–8.

studied physiology—"The movement of muscles arises from the intrinsic elasticity of fibriles" (1733)—botany—"Plants are caused to grow by water" (1733)—astronomy—"All orbits of primary planets have one focus in the center of the sun" (1730)—and, on occasion, metaphysics—"The natural world is adapted to the moral world" (1735).

The commencement theses reveal that with the introduction of Rohault into the natural philosophy course, the emphasis in physics changed from "the contemplation of natural things" (1727) to the investigation of "the general laws of nature and to apply these to a solution of particular phenomena" (1728 and later). The progression from contemplation to investigation was a significant one and, methodologically, was to introduce the Yale students to the new world of the experimental study of natural phenomena. It was not until 1734, however, that Yale undergraduates themselves were able to solve problems in physics. Before that time students read of experiments and observations by Rohault and, secondarily, Newton and others, and simply accepted the findings without question. Rector Williams evidently saw the pedagogical shortcomings of this approach, and in 1734 he, the tutors, and several gentlemen of New Haven joined forces with Joseph Thompson of London, who had donated books to the college several years before, to purchase some scientific equipment for the school.

The college appointed Henry Newman (H. 1687), who had served as Harvard's agent in England, to buy the equipment and, after consultations with various Englishmen about the items, he procured £58.7.0-worth of goods for the school. The principal purchase was a large reflecting telescope, to which Newman added "one double microscope, two prisms and one lense, one concave cylinder, one concave mirror, one barometer and thermometer, one magnifying glass added to the microscope, one day glass added to the telescope." He also bought a mahogany camera obscura, a theodolite and spirit level, a compass, a protractor, measuring wheels, a "hydrostatical Ballance and Apparatus to shew the Power and Proportion of the Leaver," and a syringe with a plug and four pipes of different sizes. So that all this equipment would not totally mystify the students, Newman included John Theophilus Desaguliers's *Course of Experimental Philosophy,* published that very year. Desaguliers's book "was a valuable manual of laboratory practice and a sound introduction to physics without mathematics."[61] The equipment and the book were neither complex nor sophisticated and, as such, were admirably suited to the needs and talents of the Yale undergraduates.

It is difficult to assess the immediate impact of this acquisition. The items arrived at about the same time as the two globes sent by Isaac Watts, so Yale possessed the basic tools for the experimental study and observation of astronomy and geography. The compound microscope, which was accompanied by ivory slides, undoubtedly furthered the study of biology, while the measuring devices certainly aided the mathematics course, especially surveying. But the rector and tutors did not have the knowledge and training to do much more with these items than duplicate some simple existing experiments. The scientific apparatus, therefore, did not advance the knowledge of science at Yale but perpetuated it. At the very least, the new equipment increased the students' perception and understanding of the physics they already knew and allowed them to substantiate for themselves the claim of the 1730 commencement thesis: "All physical knowledge is acquired from experimentation."

The physics course at Yale underwent a remarkable transformation between 1701 and 1739. From an outmoded manuscript by Rector Abraham Pierson it advanced to a relatively modern textbook which, in fact, was a disguised Newtonian treatise. Rohault's book, while scorned by the thoroughgoing Newtonians in England and probably inferior to Charles Morton's *Compendium Physicae*, which was used at Harvard, gave the Yale students of the 1730s a familiarity with the new learning in natural philosophy that their predecessors had not known.[62] Samuel Johnson, whose own college

61. Ezra Stiles, "College Records," p. 99, Yale Archives. For a discussion of this acquisition see Henry M. Fuller, "The Philosophical Apparatus of Yale College," in *Papers in Honor of Andrew Keogh*, pp. 165–68. For a particular discussion of one item in the collection, see Lorande L. Woodruff, "The Advent of the Microscope at Yale College," *American Scientist* 31 (1943): 241–45. Yale still has this microscope in the Peabody Museum, where I have examined it. For Desaguliers, see Hall, *Scientific Revolution*, p. 340.

62. Theodore Hornberger, *Scientific Thought in the American Colleges: 1638–1800*, p. 42. Several manuscript copies of Charles Morton's "System of Physicks" were in the hands of Yale students during this period. Morton, former master of Newington Green Academy in England, came to New England as Harvard vice-president in 1686. He brought a copy of his work with him and used it at Harvard. The two Yale copies were written originally by Harvard students. While the work was largely scholastic, it also was related to the Cartesian revolt against Aristotle and displayed a close familiarity with the works of Robert Boyle. Basically, how-

course in physics, taken in 1713, was devoid of any recent knowledge in the field, claimed that at the Connecticut collegiate school the Ptolemaic system was "as much believed as the Scriptures." Ezra Stiles, in a memoir written in 1760, stated that when his father Isaac (Y. 1722) was at college "the Newtonian Science had not passed the Atlantic." [63]

These charges did not apply to Yale under Elisha Williams. By the time he retired from the rectorship, Copernicus was enthroned at the college and the undergraduates were familiar with Newton. The natural philosophy notes of Solomon Welles (Y. 1739), for example, cite both Newton and Robert Hooke (1635–1703) as authorities, strong evidence that the physics course had retained its relatively up-to-date orientation right through Williams's tenure.[64] Although Yale lagged behind other colonial colleges in establishing a professorship of mathematics and natural philosophy—Nehemiah Strong was the first appointee in 1770—the college was teaching these subjects on a fairly substantial level by the 1730s.[65]

Mathematics

The content of the Yale course in mathematics also made a significant advance between 1701 and 1739. Since the knowledge of arithmetic was not an entrance requirement until 1745, many

---

ever, it was an attempt to reconcile new knowledge with the old. It was close in spirit to the work of Rohault. An extremely clean copy of Morton was owned by Peleg Heath (Y. 1721); this same copy may have been read by Samuel Pierpont (Y. 1718) and Richardson Minor (Y. 1726), as both men signed it. I have compared the Heath copy with the edition of Morton reprinted in Pub. C.S.M., 33 (1940); they correspond quite closely. Jonathan Edwards also had a copy of Morton; the original owner of this version was William Partridge (H. 1689). See William Partridge, Notebook, Yale Archives.

63. *Johnson,* 1 : 9; Ezra Stiles, "Memoirs and anecdotes of the life of the Reverend Isaac Stiles," June 15, 1760, Yale Archives.

64. Solomon Welles, Commonplace Book, pp. 19–15 (reverse pagination), photostat, Yale Archives. The book is dated 1738 in the front, but much of the material in it is dated later.

65. Theodore Hornberger, "Preface" to Louis W. McKeehan, *Yale Science: The First Hundred Years, 1701–1801,* pp. vi–vii. Thomas Clap, whose interest and talent in scientific matters were greater than those of any of his predecessors, elevated the entire physics course; his introduction of fluxions in 1758 certainly furthered an understanding of Newton. Still, Yale lagged behind other colleges in establishing a professorship of mathematics and natural philosophy. William and Mary had a man in that post in 1711, and in 1727 Thomas Hollis endowed such a chair at Harvard, occupied first by John Winthrop in 1738. Even some of the newer schools—Pennsylvania, Columbia, Princeton, and Brown—had scientific professorships before Yale.

students undoubtedly came to the college with little or no grasp of this subject. Benjamin Lord recalled that during his college years at Saybrook the mathematics course was minimal: "We recited and studied but little more than the rudiments of it, some of the plainest things in it." Samuel Johnson remembered that mathematics in the collegiate school curriculum went as far as some advanced arithmetic, along with a little surveying. Johnson's "Encyclopedia of Philosophy," written in 1714, reveals that he knew the first five rules of arithmetic and some geometry. The rules of arithmetic were numeration (notation), addition, subtraction, multiplication, and division. Johnson was also familiar with the proportion disjunct, or the Golden Rule, which was the method of finding an unknown number by the proportions of known numbers. Johnson knew this rule in its simple (use three numbers to find a fourth) and complex (use five numbers to find a sixth) states.[66]

No one was more aware of the paltriness of the mathematics course than Johnson himself. When he wanted to study Newton he found that the geometry he had learned at college hardly sufficed and that he knew no algebra whatsoever. As a tutor, Johnson undertook to compensate for his poor preparation at the collegiate school so that he could teach Newton to the scholars under his care. He studied Euclid (geometry), algebra, and conic sections, probably using as texts Johann C. Sturm's *Mathesis Juvenilis,* which had been translated into English in 1709, and Isaac Barrow's *Euclide's Elements,* which he bought from his friend and fellow tutor Daniel Brown in 1718. Johnson's notebooks show that he had prepared himself to teach a substantial mathematics course at Yale. In 1717 he composed the following scheme:

> Arithmatic is the Art of Numbering both of Integers & Fractions. Appendages hereunto are 1. Decimal Fractions. 2. Logarithms. 3. The Extraction of Roots. 4. Algebra.
>
> Geometry is the Art of measuring hereto belong the Treatises 1. of Trigonometry Plain & Spherical 2. Geodesia of Surfaces. 3. Stereometry of Solids.[67]

66. *Yale Graduates,* 1 : 116; *Johnson,* 1 : 6, and 2 : 115–37. I have used John Ward, *The Young Mathematicians Guide* (London, 1747), for information on mathematics. Ward's book, a popular text of the time, defined numeration simply as the placing of numbers in ones, tens, hundreds, etc.

67. Quoted in Simons, *Introduction of Algebra,* pp. 34–35. Simons also gives the information about Johnson's ownership of Sturm and Euclid and points out that his library in 1726 contained a copy of Ward.

Johnson and Brown succeeded in teaching most of these items to the students at New Haven. In the 1718 commencement theses the graduates displayed a knowledge of not only simple arithmetic ("A unit is part of a number") but also algebra (eight theses), geometry (seven theses), logarithms (two theses), trigonometry (two theses), and mathematical astronomy (five theses). The 1718 algebra theses are the first evidence of this subject being taught in the colonies and, while only the most basic rules were studied, Yale had forged ahead of Harvard in this one area. The geometric theses indicate that the students were prepared to demonstrate the truth of the stated propositions, and astronomy too was studied in mathematical, not simply descriptive, terms. This last observation is confirmed by the fact that Joseph Moss, who taught at Yale during these years, published *An almanack from 1720. Calculated to the meridian of Yale College in New Haven* (New London, 1720), the calculations for which may have been done by Yale students. Robert Treat (Y. 1718) was a student during these years and he too published almanacs—five of them—before, during, and after his tenure as a Yale tutor (1724–25). The astronomical observations of Yale students, however, were not always precise. On November 27, 1722, an unidentified individual at Yale observed a solar eclipse and reported his findings to Harvard Tutor Thomas Robie, who had solicited such correspondence in the two Boston newspapers several weeks earlier. Robie compared the calculations of the Yale observer with those of his acquaintances in Cambridge and found the New Haven report to be "very much mistaken," as it estimated the extent of the eclipse to be about eight digits while the Cambridge estimations found it to be above eleven.[68]

Despite such errors, it is clear that students at the college were familiar with the science of geometric astronomy and continued to practice it after the tutorship of Samuel Johnson. With regard to the last two categories in the 1718 *Mathematicae* theses, logarithms were probably taught mechanically, but the law of sines

68. Ibid., pp. 32–34. Algebra did not appear at Harvard until 1721 (see *Seventeenth-century Harvard,* 1 : 208). For information on almanacs, see McKeehan, *Yale Science,* p. 13; *Proceedings of the American Antiquarian Society,* 2d ser., 25 (1914): 93–215, has a checklist of Connecticut almanacs from 1709 to 1850. I have examined the Moss almanac. For the story of Robie's account of the solar eclipse of 1722, see Raymond Phineas Stearns, *Science in the British Colonies of America* (Urbana: University of Illinois Press, 1970), pp. 431–32.

must have been presented in connection with a limited course in trigonometry. This was a remarkable improvement over the study of basic arithmetic, but the progress was short-lived. Trigonometry and logarithms did not appear in any other commencement theses through 1740, and algebra waned after Johnson's departure. Only geometry remained a permanent fixture. In 1720 Rector Cutler used Johann Alsted's *Geometry* with the seniors and, according to Jonathan Edwards, recommended that the students procure "A Pair of Dividers or Mathematicians compasses, and a Scale which are absolutely necessary in order to Learning Mathematicks." [69] By 1722, however, the mathematics course was again minimal, as Ezra Stiles claimed that his father was "ignorant of [mathematics] beyond the 5 first Rules of Arithmetic." [70]

Aside from the Alsted book there is no evidence of required texts for the mathematics course at Yale. Johnson probably used his copy of Sturmis and may have used John Ward's *The Young Mathematicians Guide,* a text that was recommended for Yale undergraduates as late as 1778.[71] During this period the faculty probably used such books as the bases for their classroom teaching while the students, who possessed no texts of their own, wrote down the dictated rules of mathematics and solved the problems presented to them by the tutors.

During the 1720s the scope of the mathematics course at Yale was fairly wide-ranging, including some optics in 1727 and 1728 and music in 1723 and 1727. Music may have been, in part, a surrogate for algebra: a 1723 thesis argued that "In a musical progression the difference of the first and second numbers is proportional to the difference of the third and fourth according to the ratio of the first to the fourth." Most music theses, however, were less technical as, for example, the statement in 1727 that "Practical music deals with the method of modulating the voice." As

69. Jonathan Edwards to Timothy Edwards, July 24, 1719, Jonathan Edwards Collection. It is not clear which work by Alsted the students used. It could be either *Elementale Mathematicum* (1611) or *Methodus exhibens Universam Mathesin* (1641). Samuel Johnson recalled in his "Autobiography" that while he was at college the students thought of the works of Ramus and Alsted as the highest attainments in learning. It may be that the collegiate school students were using Alsted's *Encyclopedia,* a work Cotton Mather called "a *North-West Passage*" to "all the *Sciences*." See *Seventeenth-century Harvard,* 1 : 158.

70. Stiles, "Memoirs . . . of the Reverend Isaac Stiles," June 15, 1760, Yale Archives.

71. Simons, *Introduction of Algebra,* pp. 51–53.

Rector Williams was an advocate of "regular" singing—in his valedictory address John Sergeant spoke of "the tunefull notes of praise" the scholars sang in the hall—the music theses may have been designed to convince the scholars and the commencement audience that regular singing was not only more pleasant to hear but was intellectually superior.[72] By the 1730s, however, music and astronomy had been dropped from the *Mathematicae* theses. The latter was studied principally as natural philosophy and the astronomical theses under *Physicae* demonstrate that a mathematical emphasis had been retained in that subject.

Geometry theses dominated the *Mathematicae* section of the commencement sheets in 1730, 1733, 1737, 1739, and 1740. Students and/or faculty may have used Euclid at this time, an insight again provided by the poetical efforts of John Hubbard:

> The *Mathematicks* too our tho'ts employ,
> Which nobly elevate the *Students* joy:
> The little *Euclids* round the tables set
> And at their rigid demonstrations sweat,
> Till *Truth* appears in a resistless light;[73]

Hubbard implied that mathematics was used primarily to prepare the scholars to study "the starry worlds." This was a fair assessment, as mathematics and astronomy were interrelated in the college course. Geometry, in fact, was absolutely necessary if the astronomy course was to be more than a descriptive account of the workings of the universe.

The philosophical equipment purchased in 1734 undoubtedly improved the mathematics course at the college, especially its more practical aspects. Samuel Johnson stated that surveying was taught at the collegiate school in 1714, and the "theodolite and Spirit Level," the "single measuring Wheel with the Movement to use in long Mensurations instead of a Chain," and the accompanying

72. Writing to Nathaniel Chauncy (Y. 1702) in 1727, Samuel Whittelsey (Y. 1705) remarked that "The Rector is a great friend to Regular Singing." So was Chauncy: a few months after he received Whittelsey's letter, Chauncy preached a sermon to the General Association in Hartford, entitled *Regular Singing Defended, and proved to be the only True Way of Singing the Songs of the Lord* (New London, 1728). See William C. Fowler, *Memorials of the Chaunceys,* pp. 278, 109. For Sergeant's remark, see *Valedictorian Oration,* p. 30.

73. Hubbard, *Benefactors of Yale-College,* pp. 5–6.

"double measuring wheel to measure Roads" probably were used in a surveying course in the 1730s.[74]

The teaching of mathematics at Yale from 1701 to 1739, then, was somewhat uneven. In 1714 the course was little more than arithmetic with some geometry and surveying. In 1718, under Samuel Johnson, Yale mathematics reached its peak. During the remainder of this period the subject never again attained the 1718 level but remained well above the 1714 standard. The acquaintance with Euclid guaranteed the Yale undergraduates a solid grounding in geometry, and by 1739–40 the commencement theses reflected a knowledge of conic sections—"The area of a cycloid is three times that of the generating circle" (1739)—and higher plane curves—"All parallelograms described on conjugate diameters of ellipses or hyperbolas are equal" (1740). Like physics and logic, mathematics at Yale progressed between the rectorships of Pierson and Williams, and by 1740 the undergraduates were as advanced in this subject as their Harvard counterparts. But, again as with physics and logic, the progress must not be overrated. Algebra had practically disappeared from the curriculum after 1720 and it fell to Rector Clap to elevate the entire mathematics course to a more substantial and respectable level.[75]

Metaphysics

The last subject to be treated as a year-long study was metaphysics, done by the seniors. For a topic that evidently was designed to cap a four-year college course, remarkably little is known about it. There are no records of any required texts in the field, so the scholars probably learned first principles from the rector's lectures. Metaphysics was deemed essential, however, and beginning in 1730 the topic had a separate place in the commencement theses. The situation was quite different at Harvard; there, in 1723, the juniors were required to read "A System of Metaphysicks" (the text was not specified) but the commencement theses had dropped metaphysics as a distinct category before 1653. In 1678 a *Technologiae* thesis at the Bay College argued "There is no Metaphysics distinct from other disciplines." [76] Between 1730 and 1740, at least, Yale College implicitly denied this assertion.

74. Ezra Stiles, "College Records," p. 99, Yale Archives.

75. Florian Cajori, *The Teaching and History of Mathematics in the United States,* p. 32; Simons, *Introduction of Algebra,* pp. 38, 48–49.

76. *Seventeenth-century Harvard,* 1 : 147, 252–53.

According to the commencement theses, "Metaphysics deals with the existence of things, their natures and causes" (1733). This was a wide-ranging subject and the theses reveal that such topics as nature, man, and God were studied under this heading. William Ames, whose theological works were required reading at Yale, had argued in his *Disputatio Theologica adversus Metaphysicam* that metaphysics ought to be studied as a branch of theology.[77] The Yale course, however, followed the more classical view that theology—the study of God—was a part of metaphysics. Examined in these terms, theology meant natural, not revealed, theology. Statements about God were taken from the light of nature, not from the Bible. Thus, in 1730 the graduates argued that "God is the immediate cause of all phenomena in the natural world," a proposition that was repeated in various forms in 1733, 1739, and 1740. The theses also dealt with the nature of God, stating in 1740 that "The succession or change of ideas is not in accordance with a divine mind"; this thesis referred to the fact that God sees all at once. In 1730 the graduates stated this idea in another way by offering a thesis about the mind of man: "The succession of ideas is only coincidental with a mind that has been created." Other natural theology affirmations included: "Necessary existence necessarily includes all perfections" (1738) and "The absolute simplicity of divine nature implies its immutability" (1739).

Just as metaphysics dealt with the nature of God in terms of natural theology, so too the study of man was informed by man's natural light. Nature tells of God's being and general attributes but reveals nothing of Him as a Trinity or of His particular will for man. Anthropologically, nature indicates that man is a free agent designed for happiness, not that he is designed for salvation. The latter is a revealed tenet. This natural bias was made explicit in the study of ethics but was also accepted in metaphysics. In 1733 the graduates argued that "Every act of man, intellectual activity excepted, is voluntary," and clarified the exception by stating that "The immediate exertion of God is required in order to produce a simple idea." A 1735 thesis declared that "Divine foreknowledge does not abolish human liberty"; the 1739 thesis "Liberty is essential to the moral agent" offered the rationale for this view.

The natural basis for these views was expressed in the 1733 thesis "The necessity of pursuing happiness is the foundation of

77. Ibid., p. 254.

liberty." The scholars also examined the various uses of liberty. "To moderate the passions is the correct exercise of liberty" (1733) and "The highest liberty consists in extending obedience to the laws of the omnipotent" (1738) are theses that explain the natural functions of free will.

Another characteristic of the metaphysics course was its emphasis on psychology. According to the theses, Yale students were more interested in the ways in which the human mind operated than in the existence and causes of natural things. In 1730, for example, one-third of the metaphysics theses dealt with the function of the mind:

> The mind is active in the simple apprehension of ideas.
> The mind is wholly exercised in each of its operations.
> The mind always thinks.

This interest may have been a response to an acquaintance with the works of John Locke. At the very least, however, the theses indicate that by the 1730s Yale metaphysics had, on the one hand, largely abandoned the scholastic preoccupations with cause and being. On the other hand, the physics course was another domain to itself, one which served to define and explain the natural world. The natural philosophy course robbed metaphysics of its role in explaining nature. Metaphysics, therefore, tended to be, in large part, a combination of natural theology, philosophical anthropology, and mental philosophy (psychology).

9 "Their Establishment in the Principles of the Christian Protestant Religion"

The Curriculum: Part 2

Of the eight courses a student took for credit at Yale, five were offered as year-long subjects: grammar, logic, natural philosophy, mathematics, and metaphysics. Throughout his four years at college, a student took the remaining three subjects on the last two days of every week. He examined rhetoric and ethics on Fridays and read theology on Fridays and Saturdays, the last course being supplemented on other days by sermons and recitations delivered in the college hall. In terms of time spent over a four-year period, rhetoric and ethics were equivalent to year-long courses, while theology demanded almost twice as much time as any other subject.

Rhetoric

The first of the two subjects recited on Fridays was rhetoric. There is no record of a required text in this subject, but the students were probably familiar with Peter Ramus's understanding of rhetoric and may have learned the art through Alexander Richardson's *Logicians School-Master* (1657) or the *Rhetorica* of Omer Talon (1510?–62), a colleague of Ramus whose work was often bound with Ramus's *Dialecticae*. In his reorganization of logic and rhetoric, Ramus had robbed rhetoric of its traditional function of apprehending and classifying data, assigning these tasks to logic. Rhetoric, therefore, retained only *elocutio* (style) and *pronunciatio* (delivery).[1] Both Richardson and Talon also delineated rhetoric in this fashion.

Samuel Johnson's "Encyclopedia of Philosophy" (1714) reveals that this view of the discipline was accepted at the Connecticut collegiate school. Johnson recorded that the two "parts of rhetoric are elocution and pronunciation" and listed one hundred theses on elocution alone, dealing with such embellishments or tropes as hyperbole, allegory, irony, and metaphor.[2] The commencement

1. *Seventeenth-century Harvard,* 1 : 173, 177.
2. *Johnson,* 2 : 103–15.

theses reflected this understanding of the art. "Rhetoric," the graduates stated in 1718, "is the art of adapting words, feelings and voice for persuading." This was a somewhat general definition and conflated rhetoric and oratory. As later theses indicated, rhetoric, properly understood, "is the art of speaking ornately" (1733) whereas "Oratory is the art of persuading" (1730).

Classes in rhetoric, then, studied the adornments of language. The theses indicate that Yale students spent their Fridays learning the appropriate embellishments for use in orations. "No figure of speech is more excellent, more ornamental or more frequently used than metaphor" (1728) and "Irony is a figure of speech which the more it dissents with something the more clearly it illuminates it" (1723) are examples of this practical aspect of the rhetoric course. But the scholars knew that rhetoric should not be used frivolously: "That in an oration which is neither for proving, nor for depicting, nor for arousing the passions, is no real ornamentation" (1735). The students were taught that "Style ought to be regulated by subject" (1723) and that "The ornaments of rhetoric do not maintain the same use in every type of oration" (1730); in fact, "Some matters, by their intrinsic nature, deny themselves of ornament" (1738). To embellish a sermon as one would embellish a valedictory address was to do violence to the purpose of rhetoric. The graduates expressed this view in an extreme form in 1735: "It behooves one very little to treat a serious matter by using the comic and facetious." Rather, an orator should employ the figures of speech proper to his subject so as to arouse the passions and persuade the minds of his audience.

The second part of rhetoric, delivery or pronunciation, occupied a less exalted place in the Yale course, but its importance was recognized. Theses such as "The temperament of the voice is the greatest ornament of an oration" and "A becoming and proper bearing of the body does much to adorn a speech" (1718) are both concerned with the demeanor of the speaker. This aspect of rhetoric had ethical overtones, as exemplified in the 1737 thesis: "In an orator, not so much ease of speaking as an upright way of living shines forth."

The students did not have to wait until they left college and entered the ministry or politics in order to practice the arts of rhetoric and oratory. The Bible analyses at evening prayers were designed, in part, to increase the students' skill in rhetoric, and declamations and syllogistic disputations undoubtedly served the same purpose. No examples of student declamations survive, but the commencement addresses confirm that Yale undergraduates were expert in the art of writing for public address. John Sergeant (Y. 1729) offered the valedictory oration for his class, and in it he acknowledged his classmates' accomplished skill in speaking, giving a sample of ironic self-deprecation at the same time:

> When I consider in my mind the profound erudition in general, or particularly the critical knowledge in oratory, you are to so great a degree masters of; when I reflect on your refined taste, formed by all the rules of politeness, and your exact skill in the various turns of wit, which fits you to distinguish so fully between the true and the false, what can I think less than by my own words to offend your ears? [3]

Sergeant nevertheless pressed on and delivered an ornate speech praising all those who had a hand in the education of his class.

Just as the study of rhetoric prepared the scholars for public address, so the use of the syllogistic disputation trained them to defend a position clearly and cogently. Whereas rhetoric taught the style of speaking, the disputation taught the style of argument. The syllogistic disputation was the most popular pedagogic exercise at early Yale. The faculty used it in the classroom and the graduates treated the commencement audiences to abbreviated disputations on selected theses.[4] Yale undergraduates were required to dispute syllogistically five times a week after they had begun to study logic. A student might begin this task at the end of his freshman year. There were formal rules for these disputations set down by such men as Bartholomew Keckermann and Isaac Watts. Watts's scheme was the simpler, and provides a straightforward statement of how disputations were conducted:

> The tutor appoints a question in some of the sciences or arts to be debated amongst his students; one of them undertakes to affirm or deny the question, and to defend his assertion or negation, and to answer all objections against it; he is called

3. Sergeant, *Valedictorian Oration,* p. 13.

4. David Potter, *Debating in the Colonial Chartered Colleges,* pp. 12–15. The commencement theses sheets for both Harvard and Yale indicated the theses chosen for public disputation by setting them off in the text with a special mark.

> the respondent; and the rest of the students in the same class, or who pursue the same science, are the opponents, who are appointed to dispute or raise objections against the proposition thus affirmed or denied.[5]

The procedure in this exercise, for which there were many more rules, was for the respondent to offer a discourse on an assigned topic as, for example, "Simple beliefs are not able to be communicated through traditional revelation." [6] After the respondent had presented his case for or against, the first opponent raised objections which he presented as syllogisms. Keckermann, who thought of disputation as "a truth sifter," stated that the most accomplished disputants should offer few objections and press them forcefully rather than offer many and press none. The respondent then attempted to deny the objections and, if he succeeded, the opponent offered another syllogistic objection, and so on until the adversary was silenced, at which time another student became the opponent.[7]

The syllogistic disputation was cultivated at Yale until 1789, when President Stiles sadly noted its demise. There is evidence, however, that college students had disliked this rigorous exercise long before that. The Harvard student of 1721 who complained that "The Vein of Disputing is become so very common especially among the Scholars that they Can scarce ask a Question except in Mood & Figure," was undoubtedly voicing a common opinion. President Benjamin Wadsworth lamented in 1725, 1726, and 1732 that disputations at Harvard were largely neglected.[8] No Yale students left records of their distaste for this daily task, but the syllogistic disputation was waning in New Haven too. The college laws of 1748 required juniors and seniors to attend disputations only twice a week. While it lasted, however, the syllogistic disputation served its purpose well. The undergraduate participants were forced to speak eloquently and extemporaneously before their fel-

5. From Isaac Watts, *The Improvement of the Mind,* chap. 13, quoted in Potter, *Debating in the Colonial Chartered Colleges,* p. 5.

6. A logic thesis assigned for public disputation at the 1728 commencement.

7. From Bartholomew Keckermann, *Opera,* vol. 1, chap. 7, quoted in Meriwether, *Our Colonial Curriculum,* p. 241; Potter, *Debating in the Colonial Chartered Colleges,* pp. 6–7.

8. Potter, pp. 24–26.

lows and, at the same time, perfected not only their knowledge and use of logic but also their command of the physics or theology that provided the theses for debate.

Ethics

The study of ethics at Yale College was, in one sense, a dual undertaking. The students studied philosophical ethics in the college on Fridays and heard the rector explicate theological ethics on Sundays. The distinction between these two aspects of the subject was similar to the one between natural theology in the metaphysics course and revealed theology in the divinity course.

William Ames, who had argued that metaphysics ought to be subsumed under theology, also thought that ethics should be studied as a part of theology. In his *Medulla,* Ames declared that "there can be no other discipline of vertue then Divinity, which delivers the whole Will of God revealed, for the directing of our reason will, and life." He argued against those who said "that Divinity is exercised about the inward affections of men; but *Ethicks* about the outward manners" and therefore should be a separate discipline. To Ames, "morall virtue compared to spirituall is as warmth to heat" and, just as warmth and heat were taught in the same science, so too should moral and spiritual virtue be.[9] This was the context in which the students heard ethics expounded on the Sabbath.

The trustees, who did not establish texts for any other course in the curriculum, insisted that the faculty use the works of William Ames to explicate both theological ethics and revealed theology. On Sundays the rector was to expound Ames's *Cases of Conscience*. This work was a practical manual of the rules of morality that the Word of God decreed for man. The book's chief contentions were:

> 12. The Conscience is immediately subject to God, and his will, and therefore it cannot submit itselfe unto any creature without Idolatry.
>
> 13. God onely knowes the inward workings of the Conscience; he therefore onely can prescribe a law unto it, or bind it by one,

9. William Ames, *The Marrow of Sacred Divinity* (London, 1642), p. 200. For a modern rendition of this passage, see William Ames, *The Marrow of Theology,* trans. and ed. John D. Eusden, p. 226.

14. God onely can punish the Conscience when it sinneth; he therefore onely can forbid any thing to it.[10]

The volume was divided into five sections, the first on definition, the second on the state of man, the third on man's duty in general, the fourth on man's duty to God, and the fifth on man's duties toward his neighbor. The final section dealt with issues of practical morality but, like the previous four parts, it utilized scriptural texts to delineate correct behavior. Ames used the Bible to support his assertions, for he believed that only in that way could man be assured he was acting morally. While Ames asserted that even after the Fall, man had retained some innate moral principles, he thought these were too warped and weak to be reliable. *Cases of Conscience,* however, was more than a treatise on ethics. It was primarily a catechetical work that showed the reader how he could and should base his entire life, both spiritual and moral, on the precepts of God as recorded in the Old and New Testaments.

From the beginning, ethics at Harvard had followed a somewhat different route. There the faculty evidently agreed with those who saw ethics as a separate discipline and used Bartholomew Keckermann's *Systema Ethicae* as the chief text. In the 1680s Harvard switched to Henry More's *Enchiridion Ethicum,* a book still required for juniors there in 1723. In 1670, the last year in which Harvard had a category for ethics in the commencement theses, the graduates argued: "Ethics is a conception distinct from Theology." Harvard students read Ames's *Cases,* but not as a required book in the ethics course.[11]

There is no record of any texts in philosophical ethics at Yale before the early 1720s, but it is probable that the undergraduates were reading something other than Ames. In 1716 Cotton Mather had attacked the emphasis on ethicism in the two New England colleges.[12] Since it is doubtful that Mather was objecting to the use of Ames, the Connecticut collegiate school was probably teaching ethics apart from divinity. By the time Isaac Stiles attended the college (1719–22) the students were reading the *Enchi-*

10. William Ames, *Conscience with the Power and Cases Thereof* (London, 1643), pp. 4–5.
11. *Seventeenth-century Harvard,* 1 : 260–63.
12. Mather, *Diary,* 7 Coll. M.H.S., 8 (1917): 357.

ridion Ethicum (1667) of Henry More.[13] More (1614–87) was a fellow of Cambridge and one of the Cambridge Platonists. His work on ethics, translated in 1690 as *An Account of Virtue,* was an innovative and eclectic book that attempted to correlate Christian and non-Christian precepts in one system. More not only drew on Aristotle's *Nicomachean Ethics,* to which he constantly referred with obvious deference, but also on the work of Plato and others. Since More, like his fellow Cambridge Platonists, wrote principally to combat the alleged atheism and materialism of Thomas Hobbes, his main thrust was to show the compatibility of reason and revelation. While the chief authority for More's system was the revealed word of God, the purpose of his work was to stress that man's God-given reason could operate along with revelation in determining the norms of ethical behavior.

According to More, ethics was *"the Art of Living well and happily."* Happiness and goodness were synonymous, and he argued that the *"Boniform Faculty of the Soul"* was that in man which distinguished and relished the good. The Boniform Faculty (the moral sense), after appreciating that good, would then prompt man to act virtuously. More defined this operation succinctly:

> It is now manifest, there is something which is simply and absolutely good, which in all human Actions is to be sought for. That it's Nature, Essence, and Truth are to be judged of by *Right Reason;* but that the relish and delectation thereof, is to be taken in by the *Boniform Faculty.*[14]

Yale students were taught this interpretation of ethics. Since virtue consisted of living happily or in accordance with the good, and since reason was the faculty that judged the good, the Yale students were justified in summarizing More's position in the oft-repeated commencement thesis "Ethics is the art of living according to reason" (1733–40). A 1733 thesis made this view more explicit: "That which does not conform to right reasoning is not able to serve as felicity to rational beings." The term "reason," in this context, meant simply right thinking.

In studying ethics in the intellectual atmosphere of the classroom, Yale students dealt with morality for the natural man as

13. *Literary Diary of Ezra Stiles,* 2 : 349: "When my Father was in College they recited Mori Euchiridion Ethicum."

14. Henry More, *An Account of Virtue* (London, 1690), pp. 1, 6, 28.

well as for the Christian, although nearly all references to God's demands for virtue were taken from the "book of nature," not the Bible. "The obligation to virtue rests upon God alone who teaches it" (1735) and "Divine law alone makes the conscience liable to punishment directly and immediately" (1738) are statements of this natural view. The thesis "It is necessary that all ethical rules revealed in religion be included" (1735) is a clear indication that theological ethics coexisted with philosophical ethics at Yale. While the ethics course had this dual character, students spent more of their time debating the functions of man's reason than discussing the laws of God. This emphasis is reflected in such theses as "The truth of revelation must be determined by reason" (1735), "Nothing contrary to reason can be the object of faith" (1737) and "That which is repugnant to reason cannot be law" (1739).

When it came to practical rules for morality, happiness, not salvation, was the chief theme. In 1737 the graduates asserted that "The end of politics is the happiness of society" and complemented that notion with the statement "All action of society contrary to felicity is illicit." As for persons, the scholars proclaimed in 1738 that "Self-harmony is necessary for true happiness," and in 1739 that "The foundation of happiness is the rectitude of desire." Human unhappiness, on the other hand, was explained in similar terms: "The misery of the human race arises from universal error" (1738) and "The only cause of misery is the abuse of liberty" (1737). These last two theses reflect the this-worldly nature of the ethics course.

By the 1730s ethics at Yale was largely a philosophical discipline. The students still heard Ames's doctrines every Sunday, but the commencement theses—which began including ethics in 1733—reflected their familiarity with and acceptance of the ideas found in *Enchiridion Ethicum*. Ethics at the Connecticut college, then, was distinct from theology. When the graduates of 1740 argued that "The law of nature is the foundation of positive laws," and then drew the conclusion that "We are obligated through the law of nature to promote the happiness of the human race," they were expounding a position far removed from ethics derived from revealed theology. They certainly would have asserted—along with More—that God ordained the natural as well as the scriptural law but, in determining moral action, the students were more fascinated by the reliability of natural law and human reason. The Yale scholars did not claim that natural law was a sufficient guide by itself, but the commencement theses indicate that exploring the limits of natural law was a matter of intense intellectual interest. However, student interest was a matter of emphasis and does not alter the fact that, as a whole, the Yale ethics course was, like metaphysics, a dual undertaking.

Theology

The final and most time-consuming topic studied by Yale undergraduates was theology. In 1701 the trustees stipulated that the rector was to use only those systems and synopses approved by the trustees as texts to instruct the students in theology. The trustees then named the Westminster Catechism and the works of William Ames as the systems "most Conducive to their Establishment in the Principles of the Christian protestant Religion." By 1714 the theological work of Johann Wollebius had joined Ames as a required text. The students, then, read two systems of theology: William Ames's *Medulla Theologiae,* translated as *The Marrow of Sacred Divinity,* and Johann Wollebius's *Compendium Theologiae Christianae,* translated as *The Abridgement of Christian Divinitie.*[15] The study of theology was supplemented by the weekly reading of the Westminster Assembly's Shorter Catechism, the Sunday sermon, the reading of sermons in the hall in the evenings, and occasional lectures in divinity, one of which has survived. The use of the Bible in the language courses and the requirement for upperclassmen to analyze passages of Scripture gave added dimensions to this aspect of the curriculum.

Samuel Johnson recalled in his "Autobiography" that when he was at college, the students

> were not allowed to vary an ace in their thoughts from Dr. Ames's *Medulla Theologiae* and *Cases of Conscience* and Wollebius which were the only systems of divinity which were thumbed in those days and considered with equal if not greater veneration than the Bible itself, for the contrivance of those and like scholastical authors was to make curious systems in a scientific way out of their own heads, and under

15. *Documentary History,* p. 32; *Johnson,* 1 : 6. The first copy of the college laws, dated 1718, listed Wollebius as a required text; see *Yale Graduates,* 1 : 349.

> each head to pick up a few texts of Scripture which seemed to sound favorably and accomodate them to their pre-conceived schemes.[16]

Johnson's sarcastic depiction of his college theology course was not unfair in its assessment of the methodology of Ames and Wollebius. As a student, however, Johnson had displayed a reverence for these systems. The preface to his "Encyclopedia of Philosophy" announced that "we follow Ames," and at the conclusion of the theology section of his 1,267 theses on human knowledge, Johnson wrote: "See about anything D.R.G. Ames in *Medulla Theologiae* and *Cases of Conscience*." [17]

William Ames (1576–1633) wrote the *Medulla* around 1620 while residing in Leyden. A leading English Puritan, he spent most of his productive years in exile in Holland. His work, which enjoyed more influence on the Continent than in England, was considered by the New England Puritans as the best presentation of Reformed orthodoxy, and as such it was required reading at Harvard. By the last quarter of the seventeenth century Ames was joined in the Harvard curriculum by the *Compendium* (1626) of Johann Wollebius (1586–1629), a shorter work but one that retained the methodological approach of the *Medulla* (which was essentially Ramean).[18]

Ames and Wollebius shared the concern that their theological systems not be tedious but concise and straightforward. Wollebius, a pastor and professor of Old Testament theology at Basel, expressed this mutual concern for clarity and order:

> For as it concernes every Christian to be skilled in the chief Chatechistical heads at least, that by their help and guide they may with the greater profite heare and read Gods Word; so it becomes all Students in Divinity, before all things to imprint in their memories the *Anatomie* of the body of *Theologie;* that in the Common places, in the definitions and Divisions of heavenly doctrine, they may be exact and perfect.[19]

16. *Johnson,* 1 : 6.
17. Ibid., 2 : 61, 183.
18. *Seventeenth-century Harvard,* 1 : 267; Perry Miller, *The Seventeenth Century,* p. 96.
19. Johann Wollebius, *The Abridgement of Christian Divinitie,* trans. Alexander Ross (London, 1660), preface.

The two authors dealt with theology in the same basic format. Divinity, wrote Ames, 'is the doctrine of living to God" and consisted of two parts, faith (what Wollebius called knowledge of God) and observance (which Wollebius defined as worship).[20] Their theological works were divided into two books, each dealing with a part of divinity. Wollebius's treatise was the simpler, less burdened by biblical proof-texts, and probably served as an introduction to divinity for Yale undergraduates. A chief difference between the two systems was that Ames delineated church discipline in a strict Congregational way.

Both systems were products of Protestant scholasticism, written at a time when a resurgent Catholicism was putting the Reformation churches on the defensive. As attempts to settle issues arising in the Reformed tradition, both the *Medulla* and the *Compendium* adopted an anti-Arminian stance. Wollebius's work has been labeled a "faithful, positive expression of what Reformed theologians were saying in the decade of the Synod of Dort." [21] The Synod of Dort (1619) had reasserted the Calvinist tenets of divine sovereignty and irresistible grace against the followers of Jacobus Arminius (1560–1609), who had argued that God's grace was conditional and hence could be resisted by man.

While both Ames and Wollebius used the doctrine of the covenant to explicate Calvin's strong views on election and reprobation, in order to make God more reasonable and knowable, they nevertheless were Dortians.[22] Covenant theology retained the notion of God's utter sovereignty in predestining the elect to salvation but, in the case of Ames at least, predestination was not the primary consideration. Unlike strict Reformed dogmatics, which made predestination the central concern, Ames stressed the meaning of faith and the spiritual life. Covenant theology not only made the process of election more reasonable by saying that God had freely consented to bind himself in a covenant with man, offering salvation to those who entered into and abided by the contract with Him, but also presented election as a hopeful doctrine, "an incentive to introspection and personal spiritual testing." [23]

20. Ames, *The Marrow of Sacred Divinity,* p. 1.

21. John W. Beardslee III, ed. and trans., *Reformed Dogmatics,* A Library of Protestant Thought (New York: Oxford University Press, 1965), p. 11.

22. Ames, *The Marrow of Sacred Divinity,* pp. 101–03.

23. John D. Eusden, "Introduction" to William Ames, *The Marrow of Theology,* pp. 26–27; see also pp. 51–55.

Covenant theology, then, attempted to find a place in the divine economy for religious experience. This position accorded a great deal of responsibility to man but, while it opened the door to a mild form of Arminianism, its purpose was to avoid the Arminian pitfall of granting man ethical and obediential powers. It recognized that election did not depend on anything man did or was; and, because it held to the doctrine of God's sovereignty, covenant theology retained the doctrine of reprobation.

In studying Ames and Wollebius, then, the Yale undergraduates were being nurtured in the Reformed tradition as interpreted in convenantal terms. The first section of the two synopses taught them that God was in essence a spirit, eternal and infinite, and that what Ames called His "subsistences" were the properties of Father, Son, and Holy Spirit. God had created the world and governed it by His omniscient providence. He had created man and entered into a covenant of works with him, promising salvation in return for obedience. When Adam disobeyed God, the covenant was broken and mankind, which shared in Adam's fall, was damned.

But God, in His infinite mercy, established a covenant of grace with Abraham in which salvation was promised in return for faith in the coming Christ. The coming of God's Son sealed this covenant and required that man now believe in the Christ who had come. Christ, the mediator between man and God, redeemed man from his sin by his death and resurrection. Redemption through Christ became operative in certain men whom God preordained for salvation by the work of the Holy Spirit. Man thus became justified before God and was enabled to live a sanctified life, obeying God's laws and living uprightly. Such men were the saints, and they were enjoined to covenant together as a congregation of God's people to whom a minister preached the word and administered the sacraments of baptism and the Lord's Supper.

The second sections of Ames and Wollebius delineated man's proper response to God in worship and deed. Wollebius spent almost the entire section on good works or virtues as they related to the decalogue. Ames was more wide-ranging, dealing not only with virtue and good works but also with the forms of divine worship, oaths, justice, and veracity.[24]

24. Ames, *The Marrow of Sacred Divinity*; Wollebius, *The Abridgement of Christian Divinitie*. For an outline abstract of this theology see *Johnson,* 2 : 157–83.

The young scholars who learned the "definitions and Divisions of heavenly doctrine" from these systems, and who recited the Westminster Shorter Catechism, were participating in a revered theological tradition. That tradition was not only expressed in theology books; the rector and tutors also voiced the same doctrines. The only faculty lecture surviving from this period, an exposition of the seventh verse of Psalm 19 done by Tutor James Pierpont in about 1723, reveals the same allegiance to orthodoxy. While Pierpont's lecture was somewhat rambling, it nevertheless adhered closely to the doctrines of God's sovereignty and man's utter dependence on Him. Pierpont supported his every statement with an appeal to Scripture and buttressed every scriptural passage with another one. The subject of the discourse was the perfection of God's law, and Pierpont concluded with a stirring call for man's obedience to that law and a ringing condemnation of the "wickedness of the doctrines of passive obedience & non resistance as they are held by some even in such a manner as to make the laws of God to give way to the will of the prince when he becomes a tyrant." This was not only Reformed thinking but was a politically radical expression of that thinking.[25]

Though the course of study in logic, physics, and mathematics had been modernized in Yale's first four decades, the study of theology had remained static. This fact, however, does not convict Yale of backwardness. The theological heritage of Connecticut had not been altered significantly since the colony's founding; if anything, as the Saybrook Confession and the reaction to the Cutler apostasy indicated, that heritage had become more entrenched. As theological systems, Ames and Wollebius represented that tradition in its purest form—no newer synopses of divinity retained such a strict commitment to Reformed theology. For example, the works of Richard Baxter, which had been sent to the college on several occasions by various friends of the school, modified certain Calvinist doctrines. Baxter (and Baxterians) accepted the doctrine of election but ignored that of reprobation, holding to the uneasy distinction that some men are assured of salvation but that the rest are not definitely damned and might be saved.[26]

25. [James Pierpont], "The first Devinity Lecture made by me James Pierpont & published in Yale College" [1722–24], Jonathan Edwards Collection. The lecture was divided into two parts, each eight pages long.

26. Stromberg, *Religious Liberalism,* p. 113.

The trustees never permitted Baxter to be used in the theology course because his orthodoxy was flabby at precisely that point at which the Yale trustees demanded rigidity.

The religious posture of the Yale student body, however, did not derive solely from the theology course. The undergraduates also received strong doses of Reformed thinking from Rector Williams, whose surviving sermons show him to have been a bold and firm Calvinist. His sermon before the General Assembly in 1727 and one of his discourses on the doctrine of reprobation demonstrate his uncompromising orthodoxy.[27] No doubt the rector explicated similar views at morning and evening prayers and when expounding Scripture.

But other factors mitigated Yale's official religious bias. Within the curriculum itself, the study of More's *Enchiridion,* which prescribed an eclecticism in ethics, may have affected the students' attitudes toward grace and salvation. The metaphysics course permitted, and even encouraged, the scholars to think in terms of natural rather than revealed theology, a fact that may have caused some of them to adopt a more rational stance in religion. Even the study of physics had religious implications, as it offered the scholars new perceptions of reality—perceptions which may have led them to modify some theological assertions and to rephrase others. Outside the course of study, Rector Williams confessed to Isaac Watts that he feared "some unhappy Influence on the minds of our Youth" from the plethora of Arminian books in the library. As antidotes, Watts sent Yale the works of William Bates, John Howe, and Thomas Ridgley, three "moderate men," who, while not Arminians, were not Dortian Calvinists either.[28] In his request to Watts for help in counteracting Arminianism, Williams was dealing with a man who was at best a hesitant Calvinist, unwilling to relinquish the dogmas of the tradition but yet unable to affirm them boldly. Men like Watts and Boston's Benjamin Colman, his friend and correspondent, shared the eighteenth century's confidence in reason and were doctrinally timid, preferring to be broadminded and tolerant rather than theologically precise.[29]

27. Elisha Williams, Sermon on Hosea 13.9, n.d., Yale Archives.

28. Pratt, *Isaac Watts and His Gift of Books,* pp. 52, 50.

29. Stromberg, *Religious Liberalism,* pp. 95, 116. In one of his letters to Rector Williams, for example, Watts confessed that he was thoroughly perplexed by the doctrine of the Trinity and did not think that the doctrine would be clarified until the coming of Christ's kingdom. The Englishman comforted himself with the

The official theology curriculum at Yale, then, was orthodox but potentially modified by the study of Henry More, the metaphysics course, the new learning in natural philosophy, and the works of Arminians and moderate Calvinists in the library. The religious posture of the Yale undergraduates, therefore, was that of New England's founders, though it was open to (but never convicted of) a novel and ambiguous form of Arminianism. It would take the purging fire of the Great Awakening to polarize this religious and theological ambivalence and to clarify the theological stance of Yale College.

The Library

In addition to the assigned texts in the various courses and their notes from faculty lectures, the Yale students also had access to a rather substantial library. What had begun in 1701 as a few religious works donated by the first trustees had grown by 1740 to a collection of nearly 2,500 books. The library contained the works of Locke, Newton, and Boyle, the Philosophical Transactions of the Royal Society, a wealth of philosophical and theological works, and some belles lettres. It was, by American standards, a rich and varied library. It was also a dangerous one. The men who declared for episcopacy in 1722 had relied on the Yale books for their arguments, and as late as 1737 Rector Williams feared the potentially harmful effects of the Arminian and Anglican works in the library.

There is no way to tell exactly how many undergraduates made use of the library. It was certainly designed for their use, with certain limitations. At their first meeting, the trustees ordered "That undergraduates Shall at the Discretion of the Rector have the Benefit of the Collegiate Library for their assistance in their Studies." While there were few books in the early library that would have appealed to the students—indeed, it would have been all they could do to carry one of the massive tomes—the stipulation that students must obtain the permission of the rector to borrow a book meant that use of the library was limited. In 1718, after the school had finally been settled in New Haven, the trus-

---

thought that it was "a much plainer and easier Doctrine" in the days of the apostles. For a man like Williams, who was seeking support for firm doctrinal standards, Watts's caution was probably a disappointment and indicates the extent to which the rector and those who thought like him were pretty much on their own in standing up for an orthodox Calvinist position. See Pratt, *Isaac Watts,* p. 50.

tees prohibited anyone except themselves from using the library without the rector's consent. In 1723 this rule was relaxed to allow seniors and graduates-in-residence to borrow books on their own. The provision was retained in 1726, when the trustees added the stipulation that seniors could only borrow one book at a time for a period of one month. In 1727 the library laws were relaxed further so that any undergraduate could take out one book for one month. Trustees, who always had free access to the library, were prohibited from taking out books for others, and Yale graduates could only peruse books in the college.[30]

By the 1730s, then, any undergraduate could borrow from the library without clearance from the rector. Perhaps a few scholars took advantage of this freedom to read some Anglican authors, thereby prompting the rector to worry about the influence of Arminian works. This more open use of the library may explain why the trustees enacted more detailed library laws in 1740. In that year they set certain fees, which book borrowers were to deposit with the librarian, and established fines for damaged volumes. Either the students' proclivity to write in books or the possibility that some boys might read the wrong (i.e. Anglican) volumes may have influenced the trustees' decision to restrict library usage to juniors and seniors.[31]

Although the library was not available for unlimited undergraduate use throughout this period, some students read its books and some readers wrote their names and/or comments in the margins. An examination of the extant Yale Library of 1742 reveals some interesting marginal notations.[32] In about 1725, for example, Tutor Daniel Edwards (Y. 1720) read the works of Robert Boyle. He may have incorporated something from Boyle into his lectures for Benjamin Fenn and Daniel Trowbridge of

30. *Documentary History*, pp. 33, 173, 238, 265, 270.

31. Ibid., pp. 345–46.

32. I have examined every book in the extant 1742 Library, now located in the Beinecke Rare Book Library. My objective was to gain some familiarity with the works used by the students and to uncover all marginalia that might shed some light on the Yale curriculum or the intellectual preoccupations of the undergraduates. While this research yielded some rich rewards, most of the graffiti were dated after 1740 and provided valuable insights into student life and thought of the later eighteenth century. I have incorporated some of the writings from the pre-1740 period in the discussion above. All books cited are in the 1742 Library. For more on student marginalia, see my "Graffiti Olde & Bolde," *Yale Alumni Magazine*, November, 1969, pp. 38–41.

the class of 1725, and Samuel Sherman and Daniel Wadsworth of the class of 1726 all read the Boyle volumes, perhaps on the recommendation of Tutor Edwards. John Bulkley and Richardson Minor of the class of 1726 each read Jean LeClerc's *Physica* (as had Tutor Daniel Brown [Y. 1714] before them), and Elnathan Whitman (Y. 1726) read and commented on Francis Bacon's *The Naturall and Experimentall History of Winds.* Tutor James Pierpont (Y. 1718) read Descartes's *Epistolae.* And while Jonathan Edwards never inscribed his name in library volumes, his "Catalogue" of books read or to be read contained numerous entries from his years as butler and tutor, the vast majority of which probably referred to books owned by the college. Samuel Johnson also relied on the library's holdings, particularly the Dummer collection, for his teaching responsibilities at the collegiate school. Thus, at least five Yale tutors used the library and transmitted some of the information they gathered there to the students under their care.

Most undergraduates borrowed theological books from the library. They displayed catholic tastes in doing so, reading everything from biblical commentaries and Anglican expositions of the Thirty-nine Articles to defenses of Presbyterianism and Cotton Mather's *The Christian Philosopher.* Some students read books in line with their particular interests. James Davenport (Y. 1732), who was a member of a group of religious enthusiasts at Yale, read William Penn's *The Harmony of Divine and Heavenly Doctrine,* which undoubtedly bolstered his Quaker sympathies. Samuel Johnson, of course, read many Anglican books in the library and signed some of them. According to Ezra Stiles, Isaac Stiles (Y. 1722) delighted in polite writing in both poetry and prose and was familiar with the *Spectator* and *Guardian,* the works of Pope and Swift, and the lyrics of Watts and Milton while at Yale.[33] Stiles must have gleaned the college library to gain this familiarity.

Some students read books with less lofty goals in mind, and their marginalia were usually anonymous—and wisely so. Undergraduate graffiti did not really flourish until the tenure of Rector Thomas Clap, whose personality seemed to cry out for slander. Some of them, however, date before 1740. A common practice was for students to ascribe their comments to their classmates.

33. Stiles, "Memoirs . . . of the Reverend Isaac Stiles," June 15, 1760, Yale Archives.

M. C. Templero's *Physicae* contained many scrawls, one of which was this explanation: "[Abraham] Mead [Y. 1739] had this Book out of the Lybrary & [Samuel] Evans [Y. 1739] wrote all the Wrighting." Occasionally a student would dare a racy remark. After a poem entitled "Maidenhead" in Abraham Cowley's *Works,* one boy penned the suggestion that Steward Punderson had found a maidenhead. Another student appended this philosophical observation: "I dont know as I can find any more But I have found several, therefore I trust I can find more."

The library, then, had both its serious and frivolous users. A few students obviously used the library to complement their studies and a few more to expand their intellectual horizons. Others borrowed books for extracurricular reasons. On the whole, however, the library was not an integral part of the college course of study. Tutors used some books in preparation for their teaching but they rarely made additional assignments in library volumes to supplement classroom work. So in assessing the Yale curriculum from 1701 to 1740 the library is a relatively insignificant factor.

A Yale Education

By the time a student graduated from Yale College he had received a substantial and broad education. Like his counterparts in Europe, he had studied the classical curriculum in the liberal arts and sciences. The subjects he had learned were the same as those taken by boys at Harvard, Oxford, Cambridge, Edinburgh, and the various English Dissenting academies. Thus, while a claim that Yale competed with the great learned academies of Europe is slightly overblown, it is not far wrong. In the early eighteenth century, the undergraduate curriculum at Oxford consisted of grammar, rhetoric, Aristotle's *Ethics* and *Politics,* logic, economics, moral philosophy, geometry, and Greek; M.A. candidates did geometry, astronomy, metaphysics, natural philosophy, ancient history, Greek, and Hebrew. The four-year Edinburgh curriculum of 1708 included Greek, logic, metaphysics, pneumatics, moral philosophy, and natural philosophy. At Shrewsbury Academy in England, students of this period studied logic, metaphysics, geometry, astronomy, chronology, ecclesiastical history, theology, and natural philosophy. The Yale course of study was not identical to any one of these but it was remarkably parallel to all of them, except that, unlike Oxford, Yale did not divide some subjects between B.A. and M.A. students. As might be expected, Yale's curriculum was very similar to Harvard's. The 1726 course of study at the Bay College consisted of grammar, rhetoric, logic, natural philosophy, ethics, geography, metaphysics, mathematics, and theology.[34]

The Yale College course of study not only retained the structure but in many cases the content of the English curricula. Yale, like Shrewsbury, taught Burgersdicius, Heereboord, Ramus, Euclid, Gassendi, and Wollebius; like Rathmell Academy, Yale used Burgersdicius, Heereboord, Ramus, a version of *Ars Cogitandi,* Rohault, More, Ames, Wollebius, and Gassendi.[35] The Connecticut college even duplicated some of the texts used at Cambridge: Euclid, Burgersdicius, and Rohault. In preparing for classes, Yale tutors relied on other Cambridge texts such as Wells, Whiston, Newton, and Locke. Again, the collegiate school's texts were most like Harvard's. Both colleges used Burgersdicius, Ramus, the Brattle logic, More, Alsted, Gassendi, Ames, and Wollebius as well as the standard Greek, Hebrew, and Latin works in grammar.

Despite the many similarities, a Yale education differed from the English in two important respects. The first was in assigned texts. While Yale used many of the same works taught in English colleges, it rarely assigned as wide a variety of them at one time in any one course. In mathematics and physics, for example, the collegiate school used, at various times, Pierson's manuscript notes based on Magirus, Gassendi, Rohault, Alsted, and Euclid. Eighteenth-century Cambridge, on the other hand, employed: Edward Wells, *The Young Gentleman's Arithmetick and Geometry*; Wells's *The Young Gentleman's Trigonometry; Mechanicks and Opticks*; Wells's *Young Man's Astronomy, Chronology and Dialing*; Euclid's *Elements*; Phillipe de La Hire, *New Elements of Conick Sections*; William Whiston, *Astronomical Lectures*; John Keill, *Introductio ad veram phisicam*; Rohault's *Physica*; Whiston's *Praelectiones physico-mathematicae*; David Gregory, *The Elements of Astronomy*; Newton's *Opticks* and *Trigonometry*; and Thomas Burnet, *Sacred Theory of the Earth.*[36]

34. Alfred D. Godley, *Oxford in the Eighteenth Century,* p. 57; Alexander Morgan, *Scottish University Studies,* p. 73; Herbert McLachlan, *English Education Under the Test Acts,* pp. 82–83; *Seventeenth-century Harvard,* 1 : 146–47.

35. McLachlan, *English Education,* pp. 69, 82.

36. Nicholas Hans, *New Trends in Education in the Eighteenth Century,* p. 51.

While several of these works were consulted by Yale tutors and their ideas disseminated to the undergraduates, only two of them, Euclid and Rohault, were used as texts at the college. It seems apparent that colonial Yale offered a sparser diet to its scholars, perhaps because new books and theories had to travel the Atlantic to reach New Haven. But the college did a creditable job in overcoming this deficiency. The faculty familiarized the students with a significant number of these new theories, indicating that the rectors and tutors were in touch with the intellectual currents in old England and were ready and willing to channel those currents to their pupils. Thus, while Cambridge undergraduates read Locke and Newton for themselves, Yale students heard about them from their tutors. It is impossible to evaluate the precise import of this difference, as the provincial scholar may have grasped as much Newtonian physics secondhand as his cosmopolitan peer did by reading the work itself. The intellectual fare at Yale may have been less varied, but it was not necessarily less filling.

The second difference between Yale and the British colleges was in faculty. The bulk of the teaching load at Yale was carried by the tutors. These men were recent college graduates themselves and therefore were not much older than their students. No young man ever undertook the tutorship as a career, so the tenure of a given tutor was relatively brief, averaging less than two and a half years in the period 1701–40. Not only were the tutors young and their stay in office short, but they did not undergo any additional training in preparation for their jobs. Only fifteen of the twenty-nine tutors of these years had earned the M.A. when they assumed their teaching jobs, and few of them had developed any special talents in a particular subject matter. There is evidence that some, like Samuel Johnson, Daniel Brown, Robert Treat, and Jonathan Edwards, had made intellectual advancement since their undergraduate days, but most tutors simply passed on to their charges the learning they had received a few years before. Another inhibiting feature of the tutoring system was that men did not teach a subject but a class; in some cases a tutor might take a class through several years of study, but in other instances the tutor would somewhat randomly be given one class one year and another the next. This pedagogical system meant that the tutors had to be familiar with a wide range of material and that, except in a few special cases, the content of the curriculum changed slowly; only in the tutorships of Samuel Johnson and Jonathan Edwards did significant innovations occur.

In some respects the tutoring system at Yale was similar to the regenting procedure in the Scottish universities, where a regent took a given class through a four-year program of study. In 1708 Edinburgh did away with regents (Glasgow did the same in 1727) and provided instructors for each subject. The results of this change were positive; the university soon did away with Aristotelian physics and introduced David Gregory's work on optics and Newton's *Principia.* The course of study was not only modernized, but the university offered a much more expansive curriculum.[37] While Edinburgh was able to teach more subjects (usually the new courses were specialized topics in traditional subjects), Yale continued to offer the same curriculum, largely because of the conservative nature of the tutoring system.

Yale's reliance on tutors placed the college at an intellectual disadvantage in comparison to the ancient English universities. A student at the collegiate school learned physics and mathematics from, say, Tutor Joseph Noyes; an Oxford undergraduate, on the other hand, could listen to the lectures of David Gregory or John Keill and a Cambridge scholar could hear William Whiston or Nicholas Sanderson.[38] The two English universities not only had professorial chairs but filled them with first-rate thinkers. Scottish universities claimed similar talent—Gregory and Keill came to Oxford from Edinburgh—and even the Dissenting academies, while unable to boast the same caliber of intellects, had faculties of men who were aware of the new thought and theories of the time. In all cases, the English and Scottish faculties were ongoing communities of scholars where older men and young beginners shared both ideas and the teaching load. Yale was an ocean away from this active intellectual world and its educational offerings suffered accordingly. The ideas shared by Yale tutors were all derived secondhand, and since there were no academic authors on the faculty, the tutors always taught someone else's work, never a colleague's or their own.

The Connecticut collegiate school did possess one crucial ad-

37. Morgan, *Scottish University Studies,* pp. 72–73; Alexander Grant, *The Story of the University of Edinburgh,* 1 : 259–75.

38. Hans, *New Trends,* pp. 47–50, 42.

vantage over some of its English counterparts: it was not a college for the idle rich. The texts may not have been the most up-to-date nor the teachers the most brilliant, but the scholastic life at Yale was rigorous and was meant to be taken seriously. In this respect, Yale had much in common with the Dissenting academies and enjoyed a superiority over Oxford and Cambridge. While poor, hard-working students attended the latter universities and performed diligently, the most prominent aspect of learning at these two places was the cavalier and casual approach of wealthy scholars. They were there, on the whole, "to enjoy a costly luxury" and devoted more energy to "drunkenness, gambling, and an absurd attention to dress" than to education. It was not uncommon for faculty to deliver "wall lectures" to an empty hall, or for examinations to degenerate into drinking bouts.[39] Such levity and laxity were unheard of at the Connecticut college. If nothing else, faculty and students at Yale lived a more sober academic life.

Yet the college's dedication to learning could not compensate for the fact that the form and content of a Yale education were largely derivative; the colonial school was hampered by a cultural lag and innovations in its course of study occurred, on the whole, after similar innovations had been effected abroad. But although the educators of Connecticut's youth were provincial, they were at least aware of their provinciality and sought to overcome it. From the beginning of Yale's history its founders and trustees had looked to Europe and England for intellectual inspiration and educational models. They had eagerly welcomed the library sent by Jeremiah Dummer as a link with a wider intellectual world. They had tried to cultivate contacts with Englishmen such as Samuel Holden and Isaac Watts and had, perhaps secretly, rejoiced in the unsolicited attentions of George Berkeley.

This same impulse toward modernity seems to have been at work in the development of the Yale curriculum. Because Yale wanted to be up-to-date, it was not afraid to revise and change its courses. Unfortunately, no evidence survives—if it ever existed—which reveals the motivations behind the adoption of new texts by the college. But the *fact* of their adoption does exist and it is likely that such decisions were conscious and deliberate. Thus, through the development of its curriculum, Yale College over-

39. George C. Brodrick, *A History of the University of Oxford*, pp. 174–77; Godley, *Oxford in the Eighteenth Century*, pp. 178, 36–68.

came much of its provinciality and served as an agent of transfer for new thoughts and ideas.

The implications—and in some cases the content—of those new ideas were not always appreciated fully, and to this extent the college was an inadequate agent. The early eighteenth century was a time of intellectual transition, and the alterations in thought and world-view were not always smooth. Although this problem was evident in Europe as well, it was accentuated in the New World and especially at a place like Yale, which attempted to perpetuate old beliefs through new ideas. The theological import of Newtonian physics, for example, was not recognized, so that Yale, by introducing Newton to the students, unwittingly fostered a way of perceiving the world that in many ways ran counter to the religious goals of the college. This unintended subversion was the provincial's price for seeking contemporaneity.

Despite the inherent dangers of teaching the new learning to the parochial scholars of New England, Yale's achievement in enriching the curriculum was outstanding. By the 1730s the Yale curriculum compared favorably with, though it by no means was the same as, those of the more established colleges in England and Scotland. The collegiate school had come a long way from its shaky beginnings in Killingworth and Saybrook to its prosperous state in New Haven. This was not only true institutionally and financially but also intellectually. The entire course of study had become more modern and respectable. Two views of the college commencement exercises indicate this improvement. In 1714 Ebenezer Williams (H. 1709) wrote to Thomas Foxcroft (H. 1714) about an account of the graduation exercises at the collegiate school:

> I hear that the Athenian Oracle is held at Seabrook Colledge that all Notty Questions (altho twisted as hard as the Gordian one) maybe Resolved and untied; and that they'll Do it, altho with Alexanders Sword; if so for their Reward they shall have (as Alexander had) an Empire, but not of the whole known, but of the unknown world, or . . . Else the Empire of the Moon with all the principalityes adjoyning thereto, shall be committed to their trust since they are so Lunatick, and under the moons powerfull Domination.[40]

40. Ebenezer Williams to Thomas Foxcroft, Dec. 25, 1714, Connecticut Historical Society:

This lampoon of the young college, while undoubtedly in jest, is indicative of the intellectual reputation of the Connecticut school. Later, in 1738, another Harvard man, Ebenezer Parkman (H. 1721), voiced a more respectful opinion: "The [Yale commencement] Exercises and Entertainments handsome and agreeable, and especially the Valedictory Oration. . . . The Custom of giving Diploma at the time of giving the Degree is most fit and proper in my Eye and what I could wish our College would come into."[41] While the opinions of Harvard men might be suspect, in both these cases they are accurate. In 1714 the Collegiate School of Connecticut was a relatively backward institution; by 1738 it was at least possible for Yale to be seen as a model for Harvard.

41. Ebenezer Parkman, *Diary, Proceedings of the American Antiquarian Society,* n.s. 71 (1961): 432–33. Parkman, who visited Yale in 1738, was surprised to see a number of Anglican ministers at the commencement. There was nothing the trustees could do about that, but when it came time to offer honorary degrees they demonstrated where the college's sympathies lay. In 1725 Yale awarded an honorary M.A. to Gilbert Tennent, the future revivalist of the Great Awakening, and in 1737 the trustees gave the degree to John Graham, a Scottish immigrant who had won the hearts of the college supporters by engaging in a pamphlet controversy with the Anglicans. See *Yale Graduates,* 1 : 312, 570.

10 "A Succession of Learned & Orthodox Men"

Yale College was, above all, a community of young men preparing for vocations in colonial society. Both the trustees' attempts to settle and better the college and the faculty's efforts to improve the curriculum were designed to further Yale's chief purpose of educating "a succession of Learned & Orthodox men" who, in turn, would benefit the colony through "Publick employment both in Church & Civil State." [1] The history of early Yale, then, deals with more than institutional, financial, and intellectual matters: the story of the college is, in large part, the story of its students.

There are many things we can learn about the Yale undergraduates of two-and-a-half centuries ago. Thanks to the labors of Franklin Bowditch Dexter, whose six-volume *Biographical Sketches of the Graduates of Yale College* covers the classes of 1702 through 1815, we know who the majority of them were, where they came from, and what they did. From surviving letters and diaries we can discover the kind of life they led while attending the college. The story of the men who populated Yale reminds us that the high-minded intellectual, social, and religious aims of the college founders were not abstractions but were meant to be embodied in the school's living products—its graduates. Yale took boys, who often persisted in acting like boys while at school, and turned them into educated men. The ambitious goals of the original trustees were thus realized in the lives and careers of Yale graduates. This fact is readily substantiated by a survey of the 386 young men who graduated from Yale before 1740. Such statistics, of course, have limited meaning, but within those limits they reveal a great deal about the performance of the college in turning out leaders for colonial society.

The Students

One of the alleged reasons for founding the collegiate school had been the great expense of sending young men to Harvard. The Saybrook college was designed to relieve Connecticut families

1. *Documentary History*, pp. 20, 21.

of this financial burden, and it did. Whereas sixty-nine Connecticut youths had graduated from the Bay College from 1642 to 1703, only twelve did so from 1704 to 1740.[2] Most boys who would have gone to Harvard switched to the collegiate school. Four students—John Hart (Y. 1703), Jacob Heminway (Y. 1704), Azariah Mather (Y. 1705), and Jared Eliot (Y. 1706)—came to the college after spending one or two years at Harvard. Hart and Heminway took advantage of the abbreviated college course the trustees offered and graduated in three years.[3] From the outset, then, the collegiate school primarily served a local constituency. But students were few. Despite the decision of the General Assembly to offer student deferments by exempting all scholars "from watching and warding and all other such publick service," the War of the Spanish Succession took many would-be students off to fight the French and Indians.[4]

During its Killingworth and Saybrook years, the college issued only fifty-six B.A. degrees for a yearly average graduating class of 3.73.[5] The end of the war in 1713 and the settlement of the school in New Haven a few years later marked the beginning of a period of growth for newly named Yale College. During its first ten years in New Haven, the college graduated 115 students (including the six boys who took degrees at Wethersfield, one in 1717 and five in 1718), an average of 11.5 per class. Elisha Williams, who began his rectorship in 1726, supervised a time of increased prosperity and prestige for the school. Yale awarded 215 B.A.'s during his tenure and the classes averaged 16.54 graduates each. From 1702 to 1739, then, 386 young men earned their first degree at Yale, an overall average of 10.16 students in each of the thirty-eight classes. These figures indicate that the collegiate school not only took students away from Harvard but also provided the opportunity for an education to many boys who would not otherwise have had one.

2. These figures are based on the first ten volumes of *Harvard Graduates.*

3. *Harvard Graduates,* 5 : 253, 263, 283, 192.

4. *Documentary History,* p. 45.

5. All statistical information is based on my compilations from *Yale Graduates,* vol. 1. I have collected data on the 386 men who received B.A.'s from 1702 to 1739. The only source of information has been Dexter's book, and if he erred my statistics will err. Dexter, however, was a thorough and resourceful historian; the biographical sketches are based on substantial research. I have not footnoted any of the figures cited in the rest of this chapter, as all come from my compilations.

This notion is supported by the likelihood that most students came from relatively modest backgrounds. The occupation or position within the community is known for the fathers of 202 of the 386 graduates; the obscurity of the remaining 184 fathers suggests that they were probably men of small means, most likely farmers or artisans. While some of the known fathers held similar jobs, such as carpenter, weaver, mason, mariner, and trader, most members of this group were more prominent. Sixty-eight fathers of Yale graduates were ministers (thirty-two of these were also Yale trustees), ten were landowners, ten were legislators, six were judges, and two were colonial governors. The predominance of ministers' sons is understandable; with few exceptions, these fathers had college degrees themselves and envisioned the same advantage for at least one of their children. Many other fathers, about whom we have no vocational data, were active members of their communities, fifteen as prominent citizens, twenty-three as church deacons, and forty-six as members of the militia. In addition, seventy-four graduates had college-educated fathers, fifty-six at Harvard and eighteen at Yale. Another fifty-four students came from families in which some other male relative had gone to college.[6] Even so, only 33 percent of the graduates came from families with a background of college education. Again, Yale obviously served to open up educational opportunities for many New England youths.

We know the residences of 377 of these young men at the time they entered Yale. Three hundred students (78 percent of the total) came from Connecticut, forty-two from Massachusetts, twenty-five from New York, six from New Jersey, two from Rhode Island, and one each from Pennsylvania and Delaware. These seventy-seven non-Connecticut boys accounted for 20 percent of the total. Of the forty-two who came from Massachusetts, thirty-two (76 percent) came from the Connecticut River Valley or the western townships of the colony; Yale drew only eight students from eastern Massachusetts. Twenty-four of the twenty-five boys from Massachusetts who attended Yale while Elisha Williams was

6. Included in this second group are boys whose fathers had not gone to college but who had grandfathers, older brothers, and uncles or cousins who did. Of the seventy-four boys whose fathers were educated, forty had other family members who had also graduated from college. The first Yale son of a Yale graduate was Samuel Whittelsey (Y. 1729), whose father graduated in 1705.

rector were either from the valley or the western towns. Geographically, Yale had begun to dominate the interior of New England, a trend that would be accentuated during the remainder of the century.

When the college was located in Saybrook, students from Massachusetts could travel there by way of the Connecticut River. The Saybrook location was also convenient for nearby Rhode Island; but Rhode Island had no formal school system or compulsory education laws and therefore prepared few of its sons for college. Only one boy from that colony had attended Harvard in the seventeenth century, and Yale fared no better.[7] Not one Rhode Island youth attended the collegiate school in Saybrook, and the first student from that colony did not come to Yale until 1720. When the college went to New Haven, a move the trustees hoped would serve the western governments, which had no colleges, undergraduate enrollment from New York and New Jersey increased; New York had provided four students for Saybrook, and New Jersey none; but they sent twenty-one and six scholars, respectively, to New Haven.

During its first fifteen years, almost two-thirds of the collegiate school students came from seaside towns in Connecticut, a fact that certainly figured in the decision of the majority trustees to move the college to another coastal site. The move to New Haven in 1716 caused a change in the pattern of Connecticut population in the school. When the college was in Saybrook, that town sent nine boys there for an education while New Haven sent only two. After 1716 Saybrook sent only five boys to Yale while New Haven provided twenty-eight. Evidently, proximity had a great deal to do with who became educated. Stratford, Milford, and Guilford, for example, which among them had sent seven boys to Saybrook, combined to send forty-three to conveniently located Yale.

But location was not the only factor in the college's increased size. The improvement of secondary education in the colony and Yale's stability and enhanced reputation were key factors in the school's growth, and probably explain why New London and Norwich, towns near Saybrook, only sent two boys to the school there but twenty-one to New Haven. Throughout this period a growing college kept pace with a growing colony. By 1739 Yale

7. Samuel Eliot Morison, *The Intellectual Life of Colonial New England*, p. 70.

had graduated young men from fifty-four different Connecticut towns. New Haven led with thirty graduates, followed by Hartford with twenty-four. Windsor had eighteen and Milford and Guilford seventeen each; twelve towns—ten of which also provided the college with at least one trustee each—accounted for two-thirds of the Connecticut-bred scholars of Yale. By the time Elisha Williams retired, Yale had educated boys from ninety-one communities in seven colonies.

The average age of entering students was 16.44 years. While the college was at Saybrook the average was 15.71, which suggests that incoming students tended to be younger than the overall average; but since the age at entrance is computed by deducting four years from the age at graduation, the lower average age in the college's early years might be misleading. If many students took advantage of the three-year course of study, one should only deduct three years from their age at commencement. It could be, therefore, that students at the Saybrook college came, on the average, in their seventeenth year but graduated early.[8] Boys could enter Yale whenever they were able to pass the entrance examinations, so there was a vast range of undergraduate ages. Six boys were under seventeen when they graduated, the youngest being Cornelius Bennet (Y. 1726), who was fifteen; the oldest students were Benjamin Allen (Y. 1708), Benjamin Pomeroy (Y. 1733), and Hezekiah Watkins (Y. 1737), who were all twenty-eight.

Although the students came from all levels of society and many different towns, and were of varying ages, the plurality of them were eldest or only sons. The order of birth is known for 281 students, and of these 122 or 43 percent were first sons; thirty-three (11.5 percent) were second sons, thirty-five (12 percent) were third sons, fifty-one (18 percent) were from fourth up to but excluding youngest sons, and forty (14 percent) were youngest sons. Most families could only afford to send one boy to college and, according to the statistics, the eldest son usually received this ad-

8. These figures are based on knowledge of the birthdates of 362 graduates. I have subtracted the birthdate from the year of graduation to give the age at commencement. The averages for age at graduation are: 1702–16 (college at Saybrook)—19.71; 1717–26 (college at New Haven prior to the rectorship of Elisha Williams)—20.65; 1727–39 (tenure of Rector Williams)—20.54; the entire period—20.44. For more on the three-year college course, see chapter 8.

vantage. Connecticut's intestacy law, however, often wreaked havoc with this custom. Since the law provided that a man's estate be divided among his family, many individuals neglected to make out wills. For boys destined for college the result of a father's death was often disastrous. Unless his father had left him money explicitly to complete his education, a boy was forced to appeal to the General Assembly for permission to sell his estate to pay for his schooling.

At least seven Yale graduates faced this dilemma. As minors, these boys could not sell property without assembly permission and they usually petitioned the court through their guardians. (The young men obviously cherished a college education enough to sell their worldly goods to obtain one.) The case of Samuel Rosseter (Y. 1728) was typical. In 1722 his four brothers addressed the General Court on his behalf. Rosseter's father was dead and the brothers stated that Samuel "hath been kept to Gramer Learning for a Considerable Time the said Lad is very apt & forward In Learning" and desired to continue. The brothers asked leave to sell a house and a few acres left to the boy in order to pay for his education. In 1723 the brothers renewed their request, arguing that the boy "hath shued a Grate forward ness in Larning insomuch that his Life Semes to be bound upon his books and hath made sum Considerable advances." A few months later the Reverends Thomas Ruggles and John Hart testified that Samuel's "capacity, for a Liberall Education" was sufficient to warrant his encouragement. The court agreed to allow Samuel to sell part of his estate, and the boy went on to complete his degree at Yale.[9]

Upon entering college, students were "placed" or ranked in their respective classes, a practice that was undoubtedly a source of satisfaction for some and of disappointment for others. Despite

9. C.A., Colleges and Schools, 1 : 28, 29, 30. For the case of Richard Treat (Y. 1725) see p. 44; for Ichabod Woolsey Chauncy (Y. 1723) see pp. 31, 33; for Gamaliel Clark (Y. 1734) see pp. 60, 61, 62, 63; for Nathaniel Hunn (Y. 1731), see p. 65; for Hobart Estabrook (Y. 1736) see p. 68. Treat, Chauncy, and Rosseter won the assembly's approval immediately, whereas the others had their petitions turned down by either or both houses. Since all six graduated from Yale, some compromise was evidently worked out in these other cases. For the case of Samuel Cooke (Y. 1705), who also made a successful petition, see *Yale Graduates,* 1 : 29. For examples of fathers intending their sons for college, see ibid., pp. 29, 117, 268, 621. One boy went to college at the behest of his uncle; see ibid., p. 231.

the seeming snobbery of this custom, there is no record of any students objecting to it; ranking students was consistent with colonial social theory—some people were manifestly more worthy than others. The task of determining worthiness fell to the rector and tutors; in 1727 the trustees gave them this power officially, but the practice probably existed from the college's early years.[10] At their first meeting the founders had instituted degradation in rank as a form of discipline, a punishment that would have been meaningless if the students had not been placed originally.[11] For most classes, the commencement broadsides and the early catalogues of graduates are the only source of information on final class rankings. For the classes of 1728–37, however, the extant quarter bills reveal the evolution of these rankings over the course of a student's four-year career.

In placing undergraduates, the rector and tutors followed several broad guidelines. Students whose fathers held high civil office were normally put at the head of their class; thus, Gurdon Saltonstall (Y. 1725) and Samuel Talcott (Y. 1733), sons of Connecticut governors, ranked first in their respective classes. Such a ranking brought with it no special privileges, but was simply a recognition of the social status of the student. In addition to the sons of governors, boys whose fathers were members of the upper house, superior court judges, and what might be called "prominent citizens" also ranked highly. Sons of such men were ranked first in eighteen classes between 1702 and 1739. A second and more numerous category was composed of the sons of college-educated men and ministers. Ministers' sons headed seventeen classes in this period. At Harvard, boys in this group were ranked according to the year of their fathers' graduation from college. The Yale rankings did not follow this procedure with any consistency, and while sons of college graduates were usually in the top third of the class, they did not rank in any predetermined order. The sons of farmers, merchants, and artisans comprised the third and largest group of students, but lack of information on fathers' occupations prevents any appraisal of the system used in placing them. Intellectual ability and the promise of a useful career after graduation probably counted heavily, but initially these boys were most likely grouped rather than ranked. The practice of placing the students

10. *Documentary History*, p. 269.
11. Ibid., p. 32.

in this way was retained at the college until 1767, when Yale adopted alphabetical listings.[12]

At the time of a class's entrance to Yale, then, the rector had an idea of how to rank some of the students. When the class of 1732 entered college, for instance, Rector Williams ranked them on the 1728–29 quarter bills. Out of twenty-four students (twenty-three of whom graduated) the rankings of the first four and the last four remained constant from the second term of freshman year until commencement. The fifteen students in between all had their placings changed over the four-year period, probably as the rector learned more about their talents and promise. But Williams ranked the scholars in a broad division that was retained for their entire college careers. The twelve boys in the top half of the class (ten of them sons of college graduates) were still the top half at graduation although the order had been juggled, and the bottom half in 1728 was still the bottom half in 1732. No student moved out of the general category in which the rector had put him as a freshman, although most boys altered their rank within that category. During the college course the rector adjusted the rankings as he learned more about the students, so that by the time a class reached junior year it was usually in its final order. The class of 1730, for example, had been placed in its final ranking by sophomore year.

College Life

The school year began in September and was divided into four quarters: September–December, December–March, March–June, and June–September. The college laws stipulated that during an academic year the students could be absent for two months, but it was not until 1720 that the trustees formally enacted a regular vacation period. They announced that there would be a month's vacation after the commencement in September and forbade any other absences, "notwithstanding any Custom to the contrary." Though this custom is nowhere specified, it probably refers to

12. For a detailed discussion of this procedure see Clifford K. Shipton, "Ye Mystery of Ye Ages Solved, or, How Placing Worked at Colonial Harvard & Yale," *Harvard Alumni Bulletin* 57 (1954–55): 258–59, 262–63. Shipton based his findings on Harvard only, using the classes of 1724–72 for his compilations. The Harvard system was more orderly than Yale's, but the Connecticut college followed the same basic formula and reflected the same social attitudes.

the fact that students had been taking a short vacation in May following the annual elections.[13]

It seems likely that most would-be students took the entrance examination sometime in the summer and, if they passed, entered the college in early October.[14] Students no doubt came to Yale with their parents, for the trustees required that before a boy enter the college he transcribe a copy of the school laws and have his parent or guardian sign a formal "Engagement." This provision called for the parents to pledge "to submit our said Children at all Times during their Continuance in said School unto the Orders rules Discipline and Government of the Same according To the Appointments of the Reverend Trustees of said School." The students signed the same statement, promising to "Carefully Conform our Selves" to all rules set by the trustees.[15] By this time a student had already written his own copy of those laws and hence was familiar with the college regulations before he began classes. The laws, entitled "Orders and Appointments to be Observed in the Collegiate School in Connecticut," contained all the student needed to know about what the trustees expected of him while he studied at the college.

Most of the laws dealt with the student's day in the classroom, the four-year program for the degree, and the Christian nature of a college education. Other rules spelled out required behavior. Students were to honor their superiors, remain at the college at all times unless given special permission to leave, stay out of taverns, and avoid the company of all dissolute persons. No undergraduate was to go hunting or fowling or to attend election days in town unless given special leave. The most all-encompassing regulation stipulated that

> All students shall be slow to speak and avoid, and in as much as in them lives take Care that others also avoid profane swearing, lying, needless asseverations, foolish garrulings,

13. *Yale Graduates*, 1 : 348; *Documentary History*, p. 203; see also, p. 343. For reference to a postelection vacation, see Jonathan Edwards to Mary Edwards, Mar. 26, 1719, Jonathan Edwards Collection. While Edwards was talking about the students at Wethersfield, it may be that the whole college followed this custom.

14. In the 1730s, a number of freshmen delayed their arrival at Yale for up to half a year. In May, 1740 the trustees voted that any student who failed to attend classes before the end of the first quarter would be placed lowest in the class rankings. See *Documentary History*, p. 343.

15. Ibid., p. 30.

> Chidings, strifes, railings, gesting, uncomely noise, spreading ill rumors, Divulging secrets and all manner of troublesome and offensive behavour.[16]

This rule was often broken. "Strifes" were particularly frequent at the early college, as the students on several occasions openly avowed their dislike for their tutors, their living quarters, or both. Such activities had disrupted the Saybrook college and, in large part, were responsible for the trustees' decision to relocate the school. The same kind of "troublesome and offensive behavour" had also delayed the reunion of the college in 1718–19.

In 1721 matters got completely out of hand. The trouble actually started in 1720 when the undergraduates complained about the food. In April, the trustees ordered "a speedy Reformation as to the Provision & dressing" of the scholars' "dieting," and two months later hired Hannah Beacher as college cook, instructing her to provide the students with fresh meat three times a week. Widow Beacher evidently had a hard time satisfying the tastes and/or appetites of fifty young men, however, for in 1721 the students declared a food strike. Rector Cutler managed to quell this uprising, but the immediate result was that the students took to ravaging New Haven for food and to raising hell in and out of the college. Jonathan Edwards reported to his father that people were shocked by the discovery

> of some Monstrous impieties, and acts of Immorality Lately Committed In the Colledge, Particularly stealing of Hens, Gees, turkies, piggs, Meath, Wood &c,—Unseasonable Nightwalking, Breaking People's windows, playing at Cards, Cursing, Swearing, and Damning, and Using all manner of Ill Language, which never were at such a pitch in the Colledge as they now are.[17]

The rector called a metting of the trustees to deal with the difficulties: "The Schoolers were all strictly Examined in order to Detect the Shamfull Crimes Laid to their Charge by New-haven but all Prov'd unsuccessful." [18] By the fall of 1721, however, the

16. *Yale Graduates,* 1 : 347.

17. *Documentary History,* pp. 201, 204; Jonathan Edwards to Timothy Edwards, Mar. 1, 1721, Jonathan Edwards Collection.

18. Daniel Dwight to Timothy Dwight, Apr. 11, 1721, Jonathan Edwards Collection.

trustees were able to convict at least one undergraduate for his role in the trouble and suspended Ebenezer Gould (Y. 1723) "for some Atrocious Crimes." [19]

Suspension was the penultimate discipline and the trustees rarely used it. The only other instance of suspension during this period was the case of Timothy Mix (Y. 1731), whose "Miscarriages Delinquencies & Crimes" consisted of striking several of his fellow students, running away from school, and later fighting with a citizen of New Haven. In 1729 the trustees suspended Mix for one year with the provision that he could be readmitted if he reformed his ways, used the time to improve his studies, acknowledged his faults publicly, and paid his college fees for the year. Twelve months later a contrite Timothy Mix appeared before the trustees, confessed his errors, and was restored to his former rank in the college.[20]

Students were subject to other punishments as well. The trustees designated five types of discipline in the college. The rector and tutors were allowed to fine students up to five shillings for such misdeeds as missing classes or public worship, "Hallooing, singing or ringing the Bell unseasonably Firing Gunns or otherways" at public days and commencements, or playing cards.[21] A second level of punishment was public admonishment, the abridgement of certain privileges, and the requirement that the culprit perform additional college exercises (i.e. recitations). Undergraduates earned these punishments by bringing liquor to college or behaving contemptuously toward their elders. If a student was a persistent violator of college laws the faculty and two trustees could demote him. While there are no records of this punishment being used, it obviously was. Jonathan Dickinson (Y. 1731), whose father was a Yale graduate (1706) and minister (and became Princeton's first president), ranked lowest in his class of thirteen, a humiliation he undoubtedly earned as punishment for his habitual misbehavior.

Suspension was the fourth level of punishment, and expulsion, which only the trustees could impose, the ultimate form of discipline. Prior to 1739 the trustees expelled only one student, a boy

19. Jonathan Edwards to [Mary Edwards], Dec. 12, 1721, Jonathan Edwards Collection.

20. *Documentary History,* pp. 281–82, 286.

21. Ibid., pp. 47, 246, 309.

by the name of Hubbel. In 1722 he had committed the sin of fornication and had, in gentlemanly fashion, married the girl. His father asked that the boy be allowed to continue in college as he seemed repentant, but the trustees refused. It was, they claimed, "inconsistent with the Glory of God and the Welfare of the School as well as the Customs & practices of Colleges in other places" to permit Hubbel to remain at Yale.[22]

Some student delinquencies were less destructive, though not necessarily less punishable, than fornication, fighting, and firing guns. Undergraduates were prohibited from bringing rum or other strong liquor to their chambers and from going to local taverns or "victualling" houses, but they still managed to get inebriated on occasion. Samuel Johnson attested to his own guilt on this account by scrawling "I am Drunk" across a page of his college notebook.[23] The rule against drinking had been in effect from the college's early years, but it was probably easier to enforce in Killingworth and Saybrook than in New Haven. In 1722 the trustees restated the law against drinking, a sure sign that students were taking advantage of their access to spiritous liquors. There were, after all, several taverns within a two-minute walk of the college. For some, perhaps, proximity made the temptation too great.[24]

In 1738, in what may have been a common occurrence, a group of undergraduates broke the regulation against drinking with a vengeance. Ezra Clap (Y. 1740) related the incident to his classmate Nathaniel Chauncy:

> Last night some of the freshmen got six quarts of Rhum and about two payls fool of Sydar and about eight pounds suger and mad it in to Samson, and evited every Scholer in Colege in to Churtis is Room, and we mad such prodigious Rought that we Raised the tutor, and he ordred us all to our one rooms and some went and some taried and they geathered a gain and went up to old father Monsher [?] dore and drumed against the dore and yeled and screamed so that a bodey

22. Ibid., p. 224. The fornication, not the marriage, was at issue. John Smith (Y. 1727) was married while at college and was allowed to remain a student. See *Yale Graduates*, 1 : 359.

23. Samuel Johnson, Notebook, Samuel Johnson Manuscripts.

24. *Yale Graduates*, 1 : 248, 351; *Documentary History*, pp. 235–36. For the location of the several taverns see Edwin Oviatt, *The Beginnings of Yale*, p. 390, and the 1748 map of New Haven, original at the New Haven Colony Historical Society.

> would have thought that they were killing dodgs there, and all this day they [the rector and tutors] have bien a counsling to geather, and they sent for Woodward and Dyar and Worthenton, Briant and Styles.[25]

The fact that the students displayed an acquaintance with the Old Testament in naming their potent brew "Samson" probably did them little good in the face of the rector's wrath.

A student's existence, then, was not all study and prayer. The scholars evidently enjoyed these convivial and at times violent moments, but there were some sensitive boys who were deeply disturbed by disorders in college life. Jonathan Edwards reflected this feeling in the week he began his duties as a Yale tutor when he confided in his diary: "I have now, abundant reason to be convinced, of the troublesomeness and vexation of the world, and that it never will be another kind of world." No doubt this statement was motivated by practical as well as theological concerns. Timothy Allen (Y. 1736), a member of a pietistic group of undergraduates at the college, was a deeply religious boy and complained to a friend that it was *"very hard and grievous to be, as it were, under the Harrows, and at the Mercy of evil Men so long in this Place."* Samuel Hopkins (Y. 1741) entertained the same opinion of his fellow students and wrote in his autobiography that while at Yale he "avoided the intimacy and the company of the openly vicious."[26] These statements are ample testimony that student life had its rougher side and that there were those undergraduates who were not always preoccupied with religion and learning.

Yale students did not spend all of their free time in vicious pursuits, however, and life at the Connecticut college had its exuberant moments. Students at the Saybrook college swam in the ocean in summer and skated on nearby ponds in winter, recreations that probably went on in New Haven too. Such sports could be dangerous, however, as the experiences of Samuel Johnson testify. He nearly drowned when swimming in a deep channel, and his classmate Benjamin Lord fell through the ice at a

25. *Yale Graduates,* 1 : 598. The students named were all members of the class of 1740, then sophomores.

26. *Works of President Edwards,* 1 : 103; Chauncy, *Seasonable Thoughts,* pp. 214–15; Edwards A. Park, *Memoir of the Life and Character of Samuel Hopkins, D.D.* (Boston, 1854), p. 14.

skating party. Johnson crawled out on the ice and pulled his friend to safety, an act of "compassion and courage" for which Lord was still grateful over fifty years alter. The largest near-disaster occurred when ten Yale students sailed a boat on Long Island Sound and nearly perished in a storm. John Hubbard, brother of one of the students, commemorated their providential deliverance in a poem published the next year. Hubbard's title told it all: *A Monumental Gratitude Attempted, In a Poetical Relation of the Danger and Deliverance of Several of the Members of Yale-College, in Passing the Sound, from South-hold to New-haven, Aug. 20th. 1726.* According to Hubbard, only divine intervention stilled the raging storm and saved the young men from death.[27]

The most boisterous student undertaking occurred in 1738 when a substantial number of undergraduates joined some citizens of New Haven in preventing the Church of England missionary from taking possession of a tract of land near the college. As an Anglican pamphleteer later portrayed the event, the students,

> quitting soft dalliance with the *muses,* . . . roughened into sons of *Mars,* and issuing forth in deep and firm array, with courage bold and undaunted, they not only attacked, but bravely routed a YOKE OF OXEN and a poor *Plowman,* which had been sent by the then Missionary of *New Haven,* to occupy and plow up the said lot of ground.[28]

The Anglicans bitterly complained of the attack, but there is no record that any student was punished for taking part in the affair. The scholars, no doubt, were simply putting into practice the ecclesiastical bias instilled in them by the faculty.

Undergraduates did not have to go out of doors to have fun. The trustee resolution of 1734 forbidding card-playing was obviously a response to the popularity of such games with the scholars. When they were not engaged in this pastime the upperclassmen could always amuse themselves by sending the freshmen on er-

27. *Johnson,* 1 : 5. For Lord's letter of March 31, 1768 thanking Johnson for the rescue, see ibid., p. 442. John Hubbard, who also wrote *The Benefactors of Yale College,* was the brother of Daniel (Y. 1727), one of the boys involved in the incident.

28. E. Edwards Beardsley, *The History of the Episcopal Church in Connecticut,* 1 : 114.

rands. The sophomores evidently enjoyed the privilege of hazing first-year students.[29]

Not all extracurricular activities were vigorous. John Walton (Y. 1720) used his free time to compose poetry. By the end of his senior year Walton had written a funeral elegy dedicated to the memory of Massachusetts Governor Joseph Dudley and hoped to have it published, so "that this Colony as well as the other might Lament him." If the Dudley poem was successful, Walton intended to write one about Major Wait-Still Winthrop.[30] Many students undoubtedly obeyed the regulation to engage in secret prayer and some may have kept religious diaries. Jonathan Edwards, both as an upperclassman and as butler, used some of his spare moments to compose "Resolutions" of a religious nature such as:

> *Resolved,* When I think of any Theorem in Divinity to be solved, immediately to do what I can towards solving it, if circumstances do not hinder.
>
> *Resolved,* To study the Scriptures so steadily, constantly and frequently, as that I may find and plainly perceive myself to grow in the knowledge of the same.[31]

Such religious activity was a collective as well as an individual pursuit. Samuel Johnson noted that when he was at college the "scholars had private meetings for prayer and reading." Although Johnson disliked these gatherings and thought they promoted "self-conceit and spiritual pride," they probably met the needs of many young men. A similar group was formed in the early 1730s. This one was more selective than those of Johnson's day,

29. Jonathan Edwards to Stephen Mix, ca. 1720, Jonathan Edwards Collection. Edwards wrote to his uncle to complain that his cousin, Elisha Mix (Y. 1724), had been insubordinate to him. Elisha was living with Jonathan when Jonathan was butler, on the agreement that Elisha would help to serve beer at sizings. Jonathan, in turn, was to help his cousin with his studies. Elisha, however, disliked the tasks Jonathan assigned him and objected when called in from play to do chores. Jonathan asked his uncle that Elisha no longer be his roommate. Timothy Edwards also wrote to Stephen Mix about this incident. Jonathan's letter reveals that freshmen had to run errands for upperclassmen but that Elisha did little of this on account of his job in the buttery. For the hazing of freshmen, see John Cleaveland, "Diary," Jan. 15–May 11, 1742, Yale Archives. Cleaveland recorded that on February 12 "we were taken up into the Longe garret to be tormented by the Sophoimori and three of my Clase were fined for unmanners."

30. John Walton to John Winthrop, May 16, 1720, Yale Archives.

31. *Works of President Edwards,* 1 : 55–56.

and its members, too, were charged with being uncharitable and censorious. According to some of their college contemporaries, the members of this group were attracted by the zeal of one David Ferris, a Quaker, who claimed that the inner light of the Holy Spirit was the sole guide of his religious convictions. Ferris, a nongraduating member of the class of 1733, ensnared "some gloomy Persons among the *Students* . . . who having mixed something of *Devotion* with their *melancholly* Tempers, became his *Admirers*" and believed everything he said.[32]

The Quaker principles of the Ferris group were odious to many of the college students, and they kept the members under surveillance, looking for any condemning signs of heresy. The group, in turn, expressed its disdain for the religious affections of the other undergraduates. The club not only caused a minor religious furor at the school but fostered a kind of anti-intellectualism among its members. One of them, Timothy Allen, who thought Yale was peopled by evil men, quarreled with himself about remaining at college. He was convinced that his business in life was to serve God and that his years at school were being wasted. Allen was certain that the Holy Spirit would teach him all things and, as he told his classmate Daniel Bliss,

> I thought sure, the Arm of the Lord is not shortened, and therefore that I WANTED NOT HUMAN LEARNING, in order to *declare the Will of* GOD *to the World, which I see perishing by Heaps all around me;* and I desire not to come to Men with *Excellency of Speech which is of Man's Wisdom, which it seemed to me I was heaping up Treasures of.*

Allen nevertheless decided to remain at Yale, at least until God told him otherwise, and comforted himself with the fact that he had found some kindred spirits among the citizens of New Haven.[33]

While there were a few students like Allen who did not care for the intellectual atmosphere of Yale College, there were others who relished it. John Sergeant, in his valedictory address, reminded his fellow graduates of the joys of "our pleasant, free and friendly colloquies, sometimes more strictly searching the dark footsteps of truth (the aim of all our studies), sometimes with

32. *Johnson,* 1 : 11; Chauncy, *Seasonable Thoughts,* pp. 213, 211.
33. *Seasonable Thoughts,* pp. 214–15.

looser aims innocently relieving our charged minds of a good liking and similitude of manners, if with learning." Undergraduate conversations may not have been this refined, but some scholars obviously cherished the camaraderie of their fellows. Ebenezer Rosseter (Y. 1744) so enjoyed the intellectual companionship of his classmates that when he was separated from them he found himself, as he wrote to one of them, "Sitting in my Study, in a Lonesome Posture, being Destitute of the Agreeable Company of My Class which is very Trying and Troublesome unto Me. I Long to see You all and Converse with You Face to Face." [34]

Other young men retained and even intensified their scholarly pursuits after graduation. Samuel Johnson and Daniel Brown of the class of 1714 engaged in a detailed if somewhat pretentious correspondence about philosophical issues in the years between their two degrees, telling each other of books read, ideas discovered, and of each's need for the other's intellectual stimulation.[35] For still others, the life of the mind they had explored at Yale became an all-consuming passion. When Caleb Smith (Y. 1743) heard that his cousin of the same name (Y. 1744) was thinking of going to work, he wrote a long letter of objection. "For my own part," he stated,

> I think Study is one of the most pleasant & delightful Imployments in the World, and I cant but think that if it be righ[t]ly Improved it may be made very profitable, as to the things of this World, tho' I wont say the most profitable, for there are many Men of Letters that are obliged to grapple with Poverty. . . . but one would think that Learning & Philosophy should fortify a man's mind from sinking into Dejection under all the Frowns of Fortune & Hardships of Adversity.— I am poorly capable of giving Advice, but however as I have a sincere Regard for you, & desire that you may be happy both in this World which will be but short, & in another which must last always; so I have been thinking with what Advantages you could leave Studying, I mean to get a Living by some Learned Imployment, and I must needs say I think I can see nothing but Disadvantage in such a Resolution; my

34. Sergeant, *Valedictorian Oration,* p. 30; Ebenezer Rosseter to Caleb Smith, May 24, 1744, Yale Archives.

35. *Johnson,* 2 : 189–99.

> Epistle would swell to too great a Bulk, if I should put in all my Objections against Farming, Merchan[d]izing, Seafaring or any other Imployment where your Studies will not claim a Share.[36]

Few Yale graduates could afford to follow Smith's prescription for the ideal life and probably fewer still cared to. Nathaniel Clarke (Y. 1714) had no intention of living the contemplative life, but he did think that his college degree should bring him some leisure. In 1725 he petitioned the General Court that he be exempted from attending the military exercises of the local trainband and from repairing highways, on the grounds "that at great expense your supplicant has been educated in your College then at Saybrook" and that such menial tasks were "a disparaging imposition" on educated men. A few other graduates, though, used their education to live a studious life. One such man was Joseph Smith (Y. 1719), who followed no profession and was said to have lived the life of a student, deriving pleasure from his extensive library. Another was William Leete (Y. 1733) who studied for the ministry but never took a church. He became a recluse in Guilford and was known to the townspeople as "Scholar Leete." William Adams (Y. 1730) also prepared for the ministry but was never ordained and spent his life acting as domestic chaplain to a wealthy Long Island family and preaching occasionally. For the most part, however, he lived "a retired philosophic life" saying that he would be encumbered with neither a wife nor a parish.[37] Smith, Leete, and Adams, however, were obviously somewhat eccentric and their life styles were different from those of most Yale graduates. The majority of Yale students worked for a living, many of them in "Publick employment both in Church & Civil State."

The Graduates

Not many graduates resided at college after earning their B.A. The winners of the Berkeley prize were expected to live at the school for three years, but most stayed on for only one. Other resident bachelors also remained for a year or two, some, like Jonathan Edwards (Y. 1720) and Daniel Hubbard (Y. 1727), as

36. Caleb Smith to Caleb Smith, May 18, 1745, Yale Archives.
37. *Yale Graduates,* 1 : 121, 206–07, 484, 403–04.

the college butler. Most students began preparations for their chosen careers. Those intending to become clergymen often went to live with a minister who would supervise their biblical and theological studies. A number of graduates taught for a while before entering a vocation. After three years a large majority of the students returned for the second degree. A few waited beyond the three-year limit; Jacob Baker (Y. 1731), for example, took his M.A. in 1755.

Only forty-six students never took the M.A., many of them because of early death, others because of distance from the school, and some from lack of interest. One student, John Walton (Y. 1720), was refused the M.A. by the trustees on two occasions because of his ill behavior. Prior to 1740 many graduates simply showed up at commencements, expecting the degree, but Rector Clap instituted the requirement that anyone desiring an M.A. must inform him of the fact a month before commencement and must personally attend the exercises.[38] A few Yale students took a second degree elsewhere, several of them in addition to the Yale diploma. The first to attempt this feat were three collegiate school graduates who applied for a Harvard A.M. in 1709. The Harvard Corporation turned down their request, saying "that it is not advisable to admit the Persons above mentioned to their Degrees the Commencment now approaching." By 1714, however, the Bay College had relented, and after that date Yale graduates living in or visiting Massachusetts were permitted to take the Harvard degree.[39] The Connecticut college had given M.A.'s to Harvard men since the 1702 commencement, when four graduates of the Bay College became the first to have the double benefit of a Harvard education and a Yale degree. Nine Yale graduates from this period enjoyed the reverse benefit, taking the A.M. from Harvard. Two graduates took their second degree from Princeton, and Brown and Columbia each gave one Yale man an M.A.

A handful of graduates received more advanced degrees. Of the colonial colleges, Yale awarded a Doctor of Sacred Theology to three of its alumni and Dartmouth, Princeton, and Columbia each awarded one. English and Scottish universities bestowed higher degrees on seven Yale students, although none of the

38. *Documentary History,* p. 344. The first sheet of Masters' *Quaestiones* was printed in 1740. For Walton, see *Yale Graduates,* 1 : 233.

39. *Seventeenth-century Harvard,* 2 : 548.

graduates studied for the degrees. The first Yale man to study abroad was Daniel Lathrop (Y. 1733), who learned surgery in St. Thomas's Hospital in London but earned no diploma. Five graduates received M.A.'s from Oxford and two of them also received S.T.D.'s. One man received a Cambridge M.A., and Edinburgh and Aberdeen gave S.T.D.'s to two Yale men. Samuel Johnson received the most honorary degrees, an M.A. from both Oxford and Cambridge and an S.T.D. from Oxford. He was so honored not because of his intellectual prowess but because he was an Anglican convert and an S.P.G. missionary. In fact, the five recipients of English degrees and the two who received degrees from Columbia were all members of the Church of England.

The professed aim of the collegiate school founders had been to provide a college to train young men for employment in church and civil state. The actual careers of Yale graduates realized that aim (see Table 1). The vocations of 321 students are known, and of these 179 were ministers (46 percent of all graduates). The popularity of the ministry as a career was especially prevalent in the college's Saybrook years, when 73 percent of the students entered that profession. The clergy were the chief professional class in colonial New England and many fathers undoubtedly wanted their sons to achieve that status. A father's intention that his son be a minister meant that the father desired the son to have a liberal education, as the one depended on the other. When Gamaliel Clark (Y. 1734) appealed to the General Assembly for permission to sell his estate to pay for his education, he argued that his father intended him for the ministry.[40] No doubt many students came to college because they wanted to be pastors. The large majority of the ministers (83 percent) came from nonministerial families, an indication that the profession served to enhance the social status of many. Only thirty-one Yale ministers had clergyman fathers.

The Yale-educated ministers served society well, both in Connecticut and in other American colonies. More than any other occupational group, ministers spread the name and influence of Yale to new communities, as they were the most geographically mobile college graduates. Only eleven of them returned to their hometowns to take churches. One hundred (55 percent) of them

40. C.A., Colleges and Schools, 1 : 62.

served a church in a town other than their own, thirty-eight served two churches, sixteen ministered to three churches, and fourteen had four or more parishes. Extreme mobility, however, was usually a sign that the minister had a hard time getting along with his parishioners.

Like all occupational groups, many ministers held other jobs either before settling in their vocations or to supplement their income while serving a parish. The most common subsidiary vocation for clergymen was teaching. Forty-four graduates held some kind of teaching job, either in a grammar school or as college tutors, before or during their ministerial careers. Many more of them probably tutored boys for college and supervised the studies of college graduates preparing for the ministry. Phineas Fiske (Y. 1704), for example, served as a college tutor, readied boys for Yale, and taught ministerial candidates. In this last role he may have had mixed motives, however, for he managed to marry his three daughters to three Yale graduates who came to study divinity

Table 1

Occupations of Yale Graduates

Classes of:	*1702–1716*		*1717–1726*		*1727–1739*		*Total*	
Minister	41		52		86		179	
Missionary				(2)[a]	1	(4)	1	(6)
Preacher			2	(10)	4	(8)	6	(18)
Merchant	4	(1)	7	(2)	17	(3)	28	(6)
Doctor		(4)	7	(4)	17	(4)	24	(12)
Lawyer	1		7		15	(1)	23	(1)
Farmer	3	(1)	9	(2)	5	(4)	17	(7)
Public servant[b]	2	(11)	5	(17)	10	(45)	17	(73)
Teacher	1	(22)	3	(22)	5	(20)	9	(64)
Other[c]	3		4		10		17	
Unknown	1		19		45		65	
Total	56		115		215		386	

[a] Figures in parentheses indicate graduates who practiced the occupation as a secondary career.

[b] The category of Public servant refers to those graduates who held offices of public service, either elective or appointed; the category includes legislators, judges, selectmen, court clerks, sheriffs, and justices of the peace.

[c] The other occupations—with their totals—were: Business (2), College Butler (1), Innkeeper (2), Landowner (3), Mariner (2), Mercantile Business (2), Military Officer (1), "Prominent Citizen" (3), Surveyor (1).

with him.[41] The most impressive educational effort was undertaken by Joseph Bellamy (Y. 1735), who turned his home into a virtual seminary. In the course of fifty years Bellamy instructed approximately sixty ministerial candidates at his pastorate in Bethlehem, Connecticut.[42]

Nine ministers served their parishioners as doctors, thereby assuming literal responsibility for bodies and souls. Eleven of them entered some kind of public service, six of them farmed, and six worked as Indian missionaries for a time. One Yale graduate, John Sergeant (Y. 1729), devoted his entire life to missionary work.[43] Yale ministers also played a significant role in colonial higher education. Sixteen of them became Yale trustees, five were trustees of Princeton, and one served Dartmouth in that capacity. Jonathan Dickinson (Y. 1706), Jonathan Edwards (Y. 1720), and Aaron Burr (Y. 1735) all served as presidents of the College of New Jersey (Princeton), Dickinson being that college's first and Edwards its most famous president. Samuel Johnson (Y. 1714) was the first president of King's College (Columbia) and Eleazar Wheelock (Y. 1733) was Dartmouth's founder and first president. James Lockwood (Y. 1735) turned down the presidency of both Princeton (in 1758) and Yale (in 1766), preferring in each instance to remain in his Wethersfield ministry. One graduate, Timothy Allen, attempted his contribution to higher education outside the established channels. In the early years of the Great Awakening he set up his "Shepherds Tent" in New London as a school for prorevivalist students. Allen no doubt imparted his own enthusiastic Christianity to his charges, and while the school attracted over a dozen students, the Connecticut government thought it a subversive enterprise and forced Allen to move his seat of learning to Rhode Island, where it soon closed.[44]

Denominationally, the vast majority of Yale ministers were Congregationalists (in the Saybrook Platform meaning of that term for Connecticut). Twenty-five ministers were or became Presbyterians, most of them serving churches in the Middle Colonies. For a Congregationalist, this switch involved little change in ec-

41. *Yale Graduates,* 1 : 21–22. One of Fiske's daughters married two Yale graduates, but one of her husbands had not studied with her father.

42. Gaustad, *Great Awakening,* p. 137.

43. I have not included Sergeant in the total of 179 ministers.

44. Gaustad, *Great Awakening,* p. 108.

clesiastical belief, and some men moved freely between the two denominations. Jonathan Edwards, for example, began his career as a preacher to a Presbyterian church in New York City, served as minister of the Congregational church in Northampton, Massachusetts, and ended his life as President of the Presbyterian-founded College of New Jersey (Princeton).

Nineteen graduates became Anglican ministers, three others became Anglican schoolteachers, and one became a lay reader, a fact which displeased those who looked to Yale as a source of orthodox men. Most Anglicans served as S.P.G. missionaries in the American colonies. At least one Yale minister, John Walton (Y. 1720), leaned in the direction of the Baptists and published tracts supporting their tenets. On the whole, though, Yale College produced men whose ecclesiastical allegiances were consistent with the colony's adoption of the Saybrook Platform. Nearly 90 percent of the Yale ministers were either Congregationalists or Presbyterians.

Most Yale ministers lived to witness the turmoil of the Great Awakening. The Awakening had been anticipated in 1734 when Jonathan Edwards initiated a revival in his Northampton parish that soon spread to twenty-five other Massachusetts and Connecticut towns. The fervor of these early revivals cooled, only to be rekindled by the arrival in 1740 of the English itinerant minister, George Whitefield. At first, practically all New England ministers welcomed Whitefield's work in reawakening the piety and reaffirming the theology of their parishioners. But the light of the Great Awakening soon produced more heat than some clergymen could stand. Whitefield and his associates questioned the sincerity and faith of some ministers and engaged in an emotional style of preaching that offended many others. By 1742 the initial harmony of the revivals was shattered and replaced by a division in the religious establishment of colonial America; those who favored the revivals were called New Lights, those who opposed them were labeled Old Lights. We know the position of eighty-one Yale ministers in the period of the Great Awakening. Excluding the Anglicans who, led by Samuel Johnson, all opposed the revivals, the eighty-one Congregationalist and Presbyterian ministers divided almost evenly: forty-one of them were New Lights and forty were Old Lights. Most opposing ministers were older men who had graduated from college before 1726. The

New Lights tended to be younger; of the students who graduated during the rectorship of Elisha Williams, who had supported the revivals of 1734–35, New Lights outnumbered Old Lights twenty-eight to fourteen.

While the statistics suggest an even split in the Yale clergymen, the most influential graduates allied themselves with the New Light cause. Yale produced the foremost minister of the Awakening, Jonathan Edwards, who has been called the greatest theologian in the strict Reformed tradition between John Calvin and Karl Barth. The college also graduated the most vigorous and censorious New Light, Joseph Bellamy (Y. 1735), as well as the most violent exponent of the revivals, James Davenport (Y. 1732), whose itinerant preaching and emotional excesses led to his arrest in both Connecticut and Massachusetts. The courts of both colonies declared the latter insane, although he calmed down later and in 1744 published a confession of his errors. Davenport's friend and one-time associate, Jonathan Barber (Y. 1730), worked for the pro-revival cause as an associate of the Awakening's greatest figure; in 1740 he accepted George Whitefield's invitation to become superintendent and lay-chaplain of his Orphan House in Georgia. Barber remained in this post from 1740 to around 1747 and as a consequence became implicated in the attacks on Whitefield concerning the purposes and management of the orphanage. Yale turned out no comparable men of the Old Light persuasion, and the most vocal detractors of the Awakening were Harvard men, Charles Chauncy and Jonathan Mayhew.

Yale ministers also contributed to the pastoral and theological literature of eighteenth-century New England. Sixty-two graduates published sermons, tracts, and theological works. Most men published only one or two sermons, usually those preached before the General Assembly at the annual election and printed by order of the legislature. But several Yale men made substantial and enduring contributions to theological, ecclesiastical, and philosophical discourse. Jonathan Edwards was the greatest of these, and his important treatises initiated a tradition of Reformed theological thought which influenced American Protestantism for over a century. Edwards's work was furthered and systematized by two Yale graduates who studied with him in his Northampton parish, Joseph Bellamy and Samuel Hopkins. Bellamy not only wrote in defense of the Great Awakening's emphasis on experiential religion and theological orthodoxy, but also attempted to present the Reformed doctrines of sin and reprobation in more rational and enlightened terms. Hopkins's greatest contribution to the tradition was his two-volume *System of Doctrines* (1793) which delineated the Edwardsean impulse in a formal and aggressive fashion. The resulting "New Divinity" viewpoint reached its maximum national influence in the Yale-centered New Haven Theology of the nineteenth century. In opposition to these men stood Samuel Johnson, who had abandoned the tradition they sought to perpetuate; Johnson was both an apologist for the doctrines and discipline of the Church of England and the chief American expositor of the philosophical idealism of George Berkeley. Johnson's Anglicanism involved him in controversies with yet another Yale man, Jonathan Dickinson. Dickinson, an able critic of the ecclesiastical pretensions and Arminian theology of colonial Anglicans, was a central figure in the religious affairs of the Middle Colonies.

The record of the Connecticut college in training future clergymen, then, was impressive. Although 179 men became ordained ministers serving churches, many others studied theology after graduation in preparation for the ministry. One man became a full-time missionary and six graduates devoted their lives to preaching. Eighteen others, who followed different occupations, also preached at one time or another. Thus, 204 graduates were either ministers, preachers, or had preached for a time. An additional fifteen graduates became deacons or vestrymen of their churches.

The predominance of religious vocations among graduates was in keeping with the professed purposes of the collegiate school. A number of students, however, chose careers outside the church. We know the occupations of these 142 men, many of whom, like the clergymen, also served their communities in public office. Twenty-eight of them (7 percent of all graduates) became merchants, thirteen of whom served in some public position and two of whom furthered the cause of education, one as a trustee of Princeton and the other as a trustee of Brown. Twenty-three graduates (6 percent) became lawyers. Then, as now, many of those who practiced law also wanted to make law; twenty of the twenty-three Yale lawyers held public office. Two of them participated in founding new colleges—Princeton and Columbia. Twenty-four graduates (6 percent) became doctors, eight of whom were public servants. John Griswold (Y. 1721) was the first to devote himself exclusively to the medical profession, and the Reverend Jared Eliot (Y. 1706) was the first to achieve fame in the field. Eliot was not only a pastor and the foremost physician in Connecticut but also a botanist and agriculturist. He introduced the white mulberry and the silkworm into the colony and wrote *An Essay upon Field Husbandry in New-England.* In addition, he received a gold medal from the London Society of Arts for the results published in his *Essay on the Invention, or Art of making very good, if not the best Iron, from black Sea-Sand.*[45]

Seventeen graduates (4 percent) became farmers; five of them were part-time preachers and seven held public office. Another seventeen (4 percent) had no specific vocations, but devoted their careers to public service. Nine students (2 percent) spent their lives as schoolteachers, but sixty-four others taught at some time in their careers, most of them during the years right after graduation. This number does not include the many pastors who acted as professors of divinity in their parsonages and trained college graduates for the ministry. Thus, 19 percent of Yale graduates were teachers in public schools or the college at some time or another. The remaining twenty-four graduates (6 percent) whose careers are known undertook a variety of occupations, such as mariner, innkeeper, surveyor, and soldier.[46] The obscurity of the sixty-five students for whom we have no vocational information suggests that they engaged in relatively modest pursuits.

Many Yale graduates, as noted, served the civil state either as a vocation or in addition to their regular occupations. The trustees had intended that this be so, and they must have been pleased with the results. Ninety graduates (23 percent) held some civil office on either the local, county, or colony level—many of them serving on all levels in the course of their careers—and fifty-three

45. *Yale Graduates,* 1 : 54, 56.

46. A college education did not necessarily prompt a man to seek a new place of residence. With the exception of the ministers, most Yale graduates returned to their homes to pursue their vocations among family and friends. Eighty-eight percent of the farmers returned home, as did 82 percent of the public servants, 69 percent of the lawyers, 64 percent of the merchants, 62.5 percent of the doctors, and 60 percent of all others. Only 6 percent of the ministers did so.

(14 percent) served in the military, usually as officers of local militia companies.[47]

The men who served in civil offices did so in many different posts. Sixty-seven were elected to the lower house of colonial legislatures and seven of them were speakers of the house. Eighteen graduates became members of an upper house (Governor's Council); Thomas Fitch (Y. 1721) went on to become governor of Connecticut, and Darius Sessions (Y. 1737) was elected deputy-governor of Rhode Island. Nine men served as representatives to various colonial congresses. Philip Livingston (Y. 1737) represented New York in the first Continental Congress and therefore was the only Yale graduate from this period to sign the Declaration of Independence.[48] Yale men were also active as magistrates. Twenty-two were justices of the peace and twenty became either county or probate judges. Nine men attained the bench of superior courts and Yale men became the chief judges of the Connecticut and Rhode Island courts. Fourteen graduates served in county posts as court clerks and sheriffs, and seventeen participated in local politics as selectmen, aldermen, and mayors.[49]

Statistics, of course, tell only part of the story. They reveal facts rather than attitudes, stating what Yale graduates did rather than what Yale did for its graduates. It is not possible to appraise the precise impact of an early Yale education on a man's career or

47. Of the ninety men, many served in multiple positions. Thus, if all separate offices are added together they far exceed ninety.

48. Three younger Yale graduates also signed the Declaration: Lewis Morris (Y. 1746), Lyman Hall (Y. 1747), and Oliver Wolcott (Y. 1747).

49. Yale graduates not only formed a respected and useful educated class in Connecticut and other colonies but they also contributed to the propagation of that class. Three hundred and thirty-two students married a total of 455 wives; 233 men married once, 80 married twice, 15 married three wives, 3 wed four wives and 1 insatiable graduate took five brides. Fifty-four Yale men did not marry.

One hundred and twenty-three sent sons to college. Yale, naturally, admitted the large majority of the sons; 148 sons of Yale graduates graduated from Yale, four more attended but did not graduate, one received an honorary M.A., and two an honorary M.D. Twelve Yale sons graduated from Harvard and another attended there but did not graduate. Ten graduated from Princeton, five from Columbia, and three from Dartmouth. One hundred and twenty-three graduates, therefore, fathered 178 graduates of various colleges.

While the Yale men could not send their daughters to college, seventy-one of them did the next best thing and married their daughters to college graduates. Eighty-seven daughters became wives of Yale graduates, seven married Harvard men, and three married Princeton graduates.

world-view. The college did not produce a single type of graduate or perpetuate an aristocratic elite. Its students came from many social and economic backgrounds and entertained a wide range of social, political, and religious views. Yale men became wealthy and impoverished, farmers and magistrates, patriots and Tories, Anglicans and Congregationalists, Old Lights and New Lights.

On the whole, however, Yale did serve as the intellectual core of a Connecticut and interior New England societal establishment; its members sent their sons to the college and Yale's graduates served it. In this respect, the content of learning at Yale—with the important exception of theology—was not as significant as the purposes of that learning. A Yale-educated man was intended to be qualified to serve church and state, a person dedicated to perpetuating the society his forebears had created and he would inherit.

A graduate of colonial Yale bore a tremendous responsibility, for he left college burdened with the expectations of many. The purpose of Yale was either realized or squandered by every student. As Eliphalet Adams exclaimed in 1733, the college "is the Seed-plot which must furnish out the future Pastors of Churches and perhaps the future Judges and Magistrates as well as other principal Members of the Common Wealth."[50] Adams's claim echoed the argument of countless election sermons. He insisted, as did others, that Yale's benefit to Connecticut was measured by the religious and civic careers of its graduates. This standard was not imposed on the college, but was a crucial aspect of Yale's reason for being from the very beginning. It was a standard Yale met very well. Judged by the distinction of its graduates, the college fulfilled the intentions of its founders and the hopes of its friends. Nearly 70 percent of Yale graduates worked in church and civil state and many of the rest populated other useful professions. On these terms alone the venture of founding a collegiate school was a success.

50. Eliphalet Adams, *A Discourse Shewing That so long as there is any Prospect of a Sinful People's yielding good Fruit hereafter, there is hope that they may be Spared*, pp. 74–75.

11 "The Liberal, & Relligious Education of Suitable Youth"

At the first meeting of Yale's trustees in November, 1701, the seven clergymen in attendance began their deliberations by writing a statement of purpose. They recalled the "Grand errand" of their "blessed fathers" who had left Europe and come to America "to plant, and under the Divine blessing to propagate in this Wilderness, the blessed Reformed, Protestant Religion, in the purity of its Order, and Worship." The ministers went on to admit their "past neglects" of this worthy endeavor and declared their "Obligations better to prosecute the Same end." Then came the punch line: "Whereunto the Liberal, & Relligious Education of Suitable youth is under the blessing of God, a chief & most probable expedient." [1] With that goal in mind, the trustees established the collegiate school.

Although the ministers had intellectual and practical aims in mind, the religious dimension of the proposed school was paramount in their thinking. When Cotton Mather had sent them his "Proposalls for Erecting an UNIVERSITY in the Renowned Colony of *Connecticut,*" he referred to the institution as *"The School of the Churches"* and urged that it be established by a synod.[2] The original trustees did not follow his instructions to the letter but they agreed with their spirit. The collegiate school was a college of and for the churches—albeit unofficially. The first trustees and their successors were all clergymen; Yale's principal purpose was to train orthodox men in general and orthodox ministers in particular; instruction in Reformed theology was the only aspect of the curriculum legislated by the trustees; and the college laws spelled out the Christian nature of a Yale education. Finally, between 1702 and 1739, 46 percent of Yale's graduates entered the ministry. All of these factors point to the religious nature of early Yale, and the oft-repeated designation of the college as the School of the Prophets was a clear allusion to this fact.[3]

1. *Documentary History,* pp. 27–28.

2. Ibid., pp. 1–2.

3. See Stephen Buckingham, *The Unreasonableness and Danger of a People's renouncing their subjection to God,* p. 21; Jonathan Marsh, *An Essay, To Prove*

The term "School of the Prophets" was a stock rhetorical expression used by preachers to relate the college enterprise to the immemorial and half-mythic educational concerns of God's chosen people. Rhetorical or not, the term had a meaningful application to Yale. While the colonial legislators were chiefly concerned with the school's administrative and financial affairs, the ministers were mainly interested in the religious purpose and spirit of the college —ecclesiastical, theological, and spiritual. Yale was designed to produce men who adhered to the form of church government spelled out in the Saybrook Platform, who accepted the doctrines of Reformed orthodoxy, and who lived pious lives as experiential as well as intellectual Christians.

These were ambitious goals and no account of early Yale should ignore the questions of how and to what extent they were fulfilled. One central assumption emerges from an examination of these intentions: the trustees believed that liberal learning and religious education were not only compatible but were necessarily conjoined. They saw no conflict between teaching the arts and sciences and transmitting Reformed orthodoxy. Instead of creating a theological seminary, they erected a liberal arts college.

In 1701 it was possible for the ministers to undertake the errand of their fathers in their fathers' terms. At their first meeting as trustees, they had stipulated that Ames and the Westminster Catechism were to be the staples of the theology course, and reserved the right to determine which other texts could be used at the school (adding Wollebius within a few years). These decisions had seemed sufficient. The trustees believed that as long as the students read the right theology and avoided any deviant systems, orthodoxy would remain safe and strong, a belief grounded on two further assumptions: first, that the social and intellectual milieu of Connecticut would not change, and second, that the substance of the curriculum would remain fixed. They were wrong on both counts.

---

the Thorough Reformation of a Sinning People is not to be Expected (New London, 1721), p. 46; Eleazar Williams, *An Essay To Prove That when God once enters upon a Controversie, With His Professing People; He will Manage and Issue it* (New London, 1723), p. 37; Phineas Fiske, *The Good Subject's Wish Or, The Desirableness Of The Divine Presence With Civil Rulers* (New London, 1726), p. 32; Eliphalet Adams, *A Discourse Shewing That so long as there is any Prospect of a Sinful People's yielding good Fruit hereafter, there is hope that they may be Spared,* p. 73.

A Changing Milieu

At the turn of the century, Connecticut was still a relatively homogeneous society. A few seventh-day Baptists had congregated in and around New London in the 1670s and more conventional Baptists appeared in that region in the early 1700s. Quakers were even less prominent, although there had been a handful in the colony in the late seventeenth century and there would be a small organized group of them in New Milford—and at Yale—in the late 1720s and 1730s. The Anglicans, eventually the most potent dissenting force in the colony, were nonexistent in 1700. S.P.G. missionaries appeared in the colony soon after that date, but the Anglican presence did not become a genuine threat in Connecticut until after 1722.

When the collegiate school was created, therefore, the Presbyterial-Congregational establishment was firmly entrenched and happily unthreatened. There were, to be sure, varieties of ecclesiastical opinion within the establishment, but the Saybrook Platform of 1708 gave these differences an official sanction. Concern for church order persisted after Saybrook, but initially these debates related to refinements of an accepted framework. Even this harmony did not last. Isolated and insulated as it was, Connecticut was still part of the larger English world. After the revolution of 1688–89 that world had steadily become more open and libertarian. Great Britain herself led the way by permitting the coexistence of various religious groups in an atmosphere of toleration. It took time for these practices to cross the Atlantic, but they reached Massachusetts during the last years of the seventeenth century and Connecticut in the first few decades of the eighteenth. The colonial ministers and magistrates resisted and deflected the new trend, but they could not and did not stop it. In 1708 the crown directed Connecticut to allow freedom of worship to dissenters, and twenty years later the colonial government agreed to exempt dissenting church members from paying taxes to support established ministers. By 1730, Yale College existed in an open ecclesiastical milieu.

Ecclesiastical diversity, however, was only one social change that confronted the college and its purposes. Another was the matter of religious orthodoxy. In 1701, the theological consensus in the colony was such that the collegiate school trustees felt no need to establish a religious test for college officers. The Saybrook Confession, a version of the Westminster Confession as modified by that of Savoy, simply made explicit the theological convictions of the Connecticut establishment. But no effort was made to enforce those convictions, precisely because there seemed no reason to do so. The first two decades of the eighteenth century were years of theological complacency. Ministers might have been concerned about questions of church order, but they took their orthodoxy for granted. All of them accepted Westminster and preached Reformed doctrines. For its first twenty years, the college participated in the unannounced moratorium on religious debate. Rectors Pierson and Andrew never engaged in theological controversy and neither man was suspected of deviant beliefs. The collegiate school taught Ames, Wollebius, and Westminster, the students ostensibly accepted those systems, and most graduates entered the ministry. The college fulfilled its purposes.

As it turned out, the apparent religious consensus in the colony was only the lull before the storm. In fact, trouble had been simmering on several fronts for a number of years. On the one hand, church polity continued as a topic of debate, especially as it related to the issue of ministerial authority. That authority had been enhanced by the Half-Way Covenant of 1662 and bolstered by the Saybrook settlement of 1708. It had also been under attack, not only from disgruntled laymen, but from some clergymen as well. Most pastors, however, favored some form of clerical power and defended themselves against "the Vile Words that are cast about, of *Priest-Craft,* and Priest-Ridden, and an *Ambitious* and *Designing Clergy.*" [4]

Not only were there cracks in the ecclesiastical structure of the colony, but there were soft spots in the body of orthodoxy too. The Reformed tradition seemed secure in Connecticut largely because it had never been challenged. The problem was that it had not been strenuously defended either. What had taken place instead was a growing inclination among some ministers to adopt a more open-minded stance toward orthodox theology. They played down certain doctrines and emphases and concentrated on preaching a more rational form of Christianity, paying more attention to the role of man than to the work of God and appealing

4. Timothy Cutler, *Firm Union of a People Represented,* p. 55.

more to the minds than to the hearts of their parishioners. There was nothing overtly wrong with such ideas. Reformed theology had always dealt with man's religious responsibilities and had consistently spoken to the intellect. But Calvinism had traditionally placed the primary emphasis on God's grace, to which the New England Puritans added a concern with the role of piety in the life of faith. Some Connecticut clergymen, while not denying these latter characteristics of orthodoxy, evidently chose to emphasize the former. At the time, no one bothered to attack the shift in priorities.

The Cutler apostasy of 1722 shattered the prevailing calm and exposed the religious problems of the colony to open scrutiny. The Anglican issue encompassed matters of belief, order, and authority. From the time Joseph Morgan sounded the warning in the spring, the ecclesiastical issue of Anglicanism and the theological issue of Arminianism were linked as the dual threat posed by the defection. The consternation that followed Cutler's declaration was succeeded by a kind of religious revival—a self-conscious examination of the received traditions of the established churches. Ministers were now sensitized to questions of order and belief and were soon to attack each other over precisely those matters of style and emphasis that had gone unnoticed a few years earlier. It was no longer possible for pastors to take these concerns for granted; they now had to proclaim them with clarity and conviction.

The 1722 controversy struck a near-fatal blow to the purposes of the college and the practices of the colony. To some ministers, it seemed that Yale and Connecticut had gone the way of Harvard and eastern Massachusetts. The trustees, at least, took steps to prevent this occurrence at the collegiate school by requiring that all officers subscribe to the Saybrook Confession and swear opposition to Arminian and prelatical corruptions. By this belated move, the ministers acknowledged their awareness of the intertwining ecclesiastical and theological dangers posed by the defection. Of the two, the danger of polity lent itself more readily to compromise. Since it was impossible for Connecticut, as a colony of England, to keep the Anglicans out, the best solution seemed to be to coexist with them even while attacking them. The establishment adopted this tactic and pursued the latter part of it with vigor. Ministers blamed the Anglicans for the colony's troubles, for bringing the ministry into disrepute, and for fostering heretical views. At the same time, pastors continued to worry about their own church polity and to seek agreement on *"stated Methods of Procedure."* [5]

The Arminianism issue was more difficult. As long as all so-called Arminians were Anglicans, this theological deviation could be effectively quarantined and combatted. The trouble was that the established ministers perceived the Arminian threat to be more widespread. Shortly after the Cutler defection, Joseph Morgan again wrote Cotton Mather about the dangers facing Reformed orthodoxy. He lamented the fact that people were prejudiced against the Westminster Confession and went on to identify the principal source of trouble:

> Of all the engines Satan has formed against our salvation, the most effectual is Arminianism; especially so, because, while it owns most of the great articles of faith, it goes less feared and mistrusted, and, under the specious pretext of vindicating God's benevolence and encouraging virtue, and such like, it privately strikes the work of regeneration under the fifth rib, and is usually followed by Socinianism, and that by Deism.[6]

While Morgan's fear of deism was an overreaction, his concern about Arminianism was legitimate. The problem with trying to assess the strength of Arminianism in Connecticut during these years is that it is impossible to find any Arminians. This seeming contradiction can be resolved only by realizing that in the charged theological atmosphere of the 1720s and 1730s, the term *Arminianism* was used more pejoratively than precisely. It pointed to a tendency, not a position, and identified the style rather than the content of theological discourse. But the mere fact that Morgan and others discerned heretical tendencies in Connecticut in the

5. Thomas Clap, *The Greatness and Difficulty of the Work of the Ministry* (Boston, 1732), p. 21. See also [John Graham], *Some Remarks Upon a late Pamphlet* ([Boston], 1733), for a typical attack on the Anglicans.

6. Richard Webster, *A History of the Presbyterian Church in America, from Its Origin until the Year 1760* (Philadelphia, 1857), p. 337. For a discussion of Arminianism in New England during this period, see Gerald J. Goodwin, "The Myth of 'Arminian-Calvinism' in Eighteenth-century New England," *The New England Quarterly* 41 (1968): 213–37. Goodwin argues, as his title implies, that Arminianism, precisely understood, did not exist before the Great Awakening outside of the Church of England. Strictly speaking, he is correct; still, the moralistic tendencies of some Congregationalist preachers raised the specter of this heresy and caused some fears. In this chapter, I am concerned chiefly with those tendencies.

1720s reveals the radical change that had occurred in the intellectual milieu of the colony. The first trustees had established the college in an atmosphere of theological consensus; they never anticipated that it would perform its task in a climate of religious conflict. They would have found unthinkable the notion that the college itself would be implicated in that conflict.

Such, however, was the case. After 1722 Yale was forced to serve as a bastion of orthodoxy and a center of controversy in a contentious and diversified society. The ecclesiastical establishment had broken down, ministerial authority was under attack, religious pluralism was a fact, and theological sensitivity was rampant. One index of this new situation was a heightened awareness of the overt and covert threats the sermons of some ministers presented to the traditional faith. Solomon Stoddard fired the first salvo in 1724 when he condemned those preachers who implied that faith in Christ was "only a Perswasion of the truth of the Christian Religion. This is the way to make multitudes of carnal men secure, and to flatter themselves as if they were in a good Condition." Such appeals to the rational qualities of religion were pernicious and smacked of theological timidity. "Ministers," Stoddard argued, "should be Sons of Thunder" and strike fear in the hearts of their hearers. Other clergymen voiced similar concerns. "Ministers," stated Azariah Mather (Y. 1705) a year later, "should be Men of Courage, Conduct and Resolution: when they are Afraid and Cowardly in a Sacred Cause, it looks sad: they should appear boldly against Error & Erroneous Men, especially more Dangerous Errors." Mather denounced those pastors who "pretend much to Moderation & talk much of a Catholick Charity." If Calvin and Luther had been of such a temperament, he noted, there would have been no Reformation.[7]

The fact that such attacks became commonplace after 1722 does not mean the problems they confronted were new. It is probable that the tendencies Stoddard, Mather, and others found objectionable had flourished earlier but had gone unnoticed. In 1713, for example, John Bulkley had preached a Connecticut election sermon in which he argued that a principal part of the minister's work was to impart the *"Conviction of the reasonableness of Re-*

7. Solomon Stoddard, *The Defects of Preachers Reproved* (New London, 1724), pp. 14–15; Azariah Mather, *The Gospel-Minister Described, by the Important Duty of his Office* (New London, 1725), p. 22.

ligion" to the people; faith, he stated, was "assenting to the *Doctrines*" of Christianity.[8] Nathaniel Chauncy (Y. 1702) was another clergyman who fitted the pattern described by Mather. The college's first graduate had been a Calvinist in the early years of his ministry but modified his views upon reading recent English theologians who, he said, "in less room do set things in a much clearer light." Jonathan Todd, speaking of Chauncy in a funeral sermon, praised him for this "openness of mind" and linked it to his theological posture: "He was a diligent inquirer after truth; and would never suffer himself to be brought into bondage to the opinions of any party of men: And would take no doctrines of religion on trust from any man. . . . The Bible was his rule of faith." [9] Calvin, Ames, Wollebius, and the authors of the Westminster Confession were all men, and if Todd's remark is to be taken literally, Chauncy would not subscribe to any of their doctrines just for the sake of orthodoxy. Instead he appealed to Scripture; this was a classic Protestant tenet, but it obviously meant that anyone who did so was free to formulate his own theological doctrines.

Jared Eliot (Y. 1706) was of the same temperament. In a funeral sermon, Thomas Ruggles, Jr., praised Eliot's catholic spirit and disdain for differences of opinion over religious principles. Eliot abhorred "narrowness, and the mean contractedness of a party spirit" and was "an enemy to all imposition, and arbitrary dominion over other men's faith; howsoever the pretence was painted with the fair shew of the name of orthodoxy." [10] Although Eliot had toyed with Anglicanism in 1722, he, Chauncy, and Bulkley were not unorthodox; they did not openly deny Reformed doctrines or declare for deviant dogmas. They simply were not as bold and clear in preaching Reformed theology as men like Stoddard and Mather. This posture might have been acceptable before 1722, but after that date such vague and cautious views were considered dangerous. Many ministers perceived this danger and sought ways to combat it, one of which was to proclaim the orthodox position more starkly and strongly.

Such, at least, was the tactic adopted by Rector Elisha Williams.

8. John Bulkley, *The Necessity of Religion in Societies*, p. 56.

9. Fowler, *Memorials of the Chaunceys*, pp. 85–86, 105.

10. Thomas Ruggles, *The Death of great, good and useful Men lamented* (New Haven, 1763), p. 18.

After the Cutler defection it was clear that Yale could not afford to be moderate in the cause of truth. In this case, extremism was a virtue and Williams acted the part; his sermons and activities were visible expressions of his theological convictions. He gave the Connecticut legislators a pure Calvinistic sermon, sought to obtain royal sanction for the colony's ecclesiastical practices and the college's right to exist, welcomed the revivals, attacked religious deviants, and worried about the theological posture of the students. In every instance he acted boldly, so that during his tenure the collegiate school performed its mission in an aggressive style.

As the intended bastion of orthodoxy, Yale's response to the new religious milieu was to propagate Reformed orthodoxy and traditional practices all the more clearly and forcefully. This performance, however, did not protect the college from involvement in the colony's religious disputes. Even though the vast majority of the school's graduates remained within the Presbyterial-Congregational fold, the Yale student body always included a few Anglicans and occasionally some Quakers. To this extent, the external changes in colonial society impinged on the life of the college.

Not all of the school's difficulties, however, came from without. Five years after Elisha Williams took over as rector, Yale was charged with fostering Arminianism and heresy. James Pierpont, Moses Noyes, Timothy Woodbridge, Eliphalet Adams, and Benjamin Colman all voiced this suspicion. One source of the fear, of course, was the lingering specter of Anglicanism at Yale, a specter embodied not only in the ever-present Samuel Johnson, but in several undergraduates as well. But the accusation that the college had become deviant implied that the problem was more than Anglicanism. In some way, Yale had been corrupted from within.

The New Learning

The ingredients for such corruption had existed since 1701. The original trustees had deliberately set out to build an institution that would nurture the students in the ways of piety. They soon discovered, however, that talking about such an atmosphere was not the same as creating it. Still, they tried to impose this ideal through the college laws:

> Every student shall exercise himself in Reading Holy Scriptures by himself every Day that the word of Christ may Dwell

> in Him ritchly and that he may be filled with the knowledge of the will of God in all wisdom and spirituall understanding.
>
> Every student shall consider the main end of his study to wit to know God in Jesus Christ and answerably to lead a Godly sober life.

These rules established the intended religious tone of student life. Other regulations dealt with more specific requirements: the undergraduates were to attend "all publick assemblies for Divine worship," engage in secret prayer, be present at morning and evening prayers, listen to expositions on the Scripture delivered by the rector, and periodically offer an analysis of a biblical passage.[11]

In emphasizing the need for students to have an experiential relationship with God and to exercise regular habits of prayer and Scripture reading, the trustees were expressing the widely held conviction that a Christian—especially a minister—"must be a man of *true Piety*." Preachers in Connecticut repeatedly evoked this theme in their sermons. It was all very well for Christians to have what James Pierpont called "an Historical and Dogmatical Faith." But this "Speculative Knowledge" was not sufficient by itself; it had to be supplemented and completed by "Experimental" knowledge.[12] As Daniel Lewis put the issue: "A Minister should feel & experience in his own heart the power and efficacy of the Truth which he Preaches to others." Azariah Mather agreed. If ministers "have not learned of GOD," he argued, "how shall they be fit to teach others? If they be not Men of good Experience, how can we deem them fit to Undertake to lead poor Souls to JESUS CHRIST?" In religious matters, only "Experience fits men to Teach others."[13] Joseph Morgan had just this need in mind when he urged the college tutors to "teach your *Pupils* to know the *Cross of Christ*." Morgan feared, as he later put it, that the cause of Christianity would suffer irreparable harm "When men undertake to Preach the *Gospel of Christ*, who never learn'd to Know Experimentally the *Cross of Christ*: Whose Eloquent Learned Discourses can be but *with Excellency of words of Mans Wisdom*." In order to produce pious clergymen, Morgan called for rectors

11. *Yale Graduates*, 1 : 347–48.

12. Daniel Lewis, *The Good Minister* (New London, 1733), pp. 10, 13; James Pierpont, *Sundry False Hopes of Heaven, Discovered and Decryed* (Boston, 1712), pp. 16–17.

13. Lewis, *Good Minister*, p. 13; Azariah Mather, *A Gospel Star, or Faithful Minister* (New London, 1730), pp. 12–13; Stoddard, *Defects of Preachers*, p. 9.

and tutors whose experiential faith would serve as a model for the undergraduates.[14]

The trustees were well aware of this spiritual dimension of the Reformed tradition and of the college's role in fostering it. They took turns visiting the college to preach to the students, and pains to see that the religious observances at the school were performed. This attempt to infuse Yale with a spirit of piety had some positive effect. The testimonies of Samuel Johnson and Jonathan Edwards reveal that student prayer groups and personal meditation were attended and performed by a number of scholars; the young men who gathered under the spiritual leadership of David Ferris in the 1730s were perhaps the most notorious examples of this phenomenon.[15]

On the whole, however, the trustees' efforts were unsuccessful, due in large part to the nature of the institution itself. Yale was a liberal arts college, not a seminary, and no amount of legislation could impose on the school the trappings of a monastery. Students who came to the college signed no statement of faith and made no vocational commitment to the ministry. The record of student misbehavior is one sign that piety was not always foremost in undergraduates' minds, and the fact that the same laws that demanded prayer also forbade liquor is another. Yale would always contain worldly young men whose exuberant interests would militate against devotional ones.

The college's role as a nursery for experiential Christians had been an impossible one to fulfill from the outset. It was desirable, of course, for the faculty and trustees to serve as examples for the students, but there was no guarantee that the scholars would follow those models. Piety could not be produced by example or enforced by law. The rector and tutors could monitor a student's attendance at prayer but they had no way to ensure his sincerity. This problem had existed from the beginning, but with the student body increasing in size and diversity in the 1730s, the futility of the college's spiritual mission became more obvious.

The charges of religious deviance at Yale related not only to a judgment of the quality of the students' experiential faith but to

14. Morgan, *Only Effectual Remedy Against Mortal Errors,* p. 45; Joseph Morgan, *The Duty and a Mark of Zion's Children* (New London, 1725), p. 7.

15. For the remarks of Johnson and Edwards and information on the Ferris group, see chapter 10 above, notes 31, 32, and 33.

the content of their historical faith as well. The seeds of this corruption had also been planted in 1701, when the first trustees planned a college that would teach the arts and sciences, providing Connecticut youth with a liberal as well as a religious education. That seemed an uncomplicated task at the time, for the standard texts in the liberal arts curriculum posed no threats to theology. The trustees adopted that curriculum uncritically and made no attempt to specify which books should be used in the various courses. They retained control only of the theology course, where Ames, Wollebius, and Westminster were to serve as the accepted works.

The ministers' intentions, as far as they went, were realized, as Ames, Wollebius, and Westminster remained the required divinity texts at Yale for forty years. During that same period, however, the rest of the course of study underwent a process of modernization that had insidious implications for theology. These implications were not immediately apparent, for the universally held belief in the unity and compatibility of all knowledge remained strong, and men throughout the Western world failed to recognize the potentially disintegrating effects of new nontheological ideas and theories. The failure to perceive the drastic impact Newtonian physics might have on theology, for example, was not a provincial myopia but was shared by learned Englishmen and even by Sir Isaac Newton himself.

Newton, in fact, strove mightily to keep science and religion all of an intellectual piece. He confessed that when he wrote the *Principia,* "I had an eye upon such principles as might work with considering men, for the belief of a Deity; and nothing can rejoice me more than to find it useful for that purpose." Newton had no intention of removing God from active control over and interference with the workings of the universe, but even the great scientist could not prevent the implications of his work from propagating a revised view of the Creator. The metaphysics of the new science made "the ascription of ultimate reality and causal efficacy to the world of mathematics" and hence relegated God to the position of efficient first cause of the world instead of the supreme final cause of all things.[16] In an attempt to keep his religion and his scientific pursuits in concert, Newton devoted the later

16. Edwin A. Burtt, *The Metaphysical Foundations of Modern Physical Science,* pp. 288, 303.

years of his life to writing on theological subjects, but the thrust of his interests was intellectual rather than devotional, and tended to promote a belief in the Deity and to combat atheism. Newton's own work on the Trinity—which advocated a unitarian position as being most reconcilable with scientific opinion—reveals this tendency, as do the books he encouraged others to write, such as John Craig's *Theologiae Christianae Principia Mathematicae*.[17]

The potential antagonism of religion and science, therefore, remained latent and the Yale scholars who learned the new physics saw no conflict between natural philosophy and revealed theology. But the fact that such a conflict was incipient did produce some tensions. Since the students were predisposed to think of all knowledge as unified in a common source, they were prepared to accommodate the new learning to an old world-view. At the same time, however, they also found that the new learning brought with it new modes of expression and new ways of perceiving reality. To talk and think about the universe in mechanistic terms might result in talking and thinking about its creator in similar language.

What the new learning produced, then, was not so much a loss of faith as a shift in mood, a change in interests. When men became more concerned with God the Creator than with God the Redeemer, some adjustments in religious thinking inevitably followed. The spirit of such an adjustment was expressed in rather ornate form by John Sergeant (Y. 1729) in his valedictory oration. While Sergeant's later career as a missionary to the Indians showed that the new learning had not undermined his religious commitment, his words indicated the ways in which other Yale graduates might have responded to their studies. Referring to mathematical and scientific subjects, Sergeant said:

> We are sometimes also struck with admiration of the wisdom and skill of the great Establisher, when we consider the law by which He governs all in exact harmony and regular order, admiring the beautiful proportions observed now in the motions, now in the distances and now in the magnitudes of the globes that compose this our system. . . . We discover the evident tokens of superior goodness, wisdom and power of the creating, preserving and governing spirit, all the way down-

17. G. N. Clark, *Science and Social Welfare in the Age of Newton*, pp. 82–84.

ward till our tho'ts again light on this our earth, where all creation also join their universal voice to proclaim the being and excellencies of the Creatour.[18]

Similar flowery sentiments had been voiced by college graduates long before the new learning, but in the charged context of that learning such thoughts had new import. To admire God as the "great Establisher" rather than to fear him as the righteous Lord was a potentially radical notion.

Few men appreciated the impact of the new learning on theology. Those who did usually spoke in terms like those used by Sergeant. In England, Robert Boyle, an accomplished scientific thinker and a devout Christian, labored to influence the "religious experience of Englishmen by holding up to them the works of nature as objects of pious contemplation." [19] In America, Cotton Mather performed a similar task. He acknowledged that the revolution wrought by the works of Newton and others was significant, and thought that one should study them in order to contemplate the glories of God's creating work. Mather urged candidates for the ministry to get a thorough insight into "the *Principles* of our *Perpetual Dictator,* the Incomparable Sr. *Isaac Newton.*" As his own tribute to the new science, Mather wrote *The Christian Philosopher,* a book, he said, designed "to Show and Raise those Dispositions of PIETY, wherein the *Works* of the Holy and Blessed GOD invite us to *Live* unto Him; together with the *First Claim* that I have ever yet seen so explicitly made on the behalf of a Glorious CHRIST, and the Consideration due to him in our *Philosophy.*"

The study of natural philosophy became, then, a worshipful act. Mather told his readers to *"see* GOD *in every Thing!* Own Him, Fear Him, Love Him; Study *Philosophy* with a perpetual Intention to do so." [20] This was Mather's technique in *The Christian Philosopher* (1721). In the section "Of Magnetism," Mather argued that it would be idolatrous for him to worship a stone: "But then it would be a very agreeable and acceptable *Homage* unto the Glorious GOD, for me to see much of Him in such a wonderful Stone as the MAGNET. They have done well to call it the *Loadstone,*

18. Sergeant, *Valedictorian Oration,* p. 24.
19. Clark, *Science and Social Welfare,* p. 81.
20. Cotton Mather, *Manuductio ad Ministerium,* pp. 50, 51, 52.

that is to say, the *Lead-stone; May it lead me unto Thee, O my God and my Saviour!*" [21]

Mather's appropriation of the new learning for religious purposes indicated that such ideas need not cause a loss of faith. Yet when Samuel Johnson was a student at the collegiate school in Saybrook, the scholars were advised by their elders to shun the new philosophy, as it "would soon bring in a new divinity and corrupt the pure religion of the country." [22] As it turned out, the latter fear was more accurate than the former. The new learning did not introduce a new religion as much as it added novel dimensions to the old. The attempt to synthesize current scientific thinking with traditional theological formulations produced a situation in which new language was applied to old concepts. While no one denied the validity of those concepts, the changes in emphasis and expression inevitably modified their intention and meaning.

These latent contradictions would never have surfaced into full-blown conflicts had the colonists not shared the Reformed community's insistence on an educated ministry. For Quakerish zealots like Timothy Allen (Y. 1736), who had no use for a liberal education, such issues never posed a problem. He and his enthusiastic cohorts in the Ferris group clearly separated learning from religion.[23] The majority of would-be ministers, however, were continually enjoined to combine the two. Connecticut clergymen believed that an educated minister was not one who had simply studied the Scripture and theology, but one who had also learned the academic subjects of grammar, rhetoric, logic, and natural philosophy. Samuel Willard's posthumous *Brief Directions to a Young Scholar Designing the Ministry* and Cotton Mather's *Manuductio ad Ministerium,* two works that addressed this issue, both made the case for a liberal education for clergymen. The colonists generally agreed, then, that human learning was "*a necessary qualification of a Gospel Minister.*" To believe otherwise was "Strange" doctrine indeed.[24]

But of course to insist that ministers be educated was to court the possibility that their learning might overwhelm their theology.

21. Cotton Mather, *The Christian Philosopher: A Collection of the Best Discoveries In Nature, with Religious Improvements* (London, 1721), p. 114.

22. *Johnson,* 1 : 6.

23. For more on Allen and the Ferris group, see chapters 7 and 10.

24. John Graham, *The Christian's Duty of Watchfulness against Error, and Establishment in the Truth* (New London, 1733), p. 39.

Time and again clergymen warned their colleagues of this danger. Daniel Lewis advised preachers to avoid "*Sermons* fill'd with lofty Notions & curious Speculations." "A *Sermon* adorned with the flowers of Rhetorick," he continued, "and which only discovers the Profound Learning of the Preacher, will signifie very little to a poor ignorant Hearer, who rather needs to be *fed with Milk, than strong Meat.*" Azariah Mather put it most succinctly: "It is not the great Scholar, but the Humble Preacher that is most like to Convert Souls." [25] But these warnings failed to deter some ministers from flaunting their education, and it is certain that a few college graduates succumbed to the temptation and preached to the mind rather than to the heart, or talked chiefly of the powers of man instead of the glories of God. This was the danger Thomas Foxcroft had in mind when he addressed the ministers of New England in 1740:

> You are not to stand up here (*in the Pulpit*) as a Professor of ancient or modern Philosophy, nor an usher in the School of *Plato,* or *Seneca,* or Mr. *Lock*: but as a Teacher in the School of CHRIST.—*Thus saith the Prophet,* or *Thus saith the Apostle,* carries greater Weight with it both to convince and persuade, than a long Series of *Demonstrations* from remote *Principles,* tho' they should be firm and strong as those of *Euclid,* or *Sir Isaac Newton.*—'Tis the vain Exaltation of *ruin'd Nature,* that makes the *Gospel* so despis'd in our Age.[26]

The exaltation of ruined nature was, of course, the exaltation of man. Preachers who had studied Locke and Newton were struck by the wonders of the new learning and came away with an enhanced opinion of the powers of the human intellect. Their elevated anthropology may have resulted in a minimized theology. At the very least, these new ideas placed traditional theology in a new and more eclectic framework.

One example of this shift in emphasis is evident in the study of ethics. In assessing man's moral behavior, the Puritans had insisted that, despite the fact that God elected some men and not others, all men were responsible for their own ethical actions. They also declared that God's word, not human reason, must be the basis

25. Lewis, *Good Minister,* p. 19; Mather, *Gospel-Minister,* p. 28.

26. Thomas Foxcroft, *Some Seasonable Thoughts on Evangelic Preaching* (Boston, 1740), title page. Foxcroft took the quotation from Isaac Watts.

for man's moral decisions. William Ames advocated this position in his *Cases of Conscience,* a book grounded on this assumption. The Yale students who read Henry More's *Enchiridion,* however, learned a more comprehensive version of ethics. More's system retained the supremacy of revelation but it also supplemented the rules of revelation with an insistence on the trustworthiness of man's reason.

Ethics, then, was a subject apart from divinity, with categories of its own. In the context of the new learning's stress on man's intellectual abilities, the separate status of ethics had serious implications for religion. Free will, which the Westminster Confession allowed, could readily imply moral power, which Westminster denied. Graduates influenced by More might easily stress morality rather than grace as the keystone of the religious life and hence tend toward a form, although an impure form, of Arminianism. This Arminianism was not a theological stance but an intellectual disposition. It did not manifest itself in precise errors but flourished as a way of talking about the religious life in man-centered rather than God-centered terms. As such, this form of Arminianism can be attributed in part to the results of an educational emphasis on the new learning.

One man who displayed the kind of thinking derived from the new learning was Samuel Johnson, whose Anglicanism provided his opponents with ample justification for labeling him an Arminian. Although Johnson disavowed the label—he was aware of its explosive connotation in Connecticut—his sermons reveal the intellectual tendencies of the new Arminianism. In one of his discourses, Johnson spoke of moral wisdom in terms that practically denied the need for revelation. Moral wisdom, he said, "consists in finding out wherein our true happiness is placed, and proposing that as our chief end, and in discovering what are the directest and fittest means to that end, and in diligently pursuing our true happiness, by such means as directly tend to promote it." Johnson's definition of true happiness as "ease, peace, tranquillity, the enjoyment of ourselves, satisfaction, delight, and the like" was strictly this-worldly and a clear example of the vagaries of philosophical ethics.[27]

This type of thinking enraged those who styled themselves orthodox. Elisha Williams, for example, while not aiming his attack

27. *Johnson,* 3 : 395.

directly against Johnson, preached a sermon in which he delineated the implications of thinking in Johnson's terms. Williams bluntly labeled such thought as an implicit covenant of works. If any man, the rector stated,

> Has the Generall Rational belief That God is the sole fountain of True Happiness, & that His Happiness is the Enjoyment of the Divine Being His first thought then is to Ingratiate himself in the Favour of the Divine Being By Keeping His Law, the Declared Will of His Maker, Which by His first Sin He has Put himself Into an Impossible State of Perfectly obeying.[28]

Johnson, of course, would have disavowed any intention of going this far, but the thrust of his thought was to place emphasis on man's activities and abilities. Reformed orthodoxy, as presented by Williams, concentrated its attention on God's free grace. The distinction was between a man-centered and a grace-centered concern.

The Yale curriculum contained several subjects that fostered such man-centered moralism. In the metaphysics course, for example, the students studied a branch of natural theology, a mode of thinking that derived its information about God and religion from man's reason and the evidences of the natural world. In ethics, students were taught to discover the rational grounds for moral behavior. These two courses, then, were full of potential mischief for the cause of revealed religion and traditional piety. In *Manuductio ad Ministerium,* Cotton Mather attacked both of these subjects. He dismissed metaphysics with a rhetorical question: "But then to Weave any more *Cobwebs* in your Brains; to what Purpose is it?" Ethics received a more concerted treatment. Mather inveighed against it as "a *Vile Thing*" and a "*Sham*": "It presents you with a *Mock-Happiness;* It prescribes to you *Mock Vertues* for the coming at it." Ethics divorced from theology, he warned, was nothing less than "*Paganism*" and he urged students to be more Christian than to look upon the *Enchiridion* of Henry More "as *Next the Bible, the best Book in the World.*"[29] Teaching More's work at Yale may have been intellectually respectable and modern; but there were good reasons to question its compatibility with the historic Puritanism against which it was a reaction.

28. Elisha Williams, Sermon on Hosea 13:9, n.d., Yale Archives.

29. Mather, *Manductio*, pp. 37–38.

The Yale students who studied logic, natural philosophy, ethics, and metaphysics during and after the 1720s, then, were introduced to a world of learning that was very different from the education of their fathers and forebears. The emphasis of the new learning was on man's reason and abilities. It opened to the students—and to some graduates—new vistas of knowledge, and bombarded them with new perceptions of themselves and their world. Simultaneously, however, those same students continued to learn and rely on the theology of Ames and Wollebius. These were the standards for the orthodoxy the college trustees hoped to transmit to the rising generation; but they were, by this time, outdated. Ames and Wollebius wrote neither in nor for an age of reason. The orthodoxy they delineated was precise and the errors they refuted were specific. As Dortians, both men opposed an Arminianism that had been formulated in order to evade a definite and positive tenet of Calvinism—irresistible grace. Both the *Medulla* and the *Compendium* were pre-Newtonian and pre-Lockean works, and neither was designed to counteract the vague Arminianism that had been fostered in Connecticut by the new learning.

In fact, few theological works were so designed. Those eighteenth-century Reformed theologians who did deal with the new thought tended to compromise traditional doctrines in an effort to be consistent with the temper of the times. They thus countenanced rather than combated the new tendencies toward man-centered reasonableness. Jonathan Edwards was the first thinker to attempt to reassert and reinterpret Reformed orthodoxy by employing the conceptual framework of the new thought. Edwards himself was intellectually transformed by the new learning, but possessed the intellectual strength to employ that learning in the cause of Calvinism. His *A Treatise concerning Religious Affections* (1746) and *A Careful and Strict Enquiry into the modern prevailing Notions of Freedom of Will* (1754) would demonstrate, on an intellectual level at least, that orthodoxy was not tied to the world-view of a pre-Newtonian or pre-Lockean age. Edwards's work was boldly imaginative, not narrowly regressive, for he used the insights of Descartes, Locke, Newton, and the Cambridge Platonists to attack the anthropological assumptions their works had produced. Until Edwards pointed the way—which he began to do in sermons preached in the 1730s—Reformed orthodoxy proved unable to cope with many of the fresh attitudes the new learning had fostered.

Lacking any realization of what the new learning portended or how to remedy the tendencies it was creating, the college continued to teach the very works that contributed to charges of heresy among the students. Yale's role in propagating such thought and hence in nurturing these new attitudes and priorities was not a conscious one. No faculty member perceived the precise dangers inherent in the new learning; no undergraduate explicitly renounced his old faith and embraced new beliefs. The change was both gradual and subtle, neither understood nor acknowledged by those who underwent it. The reason for this ambivalence was that the new learning did not challenge the assumptions of traditional orthodoxy as much as it amplified certain aspects of that orthodoxy.

The founders of New England and their successors had always stressed the reasonableness of God in dealing with reasonable men. Seventeenth-century ministers in both Connecticut and Massachusetts constantly preached on this theme. Reasonableness was the vital core of the theology of grace. In addition, the theological systems of the Reformed tradition had always included natural theology and had confidently treated the evidences of God's providence and goodness found in the created world. At the same time, however, those ministers who spoke of reason also preached to the heart. They knew that grace and conversion were not simply exercises of the intellect but most especially activities of the soul. They also knew that the scriptural record of revealed religion deserved priority over the natural and reasonable record of creation. Here again Edwards—and then the New Light supporters of the Great Awakening—were to revivify this priority, but in the 1730s this corrective still lay in the future.

It is impossible to ascertain the precise ways in which the new learning and, more particularly, a Yale education affected New England's traditional theology. At the very least, however, such learning provided a milieu in which the intellectual facet of religion became more appealing and hence more dominant than the experiential. If this modern education produced heresy, it was, like nearly all heresy, a simplification of an existing orthodoxy rather than a denial of it. The issues at stake in the second quarter of the eighteenth century were not new; rather, some old doctrines and attitudes had gained ascendance over others. The result was that the standard expressions of Reformed orthodoxy were modified and moderated. Questioned about theological doctrines, most students probably would have given sound answers; but left to their own devices, they undoubtedly articulated novel formulations—and prompted some ever-watchful critics to cry heresy.

There was, of course, no heresy. The charges leveled by Pierpont and others in the early 1730s were overstated, and to that extent they reflected the acute theological sensitivity of the period. But those charges were nonetheless legitimate, and thus responded to the religious views of the students—views which may have been informed by the liberal arts and sciences in the Yale curriculum.

The college's theological mission, therefore, was not a simple one. Students trained under the boldly orthodox Elisha Williams still managed to appear heterodox, and even the school's graduates strayed from the paths of sound doctrine into the thickets of latitudinarian divinity. The Anglicans comprised the major portion of this group, but the wanderings of a few Congregationalists seemed more lamentable and insidious. None of these men was, strictly speaking, Arminian, although several of them were open to the charge. In 1730, for example, Jonathan Parsons (Y. 1729), suspected of Arminian tendencies, had some difficulty becoming ordained. Another graduate, Thomas Ruggles, Jr. (Y. 1723), had the reputation of possessing "a great talent at hiding his real sentiments, never coming fully out, either as to doctrinal or experimental religion." His parishioners in Guilford charged him with being "not such an edifying preacher" and "unsound in his doctrine." [30] Some people in Milford accused Samuel Whittelsey, Jr. (Y. 1729) of preaching a "system of morals" (shades of Henry More) rather than the gospel and of espousing universal redemption and the doctrine that man might fall from grace but could be regenerated by a renewal of faith. The church members declared that Whittlesey was leaning toward Arminianism.[31]

There is no way to determine whether or not these allegations were true, especially since the term—or rather, epithet—*Arminian* was used very freely. Nor is it possible to prove that the so-called

30. *Yale Graduates*, 1 : 389, 287; Bernard C. Steiner, *A History of the Plantation of Menunkatuck and of the Original Town of Guilford, Connecticut* (Baltimore, 1897), pp. 314–15.

31. Federal Writers Project, *History of Milford, Connecticut, 1639–1939* (Bridgeport, Conn.: Press of Braunworth and Co., 1939), p. 52.

Arminianism of these men was a product of their Yale education. For one thing, ministers who had attended the collegiate school long before the introduction of the new learning voiced similarly suspect theology. The sermons of Samuel Johnson revealed this novel slant. Johnson, who confronted the new learning after his graduation in 1714 and was so captivated that he later claimed he could pinpoint the date of his conversion to it, was emphasizing the reasonableness of Christianity in his sermons years before he became an Anglican. He continued to do so after he took episcopal orders. A sermon entitled *The Foundation of our Faith in Christ,* which he delivered in 1731, shows the ways in which Johnson's acceptance of an elevated view of man influenced his theology. While he cursorily admitted that God drew men to Christ, Johnson insisted that this work did not entail

> any thing that necessitates us to come, for this would be contrary to the reasonable and self-determining nature he has given us, for him to force us to come to Christ, by any irresistible operation on our minds; it would spoil all the virtue of our coming and be inconsistent with the very being of that state of probation wherein we are placed, and in short, in every respect inconsistent with the nature of things, and imply in it the greatest absurdities imaginable.
>
> The drawing therefore here spoken of must ordinarily mean such as is suited to reasonable natures, and free agents, to whom it is peculiar to be drawn by persuasion, by the force of arguments and motives.[32]

The Reformed tradition, on the other hand, insisted on irresistible grace and wholly denied that man earned any virtue by coming to Christ.

Such views were expected from Church of England ministers, but Congregationalists expressed them too. The open-minded Nathaniel Chauncy, for instance, evidently disliked the confines of orthodoxy and preferred to stake out his own theological boundaries. In his case, those boundaries were fairly undefined. In one of his sermons he spoke of Christ as one whose role "was to Instruct man in his Duty, Invite him to return thereto, and . . . to prescribe to him proper Means & Methods, that in attending on them he might experience the renewing & recovering Influences of the

32. *Johnson,* 3 : 382.

Divine Spirit." Although Chauncy recognized that man's renewal was bestowed, not earned, he clearly implied that a reasonable man need only follow certain procedures to attain grace. This was a popular theme of the new Arminianism—to pay lip service to the fact that conversion was God's work but to emphasize the necessity for human endeavor. "Such is the Nature of Conversion," Benjamin Lord (Y. 1714) preached, "that there is something for us to do in it. It *cannot* be done without God, neither *will* it be done without us." [33] Like Chauncy, Lord acknowledged God's work in the process of redemption; also like Chauncy, he preferred to stress the role of man.

Human reason was one of the main emphases of the sermons of Jared Eliot (Y. 1706) and Samuel Whittelsey (Y. 1705). Eliot attacked those who deprecated reason in order to "do the greater Honour to Divine Revelation" and argued that to condemn reason was to "undervalue the most noble Faculty of our Soul . . . promote *Enthusiasm,* and deprive Religion of one grand support." Reason, he insisted, must rule over the passions and be man's "governing Principle." [34] Whittelsey preached the same doctrine. Speaking of the minister's work, he said: "To change the Heart, and create a new Principle in the Soul, this is God's Work: We can only address to them as rational and intelligent, indued with the natural Principles of *Love* and *Fear;* and set before them such Reasons and Considerations as are suitable to operate and have Influence upon them." To achieve this end, pastors must "seek out acceptable Words, run to and fro and fetch Arguments and Reasons from every Topick" to bring men to God. People should be compelled to come into Christ's Kingdom "by the Dint of Persuasion, and all the innocent Arts of Insinuation, by all the Compulsion and Constraint that can be used with a reasonable Creature as such." [35] There was nothing heretical about these remarks, but their whole tenor was to subordinate the severe doctrines of the Reformed tradition to the less rigorous ideology of the new learning.

33. Nathaniel Chauncy, *The Faithful Servant Rewarded* (New London, 1732), p. 9; Benjamin Lord, *True Christianity Explained & Enforced* (New London, 1727), pp. 47, 51.

34. Jared Eliot, *The Two Witnesses; or, Religion Supported by Reason and Divine Revelation* (New London, 1736), pp. 64, 19.

35. Samuel Whittelsey, *A Sermon Preach'd at the Ordination of Mr. Samuel Whittelsey, jun.* (Boston, 1739), pp. 11, 14–15.

Johnson, Chauncy, Lord, Eliot, and Whittelsey had not studied the works of the new learning at the collegiate school; their education had been more scholastic. Yet their sermonic styles reflected the prevalence of the new thought in Connecticut—a prevalence which Yale, more than any other agency, fostered. To that extent, the school was responsible in part for the mild and man-centered theology which some colonial ministers articulated. The preoccupation with man and his abilities so entranced these pastors that they became wary of any aspect of humanity which seemed incompatible with this view.

Joseph Morgan, for one, perceived this wariness and attacked it directly. Reason, he warned, "is become the very *Instrument of Delusion*." It diverted men's attention from the experience of God's grace and made a "*stumbling Stone* of Christ, by devising a number of Outward Benefits by him: But none know his *real* Benefits, till they learn it by Experience." [36] Preachers like Chauncy, on the other hand, minimized experience and shunned enthusiasm and the passions. They stressed rationality. Grace became, for all practical purposes, a matter of man changing his mind rather than God breaking in and claiming his heart. These Yale ministers reflected the tendencies of the new learning without ever incorporating its substance into their sermons. They were not rationalists, just clergymen fascinated by rationality.

Yale College, however, is not noted for its graduates who modified the traditional orthodoxy, but for those who restated it. Before the Great Awakening, only one Yale graduate—indeed only one New Englander—adopted the substance of the new thought in his sermons, and he did so in order to argue against its tendencies. That graduate was Jonathan Edwards. He probably had become acquainted with the works of Locke and Newton while residing at Yale as butler from 1720 to 1722. He read Locke, he said later, with more delight "than the most greedy miser finds, when gathering up handfuls of silver and gold, from some newly discovered treasure." [37] Whereas most men either ignored Locke when they theologized or accepted only the rational impulses of the new learning, Edwards took over the categories of *Human Understanding* and applied them to his religious speculations.

In 1731, the same year in which Johnson treated his Stratford

36. Morgan, *Effectual Remedy*, pp. 2, 23.
37. Miller, *Jonathan Edwards*, p. 52.

parishioners to sublime thoughts on man's "reasonable and self-determining nature," Edwards delivered his now-famous *God Glorified in the Work of Redemption* to the citizens of Boston. In it, Edwards gave notice to all those who preached an elevated anthropology that he was to be their enemy: "So much the more Men exalt themselves, so much the less will they surely be disposed to exalt God." Edwards insisted that salvation was from, through, and in God, and God alone had the glory for this work. Man was utterly dependent on God for his redemption and could claim no credit for it whatsoever. "Hence," Edwards went on, "those Doctrines and Schemes of Divinity that are in any Respect opposite to such an absolute & universal Dependence on God, do derogate from God's Glory, and thwart the Design of the Contrivance for our Redemption."[38] Such was Edwards's challenge to the theological temper which, in a few years' time, he was to label Arminian.

Three years later Edwards published a second sermon, *A Divine and Supernatural Light,* in which he displayed the ways he was to utilize the new learning to preach Calvinism. Edwards's theme was the acquisition of divine knowledge, and he argued that such knowledge came from God, not from men. In delineating this position, Edwards spoke of the twofold nature of the mind, the "*speculative* or *notional*" faculty and the "sense of the Heart." The distinction, he said, was between the understanding and the will: "THUS there is a Difference between *having an Opinion* that GOD is holy and gracious, and *having a sense* of the Loveliness and Beauty of that Holiness and Grace." It was a difference between knowing that honey is sweet and having a sense of that sweetness. Reason, which Johnson, Eliot, and Whittelsey had made the keystone of religion, was therefore useless in the quest for divine

38. Jonathan Edwards, *God Glorified in the Work of Redemption, By the Greatness of Man's Dependence upon Him, in the Whole of it* (Boston, 1731), pp. 20, 22. For a discussion of Edwards's role in the religious controversies before and during the Great Awakening, see C. C. Goen's introduction to Jonathan Edwards, *The Great Awakening*. Goen also offers an interpretation of the Arminianism issue in New England during this period that is in line with the argument of this chapter. He writes that by the 1730s "New England churches were a mixed multitude like the ones from which their founders had fled, their outward religious life characterized largely by moral homilies in the pulpit—'Cotton Mather's "do-good" piety'—and complacent self-confidence in the pew. This is not formal or explicit Arminianism, but it is certainly the prevailing mood which evoked the outcries of 1734 and afterward" (see ibid., p. 17). I would only add that this same mood prevailed earlier and evoked outcries at Yale, at least, in 1730–32.

knowledge. It was "not a Thing that belongs to Reason, to see the Beauty and Loveliness of spiritual things; it is not a speculative thing, but depends upon the Sense of the Heart." "Reason's Work," Edwards concluded, "is to perceive Truth, and not Excellency." [39]

Edwards's imaginative use of new psychological categories to reassert Reformed theology was a unique stroke of brilliance. It was also a futile one. Edwards's efforts failed to stem the swelling tide of reasonable religion, and his disciples, his son Jonathan and Samuel Hopkins, were unable to retain the full scope of his theological views. Still, Edwards perceived the need for a new statement of Calvinist orthodoxy and fulfilled the need in the context of a new religious philosophy of nature. Elisha Williams, for one, lacked this vision. His solution was simply to state the traditional faith in traditional language. Most clergymen, however, had neither the perception of Edwards nor the persistence of Williams. Rather than confront the implications of the new thought for the old theology, these ministers preferred to bask in the bright light which that learning shed on man's rationality. These were the pastors who exemplified the effects of being captivated by their own education.

By the very nature of the college's intellectual function, then, its theological goals were always in danger of corruption or modification. Even those men who desired a learned ministry admitted that knowledge did not guarantee orthodoxy. Arius, Socinius, Arminius, and Pelagius—heretics all—were learned men, Solomon Stoddard pointed out, and simply educating the minds of future ministers was not necessarily going to prevent them from falling into the same errors: "Learning will not cure those distempers of the Heart that do expose men to false Opinions." [40] Few Yale graduates adopted any theologically false positions, but all of them had to live with the ambiguous and often contradictory requisite of learnedness. Ministers were required both to have a liberal education and to keep it in perspective—just as merchants were encouraged to work industriously but not to succumb to Mammon. The clergymen were warned to subsume learning to theology and

39. Jonathan Edwards, *A Divine and Supernatural Light, Immediately imparted to the Soul by the Spirit of God, Shown to be both a Scriptural and Rational Doctrine* (Boston, 1734), pp. 11–12, 27, 28.

40. Stoddard, *Defects of Preachers*, p. 7.

yet were tempted to use their learning to speak theologically. They were taught to celebrate the fruits of man's intellect and yet were enjoined to concentrate on God's grace. The several conflicts were seldom resolved easily.

The Spirit of Yale

In the course of its first forty years, Yale experienced numerous difficulties in fulfilling the lofty aims of its original trustees. In every instance, the religious responsibilities bestowed on the college was realized only in part. Ecclesiastically, Yale trustees wrote the Saybrook Platform, but the college later suffered the onus of the Cutler defection to Anglicanism. Theologically, Yale was established as a bulwark of Reformed orthodoxy, but the modernization of its curriculum modified that orthodoxy and the school was even charged with fostering Arminianism. Spiritually, the college was given the impossible job of producing experiential Christians, but could never be sure of its success. In all three cases, however, the immensity and complexity of the responsibility did not cause the college's supporters to give up in despair. The religious orientation of Yale remained strong and the college continued seeking to realize its goals. Azariah Mather's injunction to future ministers summarized Yale's ideal aims for its students: "Study Hard, Study Men, Study Books, especially the Book of Books, GOD's Book, Study much thy own Heart. 'Twas said of Famous Dr *Goodwin,* that he Studied Books, but he Studied his own Heart more." [41] The college could do little more than hope the same was true of its graduates.

Despite many hazards, the college's record as a training ground for learned, orthodox, and pious men was an exemplary one. The collegiate school had been established in 1701 as an alternative to a religiously declining Harvard, and over the years it continued as an orthodox foil to the Cambridge college's latitudinarianism. This fact was due, not only to the unifying nature of the Saybrook Platform and the difference between the Connecticut and eastern Massachusetts societies, but also to Yale's self-conscious adherence to the aims of its first trustees. Much of the credit must also go to Elisha Williams, who took over the rectorship at a critical moment and restored and maintained the religious thrust of a Yale education. Williams, a native of the Connecticut River Valley, no doubt

41. Mather, *Gospel-Minister,* p. 25.

brought with him that region's evangelical tradition—fostered principally by Solomon Stoddard—and imparted it to the students, many of whom, during his tenure, were also from that area. The rector himself conducted daily prayers, read sermons in the hall, and led the scholars to worship services each Sunday. At no time do the college records indicate that these religious exercises were neglected.

Harvard, on the other hand, under the tenures of Presidents John Leverett (1707–24) and Benjamin Wadsworth (1725–37), had been charged repeatedly with allowing such practices to lapse. Both presidents were theologically moderate—Leverett being the more liberal of the two—as were many of the men who presided over the college's affairs. In 1718 Judge Samuel Sewall accused Leverett of neglecting the public exposition of Scripture in the hall and in 1723 the corporation launched an inquiry into the nature of Harvard education. The report stated that many college exercises were laxly performed and that the faculty recommended no divinity books to undergraduates. Students read theology "promiscuously" and the works of Anglican authors were most popular.

Cotton Mather, who had become obsessively critical of the college, undertook his own investigation at this time and concluded that solid learning was decaying at the school. Students read too many secular books from *"Satan's library"* and were not exposed to books with "the spirit of the Gospel in them" but to those "as have many erroneous and dangerous things in them." The tutors taught principles contrary to "the *doctrines of grace*" and grossly neglected the souls of the young men. Boys lost their home-nurtured piety at Harvard. Its graduates, in order to become "excellent ministers," had to "lay aside the sentiments which they brought from the College with them." In 1732 Harvard's condition was again questioned, this time by the board of overseers. Its report declared "that the government of the College is in a weak and declining state, . . . that religion, one great end of that society, is much upon the decay: a manifest evidence of which is, that the worship of God in the Hall is scandalously neglected, or but partially and not seasonably attended by many." [42]

Such extreme charges were not hurled at Yale. The several accusations of Arminianism never implied that the rector and tutors were remiss in their duties, and only a few members of the Ferris

42. Quincy, *History of Harvard*, 1 : 494–95, 317–20, 558–60, 388.

group ever suggested that one had to disown a Yale education in order to preach the Gospel. In fact, the existence of the enthusiasts in the Ferris club at Yale was a glaring example of the differences between the Connecticut college and Harvard. The Bay College was rarely plagued by enthusiasts.

The distinctions among the college presidents further illuminate the characters of the schools. Benjamin Wadsworth was moderate and preached the old familiar doctrines of covenant theology; Elisha Williams challenged the validity of covenant thinking and reasserted strict Calvinism. Wadsworth was sedate and rational; Williams was active and experiential. And if John Leverett can be credited with preserving Harvard "from the devastating control of a provincial orthodoxy" and founding "the liberal tradition of Harvard University," Rector Williams should be credited with maintaining Yale's orthodox orientation and furthering the religious purposes of the school.[43] These differences in style and outlook mirrored the disparity between the two colleges. Harvard, located in the cosmopolitan environs of Boston, kept to the broad and catholic way during the first forty years of the eighteenth century. Yale, settled in the more insulated town of New Haven, officially retained its commitment to orthodoxy.

Yale, then, sought to preserve and perpetuate the Reformed heritage in Connecticut and, indeed, wherever its graduates settled. Buffeted by provincial pressures, lured by foreign ideologies, the collegiate school nevertheless remained true to its calling. In so doing, it served to support a colony-wide religious bias, a function most vividly described by one of its own graduates, William Livingston (Y. 1741):

> While they [the students] are in the Course of their Education, they are sure to be instructed in the Arts of maintaining the Religion of the College, which is always that of their immediate Instructors; and of combating the Principles of all other Christians whatever. When the young Gentlemen, have run thro' the Course of their Education, they enter into the Ministry, or some Offices of the Government, and acting in them under the Influence of the Doctrines espoused in the Morning of Life, the Spirit of the College is transfused thro'

43. Samuel Eliot Morison, *Three Centuries of Harvard*, pp. 74–75.

the Colony, and tinctures the Genius and Policy of the public Administration, from the Governor down to the Constable.[44]

Yale's spirit, as Livingston correctly perceived, was essentially religious, and it was this spirit which shaped and defined the college. It further molded and influenced the colony. While the purposes and hopes of the first trustees had been both bold and naive, the former characteristic counterbalanced the latter. The goal of transmitting the received religious traditions of Connecticut to the students intact was doomed to failure. At the same time, however, that goal was never forgotten and the pursuit of it never flagged. Thus, a few Yale graduates—Chauncy, Eliot, Whittelsey, and others—might have been too moderate in their zeal and too forward in stressing human powers, but they never renounced the Reformed heritage or opted for a deviant theology. Elisha Williams might have been distressed by the influence of Arminian books on the students, but at least none of the undergraduates were heretics. Religious deviations in pre-Great Awakening Connecticut—with the exception of Anglicanism—occurred within defined limits. Yale College was the institution that set those limits.

Because of its religious commitments, Yale remained more orthodox than Harvard. Its graduates were to lead the New Light faction during the Great Awakening, and the college itself to become the intellectual center of that other New England, the "Hinterland," where Edwardsean and Hopkinsian Calvinism flowered into the "New Divinity." Even the Yale graduates who opposed the Awakening did so from within the Reformed tradition and styled themselves good Calvinists. It would fall to Harvard, on the other hand, to become the source of the most outspoken Old Lights and the hub of a liberal theology that culminated, in the next century, in Unitarianism.

In 1740, the existence of two New England cultures was only vaguely apparent. Yale ministers dominated the towns in all but eastern Connecticut and had made significant inroads into Massachusetts along the Connecticut River Valley. By 1800 Yale had

44. William Livingston, "Remarks on Our Intended College," in *The Independent Reflector,* ed. Milton M. Klein (Cambridge, Mass.: Harvard University Press, 1963), pp. 175–76. Livingston wrote this remark in 1753, during the debates concerning the establishment of a college in New York. Subsequently, King's College (now Columbia University) was founded in 1754.

sent pastors throughout all of Connecticut and most of western Massachusetts and had reduced Harvard's sphere of theological influence to the seacoast.[45] Many factors, notably the evangelical revivals, contributed to this eventual bifurcation of New England, but certainly one element in it was Yale's unwavering commitment to Reformed orthodoxy and experiential piety in the years before the Great Awakening.

45. Ahlstrom, "Saybrook Platform," no. 2, pp. 7–8; Conrad Wright, *The Beginnings of Unitarianism in America,* pp. 36, 257. Wright has a list of all Arminians in New England before 1800. All eleven who graduated from college before 1740 were Harvard men. Of the entire sixty, fifty-five went to Harvard and only one to Yale (see Wright, pp. 281–88). Wright also has three maps of New England showing the location of Yale and Harvard ministers at three points of time, 1740, 1775, and 1804 (see pp. 34, 256–57). I have used these maps in describing the bifurcation of New England.

12 "School of the Prophets"

On September 12, 1739, Elisha Williams announced his decision to retire as rector. The trustees asked him to stay on and gave him a month to reconsider, but Williams's mind was set, and on October 30 the Yale trustees reluctantly released him from his duties. Thanking him "for all his past good Service" to the college, they declared the rectorship vacant and adjourned until the next morning.

We do not know what conversations and deliberations took place that night, but the issue on everyone's mind was finding a replacement for Williams. The trustees had undoubtedly been thinking about this question since September. The records do not reveal whether or not there were several candidates under consideration; they only state that the next morning, "after much Deliberation," the trustees elected Thomas Clap (H. 1722) of Windham.[1] It is likely that Elisha Williams was among Clap's strongest supporters, for the two men had joined forces in the Breck affair four years earlier and shared the same theological convictions, though not the same personal temperament. Apparently, Williams had his way, for, on the surface at least, Clap's election was conducted with dispatch and unanimity. The trustees appointed a committee to present the offer to the minister and his parishioners; on November 19, the pastor and people of Windham agreed to the election; and on April 2, 1740, the trustees installed Clap in office.

The seeming consensus on the choice of Clap, however, evidently masked some disagreement. Again, we do not know the nature of this disagreement or which trustees voiced reservations, but later evidence intimates that a few had favored another candidate. Franklin Bowditch Dexter interpreted this hint as a sign that a number of so-called Arminian trustees were opposed to the Calvinist minister.[2] This allegation is unprovable, although it

1. *Documentary History*, pp. 337–38.

2. According to a letter of Benjamin Gale (Y. 1733), written in 1755, the other nominee was Daniel Edwards (Y. 1720), a former tutor and steward who in 1739 was a lawyer and clerk of the Superior Court in Connecticut (see *Yale Graduates*, 1 : 636). For Dexter's view, see Franklin B. Dexter, "Thomas Clap and his Writings," Papers of the New Haven Colony Historical Society, 5 (1899): 253.

may be that trustees like Samuel Whittelsey and Jared Eliot, whose theological views were broad and cautious, found Clap's strident orthodoxy objectionable. Whatever doubts about Clap existed, they never materialized as open opposition—although there appeared to be some subtle pettiness. In mid-December, 1739, for instance, Clap arrived in New Haven evidently expecting to be installed as rector, only to find that there was no committee assembled to perform the service. This nonevent, Clap reported, "made some talk in the Country." [3] While it is inconceivable that the trustees had formally scheduled the installation and then reneged, it may be that certain trustees were content to let Clap think the service was planned when it was not.

Such minor acts, however, did not detract from the major fact that this was the first time the Yale rectorship changed hands in a regular fashion, and in large part this was testimony to the maturity of the college. Unlike previous periods of administrative transition, which had always occurred at moments of crisis or despair, Clap's settlement followed a period of stability. When he took over in 1740, Yale College was a firmly established center of learning in the new world. The new rector had only to improve the college, not rescue it.

Given the tribulations and frustrations of the past forty years, this was a remarkable fact. At its founding, the collegiate school had faced the possibility of interference and even disestablishment by English authorities. For its first fifteen years it had migrated from one town to another, been without a building, and lacked a full-time rector. In 1716 the college had broken up, and until 1719 it was a pawn in a political-sectional rivalry that rent the college in three. During these years the trustees had to fight to retain their decision-making independence. No sooner had this rift been healed than a more serious one occurred. Rector Cutler's defection to the Church of England practically destroyed the college, both literally and symbolically, and after 1722 the college had to deal with consistent pressure from proselytizing Anglicans. After the apostasy, Yale suffered through four embarrassing years, as the trustees' efforts to find a rector failed repeatedly. Even after the selection of Elisha Williams solved this dilemma, the college continued to have trouble. It was charged with fostering heresy in the early 1730s and suspected of Anglican leanings during the same

3. Louis L. Tucker, *Puritan Protagonist*, no. 81, p. 61.

period. Throughout these forty years, the college was in a constant state of financial insecurity, depending on the General Assembly to provide the money needed to maintain solvency.

In addition to these external difficulties, the college had faced more covert challenges to its existence and purposes. There were a few Connecticut citizens who disparaged the emphasis on education which the school propagated and claimed *"that there is too great a Spirit for Learning in the Land; more are brought up to it than will be needed, or find Improvement; hence a snare will be laid for those devoted to it, & Learning will grow into Contempt."* A smaller number of other colonists—mostly Quakers—opposed the work of the college on religious grounds, and attacked the nature of Yale's goals by denigrating "Learning in the Ministry." [4] These negative views were minority opinion, however, and were more nuisances than threats to Yale.

That the college was strong and stable in 1740 indicates the extent to which Yale's achievements and the support of the colonial establishment outweighed the failures and criticism. From a tutoring arrangement between Jacob Heminway and Rector Pierson, the collegiate school grew to a student body of around sixty with a faculty of three. From a period when the treasurer dealt mostly with farm produce, Yale developed a more systematic financial program. During these forty years, the college curriculum evolved from scholasticism to the new learning. Isolated and insulated in 1701, the school attained contacts with a wider intellectual world, and by the 1730s the college authorities and supporters were corresponding with Englishmen about academic and religious concerns. Finally, throughout this troubled period, ministers and legislators encouraged the school and worked for its improvement.

That both pastors and politicians were concerned about Yale points to a further dimension of the college: its relationships to church and state. From the beginning, the collegiate school had an ambivalent connection to both of these institutions. On the one hand, the college participated in an undefined and symbolic partnership with the churches. In one sense, Yale was a school of the colony's established churches, training the clergymen who would serve them, and teaching the orthodoxy they espoused. But

4. Jonathan Marsh, *Thorough Reformation of a Sinning People*, p. 45; Azariah Mather, *Good Rulers a Choice Blessing* (New London, 1725), p. 36.

the churches exercised no legal control over the college and to that extent Yale was independent of formal religious ties. On the other hand, the collegiate school had been chartered and partially funded by the state. Indeed, when Samuel Woodbridge referred to the college as "our Publick Nursery of Learning" he was acknowledging the fact that Yale had formal ties to the colony government.[5] There can be no doubt that such ties existed; there is much uncertainty about their precise nature. Despite the fact that the General Assembly gave the college a yearly stipend and, during Williams's tenure, provided extra monies on a regular basis, the government never dictated Yale policy. The legislators had attempted to do so during the schism of 1716–19 but had failed. College and colony, therefore, enjoyed a curious connection: financially, Yale was a public school; administratively, it was a private college. In the long run, this latter characteristic predominated, especially as it related to governance, but at no time has Yale been a wholly independent college.

The college's semiofficial connection with the state and its unofficial relationship to the church continued long after 1740. The college's religious dimension, which was ideological rather than legal, evolved and endured well into the nineteenth century, as Yale remained a theological center and sent its graduates to serve churches and missions throughout the world. Indeed, it was not until the election of Arthur Twining Hadley in 1899 that Yale had its first lay president, and not until 1905 that it had a nonclerical trustee. Compulsory attendance at daily and Sunday worship was not abolished until 1926. The college's ties to the state, on the other hand, underwent several modifications. In 1755 the General Assembly withdrew and never renewed its annual hundred-pound stipend to the college, but in 1763 some legislators attempted to have the assembly assume visitatorial rights at Yale. Thomas Clap beat back this challenge with the aid of some questionable historical interpretations, and Yale retained its decision-making autonomy. In 1792, however, the college resumed an affiliation with the state by agreeing to a charter revision allowing the governor, lieutenant-governor, and six assistants to become trustees ex officio in return for financial aid.

Ultimately, the most significant legacy of early Yale was neither its ties with the state nor its relationship to the church but its fun-

5. Samuel Woodbridge, *Obedience to the Divine Law*, p. 22.

damental nature as a liberal arts college. The original trustees' intentions to instruct young men in the arts and sciences to prepare them to serve society in positions of leadership are the most important aspects of those early years. It was this broad purpose which allowed Yale to evolve into a great university. While an understanding of the nature of early Yale demands acknowledgment of the college's religious dimension, an appreciation of Yale's subsequent history requires acceptance of this wider principle. The religious component, to be sure, persisted and influenced the college into this century and to a large extent defined Yale's spirit. But the intellectual tradition of curricular expansion and improvement, of seeking modernity in knowledge, laid the groundwork for the Yale of today.

When Elisha Williams retired, the future importance of the college he had helped to shape could have been no more than speculation. The only goal envisioned by Yale's supporters was that it continue as a School of the Prophets in training learned and orthodox men. That goal had been pursued vigorously since 1701 and the trustees' belief in it had not waned. No one could predict, however, how quickly the goal would be shaken by crisis and conflict. But even before Thomas Clap took over as rector, there were distant rumbles of the earthquake that was to come.

On March 2, 1740, Samuel Buell, a junior at the college, wrote to his friend Eleazar Wheelock. After disposing of some personal business, Buell related the latest news: "The College is Blest with Health in General, We this Week Expect the Revd Mr Clap to sustain the Place of a Rector,—and now Reverd Sir as to religion the Power of it is not very visible in this Place,—But I have Good news as to the flourishing of it att New York and Glorious Tidings from Long-Island." [6] Buell's comments were both an assessment of the state of Yale and an unwitting prediction of its future. As events were to prove, the glorious tidings from New York and Long Island, where George Whitefield and James Davenport were stunning their listeners with evangelical sermons, would have a dramatic and divisive impact on the health of the college under the rectorship of Thomas Clap.

When Clap took over in April, Yale was, he later wrote, "in the main, in a good State; yet not so perfect, but that it would admit

6. Samuel Buell to Eleazar Wheelock, Mar. 2, 1740, Yale Archives.

of sundry Emendations."[7] Perfection, or at least his version of it, was Clap's goal. He began implementing his emendations immediately. By the time six months had passed, Clap's efforts at institutional improvement were overshadowed by the phenomenon of the Great Awakening. On October 25, 1740, George Whitefield visited New Haven and preached to the students, telling them of "the dreadful Ill-Consequences of an unconverted Ministry."[8] The students were excited by Whitefield and at first the rector shared their enthusiasm. But six months later, Gilbert Tennent visited New Haven, preaching seventeen sermons in a week. His emotional style of preaching made a great impact on the undergraduates.

Its impact on Clap was equally great—and particularly negative. Clap's suspicions that the Awakening led to more excesses than conversions were confirmed by James Davenport's crazed performance in July, and by the time Jonathan Edwards offered a reasoned defense of the revivals at the 1741 commencement, Clap was firmly in the opposition camp. By the spring of 1742, religious excitement at Yale had reached such heights of enthusiasm that the college broke up. Clap's posture during these years of crisis was uncompromising and he treated prorevival sympathizers severely. He expelled David Brainerd in the fall of 1741, did the same to John and Ebenezer Cleaveland in January, 1745, ousted Samuel Cooke as a trustee later that year, and composed a declaration against George Whitefield, defending Yale against the charge that its light had turned to darkness.

Clap's performance in protecting what he understood to be the true religious heritage of Yale was, to say the least, heavy-handed and earned him lasting enemies. While the rector later shifted his position on the Awakening and joined the growing number of Connecticut New Lights, he remained constant in his handling of college affairs. The story of Clap's stormy career at Yale has been told;[9] suffice it to say here that during the twenty-six years of his tenure there were precious few moments of quiet. He succeeded to a remarkable degree in improving the curriculum and governance of the college and in defending its interests—again as he saw them—against government intrusion. But finally his despotic

7. *Yale Annals,* p. 41.
8. *Documentary History,* p. 347.
9. Tucker, *Puritan Protagonist.*

nature did him in. The students had long disliked him for his imperious ways and mocked him for his unfortunate surname. They called him "The French Pox" and in 1766 they succeeded in driving him from office.

Since Clap's time twelve other presidents have conducted Yale affairs as the Connecticut college has developed into a world-renowned university. James Pierpont and his colleagues would never recognize the Yale of today as the product of the collegiate school they created. This is as it should be, for the disparity between the two is a tribute to the vitality of the institution. From 1701 to 1740, Yale served as a School of the Prophets for colonial society. During its history the college has served the various needs of ever-widening constituencies. The one constant has been the initial dream of the original trustees: to instruct youth "in the Arts & Sciences who through the blessing of Almighty God may be fitted for Publick employment both in Church & Civil State."

Bibliography

The titles cited in the bibliography are listed alphabetically under two headings: Sources (mostly materials published in the eighteenth century) and Secondary Works (including articles and books in which sources are reprinted). The first category consists primarily of sermons and contains all such works used in the text; as sermon titles were often lengthy, some of them have been shortened to their essential components. The second section contains those books and articles which were most valuable for this study. The complete entries for those volumes mentioned in the following bibliographical note can be found in the two lists.

Bibliographical Note

The most important sources for the story of early Yale are contained in the Yale Archives. At present, these materials are deposited both in the Beinecke Rare Book and Manuscript Library and in Manuscripts and Archives, located in Sterling Memorial Library, Yale University, New Haven, Connecticut. Marjorie G. Wynne in Beinecke and Judith A. Schiff in Manuscripts have been of great assistance in facilitating the use of the collection. Since these items will eventually be housed in Manuscripts and Archives, the designation Yale Archives applies to all of them; they are most readily found by consulting the Yale Union Manuscript Catalogue in Sterling. Franklin B. Dexter reproduced the majority of these sources—principally the records of trustee meetings—in his *Documentary History of Yale University.* I have quoted the material from Dexter but have examined the originals as well. Other primary sources can be found in Henry H. Edes's "Documents Relating to the Early History of Yale University," James K. Blake's "The Lost Dukedom, or the Story of the Pierrepont Claim," and in several volumes of the Yale University Library *Gazette.*

The Connecticut Archives in the Connecticut State Library in Hartford is the second most significant depository of manuscripts used in this study. The material is indexed topically and is readily found. The most helpful collections in the archives are: Foreign Correspondence, which contains letters and reports to and from the assembly and the colony's agents in England; Colleges and Schools, which reveals much background information (committee reports, assembly communications, and votes) on decisions affecting Yale as well as the cases of boys petitioning the court for permission to sell land to pay for their schooling; Towns and Lands, which has information relating to Yale's land holdings; and Finances, which contain data on Yale's monetary dealings with the government. The archives supplement and complement the material in J. Hammond Trumbull and Charles J. Hoadly, eds., *Public Records of the Colony of Connecticut.*

The Connecticut Historical Society in Hartford has several documents relating to early Yale, and the society's collection of the Wyllys Papers has some information on the controversy surrounding the college's move to New Haven. The Massachusetts Historical Society in Boston also has some unpublished documents pertaining to early Yale. Harvard University has an interesting letter from Elisha Williams to [Benjamin Colman] about the Berkeley gift, as well as the letters of Thomas Hollis, the English benefactor of the Bay College, to Benjamin Colman and John Leverett. These were most helpful for information on Jeremiah Dummer and Timothy Cutler. Andover-Newton Seminary, Newton-Centre, Massachusetts, owns the letters to and from Jonathan Edwards and family. The letters are few but are detailed and contain precise information on the college during the tenure of Rector Cutler. Cutler's letter to Timothy Edwards of June 30, 1719, was a particularly rich find, and Jonathan's letter to his father of July 24, 1719, was the most useful document.

Several published manuscript collections of personal materials were major sources for this study. Of these, Herbert Schneider and Carol Schneider, eds., *Samuel Johnson, President of King's College; His Career and Writings,* was by far the most important, especially the first three volumes. Johnson's "Autobiography," letters, sermons, *"Synopsis Philosophiae Naturalis,"* and "An Encyclopedia of Philosophy" —the last two written during his final year at the collegiate school— shed copious light on the institutional history of Yale, the curriculum, Anglicanism in Connecticut, and the 1722 apostasy. Sereno E. Dwight, ed., *The Writings of President Edwards,* was also a valuable source, especially Jonathan's "Notes on the Mind" and "Notes on Natural Science" in volume 1. Cotton Mather's *Diary,* published in 7 Coll. M.H.S., vols. 7–8, contains many references to and ruminations on Yale; Samuel Sewall's *Diary* in 5 Coll. M.H.S., vol. 7, has some mention of Yale, as do his letters, printed in 6 Coll. M.H.S., vols. 1–2. Sarah Knight, *The Journal of Madame Knight,* has many interesting observations on Connecticut in 1704, and the *Diary* (1711–58) of Joshua Hempstead has occasional references to issues relating to Yale. In addition, documents relative to the Cutler apostasy are printed in 2 Coll. M.H.S., 2 : 129–40, and several of George Berkeley's letters to Samuel Johnson are in Pub. C.S.M., 28 : 105–10. While Ezra Stiles did not participate in the events of this period, he assiduously collected information about early Yale; this information can be found in Franklin B. Dexter, ed., *The Literary Diary of Ezra Stiles,* and in

Franklin B. Dexter, ed., *Extracts from the Itineraries and other Miscellanies of Ezra Stiles.*

Some manuscript sources were used in dealing with particular topics in the history of early Yale. For the section on Anglicanism the one essential source is the Transcripts of the Correspondence between the Society for the Propagation of the Gospel in Foreign Parts and Its Missionaries. These documents are on microfilm in an "A" and "B" series and should be used in conjunction with the first volume of Francis L. Hawks and William S. Perry, eds., *Documentary History of the Protestant Episcopal Church in the United States of America Containing Numerous Hitherto Unpublished Documents Concerning the Church in Connecticut.* Hawks and Perry printed portions of the chief letters in the S.P.G. Correspondence, as well as letters from other archives. Other relevant documents are in *Samuel Johnson: His Career and Writings* and in William S. Perry, ed., *Historical Collections Relating to the American Colonial Church,* vol. 3. Several letters written by Timothy Cutler in the late 1720s and 1730s are published in John Nichols, *Illustrations of the Literary History of the Eighteenth Century,* vol. 4. New Englanders' reactions to the 1722 defection are found in several editions of two newspapers for the years 1722–23: *The New-England Courant* and *The Boston News-Letter.*

The Yale Archives have the financial records for most of the period 1701–40. The photostated manuscript of the Yale College Treasury Book, 1701–1828, has the records for the tenure of John Alling. These are difficult to decipher but still offer an insight into the complexity of early college finances. John Prout's "Treasurer's Accounts" for 1727–37 provide a neat record of the credits and expenditures of those years. The five extant Quarter Bills are helpful indexes to the personal aspect of college costs. In addition, the library has land deeds, quit claims, and letters that deal with college finances. Ezra Stiles's "College Records; records of early gifts to the college," which he composed during his tenure as president (1778–95), has data on various donations to and acquisitions by the early college.

The Yale Archives also contain materials dealing with the curriculum. The most indispensable sources were the twelve commencement sheets for the years between 1718 and 1740. These indicated the topics and the positions the students studied and adopted. Jeremiah Curtis's notebook for 1721–22 on logic and natural philosophy, Matthew Rockwell's 1727 notebook on Newton, Asher Rosseter's freshman notes on Latin (1738), and Solomon Welles's notes on natural philosophy (1738)—all in the Yale Archives—were especially useful in assessing the dimensions of the curriculum, as were the printed compositions of Samuel Johnson and Jonathan Edwards. Edwards's "Catalogue" of books, the first several pages of which date from his years as butler and tutor at Yale, is also in the archives and reveals which works the college's liveliest intellect chose to read. Yale also has the two manuscript books Edwards owned while at Yale, both of which originally belonged to William Partridge (H. 1689): one contains "Expositiones Georgii Dounami, In Petri Rami Dialecticum catechismus" and "A compendium of logick, according to the modern philosophy, extracted from Le-grand and others their systems"; the other includes Charles Morton's "System of Physicks," a text used at Harvard. Abraham Pierson's undergraduate notebook, composed while he was at Harvard (1664–68), is also in the archives; these notes formed the basis for his manuscript physics text, which was used at the college before 1720.

"The first Devinity Lecture made by me James Pierpont & published in Yale College," done in the year 1723, is the only surviving faculty manuscript from this period and is deposited in the Jonathan Edwards Collection. John Sergeant's *Valedictorian Oration* (1729) is an interesting reflection on a Yale education as, in another way, is John Hubbard's *The Benefactors of Yale-College* (1733). The Yale Library of 1742 has been reassembled in the shelf-order devised by Thomas Clap and is in the Beinecke Rare Book Library. It contains the books used in the course of study before 1740; also, some students wrote their names in the volumes, thereby revealing which texts were consulted (or at least marked up!).

Franklin B. Dexter's *Biographical Sketches of the Graduates of Yale College with Annals of the College History,* vol. 1, contains valuable information on the 386 students who graduated between 1702 and 1739. All statistical data in chapter 10 are derived from this volume. For incidental information on students and student life, the chief sources are letters in the Yale Archives and Jonathan Edwards Collection and Samuel Johnson's "Autobiography." Some letters pertaining to David Ferris and his cohorts are in Charles Chauncy, *Seasonable Thoughts on the State of Religion in New England.*

The discussion of religion and learning at Yale and in Connecticut before the Great Awakening depends almost wholly on sermons. The Yale Archives contain a few unpublished discourses of Elisha Williams that confirm his reputation as a stern Calvinist. Election sermons and ordination sermons were the richest sources, as they often dealt with the college and addressed issues of learning, orthodoxy, and piety. The sermons published or preached in Connecticut before 1740 can be located through the first two volumes of Charles Evans's *American Bibliography: A Chronological Dictionary of all Books, Pamphlets and Periodical Publications printed in the United States of America* and read on microcards in the American Antiquarian Society's *Early American Imprints, 1639–1800.*

While the footnotes give ample testimony to the secondary works of greatest value, two of them deserve special mention. Samuel Eliot Morison's *Harvard College in the Seventeenth Century* served both as a model and a source for this study, particularly on the founding of the collegiate school and the Yale curriculum. Clifford K. Shipton and John L. Sibley's *Biographical Sketches of Those Who Attended Harvard College,* vols. 2–10, was most useful for information on Yale's original and later trustees and first four rectors. The necessary reliance on these works further indicates the extent to which Yale came out of Harvard.

Sources

Adams, Eliphalet. *A Discourse Occasioned by the late Distressing Storm.* New London, 1717.

———. *A Discourse Shewing That so long as there is any Prospect of a Sinful People's yielding good Fruit hereafter, there is hope that they may be Spared.* New London, 1734.

———. *Eminently Good and Useful Men, The Glory and Defence of the Places Where They Live.* New London, 1720.

Ames, William. *Conscience with the Power and Cases Thereof.* London, 1643.

———. *The Marrow of Sacred Divinity.* London, 1642.

Buckingham, Stephen. *The Unreasonableness and Danger of a People's renouncing their subjection to God.* New London, 1711.

Bulkley, John. *The Necessity of Religion in Societies.* [New London], 1713.

Burgersdicius, Franco. *Institutionum Logicarum Libri Duo.* Cambridge, 1666.

Burnham, William. *God's Providence in Placing Men In their Respective Stations & Conditions Asserted & Shewed.* New London, 1722.

Chauncy, Charles. *Seasonable Thoughts on the State of Religion in New England.* Boston, 1742.

Chauncy, Nathaniel. *The Faithful Servant Rewarded.* New London, 1732.

Clap, Thomas. *The Annals or History of Yale-College, In New-Haven, In the Colony of Connecticut, From the First Founding thereof, in the Year 1700, to the Year 1766.* New Haven, 1766.

———. *The Greatness and Difficulty of the Work of the Ministry.* Boston, 1732.

Cutler, Timothy. *The Depth of the Divine Thoughts.* New London, 1720.

———. *The Firm Union of a People Represented; and a Concern for it, Urged; upon All Orders and Degrees of Men.* New London, 1717.

Edwards, Jonathan. *A Divine and Supernatural Light, Immediately imparted to the Soul by the Spirit of God, Shown to be both a Scriptural and Rational Doctrine.* Boston, 1734.

———. *God Glorified in the Work of Redemption, By the Greatness of Man's Dependence upon Him, in the Whole of it.* Boston, 1731.

Eliot, Jared. *The Two Witnesses; or, Religion Supported by Reason and Divine Revelation.* New London, 1736.

Estabrook, Samuel. *A Sermon Shewing that the Peace and Quietness Of a People Is a main part of the Work of Civil Rulers, And That it is the Duty of all to Pray For Them.* New London, 1718.

Fiske, Phineas. *The Good Subject's Wish Or, The Desirableness Of The Divine Presence With Civil Rulers.* New London, 1726.

Foxcroft, Thomas. *Some Seasonable Thoughts on Evangelic Preaching.* Boston, 1740.

Gassendo, Pietro. *Institutio Astronomica.* London, 1675.

[Graham, John]. *Some Remarks Upon a late Pamphlet entitled, A Letter from a minister of the Church of England to his dissenting parishioners.* [Boston], 1733.

Graham, John. *The Christian's Duty of Watchfulness against Error, and Establishment in the Truth.* New London, 1733.

Heereboord, Adrian. *Logica.* London, 1676.

Hempstead, Joshua. *Diary of Joshua Hempstead of New London, Connecticut.* New London Historical Society Collections, vol. 1 (1901).

Hubbard, John. *The Benefactors of Yale-College.* New London, 1733.

Knight, Sarah. *The Journal of Madame Knight.* Reprint. New York: Dexter, Small, Maynard and Co., 1920.

Lewis, Daniel. *The Good Minister.* New London, 1733.

Locke, John. *An Essay Concerning Human Understanding.* Edited by Alexander C. Fraser. 2 vols. Oxford, 1894.

Lord, Benjamin. *True Christianity Explained & Enforced.* New London, 1727.

Magiri, Johanni. *Physiologiae Peripateticae Libri Sex.* Cambridge, 1642.

Marsh, Jonathan. *An Essay, To Prove the Thorough Reformation of a Sinning People is not to be Expected.* New London, 1721.

Mather, Azariah. *A Discourse Concerning the Death of the Righteous.* New London, 1731.

———. *A Gospel Star, or Faithful Minister.* New London, 1720.

———. *Good Rulers a Choice Blessing.* New London, 1725.

———. *The Gospel-Minister Described, by the Important Duty of his Office.* New London, 1725.

Mather, Cotton. *Diary of Cotton Mather, 1709–1724.* Massachusetts Historical Society Collections, 7th ser., vol. 8 (1917).

———. *Magnalia Christi Americana.* London, 1702.
———. *Manuductio ad Ministerium.* Boston, 1726.
———. *The Christian Philosopher: A Collection of the Best Discoveries in Nature, with Religious Improvements.* London, 1721.
More, Henry. *An Account of Virtue.* London, 1690.
Morgan, Joseph. *The Duty and a Mark of Zion's Children.* New London, 1725.
———. *The Only Effectual Remedy Against Mortal Errors Held Forth in a Discourse.* New London, 1725.
Newton, Isaac. *Opticks: or, A Treatise of the Reflections, Refractions, Inflections and Colours of Light.* London, 1730.
———. *The Mathematical Principles of Natural Philosophy.* London, 1729.
Pierpont, James. *Sundry False Hopes of Heaven, Discovered and Decryed.* Boston, 1712.
Ramus, Petrus. *Dialecticae Libri Duo.* Cambridge, 1672.
Rohault, Jacques. *System of Natural Philosophy, Illustrated with Dr. Samuel Clarke's Notes taken mostly out of Sir Isaac Newton's Philosophy. Translated by John Clarke.* 2 vols. London, 1735.
Ruggles, Thomas. *The Death of great, good and useful Men lamented.* New Haven, 1763.
Sergeant, John. *A Valedictorian Oration, delivered at Yale College in the Year 1729.* New York, 1882. Copy in the Yale Archives.
Sewall, Samuel. *Diary of Samuel Sewall.* Massachusetts Historical Society Collections, 5th ser., vol. 7 (1882).
———. *Letter Book of Samuel Sewall.* Massachusetts Historical Society Collections, 6th ser., vol. 2 (1888).
Stoddard, Solomon. *The Defects of Preachers Reproved.* New London, 1724.
———. *The Way for a People to Live Long in the Land that God Hath given them.* Boston, 1703.
Ward, John. *The Young Mathematicians Guide.* London, 1747.
Whittelsey, Samuel. *A Sermon Preach'd at the Ordination of Mr. Samuel Whittelsey, jun.* Boston, 1739.
Willard, Samuel. *Brief Directions to a Young Scholar Designing the Ministry for the Study of Divinity.* Boston, 1735.
Williams, Eleazar. *An Essay To Prove That when God once enters upon a Controversie, With His Professing People; He will Manage and Issue it.* New London, 1723.
Williams, Elisha. *Divine Grace Illustrious, in the Salvation of Sinners.* New London, 1728.
Wollebius, Johann. *The Abridgement of Christian Divinitie.* Translated by Alexander Ross. London, 1660.

Woodbridge, Samuel. *Obedience To The Divine Law, Urged on all Orders of Men, And the Advantage of it shew'd.* New London, 1724.

Woodward, John. *Civil Rulers are God's Ministers for the People's Good.* Boston, 1712.

Secondary Works

Ahlstrom, Sydney E. "The Saybrook Platform: A 250th Anniversary Retrospect," *Bulletin of the Congregational Library* 11, no. 1 (1959): 5–10; no. 2 (1960): 3–15.

Andrews, Charles M. "The Connecticut Intestacy Law," *The Yale Review* 3 (1894): 261–94.

Bacon, Leonard, ed. *Contributions to the Ecclesiastical History of Connecticut.* New Haven, 1861.

Bailyn, Bernard. *Education in the Forming of American Society: Needs and Opportunities for Study.* New York: Random House, Vintage Books, 1960.

Beardsley, E. Edwards. *The History of the Episcopal Church in Connecticut.* 2 vols. New York, 1865.

Bingham, Hiram. *Elihu Yale: Governor, Collector and Benefactor.* Reprint. Worcester, Mass.: American Antiquarian Society, 1938.

Blake, James Kingsley. "The Lost Dukedom, or the Story of the Pierrepont Claim," New Haven Colony Historical Society Papers 7 (1908): 258–87.

Brasch, Frederick E. "The Newtonian Epoch in the American Colonies (1680–1783)," *Proceedings of the American Antiquarian Society* n.s. 49 (1939): 314–32.

Brodrick, George C. *A History of the University of Oxford.* London, 1886.

Bronson, Henry. "A Historical Account of Connecticut Currency, Continental Money, and the Finances of the Revolution," New Haven Historical Society Papers 1 (1865): 5–192.

Burtt, Edwin A. *The Metaphysical Foundations of Modern Physical Science.* Rev. ed. Garden City, N.Y.: Doubleday, Anchor Books, 1955.

Bushman, Richard L. *From Puritan to Yankee: Character and the Social Order in Connecticut, 1690–1765.* Cambridge, Mass.: Harvard University Press, 1967.

Cajori, Florian. *The Teaching and History of Mathematics in the United States.* Bureau of Education, Circular of Information no. 3. Washington, D.C.: Government Printing Office, 1890.

Calder, Isabel M. *The New Haven Colony.* New Haven: Yale University Press, 1934.

Caulkins, F. M. "Memoir of the Rev. William Adams, of Dedham,

Mass., and of the Rev. Eliphalet Adams, of New London, Conn.," Massachusetts Historical Society Collections, 4th ser., 1 (1852): 1–51.

Clark, George Norman. *Science and Social Welfare in the Age of Newton.* Oxford: Clarendon Press, 1937.

"Dean Berkeley, Patron of the New England Colleges," Colonial Society of Massachusetts Publications 28 (1935): 104–07.

Dexter, Franklin B. *A Selection from the Miscellaneous Historical Papers of Fifty Years.* New Haven: The Tuttle, Morehouse and Taylor Co., 1918.

———. *Biographical Sketches of the Graduates of Yale College with Annals of the College History.* 6 vols. New York: Henry Holt and Co., 1885–1912.

———, ed. *Extracts from the Itineraries and other Miscellanies of Ezra Stiles, D.D., L.L.D., 1755–1794, with a Selection from his Correspondence.* New Haven: Yale University Press, 1916.

———, ed. *The Documentary History of Yale University under the Original Charter of the Collegiate School of Connecticut, 1701–1745.* New Haven: Yale University Press, 1916.

———, ed. *The Literary Diary of Ezra Stiles.* 3 vols. New York: Charles Scribner's Sons, 1901.

———, and Power, Zara J., eds. *New Haven Town Records.* 3 vols. New Haven: New Haven Colony Historical Society, 1917, 1919, 1962.

The Dictionary of National Biography. Edited by Leslie Stephen and Sidney Lee. 22 vols. London: Oxford University Press, 1949–50.

Dwight, Sereno E., ed. *The Writings of President Edwards.* 10 vols. New York, 1829.

Edes, Henry H. "The Early History of Yale University," Colonial Society of Massachusetts Publications 6 (1904): 172–210.

Ellis, Joseph J. *The New England Mind in Transition: Samuel Johnson of Connecticut (1696–1772).* New Haven: Yale University Press, 1973.

Eusden, John D. "Introduction" to *The Marrow of Theology,* by William Ames. Translated from the 3d Latin edition, 1629, and edited by John D. Eusden. Boston: Pilgrim Press, 1968.

Fowler, William C. *Memorials of the Chaunceys.* Boston, 1858.

Fuller, Henry M. "Bishop Berkeley as a Benefactor of Yale," Yale University Library *Gazette* 28 (1954): 1–18.

———. "The Philosophical Apparatus of Yale College." In *Papers in Honor of Andrew Keogh,* prepared by the staff of the Yale Library, pp. 163–80. New Haven: privately printed, 1938.

Gaustad, Edwin. *The Great Awakening in New England.* Chicago: Quadrangle Books, Quadrangle Paperbacks, 1968.

Godley, Alfred D. *Oxford in the Eighteenth Century*. London: Methuen, 1908.

Goen, C. C., ed. Editor's introduction to *The Great Awakening*, by Jonathan Edwards. New Haven and London: Yale University Press, 1972.

Goodwin, Gerald J. "The Myth of 'Arminian-Calvinism' in Eighteenth-century New England," *The New England Quarterly* 41 (1968): 213–37.

Grant, Alexander. *The Story of the University of Edinburgh during its First Three Hundred Years*. 2 vols. London, 1884.

Greene, M. Louise. *The Development of Religious Liberty in Connecticut*. Boston and New York: Houghton, Mifflin, 1905.

Hall, Alfred Rupert. *The Scientific Revolution: 1500–1800; The Formation of the Modern Scientific Attitude*. London and New York: Longmans, Green, 1954.

Hall, David D. *The Faithful Shepherd: A History of the New England Ministry in the Seventeenth Century*. Chapel Hill: University of North Carolina Press, 1972.

Hans, Nicholas A. *New Trends in Education in the Eighteenth Century*. London: Routledge and Kegan Paul, 1951.

Hawks, Francis L. and Perry, William S., eds. *Documentary History of the Protestant Episcopal Church in the United States of America, Containing Numerous Hitherto Unpublished Documents Concerning the Church in Connecticut*. 2 vols. New York, 1863–64.

Henderson, R. W. *The Teaching Office in the Reformed Tradition: A History of the Doctoral Ministry*. Philadelphia: Westminster Press, 1962.

Hoadly, Charles J., ed. *Records of the Colony and Plantation of New Haven, 1638–1649*. Hartford, 1857.

———. *Records of the Colony or Jurisdiction of New Haven, 1653–1665*. Hartford, 1858.

Hofstadter, Richard, and Metzger, Walter P. *The Development of Academic Freedom in the United States*. New York: Columbia University Press, 1955.

Hornberger, Theodore. "Samuel Johnson of Yale and King's College: A Note on the Relation of Science and Religion in Provincial America," *The New England Quarterly* 8 (1935): 378–97.

———. *Scientific Thought in the American Colleges: 1638–1800*. Austin, Texas: University of Texas Press, 1945.

Hunt, John. *Religious Thought in England*. 3 vols. London, 1870–72.

Isham, Norman M. "The Original College House at Yale," *The Yale Alumni Weekly* 26 (1916–17): 114–20.

Johnson, Thomas H. "Jonathan Edwards' Background of Reading,"

Publications of the Colonial Society of Massachusetts 28 (1935): 193–222.

Keogh, Andrew. "Bishop Berkeley's Gift of Books in 1733," Yale University Library *Gazette* 8 (1934): 1–27.

McKeehan, Louis W. *Yale Science: The First Hundred Years, 1701–1801.* New York: H. Schuman, 1947.

McLachlan, Herbert. *English Education Under the Test Acts; Being the History of the Nonconformist Academies, 1662–1820.* Manchester: Manchester University Press, 1931.

Meriwether, Collyer. *Our Colonial Curriculum: 1607–1776.* Washington, D.C.: Capitol Publishing Co., 1907.

Middlekauf, Robert. *Ancients and Axioms: Secondary Education in Eighteenth-Century New England.* New Haven: Yale University Press, 1963.

Miller, Perry. *Jonathan Edwards.* New York: W. Sloane Associates, 1949.

———. *The New England Mind: From Colony To Province.* Cambridge, Mass.: Harvard University Press, 1953.

———. *The New England Mind: The Seventeenth Century.* Cambridge, Mass.: Harvard University Press, 1939.

Morgan, Alexander. *Scottish University Studies.* London: Oxford University Press, 1933.

Morgan, Edmund S. *The Gentle Puritan: A Life of Ezra Stiles, 1727–1795.* New Haven: Yale University Press, 1962.

Morison, Samuel Eliot. *Harvard College in the Seventeenth Century.* 2 vols. Cambridge, Mass.: Harvard University Press, 1936.

———. *The Founding of Harvard College.* Cambridge, Mass.: Harvard University Press, 1935.

———. *The Intellectual Life of Colonial New England.* Ithaca, N.Y.: Cornell University Press, 1960.

———. *Three Centuries of Harvard, 1636–1936.* Cambridge, Mass.: Harvard University Press, 1965.

Morris, William S. "The Genius of Jonathan Edwards." In *Reinterpretation in American Church History,* edited by Jerald C. Braur, pp. 29–65. Chicago: University of Chicago Press, 1968.

Murdock, Kenneth. "Cotton Mather and the Rectorship of Yale College," Publications of the Colonial Society of Massachusetts 26 (1927): 388–401.

Nichols, John. *Illustrations of the Literary History of the Eighteenth Century.* 8 vols. London, 1817–58.

Nuttall, Geoffrey F. *Richard Baxter and Philip Doddridge: A Study in a Tradition.* London: Oxford University Press, 1951.

Ong, Walter J. *Ramus and Talon Inventory*. Cambridge, Mass.: Harvard University Press, 1958.

———. *Ramus, Method, and the Decay of Dialogue: From the Art of Discourse to the Art of Reason*. Cambridge, Mass.: Harvard University Press, 1958.

Oviatt, Edwin. *The Beginnings of Yale (1701–1726)*. New Haven: Yale University Press, 1916.

Perry, William S., ed. *Historical Collections Relating to the American Colonial Church*. 5 vols. Hartford, 1870–78.

Potter, Alfred C. "The Harvard College Library, 1723–1735," Publications of the Colonial Society of Massachusetts 25 (1924): 1–13.

Potter, David. *Debating in the Colonial Chartered Colleges: An Historical Survey, 1642 to 1900*. New York: Teachers College, Columbia University Press, 1944.

Pratt, Anne Stokely. *Isaac Watts and his Gifts of Books to Yale College*. New Haven: Yale University Press, 1938.

———. "The Books Sent From England by Jeremiah Dummer to Yale College." In *Papers in Honor of Andrew Keogh*, prepared by the staff of the Yale Library, pp. 7–44. New Haven: privately printed, 1938.

Quincy, Josiah. *The History of Harvard University*. 2 vols. Boston, 1860.

Schneider, Herbert, and Schneider, Carol, eds. *Samuel Johnson, President of King's College: His Career and Writings*. 4 vols. New York: Columbia University Press, 1929.

[Schwab, John Christopher]. *A Partial List of the Text-books used in Yale College in the Eighteenth Century* [New Haven?], [1901?].

Shipton, Clifford K. "Ye Mystery of Ye Ages Solved, or, How Placing Worked at Colonial Harvard & Yale," *Harvard Alumni Bulletin* 57 (1954–55): 258–63.

———, and Sibley, John L. *Biographical Sketches of Those Who Attended Harvard College*. 14 vols. Cambridge, Mass.: W. C. Sever, and Harvard University Press, 1873–1968.

Simons, Lao G. "Introduction of Algebra into American Schools in the Eighteenth Century," Bureau of Education Bulletin no. 18. Washington, D.C.: Government Printing Office, 1924.

Simpson, Alan. "A Candle in a Corner: How Harvard College Got the Hopkins Legacy," *Proceedings of the Colonial Society of Massachusetts* 43 (1966): 304–24.

Smith, Charles Henry. "The Founding of Yale College," Papers of the New Haven Colony Historical Society 7 (1908): 34–64.

Snow, Louis Franklin. *The College Curriculum in the United States*.

Contributions to Education no. 10. New York: Teachers College, Columbia University, 1907.
"Some Original Papers Respecting the Episcopal Controversy in Connecticut, MDCCXXII," Collections of the Massachusetts Historical Society, 2d ser., 2 (1814): 128–40.
Stiles, Ezra. *A History of the Three Judges of King Charles I*. Hartford, 1794.
Stromberg, Roland N. *Religious Liberalism in Eighteenth-century England*. London: Oxford University Press, 1954.
Trinterud, Leonard. *The Forming of an American Tradition: a Reexamination of Colonial Presbyterianism*. Philadelphia: The Westminster Press, 1949.
Trumbull, Benjamin. *A Complete History of Connecticut, Civil and Ecclesiastical*. 2 vols. New Haven, 1818.
Trumbull, J. Hammond, and Hoadly, Charles J., eds. *Public Records of the Colony of Connecticut*. 15 vols. Hartford, 1850–90.
Tucker, Louis L. *Puritan Protagonist: President Thomas Clap of Yale College*. Chapel Hill: University of North Carolina Press, 1962.
Van De Wetering, John E. "God, Science, and the Puritan Dilemma," *The New England Quarterly* 38 (1965): 494–507.
Walker, Williston. *The Creeds and Platforms of Congregationalism*. 1893. Reprint. Boston: Pilgrim Press, 1960.
Walsh, James Joseph. *Education of the Founding Fathers of the Republic; Scholasticism in the Colonial Colleges; A Neglected Chapter in the History of American Education*. New York: Fordham University Press, 1935.
Williams, George H. *Wilderness and Paradise in Christian Thought: The Biblical Experience of the Desert in the History of Christianity and the Paradise Theme in the Theological Idea of the University*. New York: Harper and Row, 1962.
Woolsey, Theodore D. "The Course of Instruction in Yale College in the Eighteenth Century." In *Yale College: A Sketch of its History*, edited by William L. Kingsley, pp. 495–502. 2 vols. New York, 1879.
Wright, Conrad. *The Beginnings of Unitarianism in America*. Boston: Star King Press, distributed by Beacon Press, 1955.

Index